Flyfisher's Guide to™
# Washington

# Titles Available in This Series

Saltwater Angler's Guide to Southern California

Saltwater Angler's Guide to the Southeast

Flyfisher's Guide to the Florida Keys

Flyfisher's Guide to Idaho

Flyfisher's Guide to Northern California

Flyfisher's Guide to Montana

Flyfisher's Guide to Michigan

Flyfisher's Guide to Wyoming

Flyfisher's Guide to Northern New England

Flyfisher's Guide to Washington

Flyfisher's Guide to Oregon

Flyfisher's Guide to Colorado

Flyfisher's Guide to Pennsylvania

Flyfisher's Guide to Minnesota

Flyfisher's Guide to Utah

Flyfisher's Guide to Texas

Flyfisher's Guide to New York

Flyfisher'sGuide to Virginia

Flyfisher's Guide to
# Washington™

## Greg Thomas

Wilderness
Adventures
Press, Inc.

Belgrade, Montana

*Published by Wilderness Adventures Press, Inc.*
*45 Buckskin Road*
*Belgrade, MT 59714*
*800-925-3339*
*Website: www.wildadv.com*
*email: books@wildadv.com*

*10 9 8 7 6 5*

Printed in the United States of America

Library of Congress Cataloging-in-Publication Data

Thomas, Greg.
    Flyfisher's guide to Washington  /  Greg Thomas.
       p.    cm.
    Includes index.
    ISBN 1–885106–58–0
    1. Fly fishing—Washington (State)—Guidebooks.  2. Washington (State)—Guidebooks.  I. Title  II. Title: Washington.
SH559:T48   1999
799.1′24′09797—dc21                        98–54667
                                                      CIP

# Table of Contents

# Acknowledgments

Many thanks to my Washington pals and the many biologists I contacted while working on this book; all of you gave me excellent information. Also, thanks to those who contributed the photographs that accompany the text.

Thanks also to Bill for some excellent conversation at Long Lake while our Labradors, Moose, Shadow, and Jeep, worked off energy.

My regards to Lynanne, Susette, and Brooke, my Tuesday evening thinking and drinking partners who kept me sane in Seattle.

My appreciation goes out to Tom Darlin at the Avid Angler Fly Shop for taking me under his wing and sending me abroad to fish Washington's fly waters; thanks also for the free Mariners tickets!

Most of all, thanks to my father, Fred, mother, Rita, and sister, Kim, who housed, fed, and supported me in Seattle while I worked on this project. Last, but not least, a big thanks to Moose and Shadow, my Labradors, who provided great companionship and comedy galore as we bounced in a pickup truck around the state.

# Introduction

The phone rang at 4:00AM, and the voice on the other end was way too lively for the hour.

"Listen, the ice went out on Pass Lake, and if we leave right now, we could be the first guys to fish it this year."

"Hey, I don't know," I pleaded, entirely groggy, yet very interested. "It's pretty early, and I'm supposed to go to the Sonics game with you know who. Let me know how it goes."

The voice countered, "Remember that gigantic brown trout that busted you off in the weeds last year? Well, it's waiting for you today—probably better than 7 pounds by now. Those fish haven't seen a fly in 2 months. I'd bet money that midges will come off and the trout will rise this afternoon. If not, you know their weakness for buggers. Come on. Let's go. The Sonics play again next week. Besides, they'll kill L.A. It won't even be a game. She won't mind if you go. Your absence just means she can take her mom or a friend for a change."

"All right. You are an evil man, but I'll see what I can do. I'll call you back in 5 minutes. And don't think I don't know your wife is out of town, you hypocrite."

Ten hours later, at 2:00 in the afternoon, I released my third healthy Pass Lake brown trout of the day—none equalling the fish I'd lost in the weeds, but good fish chasing the season's first flies.

By 5:00 PM, after three fishless hours, clouds dropped to the water and a cold western Washington deluge, the kind that creeps into your bones and renders fingers useless, began. I peered into the empty cooler one last time, and my thoughts changed from one more trout to my fiancé back home, sprucing up for the Sonics game.

I thought maybe I'd gone too far this time. Maybe all the flyfishing, all the spontaneous trips, and following my one-track mind would make her leave for good.

But who could blame me, I wondered, for disregarding life outside angling? In Washington, water is abundant and fishing opportunities are boundless. On any given weekend, during any month of the year, various opportunities are available to flyfishers in every corner of the state. If it's not ice-off at Pass Lake, it's giant steelhead running up the Skagit and Sauk rivers, damsels emerging at Lake Lenice, or hoppers dropping like swallows onto the surface of Rocky Ford. How about chironomids hatching at Lake Lenore or shad swarming into the Columbia River or resident silver salmon tearing up streamer flies in Puget Sound? Could you possibly miss the callibaetis spinnerfall at Dry Falls Lake or Chopaka Lake? Or what about summer-run steelhead in the Kalama, Skykomish, and Grande Ronde rivers? A guy just has to hit those streams during their prime. Right?

If one angler decided to adequately sample all the good fly water in Washington during a lifetime, it would simply be impossible. But there are flyfishers, including me, who make a serious effort to fish as much of that water as possible. For flyfishing fanatics, the need for money, status, a beautiful spouse, or the comfort of everyday life is too weak to halt our pursuit.

For the dedicated flyfisher (I didn't say demented), aquatic insect hatches, salmon and steelhead migrations, weather and road reports are all followed like scripture. Spontaneous road trips, such as my aforementioned late-winter venture to Pass Lake, are as treasured by flyfishers as the finest of cut diamonds might be to a bride (I wouldn't know for sure—she bailed out). We flyfishing bums try to cram as much angling into our daily scheme as possible, canceling reservations, calling in sick, quitting work early—or in my case, quitting work entirely—so we can hit all the prime opportunities. Unfortunately, our passion, negligence, and desire to fish catches up in predictable ways.

Today, to be soundly educated in flyfishing, to stand at a gathering and match the knowledge of other anglers, a person darn near has to live the sport. And that is where the problem lies for many of us. We struggle for and wonder if it is possible to find a balance between learning the way of the trout, salmon, and steelhead, and learning what comprises a full life. We ask if one can only be interested in fish and still enjoy other aspects of life. Or are we fanatics leading a life of fallacy, placing the importance of fish wrongfully above all else? Are we running away from society, from relationships, from responsibility? Or, we ask, are we the innovative ones, pursuing the finest in life while the majority rots in discontent? I prefer to believe the latter.

If there is a balance between flyfishing and societal norm, including a flyfisher's relationship with significant others, it treads on a thin rope, teetering precariously between right and wrong. For the novice, the experienced, or the flyfishing fanatic, lost somewhere between weekend warrior and angling oblivion, read the following pieces carefully, enjoy fully, and good luck securing your own basis for explaining this terrible affliction that haunts us all—that of having too much good water, too many good hatches, and just maybe too much wonderful fishing at our disposal. Remember, treat the land, water and your catch with respect and don't say I didn't warn you when flyfishing creeps into your soul.

—*Greg Thomas*
*Sauk River Valley,*
*Skagit County,*
*March 1998*

# Tips on Using this Book

Washington is distinctly divided in climate and culture by the Cascades. The lands to the west are characteristically wet and mild year round; to the east, the land is often hot and dry in summer, with some truly frigid winter temperatures.

West of the Cascades, the glacially carved Puget Sound has attracted shipping interests, and thus large populations, due to its mild climate and calm waters. The Olympic Peninsula, surrounded to the east by the Sound, the north by the Strait of Juan de Fuca, and the west by the Pacific Ocean, is a land of rainforests, jutting mountains, and unequalled beauty. The Cascades include active volcanoes—Mt. St. Helens and Mt. Adams—as well as some unequalled trout streams and sea-run cut-throat waters.

East of the Cascades, the populations thin immediately. All rivers here flow to the mighty Columbia, but they are as diverse as the terrain, which ranges from desert to alpine wilderness.

This book is divided into six sections covering the northwest, the Olympic Peninsula, the southwest, the Columbia Basin lakes, the northern Washington lakes, and eastern Washington rivers. The section on the northwest covers the streams flowing from the Cascades into Puget Sound. The Olympic Peninsula includes the rivers and streams flowing into the Pacific as well as those flowing into the Strait of Juan de Fuca, Hood Canal, the southern arms of Puget Sound, and the Chehalis River; all of these have their origins in the Olympic Mountains. Southwest Washington covers the rivers flowing into the Columbia west of the Cascades, as well as the lakes of Mt. St. Helens. The Columbia Basin occupies the central region of the state and is surrounded on all sides by the Columbia; the lakes of this region are fertile and offer a large and exciting variety of insect hatches. The northern Washington lakes are primarily mountain lakes and offer an alternative to those of the Columbia Basin. And, as mentioned previously, the eastern Washington rivers all flow to the Columbia; most are good trout streams, though several, such as the Klickitat, Wenatchee, Methow, and the Grande Ronde, also see runs of steelhead.

Each river and lake described in this book is followed by a summary of "stream" or "lake" facts highlighting pertinent information for the flyfisher. Trout streams and lakes where specific insect hatches are important have hatch charts telling what hatches occur and when, as well as what fly imitations to use. Each section also has a listing of regional hub cities, with information regarding lodging, camping, airline service, auto rental and repair, fly shops, and chambers of commerce numbers to call for more information.

Happy fishing!

*—The Editors*

## Washington

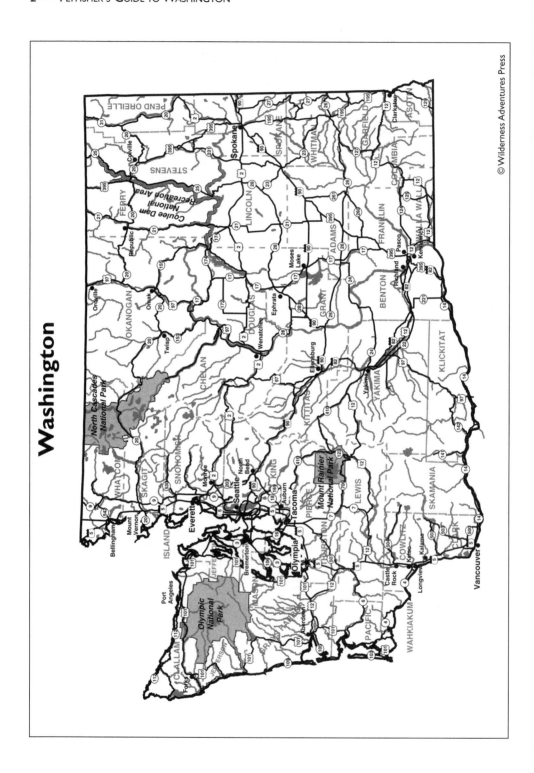

# Washington Facts

18th largest state in the union
71,302 square miles

**Elevations:**  Mt. Rainier–14,410; Pacific Ocean–sea level
**Counties:**  39
**Population (1996 est.):**  5,532,939

- 27  Indian Reservations
- 3  National Parks
- 1  National Volcanic Monument
- 4  National Historic Sites
- 11  National Wildlife Refuges
- 3  National Recreation Areas
- 7  National Forests
- 25  Wilderness Areas
- 129  State Parks

**Nickname:**  The Evergreen State
**Primary Industries:**  Forestry, aerospace, manufacturing, agriculture
**Capital:**  Olympia
**Bird:**  Willow Goldfinch
**Flower:**  Western Rhododendron
**Tree:**  Western Hemlock
**Motto:**  Alki (by and by)
**Song:**  Washington, My Home

# Stream Etiquette

I still think I should have popped him in the face. My father maintains that by turning my back and walking away, I did the right thing.

We were fishing the North Fork Stillaguamish, a river steeped in tradition and often crowded with anglers. Fortunately, on the day we chose to cast flies for summer-run steelhead, the river was nearly devoid of anglers, and nobody was fishing within a half-mile of our location.

Dad and I had just started fishing a nice run; my father was on the near, rocky bank, and I was on the far bank working the traditional riffle corner.

Another angler soon appeared and took up residence below my father, essentially limiting my dad to a 10-yard section of river to fish. He couldn't move upstream because there was a rock wall in the way, and he couldn't move downstream without being in the other angler's lap.

A few minutes later the other fisherman nearly took my father's ear off with an intentional cast. I popped a cast over his line, and he went into a tirade about, of all things, courtesy.

He crossed the river and began fishing below me. Typically, I would have worked downstream, but I didn't budge for this ass. So he moved upstream and once again the casting war ensued. I told him what I thought about his courtesy and felt the adrenaline rise—I wanted to tear that SOB's head off, snap his rod over my knee, and pitch the lot into the river. Had we been at a bar with the liquor flowing, I probably would have. We squared off momentarily, then I wandered upstream to leave that hole and the man behind.

To this day, that is the only really bad situation I've encountered on a stream, whether fishing in Washington, Oregon, Idaho, Utah, Alaska, or Wyoming. But that meeting left a very bad taste in my mouth. It didn't have to happen, and it shouldn't have.

For the most part, anglers are a congenial lot, and fishing in proximity to each other can be a bonus, not a detriment, if people apply common courtesy.

On lakes and reservoirs, that means leaving plenty of room between you and other anglers. Don't kick your float tube over an angler's line and don't make long casts toward another angler to work a rising fish. If someone is fishing from shore and you're in a boat or float tube, realize that they are limited and leave them some room to fish. Just remember to give people some distance, and encounters like the one mentioned don't need to happen.

River fishing is a little different. There are some common rules that apply to every steelhead and salmon river in the state. By following these rules, you likely will never create a nasty situation or get the cold shoulder from fellow anglers.

When you arrive at a stream, take a good look at the water you want to fish and check for anglers. If anglers are present, it's their water to fish. If you have a good second option, head for it. However, if you want to fish the run, which can extend a quarter mile or more on some of the larger streams such as the Skagit, Sauk, Skykomish, Cowlitz, and Lewis, you can do it tactfully.

To do this, walk to the top of the run—do not enter the water below anglers. When an angler is about 100 to 200 feet downstream, step in behind him. Don't push downstream quickly, don't crowd, and maintain a good distance from the other angler. He will be working downstream gradually: casting, moving 5 or 6 feet downstream, and casting again.

On the other hand, if you get to a run first and an angler works into the river above you, keep moving downstream—don't just sit in one spot or you will soon have him on top of you.

Even though tradition allows you a place at the head of a run, always say hello and ask the first-comers if they mind if you fish behind them. Just be polite—they may even offer an opportunity to step in below them.

If you are fortunate enough to hook a fish and land it, you may want to exit the river, abandon your place in line, and return to the head of the run. That is not required and nobody will fault you for keeping your place in line. However, ask yourself this: How many steelhead do you have to catch? Any more than one is a huge bonus for me. Spread the wealth.

Invariably, if you fish steelhead water correctly, especially when chasing winter fish, you will hang a few flies on the bottom. Do not wade out into the river to recover your fly. By doing so, you will spook every fish in the territory and piss off fellow anglers. Just suck it up, snap the fly off, and tie on a new one. Steelhead flies are not exceptionally difficult to replace, but your reputation, self-esteem, and streamside friends are.

By following standard stream etiquette, you should enjoy many hours on the water in proximity to fellow flyfishers without ticking somebody off. Courtesy is always the key. If you have any questions, ask somebody before you enter the river.

Most of us are disappointed to see anglers in a prime run that we are planning to fish, but it doesn't have to signal the end of the world. Look at finding other anglers on the stream as a chance to strike up some interesting friendships. You can learn many things from your fellow anglers. Sometimes free flies are offered. Almost always, conversation and a hot cup of coffee can be had.

# Catch and Release

Much has been written about catch-and-release angling, and most of those words vehemently oppose the taking of any game fish.

Articles on the subject read like this: Those who bonk a trout on the noggin will be dipped in whale oil and tossed to a pool of emaciated piranhas.

But how about a conscientious angler who likes to eat trout or salmon? Are there any situations where taking a fish actually benefits a population or, at the least, doesn't damage fishing opportunity?

My answer, although I can't remember the last fish I killed, is yes. There are certain places and conditions that allow the taking of a fish or two. However, if I see you bonking a trout on, say, the Yakima River, I just might stone your riffle.

A general rule to remember is this: take a fish or two—not your limit—from a reservoir or lake. If you are fishing a river, release trout, steelhead, and salmon.

Here's my reasoning: Trout grow large rapidly in lakes and reservoirs dining on a smorgasbord of easily caught aquatic insects, crustaceans, and fish. They have no current to battle, so very little of their energy is used maintaining a position in the water. Instead, they put their energy into quick strikes against aquatic insects or small baitfish. Extra energy is put into growth. In most cases, when a stillwater trout is harvested by an angler, it is quickly replaced by another solid specimen.

So visit an eastern Washington lake or reservoir, preferably one without special regulations, and take a fish home for dinner. Or hike into a mountain lake and satisfy your hunger with a few small trout. Mountain lakes are typically overpopulated. Taking a few fish from a lake that teems with 6-inchers can only help a population.

But remember, if you switch from a lake or reservoir to a trout river like the Yakima or Snoqualmie, among others, the whole ballgame changes.

River and stream trout grow slowly. Most of their energy is spent maintaining a hold against powerful currents and dodging logs. What is left over is divided between foraging and growth. Because survival is so trying, stream trout rarely exceed 12 inches. Those that grow bigger have survived the odds for three or four years.

To illustrate the difference between stillwater and stream trout, check this out: In northern Idaho's Lake Pend Oreille, some rainbow trout grew from fingerlings to 25-pounders in just 4 years. At least one reached 37 pounds by its fifth year!

In comparison, during a 4-year time span, a rainbow trout in the Yakima or Snoqualmie will normally not exceed 20 inches. Stream trout require lots of time to grow, and unless river anglers return their catch, all of us will sing the blues when dreaming of large river trout.

Anadromous fish are another story entirely. As you are probably aware, most of Washington's steelhead and salmon runs are seriously depressed. In my opinion, an angler should never, ever—even if the regulations allow it—take a wild steelhead or salmon from a stream. I don't care if the fish is the new world-record specimen. Take a photo and release it. People who have walls full of mounted fish are probably looking for something they will never find. People who have walls lined with framed photographs of beautiful fish that they have caught and released are cool.

If you must take a steelhead or salmon from a river (and I enjoy a barbecued salmon as much as anyone), take hatchery fish, which can be identified by their missing adipose fin.

While catch and release is a good practice, especially in rivers, it can be taken to the extreme in some cases. And my mother, Rita, holds the title.

She caught and tried to release a 125-pound halibut in southeast Alaska. My father and his friend, Ken Hagerman, quickly dispatched the fish and any hope my mother had of being the first on record to ever willingly release a legal-size halibut. In my eyes, it was an admirable attempt. She could have started a revolution.

While the situation may change from one place to another, keep in mind that catch and release is needed on most waters. When in doubt, release a fish. If you are going to keep a fish, do so on a stillwater or take a hatchery fish home from a river. Quality flyfishing, especially for large fish, relies on catch and release. Think about that the next time you want to put a fish on your wall.

# Northwest Washington

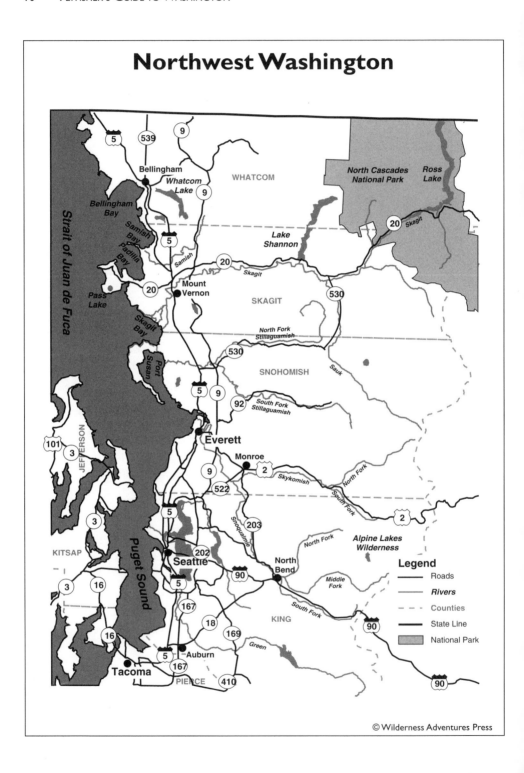

© Wilderness Adventures Press

# Northwest Washington

Damp, cold, gray skies, wind gusts, and sleet—these are the thoughts that come to my mind when considering northwest Washington, probably because I've spent so darn many days astream during fall and winter, casting flies to steelhead and salmon.

If you are a big-fish flyfisher, you regard that weather as an acceptable tradeoff. How could you not? Personally, frozen fingers, feet so cold they feel like concrete slabs, and constant shivers are bearable because of the opportunity to take a 15- to 20-pound steelhead, a 10- to 20-pound chum salmon, a heavy sea-run cutthroat trout, or a Dolly Varden trout.

It's these options, plus an abundance of quality trout lakes, that make northwest Washington such an appealing part of the state, as it has been since the days of Haig-Brown, Zane Grey, and Enos Bradner. Many of northwest Washington's waters are fabled, having been depicted in print by famous writers who stalked their banks during the good ol' days. If you compare the writings and opportunities of yesteryear to today's reality, you might pass on northwest Washington waters. Simply stated, "It ain't what it used to be."

You would be correct in making that statement, but to say that the rivers and lakes of northwest Washington are no longer worth visiting is a cop-out.

Certainly, the salmon and steelhead runs aren't what they used to be, but they remain strong enough to entice me to the banks of these fisheries all year long. And the lake fisheries, although certainly more crowded than they were earlier this century, offer excellent opportunities to take large rainbow and brown trout.

The most noted opportunities in northwest Washington include the Skagit and Sauk Rivers where some of the largest steelhead in the northwest can be taken on flies. As an added bonus, there is a catch-and-release season on this big river during its prime period, which extends from March 16 through April 30.

The Skykomish is also an excellent bet for steelhead, offering fish every month of the year. During early winter, hatchery steelhead can be caught. During late winter and spring, the big natives push upstream, offering an opportunity to catch 10- to 15-pound fish. During late fall and early winter, large, hard-fighting chum salmon are a major draw, and for good reason—they eat almost any chartreuse offering placed in front of their snouts.

The Stillaguamish River and its north fork—some of the most hallowed flyfishing ground in Washington—also offer excellent opportunities. In winter, steelhead can be pursued throughout the river. During summer and fall, there may be no better place to be than the north fork where flyfishing-only and a wild steelhead release regulations are in effect.

If you're looking for a more laid-back affair, visit the Snoqualmie River forks and cast dry flies to eager rainbows and cutthroats. Or visit Pass Lake and work nymphs, streamers, and even the occasional dry fly to some large rainbow, cutthroat, and brown trout. If luck is really on your side, you may hook an Atlantic salmon—some of them grow to 30 inches or more.

Overall, there is a plethora of flyfishing opportunity in northwest Washington, and the steelhead and salmon fisheries head that list. Oldtimers talk a lot about the good ol' days and how the fisheries have gone downhill. But immerse yourself in the Skykomish, the Stillaguamish, or the Skagit one spring, fall, or winter morning and put up with the sleet and rain and snow as long as you can. If you hook a fish, count your blessings. If you don't, say to yourself, "Maybe next time." I guarantee that if you look around at your surroundings, including massive snowcapped peaks, dark timber forests, and beautiful, large, fast-moving rivers, you won't be disappointed in your outing.

# PASS LAKE

One thing that Washington state lacks, especially on the west side of the state, is an extensive supply of brown trout. That's why Pass Lake, which lies just two hours north of Seattle near Anacortes, is such an appealing destination—it has a solid population of browns, along with lots of rainbows, cutthroats, and a few large Atlantic salmon. For those reasons, Pass Lake is an ideal weekend destination for the urban flyfisher.

What is not ideal for Pass Lake anglers is the surface water temperature during the prime late winter and spring seasons. To be blunt, it's frickin' cold, hovering between 30 and 40 degrees from November through April. For anglers who ply the water in float tubes, their legs dangling down in the drink, it's all a mind game—how much chill can you put up with?

For those who can't handle the pain, the parking lot, where a truck heater and warm coffee waits, is never far away. However, for anglers who can endure frigid water, freezing feet, and dysfunctional fingers, late winter and early spring fishing offers the best chances for large trout.

If you are a betting man, rainbows are a 5-to-1 favorite each time you hook a fish. The largest rainbows and cutthroats may stretch 30 inches long, while there may be a few old Atlantic salmon measuring 39 inches or more. Most of the Atlantic salmon, and there are very few of them, are in the 20-inch range, growing all the time but harder than hell to catch.

In fact, the Washington Department of Fish and Wildlife estimates that it takes 100 fishing hours on the lake to produce one Atlantic salmon. The fish generally stay near the bottom, traveling in fast-moving schools that are difficult to locate. Occasionally an angler will tie on a bright steelhead fly and ply the depths for salmon, but often the effort is all for naught. Atlantics are more often an unexpected, yet welcomed, catch for trout fishermen.

When you fish Pass Lake, whether focusing on rainbow, cutthroats, browns, or big salmon, you'll pit your talent against educated fish in a nasty, 100-acre theater of downed logs and submerged brush. A day on Pass is never easy and is rarely pleasant during the cold months, but it can often be very rewarding.

Despite Pass Lake's drawbacks, on any given cast an angler may land a fish of a lifetime and reach that peak called angling ecstasy.

But to catch fish, even when they are actively feeding, an angler must place a fly in what is essentially a submerged minefield. Overhanging limbs and submerged stumps and logs force anglers to cast into small snag-free channels—difficult locations to place a fly and horrendous habitat in which to land a good fish when hooked. But it can be done, and the information board at the put-in describes those huge fish, giving length and girth measurements for interested anglers.

One cold, windy, February day when I visited, the board read: January—largest brown, 28 inches; largest cutthroat, 25 inches; largest rainbow, 27 inches. Gasping material for sure!

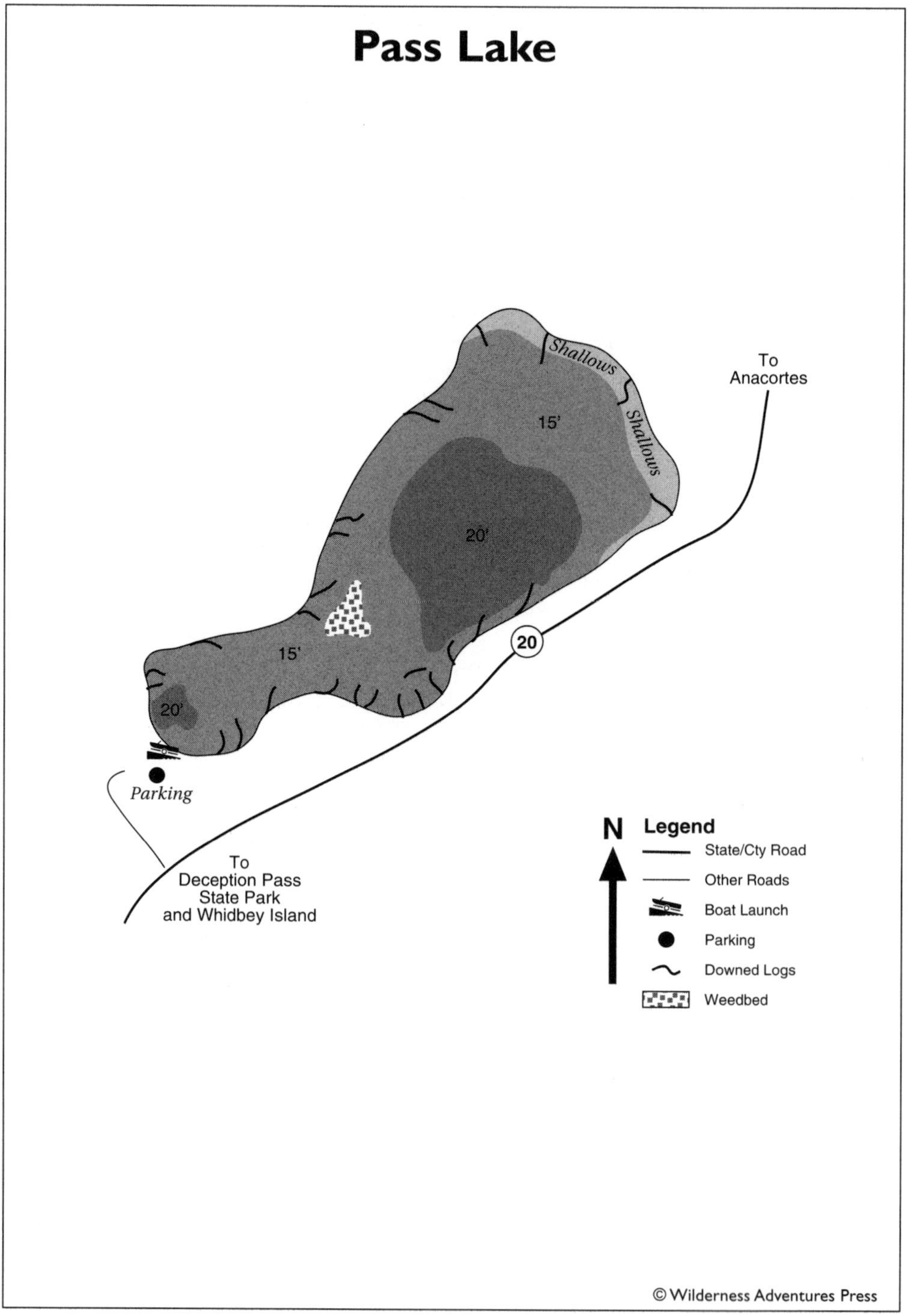

# Pass Lake

*Shallows*

*Shallows*

15'

20'

15'

20'

To
Anacortes

20

Parking

To
Deception Pass
State Park
and Whidbey Island

**N**

**Legend**

——— State/Cty Road

——— Other Roads

Boat Launch

● Parking

〜 Downed Logs

Weedbed

© Wilderness Adventures Press

Do not expect to land a trout of that length during your ventures to Pass Lake. Flyfishing the lake requires patience and dedication. You must stick it out and accept the average 10- to 16-inch fish, even when your toes feel like icicles and your hands are rendered useless. You must accept the fact that it may take many hours to catch one of those large, temperamental fish.

"An average flyfisherman on Pass Lake is going to fish two hours or more for each trout," says Jim Johnston, an area biologist. "It is not easy fishing even for accomplished anglers, but springtime, from March on into May, is the best time to fish the lake. The insects are hatching and the water warms up. Chironomids, some caddis, mayflies, and dragonflies all become active. It's a smorgasbord for the fish."

Johnston is right. As February turns to March the fish become increasingly active toward flies.

At that time, midge hatches bring rainbows away from shore and up to the surface where trout can be taken on Chironomids that range in size from #8 to #20. As the air and water temperatures rise in May, June, and July, anglers may encounter hatches of dragonflies, damselflies, and caddis, along with some small mayfly emergences like Callibaetis, Baetis and March brown drakes.

Watch for Chironomids all year long. Carry Baetis and Callibaetis patterns in April, May, and June. Caddis begin showing at the lake in late April and their presence is significant through June and July. Damselflies begin their emergence in June and dragonflies really get active in July. July and August offer minimal hatches, but caddis and even some Baetis and Callibaetis (also called speckled-wing mayflies) make cameo appearances.

Any number of proven northwest insect imitations should tempt Pass Lake's trout, but here are my favorites:

| Dragonflies and damselflies | Six pack or marabou damsel |
| --- | --- |
| Midge hatches | Suspender midge, Griffith's gnat, brassie, or palomino midge |
| Caddis | Deep sparkle pupa or timberline emerger |
| Callibaetis | Gold-ribbed hare's ear, flashback pheasant tail, Callibaetis sparkle spinner, parachute Adams, or a sparkle dun |
| Baetis | Sparkle dun, hare's ear, pheasant tail nymph, or a cripple |

When hatches are slow or off entirely, or if an angler wants to focus on large brown trout, tie on a minnow imitation, such as a silver zonker or woolly bugger. Krystal flash worked into the tail section of a woolly bugger is a good idea; fathead minnows in Pass Lake have bright silver sides and trout key on that flash. It's only natural that an offering with flash will draw more strikes than a plain, dull fly.

One frigid morning in mid-February, I cast a brown woolly bugger, which included some krystal flash, under an overhanging limb and stripped/retrieved the fly. On the third strip, a large brown cruised from the depths and nailed my offering. The fish rose straight to the surface, hurling the back of its 20-inch-plus body right out of the water, creating a small wake across the calm surface. I gasped, mumbled, "Yea, nice fish," and tried to settle my nerves. I paddled my float tube away from shore, retained tension on the rod, and prayed that the fish would follow.

Instead, with one powerful dive, the big brown plunged into the weeds and sticks and logs and snapped my 4X tippet as though it was sewing thread. That was not the first or the last time that a fish would do that to me at Pass. And it certainly won't be the last minnow imitation that gets swallowed at the lake.

"After the fish break over 12 inches long, brown trout eat a higher percentage of fathead minnows," Johnston says. "By the time they are 15 inches, the bulk of their diet is minnows. They are active all day long, but probably an hour before sunrise to an hour after sunset is the prime time to catch them. They also feed at night. I have a suspicion that there are larger brown trout in the lake than people have captured, and those fish are strictly night feeders."

Besides entertaining anglers, brown trout play a significant role in the management of Pass Lake. Due to illegal introductions of spiny-ray fishes, such as bass, perch, and green-eared sunfish, brown trout are needed to keep illegal aliens in check. However, in the past, many anglers kept any large brown trout they landed. Taking large fish from the lake only facilitated the rise in numbers of roughfish and spiny-rays. Fortunately, in 1998, the Washington Department of Fish and Wildlife made Pass Lake a catch-and-release-only water in an attempt to extend the life expectancy of brown trout. Kudos to Johnston.

Maybe the best offering for brown trout is an exact rendition of a fathead minnow. If you tie your own flies, create a streamer pattern with these characteristics: 2 to 3 inches long, silver sides and an olive/black back. The body is teardrop shaped with a slender tail and, of course, an elongated, fat head. Put a streamer with those characteristics in front of a brown, and you'll have a fight on your hands.

Leech and crayfish patterns are also good choices for Pass Lake and may hook rainbows, cutthroats, Atlantic salmon, or brown trout. These patterns are most effectively fished deep down and slow. Strikes can be jarring.

If an angler does not want to worry about the edge of the lake, where downed timber wreaks havoc with hooked fish, there are plenty of rainbows located offshore, just over submerged weedbeds. The trouble is locating the beds, which may change through the seasons, and placing a minnow imitation just over the weeds without allowing the fly to tangle in the growth.

The countdown method is the best way to keep a fly just above the weeds while remaining in that crucial zone where fish forage. A fast sinktip line will work (for that matter, a floating line with weight added is adequate), but my choice is a high density sinking line that quickly places a fly near fish.

*The author with a hard-earned Pass Lake brown trout. Winter fishing on Pass Lake is for die-hards only—the water is frigid.*

"Most of the rainbows concentrate over submerged weedbeds in water no more than 10 feet deep," Johnston says. "That's where the water is clearest, and that's where most of the insects are located. There are certain places around the lake that concentrate fish, and it takes a while to find those areas. As you find more prime areas, your catch rate will increase. When that happens, your odds of catching a fish larger than 16 inches go up dramatically."

Just about anywhere in the lake, Chironomids draw strikes from cruising rainbows and cutthroats. However, fishing Chironomids off a floating line is relatively boring. If you have the patience and a fat cigar to occupy your downtime, give it a try.

If you do that, tie a midge emerger to the end of a 15-foot leader that tapers to 6X. Above the fly, attach a strike indicator. Vary the distance of the indicator above the fly until you find what level the fish are working. Remember to cast as far from your float tube or pram as you can. Then slowly retrieve the offering or just let it sit out there in the wind, one wrist wrapped around your cork rod grip, the other around the cigar. Set up quickly when the indicator goes down. And remember: don't inhale when you get that strike. People don't want to listen to a hack-attack on a calm, quiet spring day just because you filled your lungs with an unexpected dose of smoke.

When fishing in this manner, do not expect to land any huge rainbows, although the possibility of a stray hog cruising by always exists. In fact, don't expect to catch many big rainbows in Pass Lake—those fish are the standard lowland western Washington hatchery stock that average 10 to 16 inches and subsist mostly on insects. Johnston has considered planting a Kamloops strain of rainbow, which grows larger and feeds mostly on minnows, but that would significantly lessen an angler's option to catch fish on traditional fly patterns.

"I've thought about shifting to Kamloops trout because they are more likely to eat other fish after they reach 16 inches," Johnston says. "But I wouldn't stock all Kamloops, because a lot of anglers like to fish the traditional flies. If I went to Kamloops, as soon as the fish reached 12 to 16 inches, their diet would change to fish, and the opportunity to catch fish on dry flies and nymphs would be lost."

Although there is never a truly bad time to fish Pass Lake, mid-July through early September offers the most challenging conditions. With surface water temperatures running high, the lake's fish head down to where conditions are more desirable. It takes a determined, savvy flyfisher to catch fish at that time, but for anglers willing to learn the nuances of late summer fish, the reward is significant.

"If that is the only time you can fish, you've got to find the thermocline and get right on top of it," Johnston says. "Usually, it's going to be around 15 to 20 feet deep. If it's located at 20 feet deep, fish between 15 and 20 feet and try to find places where the thermocline bumps right up against shore or submerged points. The fish will be really concentrated at that time, so if an angler can find them, he will have a much higher success rate per hour than any other time of the year."

While you might have the lake to yourself during late summer, that is not going to be the case during fall and, especially, during spring when it seems that every flyfisher in western Washington packs a boat (motors are not allowed) and his family to Pass Lake.

Johnston estimates that there are 3,000 Pass Lake visitors each year, but I can't imagine that number is correct. At times, it feels like 3,000 anglers are on the lake at one time. Maybe my timing has just been poor. If you want to avoid crowds, do the right thing: quit your job, buy a mobile home, subsist on Top Ramen, and visit Pass Lake on weekdays.

In the realm of Washington flyfishing, brown trout are one of the least encountered species. However, at Pass Lake, anglers stand a fair chance of landing a brown each time they visit. With the odds in your favor and fish to 30 inches waiting, remember, there's no time like the present. If you're sitting in an office in Seattle, Bellevue, Everett, or Timbuktu (of all places), slip a glance toward the boss's office, slide a fly rod behind your backseat, stuff a float tube in your trunk, and hit the road north. The fish are waiting.

# Lake Facts: Pass Lake

## Seasons
- Year-round

## Special Regulations
- Flyfishing only
- Catch and release only

## Species
- Rainbow trout, between 17 and 26 inches
- Brown trout, between 17 and 26 inches
- Cutthroat trout, between 17 and 26 inches
- Atlantic salmon, a few exceeding 30 inches

## Lake Characteristics
- It's a moody lake, but on a good day, Pass may place a half dozen or more big trout in your net.
- Pass offers excellent Chironomid hatches along with good damselfly and Callibaetis emergences.
- There is also good streamer fishing, and those patterns are especially effective on summer nights and again in the winter.
- Pass can freeze during cold winters, but ice doesn't remain on the lake for very long.

## Access
- A boat ramp and parking area at the west end of the lake provide easy access.
- There is very limited shore fishing, so bring a float tube, small boat, or canoe.

## PASS LAKE MAJOR HATCHES

| Insect | J | F | M | A | M | J | J | A | S | O | N | D | Flies |
|---|---|---|---|---|---|---|---|---|---|---|---|---|---|
| Chironomids | ■ |  |  |  |  |  |  |  |  | ■ | ■ |  | Brassie #16–20; Chan's Chironomid #14–18; Midge Emergers #14–18; Palomino Midge #14–20; Griffith's Gnat #16–20 |
| Callibaetis |  |  |  | ■ | ■ | ■ |  |  | ■ |  |  |  | Hare's Ear #14–16; Flashback Pheasant Tail #14–18; CDC Biot Comparadun #14–18; Callibaetis Cripple #14–18; Parachute Adams #14–18; Thorax CBH #14–18 |
| Dragonfly & Damselfly |  |  |  | ■ | ■ | ■ |  |  |  |  |  |  | Braided Butt Adams #6–8; Six Pack #6–10; Nyergess Nymph #4–10; Olive Marabou Damsel #6–10; Andy Burk's Olive Damsel #6–10; Sheep Creek Special #6–10 |
| Caddis |  |  |  |  | ■ | ■ | ■ |  |  |  |  |  | Traveling Sedge #4–8; LaFontaine Emergent Sparkle Pupa #14–16; X-Caddis #12–16; Diving Caddis #12–16; Prince Nymph #12–16 |
| Streamer | ■ | ■ | ■ | ■ | ■ | ■ | ■ | ■ | ■ | ■ | ■ | ■ | Woolly Bugger #4–8; Fathead Minnow #4–8; Egg-sucking Leech #2–6; Woolhead Sculpin #4–6 |
| Leeches | ■ | ■ | ■ | ■ | ■ | ■ | ■ | ■ | ■ | ■ | ■ | ■ | Marabou (olive, brown, black) #4–10; Canadian Mohair Leech #4–10; Kaufmann's Minileech #4–8 |
| Baetis |  |  |  | ■ |  |  |  |  |  | ■ |  |  | Sparkle Dun #18–20; Hare's Ear Nymph #18–20; Pheasant Tail Nymph #18–20; Cripple #18–20 |

# SKAGIT AND SAUK RIVERS

Each year, in late March and early April, as winter and spring lock in their eternal tug-o-war, my mind drifts north of Seattle to the Skagit River and its run of exquisitely proportioned native steelhead.

Go ahead, search the West from northern California to the middle of the British Columbia coast, and you may not find a finer race of steelhead or a better chance to land that mythic 20-pounder on a fly.

Most rivers offer 5- to 10-pound steelhead that first spawn after one or two years in saltwater (commonly called one- or two-salt fish). But the Skagit differs dramatically. For some reason, over half of its native fish make their first return after three years at sea, when they may weigh between 8 and 12 pounds. Fish that come back after a fourth year in saltwater exceed 15 pounds. A five- or even six-salt fish, having successfully negotiated a labyrinth of obstacles too numerous to list here, might weigh 20 pounds or more. And the Skagit hosts its fair share of those monsters each season.

Like any inquisitive angler, I can only imagine what lurks in the Skagit. Could there exist a steelhead exceeding 40 pounds? One that might best the 42-pound world record, which was caught on conventional gear in the saltwaters of southeast Alaska? Certainly, 30-pound fish return to the Skagit each year.

One story details Jerry Wintle's catch of a Skagit steelhead that measured 48 to 50 inches long. Imagine gently cradling a fish like that, allowing it to regain strength after a long fight. Then picture that fish cruising to the depths, its tail gently slipping from your grasp, its body slowly drifting from your sight, melting into aqua orbit. What a feeling that must have been. We can all dream, can't we? Time to spark that cigar, put the rod away for a day, if not a season, and fully appreciate the good fortune that you encountered. After that day, any advantageous event encountered in life would simply be considered frosting on an already very tasty cake.

While the Skagit offers huge steelhead, they aren't resting in every run, and by no means should an angler expect to catch a 20-pound fish on the Skagit. If it happens, it happens, and you should consider yourself one of the luckiest people alive. Most often it does not. In fact, because of its size, finding fish in the Skagit can be a monumental task, especially for novice anglers. Beginners may endure many fishless days before encountering a first strike, let alone a first fish. Even experienced anglers endure many fishless days, their motivation honed from past experience and the awesome scenery that surrounds the Skagit. When steelhead flyfishing in winter, faith and a total immersion in a beautiful landscape is everything.

One thing that tips the scale in an angler's favor is the Skagit's tendency to run clear from Ross Dam downstream to the mouth of the Sauk River at Rockport. Because of this, anglers can locate fishable water almost any time they like on the Skagit. That's something that can't be said for many western Washington rivers, especially during the heavy rain months of March and April, when mud and debris race off clearcut mountains straight into the rivers. Fortunately, much of the upper Skagit

## Skagit River
### Ross Dam to Concrete

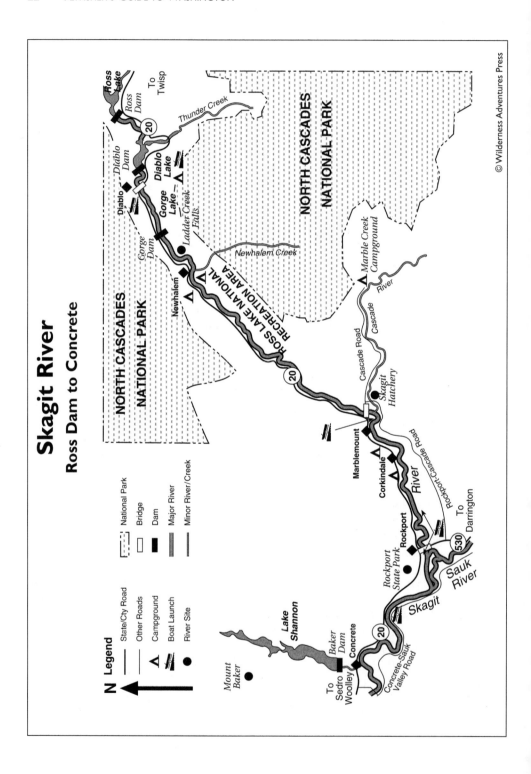

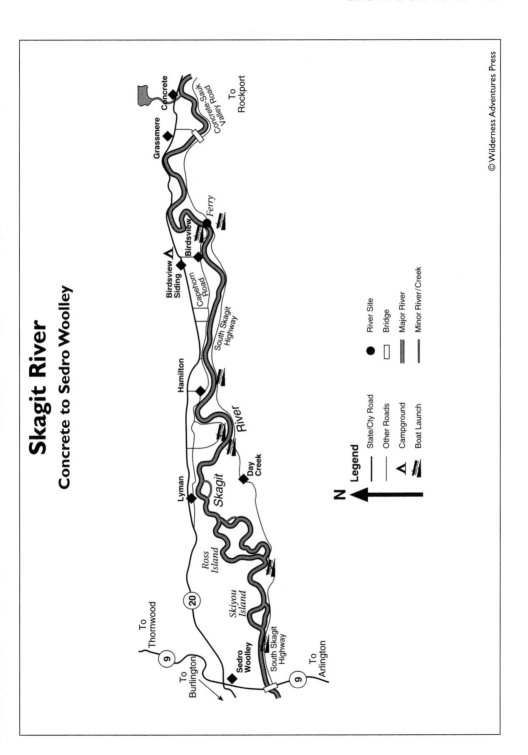

# Skagit River
## Concrete to Sedro Woolley

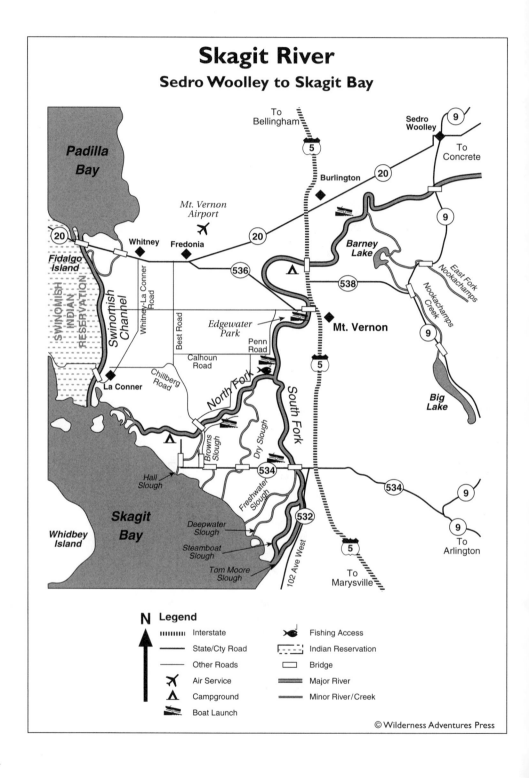

# Skagit River
## Sedro Woolley to Skagit Bay

Padilla Bay

To Bellingham

Sedro Woolley

To Concrete

Burlington

Mt. Vernon Airport

Barney Lake

Whitney   Fredonia

East Fork Nookachamps

Nookachamps Creek

Fidalgo Island

Swinomish Channel

Whitney-La Conner Road

Edgewater Park

Mt. Vernon

Penn Road

Best Road

Calhoun Road

Big Lake

Chillberg Road

La Conner

North Fork

South Fork

Browns Slough

Dry Slough

Hall Slough

Freshwater Slough

Skagit Bay

Whidbey Island

Deepwater Slough

Steamboat Slough

Tom Moore Slough

102 Ave West

To Marysville

To Arlington

**N**

### Legend

| | | | |
|---|---|---|---|
| ⊪⊪⊪⊪ Interstate | | 🐟 Fishing Access | |
| ─── State/Cty Road | | ⌐ Indian Reservation | |
| ─── Other Roads | | ▭ Bridge | |
| ✈ Air Service | | ▬ Major River | |
| ⛺ Campground | | ≈ Minor River/Creek | |
| 🚤 Boat Launch | | | |

© Wilderness Adventures Press

# Sauk River

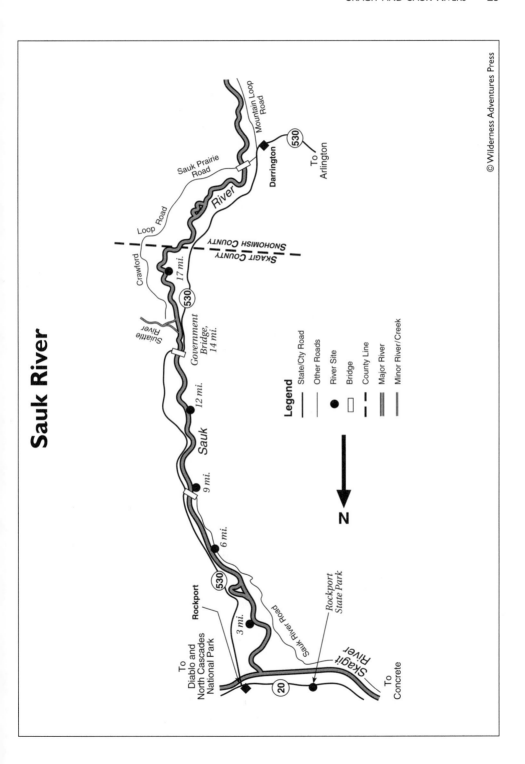

Mountain Loop Road

530
To Arlington

Darrington

Sauk Prairie Road

River

Loop Road

Crawford

17 mi.

SKAGIT COUNTY
SNOHOMISH COUNTY

530

Suiattle River

Government Bridge, 14 mi.

12 mi.

Sauk

9 mi.

6 mi.

530

Rockport

3 mi.

Sauk River Road

Rockport State Park

To Diablo and North Cascades National Park

20

Skagit River

To Concrete

**Legend**

| | |
|---|---|
| State/Cty Road | |
| Other Roads | |
| River Site | ● |
| Bridge | ▭ |
| County Line | — · — |
| Major River | |
| Minor River/Creek | |

N

© Wilderness Adventures Press

is located in North Cascades National Park and Glacier Peak Wilderness, which means it is relatively devoid of those massive clearcuts.

The Skagit begins in southern British Columbia and turns into Ross Lake, a 24-mile long impoundment that helps filter out debris, before spilling across the border into Washington. The river below Ross Dam is in the heart of the jagged, volcanically active North Cascade Mountains, which are sometimes called the North American Alps. In that stretch, extending from the dam to Newhalem, the river is fierce—splitting steep gorge walls, dropping an average of 80 feet per mile, preventing the upstream movement of steelhead—before regaining a fairly placid decline of 14 feet per mile between Newhalem and Marblemount.

It's there, beginning in that stretch, on the third largest river system in the Lower Forty-Eight, surrounded by active volcanoes that reach nearly 11,000 feet into the sky and drain more than 1.7 million acres of land, including runoff from 387 glaciers, that flyfishers pursue massive steelhead.

As mentioned, the Skagit's winter steelhead poke their noses into the system beginning in January and February. However, their concentration peaks in April, which is much later than anglers find on most West Coast winter-run rivers. Due to that fact, flyfishers actually encounter winter-runs in spring just as the water temperature warms and the days are mostly pleasant, although avid steelheaders routinely brave snow and sleet and, of course, those freezing fingers in March and April.

One of the Skagit's appealing aspects is a catch-and-release season that runs from March 16 through November 30 for native fish. The catch-and-release section extends from Dalles Bridge in Concrete to the mouth of Bacon Creek above Marblemount (about 45 miles). The catch-and-release, barbless-hooks-only season also encompasses the Sauk and Suiattle River drainages from the Sauk's confluence with the Skagit upstream to Darrington (about 16 miles). Within those boundaries, flyfishers can work the water for steelhead without worry of interruption from baitchucking plunkers.

When choosing a section of river to work, flyfishers should consider the nature of the Skagit and the effect that the Sauk and smaller tributaries have on water clarity.

The Skagit's tributaries have been logged incessantly. Many of the slopes above the rivers are virtually denuded of vegetation. When heavy rains pelt the area, as they often do in March and April, the river rises and clouds, and the Sauk adds to that mess. In fact, the Sauk, which drains glacial melt straight off the flanks of Glacier Peak, contributes the most color to the Skagit and makes fishing below its mouth a bust at times. Add to that problem Day Creek, Finney Creek, and Nookachamps Creek, which have all been logged heavily, and you have a river that is out of shape, off-color, and not fishable. When that situation occurs, it's time to hit the river above the mouth of the Sauk.

Due to clearcuts on the Skagit's tributaries, the river doesn't offer the numbers of steelhead that it used to. In fact, historical runs are estimated in the 20,000 to 25,000 fish range. Today, a typical year witnesses the return of 6,000 to 10,000 native spawners, which is up from a low of about 2,000 fish in the mid- to late 1980s.

*Dec Hogan with a mint-bright chromer from Washington's premier large steelhead system—the Skagit River. (Photo courtesy Dec Hogan)*

Despite its decline, the Skagit's future looks pretty bright. As mentioned, most of its water comes from the Pasayten and Glacier Peak Wilderness Areas and from North Cascades National Park. In those areas, logging and mining are banned, and the forests maintain their historic abundance. On the lower river outside the park and wilderness boundaries, cut-and-run logging has diminished, and past clearcuts are revegetating, which should lessen the effect of winter floods and landslides due to unstable ground. Some anglers speculate that steelhead runs could continue to climb, possibly reaching 20,000 fish per year. Of course, even with those numbers, steelhead are elusive and will make you work to find them.

When eyeing the Skagit for the first time, many flyfishers take one look at the water and feel a wave of intimidation sweep over them—the river is wide and fairly deep in many sections, and its best water is often out of reach of the flyfisher. For that reason, flyfishers must specifically seek out water that is not only approachable but relatively shallow. Fortunately, there's an awful lot of water like that on the Skagit, and much of it is located close to the banks, where most steelhead traditionally migrate.

One thing to keep in mind when fishing steelhead on the Skagit (or anywhere else for that matter) is that those fish will be moving. They are not like a stream trout that stakes its claim to a prime piece of water and sets up camp. Remember, steelhead migrate, sometimes many miles in a day, so a run that might be empty in the

*A typical cold winter day on the Skagit. (Photo by Dec Hogan)*

morning could be loaded in the afternoon. So it makes sense to fish through the best water first and return later if you have time.

What's a prime piece of flywater on the Skagit? Look for water in the 3- to 6-feet deep range with a relatively gentle flow that allows a large fish quick access to cover, meaning a riffle, deep hole or some broken surface that masks a fish from view. According to Dec Hogan, a top guide on the Skagit who's caught his fair share of fish, successful anglers have the ability to locate "a stream within a river" when fishing the Skagit. That task is not always an easy one.

"The good water can be really subtle on the Skagit," Hogan says. "You want to find places where the current slows. That could be where two currents meet, or it might be a riffly, choppy piece of water that breaks out into a slow section. But most important is (water) depth and speed. You want to fish water that moves at a walking pace. That walking speed water may only stretch 5 feet wide, and it might have fast

*The Skagit is a broad river that requires long-distance casts and a strong measure of patience. Because they throw a lot of line, the Skagit's devoted anglers prefer two-handed rods. (Photo by Dec Hogan)*

water on either side. On most rivers you see a defined choppy head with fast water on one side and slow water on the other. That's not often the case on the Skagit. You really have to study the water.

"One place that is always worth exploration is an exposed gravel bar," Hogan adds. "When you see an exposed gravel bar, it means there is a bottom that slopes gradually into the main river. Where there is a sloping gravel bar there is walking speed water and, normally, a rocky bottom. Steelhead like rocks.

"You won't find a bunch of boulders in the Skagit, but you do want to locate a hard bottom—the bigger the rock the better. But don't be deceived by a golf-ball-sized rock bottom. As long as you stay off the sand, you're in there."

If you locate the productive water and work it thoroughly, you just might be rewarded with a mint-bright buck or a heavy hen. If it's your first steelhead caught on a fly, pause for a moment before letting go of the tail—the first fly-caught steelhead is an amazing event in the progression of a flyfisher, a real stepping stone. Releasing your first steelhead is a moment that will be recalled through your life. One special fish. And not one damn moment too soon, I can hear you say.

While locating prime water is paramount, fly presentation is equally crucial. If a fly is not placed in a steelhead's immediate area, meaning that it's about to bump into the fish's snout, you are likely not going to hook that fish, although there is always the potential to nail the oddball chasing a fly out of the depths and into shallow water at your bootlaces.

One trait that is true of steelhead no matter where you find them, especially winter-run fish, is their propensity to sit tight-finned to the bottom. That's where a fly needs to be placed on the Skagit if you hope to land a fish. And don't be fooled—using a sinktip line does not assure your fly a deep drift. Sinktip lines do encourage a deep drift, but short leaders are equally important. A 9- or 10-foot leader, for instance, allows a fly to drift high in the water column. Short leaders of 3 or 4 feet follow a sinktip down and assure deep drifts. Hogan fishes short leaders in 10-pound test Maxima.

If you can reach a fish with your fly, it will likely eat it. On the Skagit, most anglers agree, success is more a matter of finding fish and getting a fly to them than the selection of one particular "hot" fly. But there are times when one fly is definitely a better choice than another.

"Conditions mean everything in fly selection," Hogan says. "You have to change flies accordingly, but you can get away with just a few patterns. If I could only use three flies on this river, I would choose marabou flies—one black, one purple, and one orange. But general practitioners work well, too. I also tie a fly that I call the Olive Garden [yes, Hogan digs pasta] that is a drab olive, natural tone. When the weather is sunny and clear, as it can be in April, that fly works particularly well."

Rod selection can also influence an angler's success or lack of it. On the Skagit, most serious flyfishers throw two-handed rods. That does not mean that your standard, single-handed rod won't work—you just won't stand out as a local.

"If you want to be up to par with the serious, hard-core guys, you use a two-handed rod," Hogan said. "I think a 14-foot, 9-weight is probably the most popular rod. But, single-handed rods work, too. If you have a 9- or 10-foot, 8 or 9-weight, you'll do fine.

"But it helps to be able to cast as far as possible on the Skagit," Hogan adds. "To cover the river really effectively, you need to cast between 60 and 70 feet. It's not an endurance competition—you just really have to pop it out there. I have clients who can barely cast 50 feet, but they catch fish. Then again, they are fishing with me, which helps. A guy that just shows up to fish the river for the first time is going to be limited if he can't distance cast."

Whether you are able to cast a fly 70 feet or not, a drift boat or raft increases odds of success, whether floating the Skagit or the Sauk where most of the big river's fish turn southeast to spawn.

"Drifting the river really helps as far as gaining access," Hogan says. "You can't just drive along the river and say, 'That looks like a nice hole, I'll fish there.'

"A couple of very nice, fullday floats run from Marblemount to Rockport and from Rockport to Concrete. The actual floating time is quick, but there is an awful lot of fishing on those floats if you get out of the boat and work the water. There are boat ramps between those sites also, so you can make the float as long or short as you like.

*If you are looking for a giant steelhead, test the Sauk River. Here, the author works its broad current.*

"On the Sauk, there are two excellent floats, but they have primitive access sites," Hogan explains. "You aren't going to pull up there in a Toyota Camry and drop the boat in. If you have a good vehicle, put in at Darrington and float to the Suiattle River. Or you can float from the Suiattle to Native Hole, which is located at the SR 530 Bridge that crosses the Skagit. However, I'll warn people about the Sauk—it will kill you if you aren't careful. There aren't any big waves or rapids, but you can't get complacent—you have to keep an eye on the river. The Skagit is a great place for a drift boat rower-in-training, but you have to keep an eye peeled there, too."

No matter whether you fish the Skagit or Sauk, float or wade, don't hit the river with inflated expectations. Yes, the Skagit system harbors some of the largest steelhead in the world, but they aren't easily taken. Would-be Skagit flyfishers should, instead, visit the river to enjoy the scenery, to merge with the river and feel its currents. If a steelhead happens to be landed, so much the better. If a fish exceeds the magical 20-pound mark, consider your good fortune. But never, ever judge the Skagit solely on your ability to produce a 20-pounder from its depths. You'll only be disappointed.

"On the Skagit you have to look at searching, reading the water, and the anticipation as your recreation," Hogan stresses. "No whiners need apply. If we went out there and caught 10 steelhead a day, it wouldn't be the same. But you have to be confident. If you are not confident in your ability, it's hard to hang in there. I've put in enough time that I don't question myself or my method. If I don't catch a fish, I just chalk it up to steelheading.

"As far as hooking one, work ethics are the key. You don't just fish the sweet spot. Fish the run from head to tail. No stone goes unturned. When you think you started at the top of the run, start a little higher. If you think you fished the run thoroughly, fish it some more."

Concerning 20-pound fish, maybe Hogan's experience sums up the river best. He's fished the Skagit and Sauk religiously since the mid-1980s, and his first 20-pounder arrived in 1997.

"You can hook truly big fish here, but it's not the reason a guy should come here," he said. "I'm on that river with capable anglers and I see slightly less than one of those 20-pound-plus fish each year.

"You have to think, 'How big do I need?' Fourteen pounds is a huge steelhead, and you are more likely to see a 14-pounder than a 20-pounder. And you are more likely to see a 12-pounder than a 14-pounder. The fish average 9 to 14 pounds, and that is big. You'll catch some 7-pounders here, and you'll catch some 15-pounders. Some years they might even average 14 pounds. But, there is always that chance. To this day, when I hook a fish, my heart jumps into my throat because I never know what it will be. You may have your hands seriously full on the Skagit."

That's exactly what Hogan found when he hooked his 41-inch, 20-pound buck in 1997. After waiting so many years for a shot at a fish like that, Hogan fully appreciated his opportunity.

"I wasn't really looking for a 20-pounder," he said. "In fact, I wasn't necessarily expecting to catch a fish. The river wasn't in ideal shape, and most people stayed home that day.

"After I hooked the fish, it jumped five times. I said 'Holy shit, it's about damn time.' When he came into the shallows it was awesome. It was like it wasn't even a fish. It was like an animal, a prehistoric creature. It had a look of its own. I was so damn excited. I'm glad I got a taste of that.

"When I let him go, I didn't say, 'That's all I ever want to catch.' I just figured a fish like that was a bonus. But I'm not going to measure all of my fish against that one. They are all different, special. They're all bitchin'."

If you choose to fish the Skagit and Sauk some day—and I suggest you do just that—allot enough time on the water to give yourself a chance at success. Persistence is key for winter steelhead, and you have to give yourself the best shot.

# Stream Facts: Skagit River

## Seasons
- From Dalles Bridge at Concrete to Bacon Creek: Open June 1 through March 15 for trout, including Dolly Varden; from March 16 through April 30, it's catch and release on all game fish with selective gear rules applying.
- From Bacon Creek to Gorge Dam: Open June 1 through February 28.

## Special Regulations
- Catch and release on steelhead and trout March 16 through April 30.
- Wild steelhead can be retained from December 1 through February 28, but they should be released.
- Check the regulations booklet thoroughly—rules on the Skagit are changed regularly.

## Species
- Steelhead
- Dolly Varden
- Sea-run cutthroat
- Chum, pink, king, and coho salmon

## Stream Characteristics
- The Skagit is a huge river system, and it produces steelhead to match. A few 20-pound-plus fish are produced each season, with some monsters going better than 30 pounds. Flyfishing options are best during the catch-and-release season.

## Access
- Wade fishing is possible, but an angler should be ready to beat some brush to reach the river. A better option is to float the river in a drift boat or raft. There are many public access points sprinkled along the river.

# Stream Facts: Sauk River

## Seasons
- June 1 through February 28.
- March 1 through April 30: Catch and release only.

## Special Regulations
- March 1 through April 30: Catch and release only.
- Selective gear rules apply March 1 through April 30: 20-inch minimum on Dolly Varden; 14-inch minimum on trout.

## Species
- Steelhead
- Dolly Varden
- Sea-run cutthroat

## Stream Characteristics
- The Sauk is a wide, brawling river but not quite as big as the Skagit.
- The Sauk receives Skagit River steelhead that run in excess of 20 pounds.
- An average steelhead weighs between 10 and 14 pounds.
- March 1 through April 30—catch and release season—offers the best opportunity for flyfishers.

## Access
- The Sauk can be waded successfully, but floating is an excellent way to cover lots of water thoroughly.
- Excellent access points exist on the river, and there are several prime floats to be had (see Sauk River map).

# SAMISH RIVER

The Samish River has endured its problems, but this small, forested river still attracts a modest run of king and coho salmon, supplemented by mostly hatchery steelhead and a push of fall-run chum salmon.

Located south of Bellingham and west of Sedro Woolley, the Samish and its tiny tributary, Friday Creek, used to be so good they nearly expelled one of my father's friends from Western Washington University—he spent too many days on the water chasing steelhead and too few in the classroom.

Today, this brushy stream still offers decent fishing during fall and winter. From late August extending through September and into October, some nice kings, plus their little brothers (jacks) can be tempted. During October the Samish sees decent numbers of jack and adult coho salmon. In November, chums push into the system, and, like chums everywhere, they're aggressive toward chartreuse streamers.

The lower river, from the mouth of the Samish to Thomas Road Bridge, is open for salmon July 1 through December 31. From Thomas Road bridge to the I-5 Bridge, the river is open October 16 through December 31. Before you cast a line for salmon, take a strong look at the regulations for the Samish—they are diverse and can change from year to year.

Steelhead fishing is open from June 1 through March 15, but the best action occurs in December, January, and February. Wild steelhead must be released.

To reach the lower Samish, follow I-5 to the exit just north of Burlington. To reach the upper river, take the Bow Road exit off I-5 and follow Prairie Road.

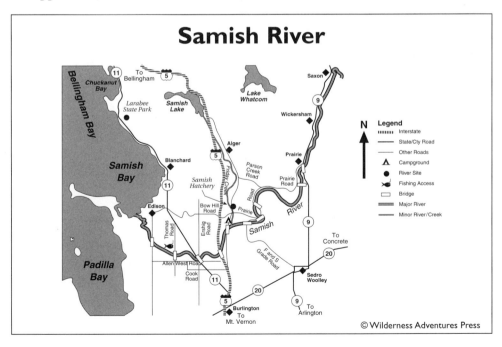

Samish River

© Wilderness Adventures Press

# Stillaguamish River

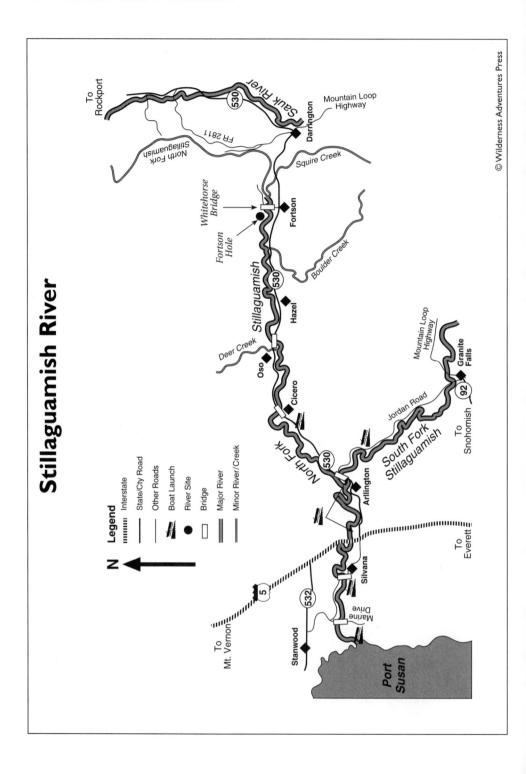

# STILLAGUAMISH RIVER

When considering the angling tradition, history, and literary acknowledgment of a river, no stream in Washington (and few hallowed waters in the Northwest) offers a resumé as loaded as the Stillaguamish. Unfortunately, its salmon and steelhead runs have atrophied over the years.

The Stillaguamish begins as two small forks, the north and south, that twist out of the North Cascade Mountains and the Mount Baker/Snoqualmie National Forest about 75 miles north of Seattle. Where the forks meet near Arlington, the main Stillaguamish is born, and it carries water about 15 miles before dumping its flows into the saltwaters of Port Susan just south of Stanwood.

Historically, the Stillaguamish and its fabled tributary, Deer Creek, hosted one of the best runs of native summer steelhead in the West. Pioneering anglers, including Zane Grey and Roderick Haig-Brown, made expeditions to the river in the early 1900s and found fantastic summer-run steelhead and pristine surroundings. In 1949, the North Fork Stillaguamish, thanks to farsighted flyfishers, became the first flyfishing-only steelhead water in the world. By 1950, the North Fork received its first returns of hatchery-origin summer-runs, spawned from the local Deer Creek stock. The future looked good for this fishery.

However, in the late 1940s and 1950s, loggers found the Deer Creek watershed and cut it ruthlessly. They turned the crystal clear runs and pools of this stream into a muddy, silt- and debris-laden mess. The hills above Deer Creek, previously first-growth rainforest, resembled a lunar landscape. Most of Deer Creek's native summer steelhead, possibly the best summer-run in history, perished.

A few Deer Creek natives persist today, but that story is a sad commentary, one that can be applied to every Puget Sound stream, if not every waterway in the state.

Today, the North Fork offers Deer Creek origin summer-runs, but nobody will tell you that the Stillaguamish's fishing is as good it used to be. Still, due to its tradition and some good summer-run and winter-run options, the river draws a fair amount of pressure.

Summer steelhead show up in the North Fork in June, but the bulk of the run enters in July and August. Native Deer Creek fish move through the system slowly, then make a left-hand turn up Deer Creek when they smell their natal waters. Sometimes, if conditions aren't quite right, Deer Creek fish hold at the mouth of the creek, waiting patiently for a rain to push conditions in their favor. When the Deer Creek watershed receives a freshet, fish fire upstream to spawn. All of Deer Creek is closed to angling.

Traditionally, hatchery-origin steelhead moved through the North Fork at a moderate speed. However, the lower North Fork's pools continue to fill with sediment and debris, which leaves steelhead little holding water. Today, hatchery fish move through the lower river quickly. But they slow down when they hit their imprinting areas (where they were released by hatchery workers), including these spots—White Horse Bridge, the mouth of Boulder Creek, Hazel, Whitman Bridge, and Fortson Hole, among other locales.

*Is there a more hallowed steelhead water in Washington? Here the author probes the North Fork Stillaguamish for summer-run steelhead.*

As they move up the North Fork, hatchery summer-runs and even a few wild, native fish, hold in traditional steelhead water. Anglers should pay close attention to pools and runs that range between 4 and 10 feet deep. Look for areas of moderate water speed—a walking pace is best. As the water lowers in July and August, fish seek security. At that time, heavy riffles, undercut banks, rock or riprap banks, downed logs and, again, the deeper pools could hold fish, and those areas should be worked thoroughly.

Unfortunately for the North Fork's steelhead, during late summer and fall, they must share prime holding water with large king salmon (kings are not open for fishing). Kings are superior specimens, and steelhead must accept second-rate security water when the larger fish are about. But that doesn't mean anglers should immediately think there are no steelhead present if they see a big king roll.

*The North Fork's demise was caused by logging. Wholesale timber cutting continues today, as shown by this operational mill near Darrington.*

According to Dennis Dickson, a former biologist who runs Sauk-Suiattle Flyfishing and spends generous portions of time on the Stillaguamish (he lives at the forks in Arlington), steelhead often hold near big kings.

"They look for the security of deeper water, but they are moved around by chinook," Dickson says. "They'll lie above and below the chinook, at the heads and tailouts of pools, so you have to fish around the Chinook to get at the steelhead."

Flyfishers encounter similar situations on the South Fork Stillaguamish, which also receives summer- and winter-run steelhead, plus kings (again, they are not open for angling). The South Fork does receive some wild steelhead, but the overall fishery is not regarded as highly as the North Fork, possibly because it lacks flyfishing-only restrictions. Places to look for summer fish on the South Fork include the mouth of Canyon Creek, the Gold Basin area, Rogue Valley, and Red Bridge.

While steelhead can be caught from the North and South Forks as summer dwindles and fall begins, late August and September are incredibly challenging times—the water is low and clear, and the fish have seen it all before.

Flyfishing perks up in October when the first rains arrive and fresh fish push into the system. Also, Dickson says, a strange phenomenon occurs at that time that is well worth trying to exploit.

*Fly-only water at Fortson Hole on the North Fork Stillaguamish.*

"When the first fall rains come, steelhead from both forks bail out and head for the Fortson Hole area," he says. "You might have as many as 200 steelhead show up in the Fortson area at one time. It's just an amazing thing that happens. If an angler can hit that right, there are days upon days where you can really get them. My personal best when I encountered that situation was 20 fish hooked, 11 landed."

Although it's quite feasible for an accomplished fly caster to stick a couple summer-runs a day on the Stillaguamish, a multiple-fish tally should never be expected. In fact, because the Stillaguamish gets pounded, its fish wise up to the way of the angler. When that happens, precise techniques and patterns are required to score.

"During the early season, it you can put a fly in front of a fish, it doesn't matter what pattern you are using or what leader you have on, they'll take it," Dickson says. "The native Deer Creek fish, especially, have an affinity for taking flies from the surface. In fact, I think they take from the surface as well, if not better, than underneath. If you get into a pod of Deer Creek fish that want to eat off the top, you'll think life is wonderful."

When fishing on top, Dickson goes with size 6 to 10 bombers in color combinations of black, brown, and orange. He's also very confident with a size 10 October caddis or a size 8 royal Wulff. When considering surface options, Dickson looks for days that offer clear water and dark, overcast skies. When fishing below Deer Creek for natives, Dickson goes with a 12-foot leader, tapered to 0X, which equals about 8-pound test.

If fishing above Deer Creek mostly for hatchery fish, Dickson ties his flies on with a riffling hitch. Muddler minnows and the aforementioned bombers and skaters are good surface options over that water.

"I fish the skaters over glassy pools and tailouts," Dickson explains. "In the choppy water and riffled heads and tailouts, I prefer muddlers and bombers."

When fishing over hatchery steelhead, especially late in the season when the water is low and clear, anglers need to incorporate stealth to their routine—these are incredibly wary, skeptical fish that don't come easy.

"If we have a pulse of rain, I may go with a 9-foot leader," Dickson says. "If the water is low and clear and the light is bright, I'll go much longer, up to 15 or 18 feet. If I feel the fish have been pounded, I like to go with a skating fly. I've even gone with small dry flies; once I landed a nice summer-run on a size 20 parachute Adams. That's the extreme, but it can be done. Most of the fish are real receptive to size 8 through 14 trout flies. I use hare's ears, Prince nymphs, and pheasant tails. Once, after the rains had come and the river dropped back to gin clear, I caught five steelhead on seven casts using a San Juan worm. Really, once the water gets low and clear, you have to treat these fish like a big trout, not a steelhead. They've avoided snaggers, swimmers, and catch-and-release fishermen like me, and they see everything—they can tell you the size, pattern, and who tied a fly that drifts by."

It's a fact: Bright, gaudy flies do not draw takes when the water is low and clear. Anglers may want to shelve traditional patterns, such as the green butt skunk, in favor of toned down flies in natural colors like green, brown, and black.

"It's like hunting pheasants late in the season," Dickson says. "No longer are you shooting at the young, dumb birds. Instead, you've got the old roosters that flush from the far side of a field when you shut the door of your truck.

"Late season steelhead are not dumb, and they realize that things like line shadow are things that create hurt for them. They wise up and become more oriented to insects. They may say, 'Here comes a green butt skunk, get out of the way.' They are in an avoidance pattern, and one of the things they do to avoid anglers and fly lines is to suspend themselves midlevel in the stream. Typically, you can put a fly on the bottom or on the top, and you are in a steelhead's strike zone. But late in the season, especially where steelhead stack up in places like Fortson Hole, you can find them suspended, and you have to put a fly in front of them."

To do that, Dickson often opts for a sinktip line. Sinktips are effective every day of the year on the Stillaguamish, even during low-water periods. However, an angler should carry a variety of lines to match flow conditions.

"Sinktipping is very effective, but I go small and subtle," Dickson says. "For the wild fish, I use a lot of marabou flies in small sizes. Woolly buggers and hare's ears in natural colors are also good choices. Again, things that look like insects work best. The only time I go with something bright, such as a royal coachman or green butt skunk, is when the light is low in the morning and evening. But during summer, that only lasts an hour or two."

One tactic that can place a fish in your grip when other flyfishers sing the "unproductive" blues is to change tactics and show steelhead something they haven't seen before. For me, that tactic has worked on Rocky Mountain tailwater fisheries, on eastern Washington's Columbia Basin lakes, on Alaska's coho salmon, and even on tarpon in the Florida Keys. It works on the Stillaguamish's steelhead, too, much to Dickson's delight.

"When everyone is going with a sinktip on the bottom, I like to put on a floating line and work the top," Dickson offers. "A lot of guys believe that hatchery fish won't come up top to eat, and I tell them, 'Oh, you're probably right.' Then I go out and do it, and that tactic works really well for me."

While summer-run steelhead attract most of the attention on the Stillaguamish, its winter offerings should not be overlooked. The flyfishing-only season on the North Fork runs from April 16 to November 30, so flyfishers may have to rub elbows with the bait and tackle crowd during winter, but that can be tolerable.

Both the North and South Forks receive winter steelhead, but the run is more pronounced on the North Fork. Productive winter steelhead fishing occurs from February through May, and anglers who tie into those fish do so with sinktip lines. The standard down-and-across steelhead swing is the most effective presentation. Look for steelhead to hold in the pools and in mid-depth, walking-speed runs.

"During their exploration of the North Fork, guys should fish the winter run—it's one of the most underrated fisheries around," Dickson says. "Fish that enter from February through May are phenomenal. Most are wild fish that are mainstem spawners, but they do cruise up Squire Creek, too. I enjoyed lots of days in April and May where I've hooked four or five fish in a day. I think the best winter run fishing occurs from Deer Creek up to Whitehorse because that's where the best spawning gravel is."

Sea-run cutthroats also provide excellent opportunities on the Stillaguamish. They are present in good numbers below the forks, extending to the mouth of the river. Fall is the best time to pursue 10- to 16-inch fish, and they can be a blast.

When I was cutting my flyfishing teeth, too afraid to ask for advice, an older man approached me at the Silvana access site. Obviously, he'd seen my futile attempts and politely offered advice. We engaged in quality conversation (no attitude on his part), then he pulled out a stocked fly box and presented me with a couple dozen (a couple dozen!) supremely tied sea-run cutthroat and summer steelhead flies. I wish I had taken his name and phone number down because generous people are few and far between. Anyway, I took his brief cutthroat dissertation, plus those flies, downstream and hooked up on a couple of wonderful fish. (Sir, if you read this, I offer my thanks. I saved some of those flies for reference, and I've used those patterns successfully on many rivers.)

The top months for sea-runs are September and October, and they can be taken on many traditional patterns, such as the yellow spider or a sunken coachman. But

*Steve Winder with a big, native buck steelhead from the North Fork Stillaguamish. (Photo courtesy Salmon Bay Tackle)*

sea-runs also accept cranefly and grasshopper imitations. Yellow sally patterns, such as a size 14 stimulator, also draw takes on the surface.

No matter when or where you choose to fish the Stillaguamish, you should surround yourself with a sense of history. Read the Stillaguamish's great authors, such as Grey, Haig-Brown, Steve Raymond and Enos Bradner—their historical perspectives on the Stillaguamish indicate how good fishing used to be in western Washington. Their stories can be applied to most waters in the state and their words explain why it is so important to protect what we flyfishers have left.

On the other hand, don't let stories about how good it was in the good old days and the subsequent demise of anadromous fish runs in western Washington keep you away from the river. The North Fork of the Stillaguamish remains wonderful water to fish and one of my favorite places to cast a fly. Tie into a stubborn, resourceful native steelhead or even one of its hatchery brothers and you should realize why the Stillaguamish remains one of the most revered steelhead streams in the Northwest.

# Stream Facts: Stillaguamish River

## Seasons and Special Regulations
- Steelhead: Open March 1 through November 30. Flyfishing only April 16 through November 30.
- From December 1 through February 28, statewide rules apply.

## Species
- Steelhead
- Sea-run cutthroat
- Dolly Varden
- King and chum salmon

## Stream Characteristics
- In the flyfishing-only waters of the North Fork, steelhead hide in the deeper pools and runs.
- Most of the river can be covered with a cast from a single-handed rod.
- The North Fork's summer-run steelhead are inclined to take surface flies.
- The river's late summer and fall run of king salmon are off-limits to anglers.
- In the South Fork, fly rodders rub elbows with bait and hardware anglers for summer-run steelhead.
- The lower river, below the forks, holds some steelhead, but it is more highly regarded for its sea-run cutthroat fishing. September and October are the prime months for sea-runs.

## Access
- The Stillaguamish forks are best waded, and there are numerous spots to jump off the highway and get on the river.
- The lower river, below the forks, also provides excellent wade fishing.
- If an angler has to fish out of a boat, there are crude put-in and take-out spots located all along the river.

# SKYKOMISH RIVER

Under the watchful eye of towering Mount Index, surrounded by thick evergreen forests and cascading waterfalls, the Skykomish River offers Washington anglers some of the most spectacularly imposing scenery in the West, along with great opportunities to catch large steelhead and salmon on a fly rod.

In fact, blessed with both winter- and summer-run steelhead and a variety of salmon species, including king, chum, coho, and pink, the Skykomish offers decent opportunities every month of the year.

Due to these opportunities and its proximity to major metropolitan centers (the Sky is just an hour's drive northeast of Seattle), the river is one of Washington's most popular and heavily-fished waters. Unfortunately, it does not offer a fly-only section. But that doesn't really matter. Even for those of the solitary persuasion, a short hike assures uncluttered rapids and prime runs that can be fished at a leisurely pace. The Sky has so much appealing water it's never a question of, "Is there enough room for me?" Instead, the pertinent question is, "Where should I fish?" when so much appealing water is there for the taking.

If you prefer a typical small river environment—small being relative here since the Skykomish drains hundreds of square miles of soggy terrain and is prone to blowout floods—you stick to the north and south forks where trout and steelhead hide in pronounced riffles and runs or behind giant boulders. If you are looking for the classic big water environment, fish downstream below the town of Goldbar, where metalheads and salmon hold to subtle, submerged structure, such as gravel bars, boulders, and logs. Big rods, shooting heads, and sinktip lines are the common tackle used here.

No matter where you choose to fish the Skykomish, its quality fishing is dependent on the return of salmon and steelhead from the Pacific Ocean and Puget Sound. Because these fish face many obstacles at sea and an equal number on their upriver trip to spawning grounds, the quality of fishing varies from season to season.

During good years, the Skykomish can be loaded with steelhead. A good salmon season witnesses the return of about 10,000 chums, 5,000 cohos, and 120,000 pinks. (Note: Pink salmon returns are highest during odd-numbered years. On even-numbered years, just 3,000 or 4,000 pinks return.) A summer king salmon run also enters the Skykomish, but their numbers are so low that they are listed on the endangered species list. Fishing for king salmon is forbidden on the Sky. Sea-run cutthroat trout (also called harvest trout) and Dolly Varden char can be encountered anywhere on the Skykomish. Sea-run and Dolly numbers are typically strongest during fall.

No matter what kind of fish you encounter, the Skykomish is a treat on which to cast a fly. I began my forays to the Sky when I was five, accompanying my father on winter steelhead trips to the north fork. I was too young to carry a rod, but I remember my father hooking huge steelhead from beautiful runs on some absolutely dreadful, sleeting days. In particular, I remember him hooking a huge metalhead, maybe

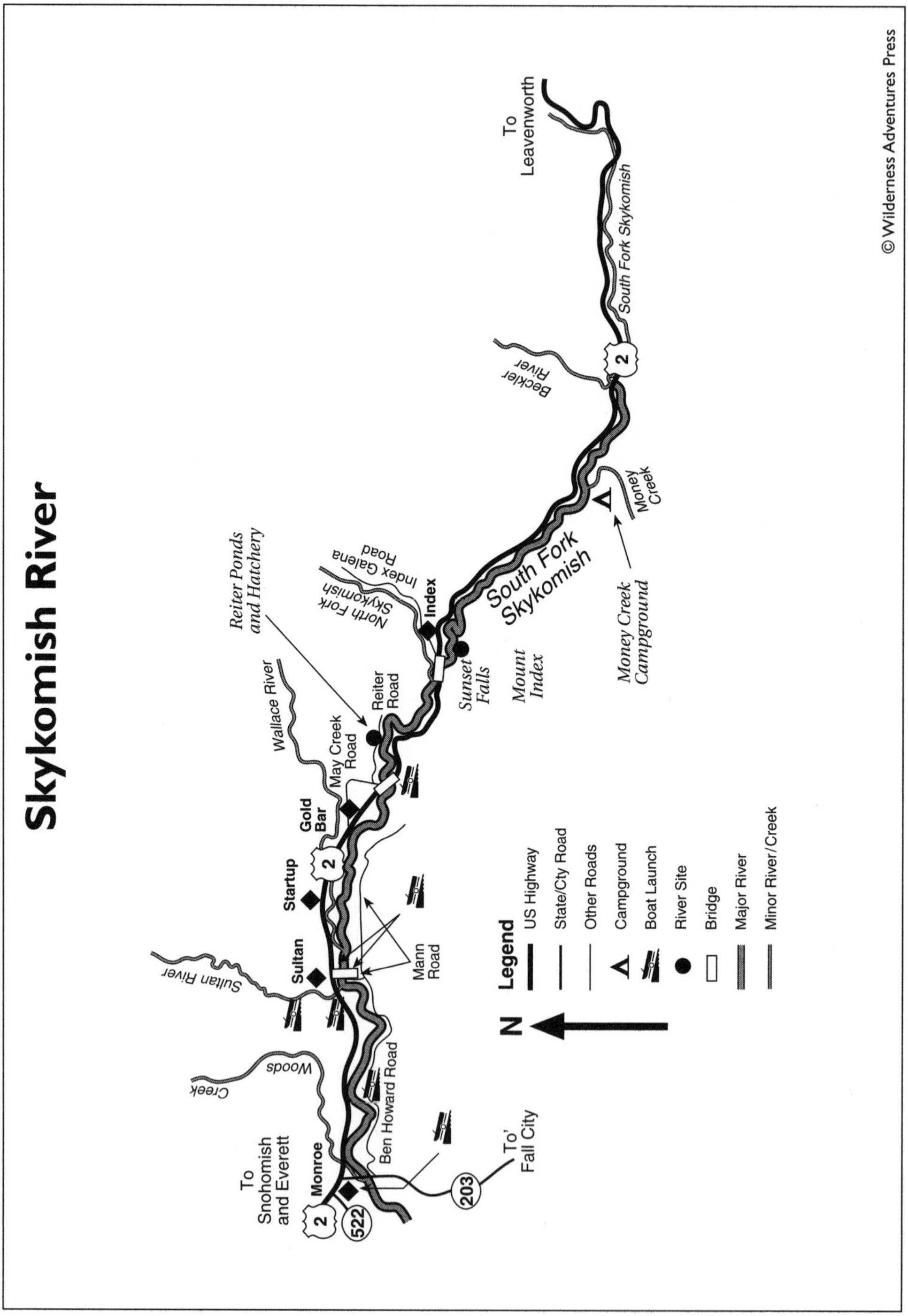

# Skykomish River

Legend

N

US Highway
State/Cty Road
Other Roads
△ Campground
Boat Launch
● River Site
□ Bridge
Major River
Minor River/Creek

To Snohomish and Everett
Monroe
2
522
To Fall City
203
Ben Howard Road
Woods Creek
Sultan River
Sultan
Mann Road
Startup
Gold Bar
2
May Creek Road
Wallace River
Reiter Road
Reiter Ponds and Hatchery
North Fork Skykomish
Index Galena Road
Index
Sunset Falls
Mount Index
South Fork Skykomish
Money Creek Campground
Money Creek
Beckler River
South Fork Skykomish
2
To Leavenworth

© Wilderness Adventures Press

the biggest he'd ever fought, only to lose it when some numbskull cast over his line. I learned a few new words that day.

In high school, when my friends were old enough to drive, we took their old beater cars to the Skykomish—the river was far enough away to give the impression that we were embarking on a huge expedition, yet close enough that we could phone our parents, relate our sob stories, and ask for a ride home when the vehicles broke down.

In college, the Skykomish was close enough to hit after Saturday morning basketball practices. I remember one very cold February day upstream from Monroe, when a massive native steelhead devoured my offering and took off for the Puget Sound. I clamored along a steep bank, rod held high in one hand, the other grasping tree limbs, my felt-soled wading boots sliding on mud. That I did not snap a limb and plunge headlong into the river is surprising. Unfortunately, my luck didn't hold—the steelhead, a beautiful, colorful fish that I estimated between 12 and 16 pounds, took out nearly all of my line and shook the hook. I reeled in slack line and climbed the bank to level ground and sat down.

Today, the Skykomish still holds promise every time I visit. It may not seem the long, adventurous trip that it once did, but the scenery is still there, the salmon and steelhead runs are stable, and I hit the river every opportunity I get. Because it is not a long drive from Seattle, I can write in the morning, then skip town and fish the afternoon hours. On warm sunny days, when the summer-runs are stacked up in the forks, there's no better option.

If you choose to fish the Skykomish, you really can't pick a bad time unless you hit the river during one of its common November or December floods. After those floods, which may last a week or more, the Skykomish takes another week or so to clear up and drop. That's why it always pays to call a tackle shop or a guide before visiting the river. There's nothing worse than driving an hour or two to find the river blown and your angling adventure shot for the day. No matter what anyone tells you, a full day in a Snohomish Valley bar does nothing to promote your chances of catching a fish.

During January and February, the Sky gets the bulk of its hatchery steelhead returns, all of them headed for the hatchery at Reiter Ponds. By early February, some wild, native fish start showing up in the Snohomish, and soon they are into the Sky, sucking down flies near Monroe. The bulk of the wild winter-runs are spread through the system by March 1, but their numbers peak in late March and April. During that time, it is not uncommon for dedicated anglers to hook steelhead that range between 8 and 16 pounds. A few big brutes in the 20-pound range show each season, as well.

"Skykomish steelhead run average size for Puget Sound river fish," says Kurt Kramer, a biologist for Washington Department of Fish and Wildlife in Mill Creek. "Compared to Skagit River fish, they aren't big; there are not nearly the numbers of 20-pound fish in the Sky. But I have seen steelhead taken on the Skykomish that weighed in the high 20s. In fact, we've creel-checked several fish over 25 pounds."

*A lovely, broad run on the mainstem Skykomish, near Sultan.*

While wild fish scatter throughout the entire Skykomish system, including the north and south forks, most of the steelhead stop their migration before reaching Goldbar. The forks don't hold nearly as many fish as the downstream reaches. The densest redd counts are usually tallied below Monroe.

According to John Farrar, a dedicated fly bum who works at Patrick's Fly Shop in Seattle and has been fishing and guiding the river for 20 years, good flyfishing opportunities can be found throughout the system, even below the Skykomish in the Snohomish River.

"There is excellent water all the way down the system into the Snohomish," he says. "In fact, when the water is extremely low and clear, you might have to drop into the Snohomish to find the fish. Sometimes they stack up below the mouth of the Skykomish to wait for better conditions.

"The section from Monroe to Sultan has numerous gravel bars with excellent water. The Sky has enough bars, with excellent water, that you could fish bars the entire season and not exhaust the possibilities.

"There is good winter-run water upstream, too," Farrar adds. "The braided water between Sultan and Goldbar has lots of pockets and interesting developments that change each year due to floods."

Finding good water on the Skykomish is no different than finding quality water on any other Puget Sound steelhead stream: Look for medium-depth water in the

*The North Fork of the Skykomish offers decent summer-run steelhead action.*

3- to 6-foot range with a walking pace speed, a rocky bottom, and nearby deep water that allows a fish quick access to safety. Sinktip lines, short, 3- or 4-foot leaders, and weighted flies help reach fish that sit tight-finned to the bottom.

As is true with any steelhead river, flyfishers should avoid the deep, sexy water—to catch winter fish, flyfishers must place an offering near the bottom, and that just isn't going to happen if you cast to deeper runs. Obviously, that water holds fish; it just can't be fished as effectively.

If you can find productive water and fish it meticulously, a steelhead will likely eat your fly, whether you fish a marabou, woolly bugger, the classic skunk or any number of historic favorites. However, fly selection does change with varying weather conditions, and Farrar assures that fly selection will affect success.

"I would say I usually fish the marabou, spey-style flies in sizes 0/2 to 2," Farrar says. "But the general practitioner in a variety of colors is also a good choice. On bright days, as long as the water is clear, I feel comfortable fishing dark flies like blacks and purples. On dark days or if the water is cloudy, I like orange. A black over chartreuse marabou is always a good choice, too."

Because the Sky is a wide, deep stream, selection of fly rod can be crucial to your success. A big river calls for fairly heavy rods in the 7- to 10-weight range. Anything less and you might burn your shoulder out trying to stretch a cast to a perfect run 60 or 70 feet distant.

Like many area waters, the Sky has witnessed a steady increase in two-handed spey rods along its banks, and Farrar is among those who like to pitch flies with the long rods.

"I don't discourage people from using single-handed rods in the 7 to 9-weight range, but the two-handed rods are a lot of fun, and I fish them more than anything else. During winter I use a 14- or 16-foot, 8-weight. During summer I fish a 13.5-foot rod for an 8-weight line.

While the Skykomish is usually fishable in some capacity, it is prone to "coloring up" after a rain storm or when the temperature and surrounding snow level rises. If the snow level rises suddenly, realize that snowmelt will certainly raise and cloud the river. Rising water will move fish into the system, but they can be extremely difficult to coax to a fly at that time. However, just after the river has risen, a cold spell can start the water dropping and clearing. That is the time to fish.

"Personally, if the river is rising and coloring, I don't bother fishing," Farrar says. "But if it's falling and clearing with a couple feet of visibility, that's a good time to fish. At that time, steelhead lie closer to the bank and take up new holes. It can be really good like that."

Whether the river is rising or falling, Farrar rates February through April 1 as the prime time to fish the Skykomish. Like most avid steelhead fishermen, Farrar would much rather chase and catch wild fish than their hatchery impostors.

"I think you just can't beat the opportunity to catch wild fish," he says. "In December and January, we are primarily fishing hatchery steelhead, and they move through the system quickly. In February you start to see the wild fish, and it just gets better in March and April."

While winter steelheading has its merit, for me there's nothing like chasing 5- to 10-pound sea-run rainbows during the summer months with a light fly rod and small flies. And the Skykomish is an excellent place to do just that.

What could be better than hopping along a rocky bank on the north fork, searching the pools and riffles with skating and waking surface flies? I've spent many July, August, and September afternoons searching the Skykomish for fish, and I have never walked away from the river disappointed. That is not to say I've caught or even raised a fish on every trip. It's just a reflection on the sunny western Washington days when I can wet-wade the clear river, the evergreens offering that pungent aroma, and everything in life seems just about right.

Summer steelhead enter the Skykomish in May, and they are present when the river opens June 1. At that time, most of the summer-runs are holding or moving through the Monroe to Goldbar section. Later, around July 4, many fish can be found upstream in the north and south forks.

One thing to consider when chasing summer steelies is water condition. The Skykomish usually endures its heaviest runoff during May and June. That does not mean that the river is necessarily blown out and flies won't work. However, high water can make fishing the upper river, including the forks, difficult.

*The Skykomish River carves through some of Washington's most impressive, rugged country and offers winter and summer-run steelhead to 20 pounds. Here, avid flyfisher Jeff Bobin surveys the water.*

That's why Farrar prefers to fish the lower river, from Sultan downstream, during early summer. After July 4, as water conditions settle, Farrar starts looking upriver. "June is a great time for summer-runs, and they are tremendously active and strong at that time," he says. "They can rip out a hundred yards of line real quick. But during that time, we've often got high water. It's clear and fish move in it, but it's hard to get around on the upper river when conditions are like that. At that time, I really enjoy fishing the lower river from Sultan to its mouth. There are lots of gravel bars, and the fish will be there.

"From mid-July on, the fish will be higher up in the forks, and it's beautiful water to fish," he adds. "There are beautiful runs and rock-studded holding water to work."

Unlike some western Washington summer-run streams, the Skykomish does not offer classic spot and stalk opportunities. Instead, due to its depth, the Sky demands traditional steelhead fishing methods. When working dry flies, anglers must cover all of the prime water. The same is true when fishing subsurface patterns with the traditional downstream steelhead swing. Whether going with a dry fly or streamer, concentrate on the riffles and fast runs where summer-runs seek aerated water.

An ideal summer-run rod is a 9-foot, 7-weight, although some anglers prefer to fish a 6-weight, and others wouldn't approach the river without a 10-foot, 8-weight. No matter what weight rod you bring, fish summer-runs with a sinktip or floating line and fairly long, light tippets in the 10-foot, 1X to 3X range. Vary the strength of your tippet, depending on the attached fly. If you fish a size 8 or 10 fly, go with 3X. If you offer a size 4 or 6 fly, use a heavier tippet.

One place you can count on finding summer-runs, whether you chase them in July, August, September, or October, is the Reiter Ponds stretch. Hatchery fish hold above and below the hatchery that is located there, and they are often willing to take a fly.

Speaking of flies, any of the low-water patterns work well on the Skykomish. Local favorites include the Skykomish sunrise, Brad's brat, fall favorite, comets, steelhead caddis, bombers, moose turds, and muddlers.

Farrar's favorite summer-run fly is a black woolly worm, size 8. He fishes that pattern during June before switching to topwater patterns when the water reaches 52 or 53 degrees.

"In June, I might fish woolly worms off a sinktip line, but when the water warms, I switch to a floating line and topwater flies. Any deer-hair waking pattern will work on top."

The south fork Skykomish offers some particularly interesting summer and fall fishing options. Decent numbers of steelhead enter the south fork, but their upstream migration stalls at a natural falls that keeps fish from moving upstream. To help the fish and allow them to reach some excellent spawning grounds, WFW trucks about 800 wild summer-runs and "several hundred" hatchery fish above the falls. Those fish are complemented by a decent population of wild rainbow trout that range between 12 and 20 inches. The largest of those resident trout, assures Kramer, rest away from easy access points. If anglers are willing to hike away from the highway and the easily accessed waters, they will likely tangle with a few trout over 15 inches in a day. A steelhead attached to your line, tailwalking in midriver, is icing on the cake.

While steelhead draw most anglers to the Sky, the river's salmon opportunities cannot be overlooked. Because of their low numbers and endangered species listing, king salmon are a moot point. Coho, pinks, and chums are a different story.

Pinks and coho move into the Skykomish in August, and their numbers peak in mid to late September. Kramer estimates that 4,000 coho return each year and about 120,000 pinks every other year. While cohos offer limited opportunities, they can be found in schools, and any bright streamer pattern, including marabous, will draw strikes. If you catch one coho, sit on that spot because other fish are likely nearby.

*Byron Vadset hoists a hard-earned hatchery steelhead that Fred Thomas caught on the Skykomish River. To fish the Sky during winter, flyfishers need patience and a strong will to stave off the cold. (Other necessities will also do the trick—note the contents of the boat.)*

Pinks attack smaller flies, such as sand shrimp imitations and small marabous. Pinks spread out through the entire system and remain in the river through the fall, although, like other salmon, their body quality diminishes the longer they remain in freshwater.

Chum salmon offer the best big-fish opportunities on the Skykomish. Look for chums to enter the system in late October or early November. Thanksgiving always assures good chum numbers and is a prime time to hit the river—as long as it's not flooding.

"Sometimes we'll have fishable numbers by October 20th, and other times it won't be until November 10th," Kramer says. "In the odd-numbered years, we see about 10,000 chums return. In even years, we see about 28,000. Those are primarily wild fish, and they tend to concentrate in the lower river, although we see good numbers all the way to Sultan. They average 8 to 17 pounds, and they are strong fish that put up a good fight."

While Farrar shies away from coho and pink salmon options, preferring instead to chase summer-run steelhead in the Columbia Basin, he returns to the Sky during late fall to tackle chum salmon (also called dog salmon) with his fly rod.

"They are a great, strong fish and there are just tremendous numbers of them," he says. "They take a fly real well, and anything from a straight skunk to chartreuse marabou patterns will work.

"The run peaks around Thanksgiving, and at that time, there are so many fish around, you just cover the water. They hold pretty close to shore, which is an advantage. You can cast downstream and let a fly swing, and they will pound it. I think they take it more out of territorial aggression than anything else. If they see a fly, they grab it."

Whether chasing salmon or steelhead, the Skykomish and its fish are easy to reach. From Seattle, take I-5 north to the Alderwood Mall Boulevard Exit and turn onto I-405 south. Take the Monroe/Stevens Pass exit and follow to Monroe. Turn left at Monroe and follow Sr 2 east. The river parallels the highway toward Stevens Pass.

If you can swing it, a boat should be hooked up to your truck when you visit the Skykomish. An angler can reach most of the prime runs by wading, but the river is big and powerful and often dangerous for wade anglers. A boat allows anglers to cover any piece of water in relative safety. A boat also allows first-time anglers a good overview of the river. Later, favorite runs can be visited on foot if water conditions allow. Standard drift boats, like Lavro's (built in Monroe), Hyde's, Roe's, Clackacrafts, and Willie's work fine along with Avon and Achilles rafts if they have secure rowing frames.

"A boat really helps a guy—it's an asset," Farrar says. "There is hardly a drift that you can't get to on your feet, but it will take dedication and planning. With a boat you get to feel the mood of the river and see all of it."

Sometimes the Skykomish River gets lost in the aura of the Skagit and Sauk Rivers to the north and the Olympic Peninsula streams to the west. Those rivers offer the greatest concentrations of big, wild fish, and there are great flyfishing traditions built around them. However, for me, the Skykomish will always beckon—it's close to home, it receives generous runs of steelhead and salmon, and its scenery can't be beat. Sure, there is heated competition from spin and bait fishers, some of them cruising the river in obnoxious jet sleds, but I can always find a place to fish the river in relative solitude. If you join me on the Skykomish some warm summer afternoon, take a moment to peer upriver toward Mount Index and the surrounding valley walls, most blanketed in dense timber. Listen to the river and ask yourself this question: Is this a little taste of heaven?

# Stream Facts: Skykomish River

### Seasons
- Open for trout and steelhead June 1 through February 28, including south and north forks.
- Catch and release from March 1 through April 30 from mouth to Sultan River.
- From Sultan to Forks open June 1 through March 31.

### Special Regulations
- Wild steelhead can only be retained (they should be released) from December 1 through February 28.
- Salmon restrictions apply.
- Check regulations booklet thoroughly before fishing the Skykomish.

### Species
- Steelhead
- Coho, pink, king, and chum salmon
- Sea-run cutthroat
- Dolly Varden (bull trout)

### Stream Characteristics
- A mountain freestone river, the Skykomish is a medium-sized river through its forks.
- Downstream stretches are broad.
- The Skykomish offers winter- and summer-run steelhead to good size.
- A good winter fish pushes 15 to 20 pounds.
- Summer-runs range from 5 to 15 pounds.

### Access
- Boats or rafts offer almost unlimited access to the Sky. Numerous launch and take-out sites are located along the river.
- Bank anglers also find plenty of access, some over private land (with permission), some on Forest Service ground, and some managed by Washington Department of Fish and Wildlife.

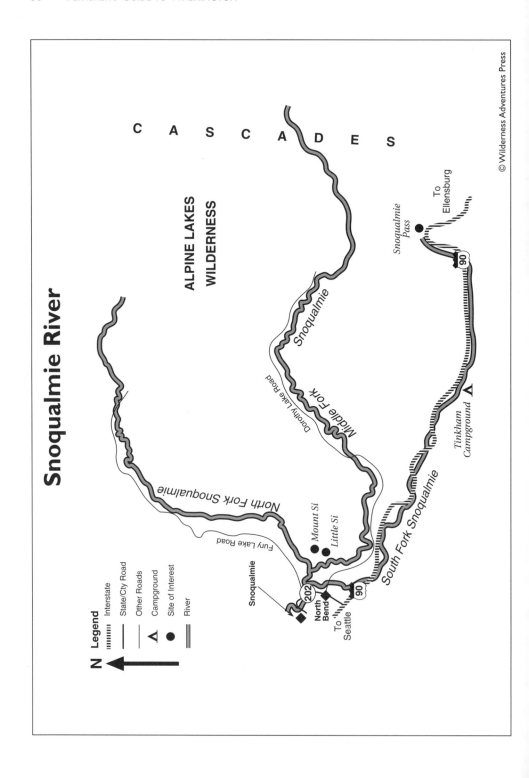

Snoqualmie River

# SNOQUALMIE RIVER

Although the Snoqualmie River may never be mentioned in the same breath as Washington's Yakima River and Rocky Ford Creek, it is a pleasant place to fish, and its trout, if not large, are appealing for this reason: they are all wild and are just 45 minutes away from downtown Seattle.

Just imagine: you are whiling away the hours at a Columbia Tower office on a June afternoon, and the sun has been pounding the Seattle asphalt relentlessly. All day, you've been peeking out the window and chastising yourself for living the inside life. Money versus freedom. Money versus freedom. Money versus freedom. A co-worker tells you to shut up, "You're bugging me." Not good, this. How bad, you ask yourself, do you want to be outside in that treasured sunshine, especially on a river with fly rod in hand?

You consider your options: The Yakima is just a little too far away. Rocky Ford Creek is a weekend expedition at best. The lowland lakes are frothing with hatchery trout, carp, and a bunch of baitchuckers. And the summer-run steelhead just haven't come in yet. You consider eastern Washington's desert lakes, but you have to be in the office in the morning or the boss will have your ass.

That's when the notion strikes: You can leave at 3:00, beat traffic across the I-90 bridge, and slide waist deep into the Snoqualmie, casting dry flies, by 4:30PM. And that's exactly what you do. See, life isn't so bad, and because of that job, you've got a hell of a lot more money to play with than I do.

The Snoqualmie River begins as three distinct forks in the Cascade Mountains east of Seattle near Snoqualmie Pass. Each is a swift stream, carrying snowmelt, spring water, and groundwater runoff down the flanks of the Cascades. Where the forks meet, just above Snoqualmie Falls, the main river begins. However, for a fly-fisher's purpose, the forks represent the best option. Downstream, the Snoqualmie is a deep, slow-moving river that harbors steelhead and salmon seasonally, but it is not overly conducive to a fly.

The forks, which slice through dense timber and the nearly impenetrable west-side brush, offer decent action on wild rainbow and rainbow/cutthroat hybrid trout in the 8- to 12-inch range with an occasional 15-inch monster falling for a fly. If you must catch large trout to feel refreshed, don't bother fishing the Snoqualmie. Stay in Seattle and swelter in your office.

However, if you can accept the limited size of its fish, the Snoqualmie offers much to the urban-bound flyfisher. In fact, the Snoqualmie's small fish should not be ignored even if you are a chaser of trophy trout. I have been called "a big trout snob" (there are worse things to be called), but I, too, find merit in fishing the Snoqualmie.

Each time I visit the river, I realize what a good time can be had on a small stream with a light fly rod and a box full of dry flies. Cast a parachute Adams here, toss an elk hair caddis there, run a Prince nymph behind an exposed boulder or drift a grasshopper through a shallow riffle—a trout will eventually eat it. And if I miss a fish on the take or allow it to shake a fly loose during its spirited, if short, fight—hey, no sweat. The pace is slow, the pressure low, and there are always more eager trout around every bend. That's an attitude that differs dramatically from times when I've lost large trout on the Yakima or one of the eastern desert lakes, and it's a refreshing change.

When I do land a Snoqualmie trout, which has occurred as many as 25 times in a day, I'll hold it in the water and examine its shape and color. By no means does a small fish pale in comparison to a large fish in regard to color and beauty. Bright silver on the side accentuated with a red slash, its back a dark olive splashed with ebony spots, a Snoqualmie rainbow is a fish to appreciate. I often wonder why I don't fish small streams more frequently.

When choosing a place to fish on the Snoqualmie, anglers must make several important decisions—what size stream they want to cover and how much energy to expend to reach it.

If looking for a medium-sized stream, fish the middle fork and adhere to its catch-and-release regulation. If looking for even smaller water, try the south or north forks, which can be easily covered bank to bank with a cast, and honor the selective fishery regulations.

The south fork is the most easily accessible fork. Anglers can fish right in the town of North Bend or travel slightly farther east on I-90 to Twin Falls where there is also good access. Continuing past Twin Falls, I-90 crosses the river a few times. There are numerous exits that provide access at bridge crossings, and anglers can wade up or downstream as they please. Remember, the farther an angler battles the brush to get away from bridge accesses, the better off he'll be.

To reach the north fork, anglers must follow a county road through North Bend, which turns into a dirt road a few miles upriver. The road cuts primarily through private lands for 8 to 10 miles, but it offers public access above that point.

To reach the middle fork and its gorgeous water, anglers should take Exit 34 off I-90 and follow the Middle Fork Road southeast. Middle Fork Road turns into Lake Dorothy Road and then parallels the south fork for 16 miles. Through that stretch, anglers can hop off the road wherever they see prime water and wade into the river.

No matter what fork is chosen, anglers will encounter some of Washington's most beautiful scenery. And they'll find trout that are very willing to scarf flies between the June 1 opener and the October 31 closing date. And I'm not talking about exact imitations here. Forget the no-hackles and bring out the traditional hairwing and parachute patterns.

All of the forks are characterized by excellent pocketwater with a few deep runs and numerous shallow riffles thrown in on the side. Often, deep pools are formed by logjams and downed trees, and the Snoqualmie's trout love those dark lies. During the heat of the day, especially if the sun is high, look for trout holding in the riffles where broken surface current offers ample cover. Early and late in the day, as temperatures drop and the sun moves off the water, fish will spread out a bit, and anglers should systematically cover all the good spots.

*Prime rainbow water on the Snoqualmie River.*

As mentioned, basic attractor flies such as a parachute Adams, humpy, elk-hair caddis, royal Wulff, Joe's hopper, black ant, beetle, stimulator, and light cahill will draw trout to the surface. However, fish do key in on specific hatches, and when they do, an angler needs to inspect the surface to find out what's happening.

In June, look for morning emergences of midges, followed by a caddis hatch that gets rolling around 2 PM and peaks at dark. Baetis mayflies may also be encountered in the afternoons.

In late June and July, look for a solid hatch of pale morning duns that emerge around 11 AM and extend through the afternoon. During summer, make sure to carry a few terrestrial patterns, such as hoppers, ants, and beetles. Often, when fish shun your exact mayfly and caddis imitations, they'll still rise to a terrestrial.

Terrestrials will draw strikes through closing day, but anglers should also take fall Baetis imitations and some large caddis to match the giant October caddis, which can be seen on the river from late September through October.

If you visit the river in June or early July, expect some healthy water conditions. During that time, the spring thaw is just ending, and the water can still be relatively high and slightly off-color.

If you encounter such conditions, try attractor patterns in the size 12 to 16 range or go underneath with nymphs. Basic patterns such as a beadhead hare's ear, pheasant tail, halfback PMD, cased caddis, olive caddis pupa, and a deep sparkle pupa should draw strikes.

In high water conditions, the Snoqualmie's trout will search for mild currents where they can rest and still find food. Anglers should test slackwater pools behind boulders, the inside seam of riffles, backeddies and slow moving side channels. Also, if you visit the river early in the season, pack a pair of waders—at that time, the water can make you sing the high-pitched blues if you wade deep. Later in the season, a pair of shorts and felt-soled wading boots should suffice.

When fishing the Snoqualmie's forks, light, fast-action rods work best. I fish a 4-weight Scott that performs wonderfully with a weight-forward floating line. That rod offers enough backbone to cast nymphs, yet it's delicate enough to throw small dry flies to the wariest of rainbows.

For leaders and tippets, Snoqualmie flyfishers should go with 9-foot, 4X leaders during the early season when conditions offer high water and somewhat limited visibility. As summer progresses and the water drops and clears, 9-foot leaders, tapered to 5X or even 6X, allow more strikes.

Snoqualmie is not a trophy trout stream. However, for western Washington anglers who desire a match-the-hatch, dry-fly scenario, the Snoqualmie is a godsend. True, its rainbows and cutthroats are not huge, but they are located in a place that is not only beautiful but close to the giant city. When the hectic pace of Seattle and the surrounding suburbs becomes too much, the Snoqualmie is the place to go.

Note: The South Fork and North Fork Snoqualmie are managed under a 2-fish over 10 inches per day regulation. However, flyfishers should practice catch and release on the forks. In a high mountain environment, where water temperature is very cold eight or nine months of the year, trout grow slowly. Take too many large fish (that description is relative on the Snoqualmie), and we'll all be stuck with 6-inchers. Consider the fishery when you hook up.

# Stream Facts: Snoqualmie River

### Seasons
- From mouth to Snoqualmie Falls: June 1 through March 31.
- North and South Forks: June 1 through October 31.
- Middle Fork: Year-round.

### Special Regulations
- Selective gear rules apply in some sections.
- Catch and release on North and South Forks from November 1 through May 31.
- Catch and release only and selective gear rules on Middle Fork year-round.
- Other restrictions do apply. See regulations booklet for details.

### Species
- Rainbow and cutthroat trout. Most go 6 to 12 inches, but some 14- to 16-inch fish exist.

### Stream Characteristics
- The Snoqualmie's forks offer decent pale morning dun and Baetis mayfly emergences plus solid caddis hatches throughout summer. Attractor dry flies and standard nymphs draw strikes.

### Access
- The forks are highly accessible, and there is plenty of wade fishing available. A boat is not needed.

# THE ALPINE LAKES WILDERNESS

Carving through Washington state from north to south, the Cascade Mountains and their alpine lakes offer a sanctuary for flyfishers who are fed up with crowded conditions and wary trout at the highly accessible, pressure-pounded lowland lakes and streams.

However, prospective high mountain lake fishers pay a price to reach the Cascade's isolated waters—anglers must burn some leg muscles and lungs, under heavy burden of backpack and fishing gear, to reach these waters. Unless, that is, you have the liberty to take along a couple of horses and allow them to shoulder the load.

Either option provides some memorable days in the high country. The Cascade Mountains have been called the American Alps, and they deserve that recognition: towering rock spires, vast tracts of deep timber, and beautiful, lush green mountain meadows cover the Cascades.

Washington Department of Fish and Wildlife periodically stocks the mountain lakes with trout, so some waters harbor mostly small, yearling trout while others may offer 12- to 18-inch carryover cutthroats, golden trout, or rainbows. Some lakes may be too sterile for trout.

Trout in the alpine lakes are not difficult to catch, but they can be challenging to reach without the mobility that a float tube offers. Yes, a pair of waders, swim fins and a float tube is an awful lot of extra weight to pack into a lake, but those items can make the trip much more enjoyable.

Because most mountain lakes offer a fairly sterile environment—meaning there isn't a lot of food for trout to eat— rainbows, cutts, and goldens pound standard insect imitations.

Traditional Washington fly patterns such as the Carey special, double gray, Conway special, Brad's brat, dandy green nymph, cherry spinner, grizzly king, buck-tail coachman, mosquito, Chironomid pupa, alder fly, black leech, Terry's black ant, gray Wulff, and parachute Adams all draw hearty strikes. Specific insect imitations are not required, but they'll work fine, too.

When visiting the alpine lakes, you'll want to bring a floating line and a sinktip or full-sinking line, preferably all three. When trout feed off the surface, you can use the floating line and a leader tapered to 5X to tempt fish. Early in the morning or during the afternoon, you may find trout feeding subsurface on nymphs. That's when the sinktip and full-sink lines come into play.

While trout can be found just about anywhere in an alpine lake, flyfishers should concentrate efforts at shallow bays, rock drop-offs, and, especially, near inlet and outlet streams if applicable.

One of the beauties of fishing in the alpine country is the chance to fish several lakes during one trip. Mountain lakes are sprinkled throughout the high country, and a little time spent studying a map can offer a path that winds by one or more lakes. And it pays to have a second option.

*Washington's Alpine Lakes Wilderness offers lots of rainbow and cutthroat trout, along with a smattering of golden trout. Here, John Huber celebrates an imminent high mountain trout dinner.*

During severe winters, lakes may freeze over, offering no oxygen, and that may cause trout to perish. However, just over the hill from a winterkill water, another lake might have had just enough oxygen and food for trout to survive. By honing in on areas that offer plenty of options, you won't be too disappointed when one lake fishes poorly. Just hop over the next ridge or saddle and see what might be waiting.

Trying to choose a mountain lake destination is a major problem—there are so many good options, so much beautiful country to see that picking one spot is an awful challenge.

Your best bet is to check with Washington Department of Fish and Wildlife to gain current stocking information. They'll tell you which lakes were stocked recently and which lakes might offer large, holdover trout. They may even tell you which lakes suffered winterkill.

One of the best high country options is the Alpine Lakes Wilderness Area, which takes in a beautiful chunk of terra firma that stretches from I-90 and Snoqualmie

Pass north to Stevens Pass and SR 20. In that area, more than 200 lakes can be found, and many of them harbor trout. Some of the lakes are quite small—essentially pot-holes—while others are large, windswept waters.

When I was in high school I always dreamed of setting out to hike and fish from one highway to the other. My dream never materialized, but someday it might. Several times, I hiked into backcountry lakes and caught piles of rainbows and brookies. One time, I hit a lake stuffed with carryovers, and by the end of the day, I'd landed more than 40 trout over 12 inches. That's high lake fishing at its best.

Most of the Cascade lakes aren't accessible until the snowpack has melted some-time in July. As soon as the snow is gone and ice burns off the lake, some excellent fish-ing can be found, but it tails off just as quickly as it arrived. In fact, by September snow may blanket the high country. In October, count on cold conditions again.

Whether you visit a high mountain lake during the hottest days of August or later in the fall, take along all the emergency and survival gear you need. There are no hos-pitals in the backcountry—you're on your own. Before you leave on your trip, make sure you tell someone responsible where you are going and when you will be back.

When you fish the mountain lakes, don't be afraid to harvest a couple of trout for dinner. Those fish, having prospered in cold, clear water, taste great. And you aren't going to severely impact the trout population by frying a few. In fact, you will proba-bly help the population; mountain lakes often suffer from overpopulation, which stunts trout growth.

Camping sites are abundant in the mountains. Pick a level spot and pitch your tent. There are no fees or reservations. Just make sure you camp away from the lake and try to use low-impact techniques. Brochures explaining low-impact techniques are available from the Forest Service. Remember to store your food appropriately; the Cascade Mountains host black and grizzly bears.

An excellent map of the Alpine Lakes Wilderness Area can be acquired from the Alpine Lakes Protection Society at Route 1, Box 890, Ellensburg, Washington 98926. Maps can also be purchased from the Forest Service. Call the Mount Baker-Snoqualmie Ranger District at 360-677-2414, for more information. A parking permit is required and may be purchased from the District Office or at area outdoor stores.

# Lake Facts: Alpine Lakes Wilderness

### Seasons
- The Cascade Mountain lakes open once snow melts off the high slopes so anglers can reach them.

### Special Regulations
- Most of the mountain lakes are managed under statewide rules.

### Species
- Rainbow, brook, golden, and cutthroat trout
- Most fish average 6 to 8 inches, but larger fish surprise anglers.

### Lake Characteristics
- Relatively sterile environments, the mountain lakes don't offer huge trout, but they make up for it in numbers of fish.

### Access
- Once the snow melts, anglers can hike or ride horses into the remote lakes. Take plenty of food and survival gear. A float tube allows unlimited access and is worth the trouble to pack in.

# Green River

## Legend

**N**

| | |
|---|---|
| ● | River Site |
| ⚞ | Fishing Access |
| ▯ | Bridge |
| ▮ | Dam |
| ▬ | River |

| | |
|---|---|
| ‖‖‖ | Interstate |
| — | State/Cty Road |
| — | Other Roads |
| ✈ | Air Service |
| 🎣 | Boat Launch |

To Renton
(167)

To Seattle
5
Duwamish Waterway

SeaTac

SeaTac International Airport

Green

Kent
516

(167)

To North Bend
18

516

(167)

516

18

Kent-Kangley Road

Kangley

To North Bend

Kanaskat Selleck Road

Green River Rearing Pond

FR 54

Howard Hanson Dam

Kanaskat-Palmer State Park

Franklin-Enumclaw Road

Green River Gorge Road

Black Diamond

Auburn-Black Diamond Road

SE Green Valley Road

River

Whitney Bridge

Flaming Geyser State Park

(169)

Enumclaw

5

Federal Way

Auburn
18

(167)

To Puyallup

To Tacoma

© Wilderness Adventures Press

# GREEN RIVER

Best known as the dumping ground for an elusive serial killer, the Green River offers excellent winter and summer steelhead options, plus decent action on fall-run coho and chum salmon.

Once regarded as a top-10 Washington steelhead river, the Green has fallen from that rank in direct relation to its decline in hatchery-origin metalheads.

In fact, since a huge hatchery steelhead run in 1985, hatchery steelhead returns have decreased each year. Today, maybe a thousand hatchery fish reach the river each season. Fortunately, the Green's wild steelhead seem to be holding their own, with 2,000 to 3,000 making a successful return each year. For those who understand the merit of wild fish, that's great news.

The Green opens for steelhead June 1, and through most of its sections remains open until March 15. There are some exceptions, so check regulations thoroughly before you hit the river.

Hatchery-origin, summer-run steelhead are present in the river on opening day, but fishing doesn't pick up until late June. Prime action extends through early September, but flyfishing conditions become extremely challenging as the water drops in early to mid-July. According to Keith Willits, who manages Salmon Bay Tackle in Ballard and fishes the Green extensively, it's a game of stealth when the water recedes.

"It can be really tough, because the water is low and clear," he says. "The best fishing is in Flaming Geyser Canyon, and it's easy to spot fish in that section of river. But they can see you, too. Really, you have to fish early in the morning, before bright light hits the water, to do well."

When chasing summer-runs, flyfishers may want to focus their efforts from just downstream of Flaming Geyser State Park to Kanasket-Palmer State Park. There are no native summer-runs on the Green so, for most fish, their upstream progression ends there.

The summer-runs range between 6 and 16 pounds, and they are fond of size 6, 8, and 10 bosses and stonefly nymphs. Traditional low-water, sparsely-tied steelhead flies do the trick here.

Summer-runs remain in the system through December, when their numbers are supplemented by early arriving, hatchery-origin winter steelhead. That declining hatchery run peaks in December and January, but the prime fishing begins when native steelhead point their snouts into the Green in mid-January.

"The winter-run hatchery fish are pretty small, maybe 6 to 10 pounds, but the wild fish can be huge," Willits says. "The largest wild fish I landed weighed 18 pounds. Some friends of mine who fish hardware have broken off huge fish—20 to 25 pounds. The best thing about the Green's winter-run fishery is that it doesn't get too much pressure. You can't whack the wild fish, so a lot of guys stay away."

To catch winter steelhead on the Green, flyfishers should seek water that holds steelhead and work it thoroughly. Look for walking-speed water, sprinkled with rocks and boulders. Don't overlook the tailouts of pools, the inside corners of riffles, and the seams between speedy currents. And finally, if you feel like it, cast into the deeper pools and try to maneuver a fly toward the bottom. Pools are not defined as classic steelhead flywater, but they do hold fish.

"This isn't a real large river; it's a quaint stream," Willits says. "It's similar in size to the North Fork Stillaguamish, so you can work the water thoroughly. I like to fish a mile section and get to know it well. I learn that water, and each time I return, I can go to that section and expect to find fish somewhere in it. That's a good tactic as opposed to just running all over the place looking for fish."

As in summer-run fishing, Flaming Geyser Canyon is a good place to look for winter fish. Anglers can gain access to the river at Flaming Geyser State Park and wander upstream or downstream—either direction holds good water and heavy, wild fish. Excellent water also extends upstream as far as Howard Hanson Dam, but access is more difficult. Some private property may be encountered and a bit of bushwhacking will definitely be required to reach the river.

One place that is particularly popular and productive is the hatchery hole at Kanaskat-Palmer State Park. Steelhead stack up below the rearing ponds, but spin casters hit the hole relentlessly. Weigh the merit of solitude vs. piles of fish when you consider fishing this water.

While the Green offers excellent wade fishing, floating the river in a drift boat or raft allows flyfishers a good overview of the river, plus lots of prime water to fish. Just remember: you can't fish from a boat on the Green—it can only be used to transport anglers.

There are many prime floats on the Green, but one of the best extends from the boat launch at Kanaskat-Palmer State Park downstream 7 miles to Flaming Geyser State Park. Another excellent float, Willits' favorite, runs from Flaming Geyser State Park downstream about 8 or 9 miles to the public takeout just above the SR 18 bridge.

"I think the best steelhead float is from Geyser down to the SR 18 bridge," Willits says. "There is so much good water in there that you have trouble deciding where to pull off and fish. If you just float, it doesn't take too long to cover that water, so you can make the trip as long or short as you like. Just watch out for sweepers (logjams). The river changes each year."

If Willits was restricted to a two-week period on the Green each year and could only fish one fly, he'd fish the first two weeks of March and would be throwing a black and orange or black and chartreuse marabou fly. His second choice would be a similarly colored bunny leech, wrapped with lead, and having copper bead eyes.

"A lot of flies work on the Green, but in winter you want something big and flashy, so I go with large marabous," Willits says. "The standard winter steelhead flies work, too. You just have to get it near bottom. Sometimes that requires a sinktip line, and other times you can get away with a floating line and a long leader that runs about 8-pound test."

While the Green's steelhead are its big draw, the river also offers coho, king, and chum salmon in good numbers. Kings are restricted heavily, so they aren't even a

*Often overlooked by Puget Sound area flyfishers, the Green River boots out good numbers of native steelhead each winter. This 15-pound buck, pictured with David Boehm and Trevor Gong, is a typical fish. (Photo courtesy Salmon Bay Tackle)*

viable option anymore. However, cohos return in good numbers and can be taken by flyfishers on the lower river. Try flashy red flies loaded with krystal flash. Chums will also attack flies and are fond of chartreuse streamers. Sinktip lines are a must when fishing chums. Look for them holding in the slow side of seams, the inside corners of riffles, and even in the deeper holes.

The Green also offers this surprise: Puget Sound, pen-raised Atlantic salmon escapees. They hone in on the Green each year and can be taken on a fly rod. Washington Department of Fish and Wildlife has classified them as an official game fish, but feel free to whack one on the head if you want. Take it home instead of a native, wild steelhead; it is legal to keep wild steelies on the Green at certain times of the year, but almost all flyfishers release these gems.

To reach the Green River, take State Route 167 to SR 18 and follow it east through Auburn to Green Valley Road. Turn east on Green Valley Road, which follows the river.

# Stream Facts: Green River

## Seasons and Special Regulations
- Steelhead: Open June 1 through March 15 in most sections.
- Salmon: October 1 or October 16 opener for salmon, depending on section.

## Species
- Steelhead
- Coho, chum, and king salmon

## Stream Characteristics
- A brushy-banked, medium-sized river sprinkled with blowdowns and logjams.
- Best opportunities for steelhead exist through Flaming Geyser Canyon.

## Access
- Two state parks offer good access above and below Flaming Geyser Canyon.
- Drift boats can be launched at Flaming Geyser State Park and taken out at the SR 18 bridge about 7 miles downstream.

# SEA-RUN CUTTHROAT TROUT

While reading this book, you may notice a lack of recognition for the sea-run cutthroat trout. In many chapters on coastal rivers, I've only made brief mention of this fish simply because you might bump into one while fishing for summer-run steelhead or fall salmon.

That brief acknowledgment by no means suggests what the sea-run cutthroat is worth to flyfishers: sea-runs are extremely beautiful, hard-fighting fish with an eagerness to take flies in salt- and freswater and a propensity to jump. Compared to inland rainbow, cutthroat, and brown trout, the sea-run cutthroat is a superior physical specimen.

My father, who has fished around the Northwest for salmon, steelhead, and trout, says, "Pound-for-pound, the sea-run cutthroat is the best fighting, strongest fish in the Northwest." I can't argue with him, and I imagine that few people who have caught many sea-run cutthroats, especially in saltwater, would disagree.

My first experiences with sea-run cutthroats took place in Hood Canal, where our family owns 17 wooded acres. We've cared for that property for more than a half century, and during that time, we've fished often for sea-runs. Our property abuts the head of a small bay. Just below our old cabin, we can launch a boat into the bay and row to its mouth. A spit covers most of that mouth, but a small opening allows water in and out as the tide ebbs and flows.

On an incoming tide, sea-runs race through the gap and spread out over clam and oyster beds, munching any little baitfish they can catch. During my youth, I trolled little spinners over those flats and caught lots of nice sea-runs. I've seen home movies of my father, in his youth, hoisting sea-runs that must have weighed 5 pounds, which he caught out of the bay. Five pounds is huge for a sea-run cutthroat. Most of them average 12 to 16 inches long, rarely longer. However, I keep an ear directed toward conversation whenever I hear sea-run cutthroat mentioned, and I've heard some tales of sea-runs stretching into double digit weights.

For those who know the sea-run cutthroat, taking a fish over 10 pounds, even a fish over 5 pounds, would be similar to catching a 50-inch steelhead or a 30-inch-plus brown trout from a river. Big sea-runs are just so rare that you can't even head out on the water with the thought of catching one over 18 or 20 inches.

During high school, I made frequent forays to Hood Canal and the cabin where I launched our wood boat (the bottom through which my uncle once shot a spear) and rowed to the mouth of the bay. By that time, I had a fly rod in my hand and a catch-and-release ethic in my soul—no more cutthroats ended up in the frying pan.

I remember taking my grandmother, who was in her early 70s, out on the water several times for sea-runs. I rowed while we dragged flies and spinners behind the boat. On one of those days, she landed two identical sea-runs, both 16 inches long. I remember her whooping when one of the fish leaped high in the air and exclaiming, "Beautiful!" And they were. Each displayed a dark green color on its back and head, a yellowish-brown on the sides, speckled by hundreds of small, black dots.

And, of course, they each sported brilliant orange slashes around the gill plates, their trademark. Those fish and that day remain one of my fondest memories—a special time. Now that she is in her mid-80s, I can only hope we get the opportunity to chase sea-runs again. There's no doubt my grandmother still has the fire burning and would join me if asked—she's a fireball.

But back to cutthroats. Sea-runs are still relatively abundant in Puget Sound and Hood Canal, and they ascend most of the large rivers, medium-sized streams, and small creeks that drain into Washington's saltwater coast. However, sea-run cutthroat have not escaped the downsizing of fish runs in the Puget Sound area—the population of wild, native sea-runs has diminished substantially as urban populations have grown. Today, all wild cutthroats must be released.

If you consider the life history of sea-run cutthroat and count the difficulties they must endure to reach maturity, you'd probably release them without that regulation —an acknowledgment of this tough creature, a toast to a fish that has battled its way through a tumultuous life. If sea-run cutthroats were human, they'd have weathered the depression, been drafted into and fought valiantly in several wars, then passed on those strong attributes to offspring just as proud and relentless in their pursuits as those who preceded them. We're not talking sissy fish here.

Sea-run cutthroat begin their life in freshwater streams, hatching from eggs to become fry or parr. At this stage of life, small cutts must compete against burgeoning numbers of salmon smolts. In that competition, cutthroat are inferior opponents, and many perish. Because they are forced into second-rate habitat— salmon control the prime spots—sea-runs must survive on a limited food supply, and many just can't make it.

To rid themselves of salmon competition, adult sea-runs seem to seek out the very highest tributaries and even very small streams to spawn. By doing so, they separate themselves from most salmon, which require fairly sizable streams in which to spawn. This gives sea-run prodigy time to feed and grow without having to deal with salmon smolts.

Sea-run cutthroats are vulnerable to overharvest when sitting on their spawning beds. Because they choose water that is relatively shallow, maybe 2 feet deep or less, with a slow flow, anglers can spot them on redds and cast without mercy to them. That's not good sport, and it isn't in the best interest of sea-run cutthroat. So if you do find them on the their spawning beds, please take a moment to appreciate their beautiful color and the unique nature of this fish, count yourself fortunate, and move on.

It is often an accepted fact that in large rivers, such as the Skagit, sea-run cutthroats may never actually make it to saltwater, choosing instead to feast in a river environment and possibly slipping into Skagit Bay to chase minnows where fresh and saltwater meet. They may never truly enter Puget Sound, the Strait of Juan de Fuca, or the open Pacific Ocean.

However, because many sea-runs spawn in small streams, which provide excellent juvenile habitat but not enough food to sustain a mature fish, many move out into saltwater to grow. It's that trait that places them in the range of saltwater flyfishers.

Sea-runs can be found throughout Puget Sound and Hood Canal. I've seen cutthroat along many Hood Canal beaches, but I've also spotted them in the water off Whidbey Island and in Skagit Bay off Camano Island. I've even seen them off the sand beaches just north of Seattle. The Bainbridge Island area, Liberty Bay, Thorndike Bay, the Belfair area and Lynch Cove, Sinclair Inlet, Oyster Bay, Dyes Inlet, Dabob Bay, the Kingston area, Port Gamble, the Tacoma Narrows, and Budd Inlet are just a few locations that sea-runs are known to prowl.

To locate hot spots for cutthroat, which are heavily guarded secrets, you can take several routes: spend lots of hours on the water searching for prime areas; get information from acquaintances; or visit a fly shop and pry information from guides and shop owners.

Really, locating sea-runs is not a huge problem, especially for those with a boat —even a 12-foot, V-bottom with oars or a 6-horse outboard motor will work fine.

If you have a boat, cruise the beaches on incoming and ebb tides and watch for the presence of small baitfish. Birds feeding in an area may alert you to baitfish. More encouraging is sighting a couple of splashy rises, indicating that sea-runs are present. Typically, if you find one cutthroat, more can be located nearby—they often travel in schools.

If you don't have a boat, pull on a pair of waders and hit the salt. Wade fishing is productive in all the estuaries of large rivers, and often it's productive at the mouth of small creeks, as well. Other prime wade areas include oyster beds, mouths of bays (especially if they are narrow), and sandy beaches where sea-runs spread out in search of sand eels, shrimp, and baitfish.

Although I've taken sea-run cutthroat on dry flies from saltwater, they are most often hooked under the surface on minnow and shrimp imitations. Floating lines can be used; however, sinktips are a nice option. If you do go with the dry-fly option, you'll want to use floating line and place a size 10, 12, or 14 dry fly in the rings of any rises you spot. If the fish doesn't immediately swallow your offering, give it a few quick strips to draw attention. I've used double humpies on the protected waters of southeast Alaska and taken some dandy cutts off the surface. They seem to work best on an incoming tide in protected bays when the surface is calm.

In saltwater, patterns that imitate eels, shrimp, and candlefish are most effective. Place one in front of a cutthroat, and it is not likely to pass on an easy meal. Some popular saltwater patterns include the candlefish, sea sculpin, Borden special, JR's shrimp, purple Joe, Mickey Finn, red and white bucktail, and the professor. These patterns are best tied in size 2, 4, and 6 hooks.

While the best time to find cutthroat in saltwater extends from February through August, there are good numbers of fish in saltwater all year. However, many adult fish move toward their freshwater spawning grounds beginning in August. They remain in freshwater through winter.

Remember, after fishing saltwater, hose down your gear thoroughly. You don't want saltwater corroding your gear.

In freshwater, sea-runs take typical trout fare, such as elk hair caddis, beetles, hoppers, gray drakes, and Baetis. Underneath, they grub cased caddis, all sorts of mayfly nymphs, roe patterns, and even flies that imitate emerging salmon fry.

Some classic sea-run stream flies include the badger yellow, Conway special, grizzly king, shammy royal, Brad's brat, chappie, Dave's two-egg sperm fly, fall favorite, fry fly and the surgeon general, among many others. These patterns are most effective when fished in the fall. Sea-runs typically ascend streams extending from August through November—hence their label as the "harvest trout."

Some flies fish best depending on stream conditions. It always pays to check with a fly shop before you head astream as they can suggest a hot pattern. It's also advisable to get your hands on a copy of *Flies of the Northwest*, a small spiral-bound book that is now published by Frank Amato Publications in Portland, Oregon. The book was originally produced by the Inland Empire Fly Fishing Club in Spokane, Washington, and it is a valuable source of proven patterns, complete with tying instructions for many salmon, steelhead, and sea-run cutthroat flies.

While sea-run cutthroat may never attract the respect and admiration directed toward its larger cousins, the salmon and steelhead, it is a wonderful game fish that can provide all the challenge and fight needed when fishing with a light fly rod. Sometime between April and December, string up your 4- or 5-weight outfit and hit a saltwater estuary or head up a stream and search for cutthroat. If the thrill of pursuit, of new discovery, and the beauty of an interesting fish is what you're after, spend some time on the lonely estuaries and oyster beaches of western Washington or crawl through a tangle of brush to find your own cutthroat haven on one of western Washington's small streams. Solitude and a very interesting fish await you.

# Stream Facts: Puget Sound and Hood Canal (Sea-run Cutthroat)

### Seasons
• Year-round

### Special Regulations
• Limit is 2 fish over 14 inches.
• Release of wild cutthroat trout is mandatory.
• Check with Washington Department of Fish and Wildlife for any emergency closures.

### Species
• Sea-run cutthroat trout to 18 inches.

### Saltwater Characteristics
• Sea-run cutthroat anglers concentrate on the shallow beach areas, mudflats, stream inlets, and oyster beds on incoming and ebb tides.
• Watch for the splashy rise of sea-runs—where you see one fish, more are generally present.

### Access
• Boat launches are sprinkled throughout Puget Sound and Hood Canal. A boat is always a benefit, although beach areas and creek mouths offer some opportunity for a wade fisher.
• If you plan to wade fish, bring 5mm neoprene waders—Puget Sound and Hood Canal waters are always cold.

# NORTHWEST HUB CITIES

# Seattle

### Elevation–0 • Population–491,400

## ACCOMMODATIONS

**Airport Executel,** 20717 International Boulevard / 206-878-3300
**Airport Plaza Hotel,** 18601 International Boulevard / 206-433-0400
**Best Western Airport Executel,** 20717 International Boulevard / 206-878-3300
**Comfort Inn at Sea Tac,** 19333 International Boulevard / 206-878-1100
**Days Inn Hotel,** 19527 Aurora Avenue North / 206-542-6300
**Days Inn Seatac Airport,** 19015 International Boulevard / 206-244-3600
**The Edgewater,** Pier 67 / 206-728-7000
**Embassy Suites Hotel,** 15920 West Valley Hwy (Tukwila), 425-227-8844
**Executel Airport,** 20717 International Boulevard / 206-878-3300
**Hampton Inn Seattle Airport,** 19445 International Boulevard / 206-878-1700
**Ho Jo Inn by Howard Johnson,** 20045 International Boulevard / 206-878-3310
**Inn at the Market,** Pike Place Market / 206-443-3600
**Quality Inn,** 17101 International Boulevard / 206-246-7000
**Ramada Inn,** 2200 5th Avenue / 206-441-9785
**Ramada Limited,** 22300 7th Avenue South / 206-824-9920
**Red Lion Hotel Seattle Airport,** 18740 International Boulevard / 206-246-8600
**Rodeway Inn Sea Tac,** 3000 South 176th Street/ 206-242-0200
**Seatac Valu Inn,** 22246 Pacific Hwy South / 206-878-8427
**Seattle Airport Hilton,** 17620 International Boulevard / 206-244-4800
**Travelodge Airport North,** 14845 Pacific Hwy South / 206-242-1777

## CAMPGROUNDS AND RV PARKS

**Holiday Resort Mobile Park,** 19250 Aurora Avenue North / 206-542-2760

## RESTAURANTS

**Applebee's Neighborhood Grill & Bar,** 17790 Southcenter Parkway /
    206-575-4700
**Ballard Firehouse Food & Beverage Company,** 5429 Russell Avenue Northwest /
    206-784-3516
**Benihana Restaurant,** 5th & University / 206-682-4686
**Best Western Airport Executel,** 20717 International Boulevard / 206-878-3300
**Stuart Anderson's Black Angus Restaurant,** 15820 1st Avenue South /
    206-244-5700
**Cafe Minnies,** 101 Denny Way / 206-448-6263
**Canterbury-ale & Eats,** 534 15th Avenue East / 206-322-3130
**The Crabpot,** Pier 57 / 206-624-1890
**Cucina Cucina Italian Cafe,** 901 Fairview Avenue North / 206-447-2782
**Cutters Bayhouse,** 2001 Western Avenue / 206-448-4884

**Denny's Restaurant,** 17206 International Boulevard / 206-246-6076
**The Edgewater,** Pier 67 / 206-728-7000
**El Puerco Lloron,** 1501 Western Avenue / 206-624-0541
**Elliott's,** Pier 56 / 206-623-4340
**Grazie Caffe Italiano,** 16943 Southcenter Parkway / 206-575-1606
**Ivar's Restaurant,** Pier 54 / 206-624-6852
**Kell's Irish Restaurant & Pub,** 1916 Post Alley / 206-728-1916
**Marie Callender's Restaurants & Bakery,** 9538 1st Avenue Northeast /
    206-526-5785
**The Old Spaghetti Factory,** 2801 Elliott Avenue / 206-441-7724
**Osaka Grill Teriyaki & Deli,** 128 Pike Street/ 206-340-1793
**Outback Steakhouse,** 13201 Aurora Avenue North / 206-367-7780
**Steamers Seafood Cafe,** Pier 59, 1500 Alaskan Way / 206-624-0312
**Stuart Anderson's Black Angus Restaurant,** 15820 1st Avenue South /
    206-244-5700
**Toscana,** 1312 Northeast 43rd Street/ 206-547-7679

## VETERINARIANS
**Airport Veterinary Clinic,** 14636 Military Road South / 206-243-7777
**Aurora Veterinary Hospital,** 8821 Aurora Avenue North / 206-525-6666
**Bean Animal Hospital,** 12705 Renton Avenue South / 206-772-1270
**Blue Cross Veterinary Hospital,** 2227 4th Avenue South / 206-623-1932
**Des Moines Veterinary Hospital,** 21935 Pacific Hwy South / 206-878-4111
**Elliott Bay Animal Hospital,** 2042 15th Avenue West / 206-285-7387
**Emergency Veterinary Service,** 112 Southwest 157th Street/ 206-246-1211
**South Seattle Veterinary Hospital,** 11033 1st Avenue South / 206-242-8338

## FLY SHOPS AND SPORTING GOODS
**The Angler's Workshop,** 1350 Atlantic, Woodland / 360-225-6359
**Avid Angler Fly Shoppe,** 11714 15th Avenue Northeast / 206-362-4030
**Creekside Angling Company,** 1660 Northwest Gilman Blvd #C-5, Issaquah /
    425-392-3800
**Kaufmann's Streamborn, Inc.,** 1918 4th Avenue / 206-448-0601 / also in
    Bellevue: 15015 Main Street / 425-643-2246
**Morning Hatch Fly Shoppe,** 3640 South Cedar, Suite L, Tacoma / 253-472-1070
**Orvis Seattle,** 911 Bellevue Way Northeast, Bellevue / 425-452-9138
**Outdoor Emporium,** 420 Pontius Avenue North / 206-624-6550 / Some
    flyfishing supplies
**Patrick's Fly Shop,** 2237 Eastlake Avenue East / 206-325-8988
**Salmon Bay Tackle Guides & Outfitters,** 5701 15th Avenue Northwest /
    206-789-9335
**Swede's Fly Shop,** 17419 139th Avenue Northeast, Woodinville / 425-487-3747
**Ted's Sport Center,** 15526 Hwy 99, Lynnwood / 425-743-9505

**Warshal's Sporting Goods,** 1st & Madison / 206-624-7301 / Some flyfishing supplies

**Big 5 Sporting Goods,** 1133 North 205th Street / 206-546-4443
4315 University Way Northeast / 206-783-0163
2500 Southwest Barton Street / 206-932-2212 / Some flyfishing equipment

**REI,** 1525 11th Avenue / 206-323-8333 / No flyfishing equipment

## AUTO REPAIR

**AAA Automotive Auto Repair,** 937 North 96th Street/ 206-522-6100

**Affordable Auto Service,** 9606 4th Southwest / 206-763-4474

**All Tune and Lube,** 16310 International Boulevard / 206-433-0766

**Associated Auto & RV Service, Inc.,** 16616 International Boulevard / 206-244-7746

**Ballard Auto Repair, Inc.,** 1546 Northwest Leary Way / 206-789-5516

**Car Tender, Inc.,** 1706 12th Avenue / 206-324-0345

**Checker Auto Repair,** 10710 East Marginal Way South / 206-764-0697

**Downtown Auto Care,** 1614 6th Avenue / 206-343-9121

**Econo Lube 'n Tune,** 12248 Aurora Avenue North / 206-362-5517

**Firestone Tire & Service Centers,** 1145 Northwest Market Street/ 206-782-6563

**Midway Auto Repair,** 2802 South Kent Des Moines Road / 206-878-8870

**Super Tune & Brake,** 20309 Ballinger Way Northeast / 206-367-4174

**Village Autocare,** 2724 Northeast 45th Street/ 206-526-2345

## AUTO RENTALS

**Alamo Rent-A-Car Downtown,** 1301 6th Avenue / 206-292-9770

**Dollar Rent-A-Car Auto & Truck Rental,** 17600 International Boulevard / 206-433-6777

**EZ Rent-A-Car,** 16325 Military Road South / 206-241-4688

**Enterprise Rent-A-Car,** 15667 Pacific Hwy South / 206-246-1953

**National Car Rental,** Seattle-Tacoma International Airport / 206-433-5501

**Thrifty Car Rental,** 18836 International Boulevard / 206-246-7565

## MEDICAL

**Harborview Medical Center,** 4101 1st Avenue South / 206-731-3074

**Northwest Hospital,** 1550 North 115th Street/ 206-368-1783

**Providence Seattle Medical Center,** 500 17th Avenue / 206-320-2161

**Swedish Medical Center,** 5401 Leary Avenue Northwest / 206-781-6362

**University of Washington Medical Center,** 1959 Northeast / 206-548-4333

**Virginia Mason Medical Center,** 2720 East Madison Street/ 206-223-6616

## FOR MORE INFORMATION

Greater Seattle Chamber of Commerce
1301 5th Avenue, Suite 2400
Seattle, WA 98101
206-389-7229

# Auburn

**Elevation–700     Population–142,517**

## Accommodations
Best Western Pony Soldier Motor Inn, 1521 D Street Northeast  /  253-939-5950
Nendel's Valu Inn, 102 15th Street Northeast  /  253-833-8007
Comfort Inn, One 16th Street Northeast  /  253-833-1222
Howard Johnson, 1521 D Street Northeast  /  253-939-5950  /  Pets $5

## Restaurants
British Market Place, 26 B Street Northeast  /  253-833-2404
Denny's Restaurant, 502 15th Street Northeast  /  253-939-7931
Flapper Alley Saloon & Eatery, 18 Auburn Way South  /  253-833-6960
Gerry Andal's Ranch Restaurant, 635 C Street Southwest  /  253-833-5251
The Great Steak and Potatoe Company, 1101 Supermall Way  /  253-939-2038
La Posada Mexican Restaurant, 1403 Auburn Way South  /  253-939-2540
Raden's Steak & Seafood House, 1815 Howard Road  /  253-833-7980
Warehouse Sandwich Shop, 3411 C Street Northeast  /  253-939-7270

## Veterinarians
Auburn Veterinary Hospital, 718 Auburn Way North  /  253-833-4510
Forest Hill Veterinary Hospital, 3240 Auburn Way South  /  253-833-9100
Valley Animal Hospital, 3615 West Valley Hwy North  /  253-833-6701

## Fly Shops and Sporting Goods
Auburn Sports & Marine, 810 Auburn Way North  /  253-833-1440  /  Some flyfishing equipment
Diamond Sports Shop, 30848 3rd Avenue, Black Diamond  /  360-886-2027
Shoff's Tackle, 214 West Meeker Street, Kent  /  253-852-4760
Wal-Mart, 1425 Supermall Way  /  206-735-1855

## Auto Repair
Auburn Car Repair Co., 328 37th Street Northwest  /  253-939-5019
Firestone Tire & Service Centers, 535 15th Street Northeast  /  253-833-8155
Grease Monkey, 202 15th Street Northeast  /  253-735-3690
Mobile Mechanic, 37061 55th Avenue South  /  253-833-0376
Valley Auto Clinic, 4725 Auburn Way North  /  253-850-1538

## Auto Rental
Enterprise Rent-A-Car, 2806 Auburn Way North  /  253-939-4690
Snappy Car Rental, 1919 Auburn Way North  /  253-735-5983
U-Save Auto Rental, 3405 Auburn Way North  /  253-735-8374

## Airport
City of Auburn Airport, 400 West 23rd Northeast  /  253-931-3026

## MEDICAL
**Auburn Regional Medical Center,** 202 North Division Street / 253-833-7711
**South Auburn General Medical,** 3830 A Street Southeast / 253-939-6703
**Auburn General Hospital,** 20 Second Street Northeast / 253-272-8180

## FOR MORE INFORMATION
Auburn Chamber of Commerce
228 1st Street Northeast
Auburn, WA 98002
253-833-0700

# North Bend

### Elevation–820 • Population–13,700

## ACCOMMODATIONS

**Edgewick Inn,** 14600 468th Avenue Southeast / 425-888-9000
**Mt. Si Motel,** 43200 Southeast North Bend Way / 425-888-1621
**North Bend Motel,** 322 North Bend Avenue East / 425-888-1121

## CAMPGROUNDS AND RV PARKS

**Norwest Inn & RV Park,** 45810 Southeast North Bend Way / 425-888-1939
**Norwest RV Park,** 45810 Southeast North Bend Way / 425-888-1939
**Olallie State Park,** 52000 Southeast Homestead Valley Road / 425-888-3325

## RESTAURANTS

**Giuliano Ristorante Italiano,** 101 West North Bend Way / 425-888-5700
**Main Street Eatery,** 461 South Fork Avenue Southwest / 425-888-4545
**Mom's Kitchen,** 247 North Bend Avenue East / 425-831-6975
**North Bend Tavern & Eatery,** 228 North Bend Avenue East / 425-888-9149
**The Reef,** 426 Main Avenue South / 425-888-2424

## VETERINARIANS

**North Bend Animal Clinic,** 1308 Boalch Avenue Northwest / 425-888-3300
**Whitfield Hardware Do It Center,** 209 Main Avenue South / 425-888-1242

## AUTO REPAIR

**Arco Full Service,** 225 North Bend Avenue East / 425-888-0233

## AUTO RENTAL

**G & S Rent-A-Car,** 225 North Bend Avenue East / 425-888-0233

## MEDICAL

**Virginia Mason Clinic,** 100 Northeast Gilman Boulevard (Issaquah) /
425-557-8000

## FOR MORE INFORMATION

Upper Snoqualmie Valley Chamber of Commerce
P.O. Box 357
North Bend, WA 98065
425-888-4440

# Everett
### Elevation–0 • Population–80,000

## ACCOMMODATIONS
**Holiday Inn,** 101 128th Street Southeast / 206-337-2900 / 249 rooms, pool, hot tub, restaurant, lounge

**Best Western,** 2800 Pacific Avenue / 206-258-4141 / Downtown access, free breakfast

**Motel 6,** 224 128th Street Southwest / 206-353-8120 / Cable TV, pool

## CAMPGROUNDS AND RV PARKS
**Lakeside RV Park,** 12321 Highway 99 South Everett / 206-347-2970 / Full hook-ups, laundry, showers

**Silver Shores RV Park,** west side of Silver Lake / 206-337-8741 / 11 tent sites, 50 RV sites, swimming, boat launch, 7-day limit

## RESTAURANTS
**Anthony's Homeport,** 1726 West Marine View Drive / 206-252-3333 / Great seafood, pasta, steaks

**Ivar's Mukilteo Landing,** 710 Front Street / 206-347-3648 / Waterfront view, fish and chips, clams, mussels, salmon, halibut, ling cod

**Olive Garden,** 1321 Everett Mall Way / 206-347-9857 / Lunch and dinner, Italian dishes

## FLY SHOPS AND SPORTING GOODS
**Ted's,** 15526 Hwy 99 West (south of Everett in Lynnwood) / 425-743-9505 / Fly tying goods, rods, reels and lines, waders and boots

**Fly Smith, The Fly Fishing Outfitters,** 1515 5th Avenue, Marysville  /  360-658-9003

**K-mart,** 8102 Evergreen Way / 425-290-7245

**Target,** 405 Southeast Everett Mall / 425-353-3167

## AUTO RENTAL AND REPAIR
**All Tune and Lube,** 46 Southeast Everett Mall Way / 206-355-2900

**Aj's Auto Repair,** 2110 25th St / 206-258-2400

## AIR SERVICE
**Paine Field,** 3220 100th Street Southwest / 206-353-2110 / Aircraft rental, maintenance

Closest commercial service: Seattle-Tacoma International

## MEDICAL
**Providence General Medical Center,** 1321 Colby / 206-261-2000

## FOR MORE INFORMATION
Everett Area Chamber of Commerce
1710 West Marine View Drive
Everett, WA 98201
425-252-5181

# Monroe

### Elevation–68 • Population–6,555

Located on the banks of the Skykomish River and home to Lavroe Drift Boats, Monroe is an angling town and a prime place for steelhead and salmon flyfishers to stay.

## ACCOMMODATIONS

**Best Western Baron Inn,** 19233 Hwy 2 / 360-794-3111 / 58 units, pool and hot tub

**Fairground Inn,** 18950 Hwy 2 / 360-794-5401 / 60 units, hot tub, restaurants close

**The Frog Crossing Bed and Breakfast,** 306 South Lewis / 360-794-7622 / Victorian style, phone, cable TV, fireplace, continental breakfast

## CAMPGROUNDS AND RV PARKS

**Evergreen State Fairgrounds,** Hwy 2 West / 360-794-4344 / 300 RV spaces, full hook-ups

**Wallace River State Park,** 36010 Hwy 2 / 360-568-2274 / 10 miles east of Monroe, RV sites available

**Flowing Lake Park,** Hwy 2, 10 miles northwest of Monroe / 360-568-2274 / Full hook-ups, 40 RV sites, tent sites

## RESTAURANTS

**Petosa's Restaurant,** 191 State Route 2 / 360-794-4436 / 6AM–2am / Pies, home-cooked meals, coffee

**Buzz Inn Steak House,** 18960 State Route 2 / 360-794-3838

**Toshi's Teriyaki,** 19821 State Route 2 / 360-794-6130 / Fast oriental food

**Subway,** 19636 State Route 2 / 360-794-0786 / Sub sandwiches and snacks /

## FLY SHOPS AND SPORTING GOODS

**Coast to Coast,** 17150 162nd Street Southeast / 360-794-7564

**Sky Valley Traders,** 18600 State Route 2 / 360-794-8818

## AUTO REPAIR

**Monroe Auto & Truck Repair,** 18980 State Route 2 (behind Del's Feed Store) / 360-794-5858

## MEDICAL

**Valley General Hospital,** 14701 179th Avenue Southeast / 360-794-7497

## AIR SERVICE

**First Air Field,** 13812 179th Avenue Southeast / 360-794-8570

## FOR MORE INFORMATION

Monroe Chamber of Commerce
111 South Lewis Street
Monroe, WA 98272
360-794-5488

US Ranger Station, Skykomish
360-677-2414

# Mt. Vernon

### Elevation–35 • Population–23,000

## ACCOMMODATIONS

Cottontree Inn & Convention Center, 2300 Market Street / 360-428-5678

Days Inn, 2009 Riverside Drive / 360-424-4141

Travelodge, 1910 Freeway Drive / 360-428-7020

Tulip Valley Inn, 2200 Freeway Drive / 360-428-5969

## CAMPGROUNDS AND RV PARKS

Blake's RV Park & Marina, 1171 Rawlins Road / 360-445-6533

Mt. Vernon RV Park, 1229 Memorial Hwy / 360-428-8787

Riverbend RV Park, 305 Stewart Road / 360-428-4044

## RESTAURANTS

Big Lake Bar & Grill, 1821 Hwy 9 / 360-422-6411

Buzz Inn Steak House, 1115 Riverside Drive / 360-424-0303

Cranberry Tree Restaurant, 2030 Freeway Drive / 360-424-7755

Denny's, 300 East College Way / 360-424-7500

Farmhouse Inn, 1376 LaConner Whitney Road / 360-466-4411

Los Arcos Mexican Restaurant, 2121 East College Way / 360-424-5886

Reef Broiler, 2401 Riverside Drive / 360-428-5726

Skagit River Brewing Co., 404 South 3rd Street / 360-336-2884

## VETERINARIANS

Animal Hospital of Mt. Vernon, 1310 North Laventure Road / 360-424-7138

Mountain View Veterinary Clinic, 1911 East Division Street / 360-424-4455

Parker Way Veterinary Clinic, 1515 Parker Way / 360-424-7387

## FLY SHOPS AND SPORTING GOODS

Ace Hardware, 1420 Riverside Drive / 360-428-6977

## AUTO REPAIR

Alternative Automotive, 1552 Memorial Hwy / 360-424-2195

Budget Towing & Auto Repair, 1675 Old Hwy 99 South / 360-424-4517

J & K Automotive, 1225 Riverside Drive / 360-428-2601

John's Auto Repair, 1824 South Woodland Drive / 360-424-3462

Walt's Automotive, 1685 Milltown Road / 360-445-2171

## AUTO RENTAL

Agency Rent-A-Car / 360-336-5822

Enterprise Rent-A-Car, 2222 Riverside Drive / 360-757-6477

## MEDICAL

Skagit Urgent Care Walk-in Clinic, 809 South 15th Street / 360-428-6434

## For More Information

Mt. Vernon Chamber Of Commerce
1700 East College Way
Mt. Vernon, WA 98273
360-428-8547

# Bellingham

### Elevation–68    Population–61,240

## ACCOMMODATIONS
Bay City Motor Inn, 116 North Samish Way / 360-676-9191
Cascade Inn, 208 North Samish Way / 360-733-2520
Comfort Inn, 4282 Guide Meridian Road / 360-738-1100
Days Inn, 125 East Kellogg Road / 360-671-6200
Hampton Inn, 3985 Bennett Avenue / 360-676-7700
Holiday Inn Express, 4156 Meridian Street / 360-671-4800
Quality Inn Baron Suites, 100 East Kellogg Road / 360-647-8000
Ramada Inn, 215 North Samish Way / 360-734-8830
Travel Lodge, 101 North Samish Way / 360-733-8280

## CAMPGROUNDS AND RV PARKS
Eagle's Haven RV Park, 2924 Haxton Way / 360-758-2420

## RESTAURANTS
Alger Bar & Grille, 176 Old Highway 99 North / 360-724-3291
Boundary Bay Brewery & Alehouse, 1107 Railroad Avenue / 360-647-5593
Cafe Toulouse, 114 West Magnolia Street / 360-733-8996
Cathay House, 950 Lincoln Street / 360-676-9100
Cliff House, 331 North State Street / 360-734-8660
Colophon Cafe, 1208 11th Street / 360-647-0092
Denny's Restaurant, 161 Telegraph Road / 360-676-0173
Dos Padres Restaurant, 1111 Harris Avenue / 360-733-9900
Fisherman's Market, 514 West Holly Street / 360-733-3200
Ivar's Seafood Bar, 1 Bellis Fair Parkway / 360-734-9169
Mt. Baker Brewing Co., 1408 Cornwall Avenue / 360-671-2031
Old Town Cafe, 316 West Holly Street / 360-671-4431
Pepper Sisters, 1055 North State Street / 360-671-3414
Stuart Anderson's Black Angus Restaurant, 165 South Samith Way /
    360-734-7600
Wild Garlic, 114 Prospect Street / 360-671-1955

## VETERINARIANS
Bellingham Animal Hospital, 720 Virginia Street / 360-734-0720
Fairhaven Veterinary Hospital, 2330 Old Fairhaven Parkway / 360-671-3903
Mountain Veterinary Hospital, 3413 Mt. Baker Hwy / 360-592-5113
Vetsmart Pet Hospital & Health Center, 4379 Meridian Street / 360-734-9459

## FLY SHOPS AND SPORTING GOODS
The Guides Fly Shop, 3960 Suite C, Meridian / 360-527-0317 / Fax 360-527-0853
H & H Outdoor Sports, 814 Dupont Street / 360-733-2050 / Carries fairly large
    amount of flyfishing supplies
R & R Tackle & Fly Shop, 109 East Woodin Road, Sunnyside / 509-837-2332

Big 5 Sporting Goods, 1 Bellis Fair Parkway Ste 202 / 360-734-7802 / Some fly-fishing equipment
K-Mart Stores, 1001 East Sunset Drive / 360-734-9550
Wal-Mart, 4420 Meridian Street / 360-647-1400

### Auto Repair
All Towing & Automotive, 5493 Guide Meridian Road / 360-398-8697
Autotech, 106 East Axton Road / 360-398-9197
Chuck's Midtown Motors, 1058 North State Street / 360-733-1527
Earl's Auto Tech, 1025 Pasco Street / 360-738-9490
Penske Auto Center, 1001 East Sunset Drive / 360-734-9565

### Auto Rental
Avis Rent-A-Car, Bellingham International Airport / 360-676-8840
Budget Rent-A-Car, Bellngham International Airport / 360-671-3802
Enterprise Rent-A-Car, 1407 Iowa Street / 360-733-4363
Hertz Rent-A-Car, Bellingham International Airport / 360-733-8336
National Car Rental, Bellingham International Airport / 360-734-9220

### Airport
Bellingham International Airport, 4255 Mitchell Way / 360-734-3009

### Medical
St. Joseph Hospital, 2901 Squalicum Parkway / 360-734-5400

### For More Information
Bellingham Whatcom Chamber of Commerce
1801 Roeder Avenue, Suite 140
Bellingham, WA 98225
360-734-1330

# Olympic Peninsula

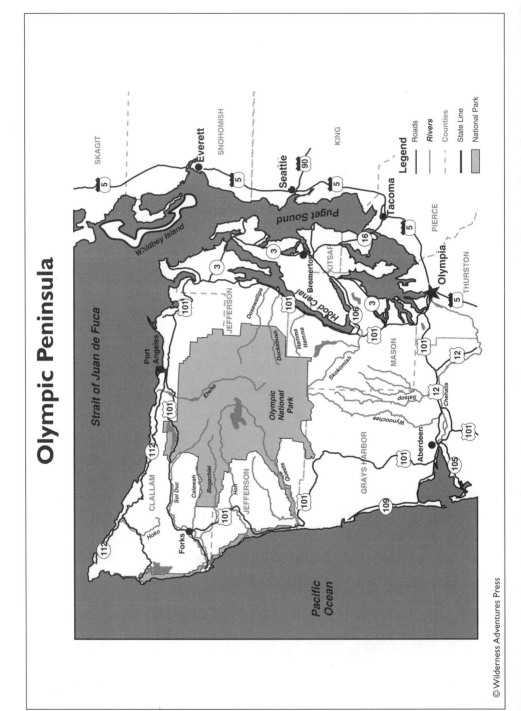

# Olympic Peninsula

With flows originating on the flanks of the Olympic Mountains, the Olympic Peninsula offers dozens of beautiful, freestone rivers that beckon anadromous fish. Steelhead, sea-run cutthroat, Dolly Varden, as well as the salmon species, including chums, cohos, and kings: all call these rivers home.

Unfortunately, many of these streams have been sabotaged by consumptive interests, and while many fish runs are simply depressed, some have disappeared. Today, some of these waters are but skeletons of what they used to be. That is particularly true of the streams that drain the east side of the Olympic Mountains, with flows spilling into Puget Sound. However, even these streams offer seasonal options, although most of their fish are comprised of hatchery impostors.

Today, when the Olympic Peninsula is brought up in coffee-table discussion, most anglers conjure images of the western peninsula's major steelhead rivers, including the Hoh, Queets, Sol Duc, Calawah, and Bogachiel.

These rivers, although hammered mercilessly by tribal netting and other consumptive interests such as logging, still provide excellent flyfishing options, especially for sea-run cutthroat and large native steelhead.

Steelhead to 30 pounds have been landed on these waters, and fish to 20 pounds are relatively common, especially late in the winter season, say March and April. Prior to this time, large wild fish are outnumbered by hatchery stocks that range in size from 6 to 15 pounds.

Because these streams flow through the Olympic rain forest, they are heavily timbered along their banks and are temperamental due to the massive amounts of rainfall each year. One day a river can run in perfect shape, but overnight it can be transformed into a monster. For this reason, visiting these streams from any distance is a gamble. But it's a gamble most serious flyfishers are willing to take.

Steelhead are not the only game in town. Sea-run cutthroat are present most of the year. Fishing for them picks up when the first fall rains occur. Then, sea-runs rocket into the river systems and can be taken on a variety of dry flies, including big, size 4 muddler minnows floated on top. When the fish are on, pounding every dry fly in sight, it's tough to imagine a better time on the water.

If you are looking for truly huge fish, you'll want to test these peninsula streams in the fall when giant king salmon arrive. Like sea-run cutthroat, kings move into the river when the first fall rains arrive. If you do choose to pursue these fish, take a stout rod and heavy leaders—you might tie into a specimen that exceeds 50 pounds.

For those who prefer rainbow trout, the Elwha River, which flows into the Strait of Juan de Fuca, is the place to be.

The Elwha hosts a few steelhead and salmon in its lower reaches, but prime fishing occurs above its reservoirs, deep within Olympic National Park. Prime time on the Elwha arrives post-runoff, when caddis and mayfly hatches bring rainbows to the top. Elwha's fish commonly stretch between 8 and 17 inches, but an angler who wants to catch them must hike in on the Elwha River trail. A four- or five-day hike-in camp trip along the Elwha rates as one of Washington's best summer activities.

Overall, even though the Olympic Peninsula streams are not what they used to be, many are still quite good, offering kings, sea-run cutts, and that glory fish, the steelhead. For those who aren't afraid of a little rain, the Olympic Peninsula is a great place to spend a week, a month, or even many years. There is enough quality water around to keep the most avid angler busy.

# ELWHA RIVER

There have been a lot of dams built across the rivers of Washington, but it's possible that none are more hated than those that lie on the Elwha River watershed. These dams, built without fish passage consideration, wiped out one of the greatest, if not the greatest, chinook salmon runs on the globe. We're talking some Kenai River-type kings. Fish over 50 pounds were commonly taken. Fish exceeding 100 pounds were possible.

Not today. The Elwha, located at the north end of the Olympic Peninsula, still hosts some king salmon, but only in its lower 5 miles—that's as far as anadromous fish can go (the Elwha had them: all Pacific salmon species, plus sea-run cutthroats, Dolly Varden, and steelhead). Along with kings, the Elwha offers a few winter- and summer-run steelhead, but certainly not like it used to.

Today, the Elwha is noted for its rainbow trout fishing, along with an opportunity to hook and release large bull trout. However, that may change if a plan to remove both Elwha dams pushes through. Then, given time, the river may once again be heralded for excellent anadromous fish runs, including giant king salmon. If you're 30, as I am, it's a toss-up whether you will see the return of runs in your lifetime. (The genetic integrity of the Elwha's chinook has been preserved, but we'll get to that later.) For now, we'll take a good look at the Elwha's current attributes.

Some anglers view a hike-in fishery with trepidation, because they just don't like to work very hard to reach the water. Others view the challenge of a hike-in fishery as the best of angling options. They see limited access and visualize a pristine setting, plenty of solitude, and lots of beautiful, aggressive fish. For anglers who like to hike, the Elwha is a dream stream.

To reach the Elwha's best water, an angler must follow the Elwha River Road (Olympic Hot Springs Road) to the north end of Lake Mills, above the second dam. From there, anglers can hike as far as they want and fish the river wherever they please, with the exception of several canyon sections that are mostly inaccessible. Throughout the upper river, which carves through densely timbered old-growth forest, flyfishers can expect to hook rainbow trout ranging from 6 to 18 inches. While most of them range between 9 and 14 inches, a dandy occasionally shows itself.

"All of the upper Elwha is a good fishery," says John Meyer, a biologist for Olympic National Park. "There is good fishing right when you start up the trail, and it extends into the very headwaters of the river, but the best fishing seems to occur between 12 and 22 miles. That's some pretty darn good trout fishing. We collected fish for our brood stock program through that section, and we found a lot of trout between 12 and 18 inches. There are even bigger fish in there, including some Dolly Varden (bull trout) in the 5- to 10-pound range."

Although rainbows and Dollies remain in the river all year, there are several factors that could influence the success of your trip. First, coastal Washington's weather can be atrocious during late spring and early summer, rendering even the most experienced camper soaking wet. Also, June marks the peak of spring runoff that can lead to

# Elwha River

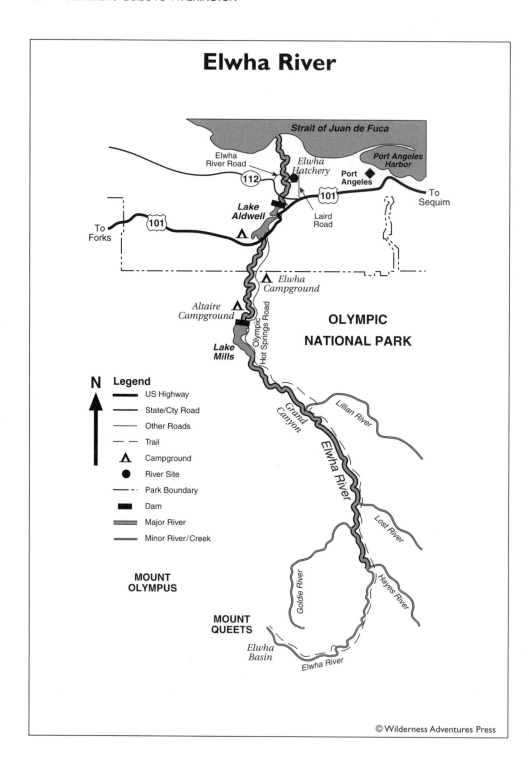

Strait of Juan de Fuca

Elwha River Road

Elwha Hatchery

112

Port Angeles Harbor

Port Angeles

To Sequim

101

Laird Road

Lake Aldwell

To Forks

101

Elwha Campground

OLYMPIC

NATIONAL PARK

Altaire Campground

Olympic Hot Springs Road

Lake Mills

**N**

**Legend**

US Highway

State/Cty Road

Other Roads

Trail

Campground

River Site

Park Boundary

Dam

Major River

Minor River/Creek

Grand Canyon

Lillian River

Elwha River

Lost River

Goldie River

Hayes River

MOUNT OLYMPUS

MOUNT QUEETS

Elwha Basin

Elwha River

© Wilderness Adventures Press

poor river conditions. The Elwha is partially fed by glaciers and can run silty, reducing visibility to inches.

Second, as the season progresses into late September and October, the Elwha's rainbows may move great distances and take up residence in certain sections of the river. Meyer isn't sure exactly why or where the trout go, but his guess is the lower section of the upper river.

"They just disappear from the upper headwaters," Meyer says. "I doubt they go into the canyons, but they probably opt for some of the slower, deeper holes."

Prime time on the Elwha occurs between July 1 and the end of October. At that time, flyfishers should expect decent mayfly emergences, such as hatches of pale morning duns and some Baetis, but the big draw is the caddisfly hatch. During summer, you can count on caddis each evening, especially during the last hour of light.

"You can expect a caddis hatch every day on the Elwha," says Tom Thompson, who runs Greywolf Angler in Sequim and fishes the Elwha whenever he can. "Most people prefer to fish it in the evening, because that's when the best hatches occur, but it can be good during the afternoon, too. It's not very technical—just use an elk hair caddis, size 14, 16, or 18, depending on the size of the insect. An Adams or stimulator works, too."

Anglers who are familiar with a caddis hatch understand that most of a trout's evening feeding activity on caddis is directed toward emerging insects. Most often, an elk hair caddis draws plenty of strikes during an emergence, but it actually imitates an adult caddis. To mimic emerging caddis, try an X-caddis or a LaFontaine sparkle emerger during evening. By doing so, you could double your trout tally for the evening.

While anglers usually catch the Elwha's rainbows on the surface, nymphing is very productive, too. Any of the standard beadhead offerings, such as a hare's ear, pheasant tail or Prince nymph, should draw takes when dead-drifted through the medium-depth runs and riffles. Most anglers fish these offerings under a strike indicator, which helps a flyfisher sense subtle subsurface takes. Deep sparkle pupa and a free-living caddis are also excellent nymphal patterns to carry up the trail with you.

As they do wherever they are found, whether on the Elwha, Montana's Madison, or even in New Zealand's crystal-clear waters, rainbow trout eat streamers. Size 2, 4, and 6 woolly buggers, zonkers, muddler minnows, and rabbit strip leeches all draw strikes on the Elwha. Anglers should work those streamers through the deep slots, heavy riffles, and even in the deep holes. And be aware that a huge fish could latch on. The reason: the Elwha hosts Dolly Varden. They typically hold in the deeper water and smack streamers with abandon. If you expect to land a Dolly that might reach 10 pounds, tie on 3X leader before running a streamer through a hole.

However, when fishing streamers, it's important to realize that the Dolly Varden is not doing well throughout its range. Anglers are not allowed to specifically target Dolly Varden in the Elwha, but they have a good chance of hooking one while fishing for rainbows. If you hook a Dolly, play it quickly; don't let it dog down deep, wasting all of its energy. Try to keep a fish in the water when you land it and quickly remove the hook (make sure you take forceps with you). Then gently move the fish forward and backward in the water to oxygenate its gills. When the fish is strong, let go of the tail and enjoy the sight of it returning to the river.

When fishing the Elwha in July, August, September, and October, the water should run low and clear. Anglers must use a little stealth, including light leaders and delicate presentations, to score on those rainbows.

"The fish aren't too wary, but you can't go splashing into a riffle or run and expect rainbows to stick around," Thompson says. "You'll want to use as light a leader as you can. Typically, you can get away with a 5X tippet, but sometimes 6X is better."

During summer, make sure you cover the fast, roily water that is heavily oxygenated—that's where the fish congregate during the hot periods of July and August. As September brings a weather change, look for trout to spread out into moderate flows. You may not catch them at the head or in the middle of a riffle, but you can take them in the tailout or along the inside corners and current seams.

September and October are prime times to fish the Elwha for several reasons. First, rainbows feel the weather change and realize it's time to engage in one last feeding binge before winter brings measly pickings. Second, fewer people hike up the Elwha River Trail at that time, and solitude abounds. Also, you may be fortunate enough to hear the whistle of an elk in rut. Almost certainly, you'll see some elk, not to mention plenty of black-tailed deer and, possibly, a black bear or two.

"There are always people on the trail during July and August," Meyer says, "but by September it clears out. It's never really crowded at any time, and you can fish just about anywhere you want without encountering another angler."

During summer, flyfishers can wet-wade extensively. However, you should wear a pair of felt-soled, studded wading boots since the river bottom is rocky and slick. During fall, a pair of lightweight waders should work. If the weather is uncharacteristically cold, pack in a pair of 3mm neoprenes.

If hiking in to the upper Elwha isn't your game, you aren't totally out of options. In fact, the middle Elwha, which twists seductively between the two dams, offers special regulations and some decent fishing for rainbows. Plus, a road parallels the river through the entire section, and there are two campgrounds available for those who opt for an overnight trip.

"This section is managed as a quality fishery, with a single, barbless hook and no bait restriction, plus a limit of 2 fish over 12 inches, but it's not a great fishery, not nearly as productive as the upper river," Meyer says. "The section gets pounded by anglers, and we've found that the mainstem spawning areas are pretty much gone and the tributary spawning is pretty minimal, too. There are still a few fish to good size, but not many."

The lower Elwha also provides limited opportunities. Flyfishers can pursue summer-run steelhead and a few sea-run cutthroat from late June through August.

Of course, all of this information may change if the Elwha's dams are indeed removed. If that happens, all of the river's anadromous fish would be restored.

*Washington's hike-in rainbow trout gem— the Elwha River.*

"When they take out the lower river dam, it won't cause a tremendous amount of change in the fishery," says Brian Winter, a biologist for Olympic National Park. "But for the first time in 90 years, we'll see anadromous fish to mile 13. However, if we can get both dams out, I'm fully optimistic that we could restore the stocks. If we took both dams out at the same time, we expect it to take 30 years to rebuild full stocks. Unfortunately, it looks like one dam will be removed, then the other at another time. That will slow down the recovery process."

If the dams are removed, anadromous fish are expected to infiltrate the river up to mile 42. What that will do to the resident rainbow fishery is anyone's guess. Only time will tell.

The Elwha is an Olympic Peninsula treasure, a solid rainbow trout river that flows through some of the most pristine, impressive country in Washington. Take a

*The scenic Elwha River runs through some of Washington's most pristine forest.*

week this summer or fall and backpack into the upper river. The solitude, the amazing rainforest scenery, and the powerful rainbows shouldn't disappoint.

To reach the middle and upper Elwha, follow Hwy 101 west from Port Angeles or east from Sequim and turn south on Olympic Hot Springs Road. Follow the road upstream. When leaving Sequim, make sure to stop at Greywolf Angler and talk to Thompson. He has a full selection of flyfishing gear, as well as information on the Elwha's conditions.

# Stream Facts: Elwha River

### Seasons and Special Regulations
- Mouth to Aldwell Lake Dam: Trout, steelhead, and salmon open June 1 through February 28. Bank angling only. Salmon open October 1 through November 15 (coho only).
- Lake Aldwell to 400 feet below spillway at Lake Mills Dam: Trout and steelhead from June 1 through October 31. Selective gear rules apply.
- Elwha through Olympic National Park: Check current park regulations.

### Species
- In its lower portions, the Elwha offers steelhead, cutthroat, and coho salmon. A few Dolly Varden may be present.
- Above the lakes, the Elwha supports rainbow trout and large Dolly Varden.

### Stream Characteristics
- The best portions of the Elwha exist above the dams in Olympic National Park.
- Excellent rainbow trout fishing and large Dolly Varden draw numerous back-packing flyfishers during summer and fall months.
- Look for rainbow trout holding in the pocketwater and eddies.
- Bull trout dwell in the deep holes.

### Access
- Access abounds on the Elwha.
- The lower portions are easily reached.
- The upper reaches, above the dams, require a hike to reach. The severity of the hike depends only on how far your feet are willing to take you.

# Hoko River

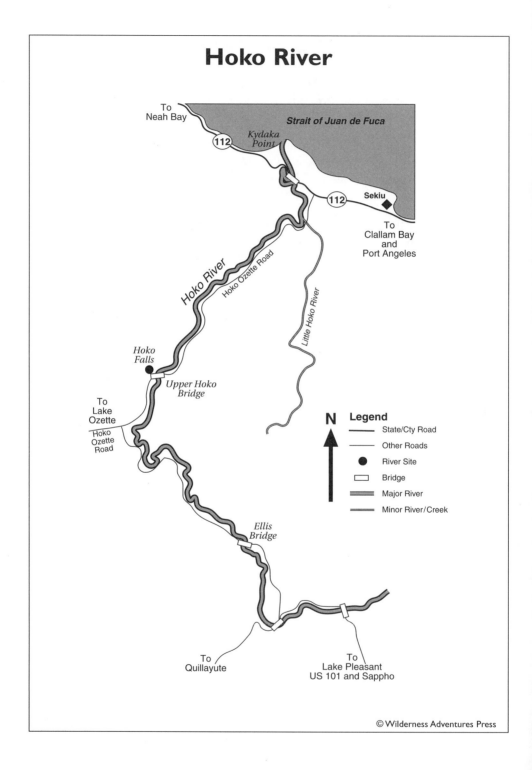

To
Neah Bay

**Strait of Juan de Fuca**

112

*Kydaka Point*

112    Sekiu

To
Clallam Bay
and
Port Angeles

*Hoko River*

Hoko Ozette Road

*Little Hoko River*

*Hoko Falls*

*Upper Hoko Bridge*

To
Lake
Ozette

Hoko
Ozette
Road

**N**

**Legend**

———  State/Cty Road

———  Other Roads

●  River Site

▭  Bridge

━━  Major River

━━  Minor River/Creek

*Ellis Bridge*

To
Quillayute

To
Lake Pleasant
US 101 and Sappho

© Wilderness Adventures Press

# HOKO RIVER

One of the smaller Olympic Peninsula steelhead streams, the Hoko River often makes a flyfisher's hit list because it offers a flyfishing-only section and some excellent opportunities for hatchery-origin metalheads.

The Hoko is not a large river and can be easily wade-fished. Most flyfishers avoid the lower river, from upper Hoko Bridge to its mouth, due to the presence of bait- and spinchuckers. There is a 2 steelhead over 12 inches limit on the lower river, and unfortunately, anglers can retain wild fish between December 1 and March 15—go figure.

Fortunately, once fish swim past the upper Hoko Bridge extending to Ellis Bridge at river mile 18.5, it's flyfishing-only. Flyfishers are legally allowed to harvest hatchery steelhead, but most are released anyway.

Most hatchery-origin steelhead return to the Hoko in December and January, but wild fish keep pushing into the system in February and March. Fishing remains good in the flyfishing-only section throughout the season, which opens June 1 and closes March 31.

The Hoko also offers sea-run cutthroat in good numbers. They push into the system as early as late August, but fishing doesn't really pick up until the end of September. October and November can offer prime sea-run fishing. Wild cutthroat must be released.

To reach the Hoko, follow Hwy 112 west past Sekiu. Two miles past Sekiu, turn south on the Hoko-Ozette Road, which follows the river upstream.

# Quillayute River System

© Wilderness Adventures Press

**Legend**

N

- US Highway
- State/Cty Road
- Other Roads
- ▲ Campground
- Boat Ramp
- ● River Site
- Park Boundary
- Major River
- Minor River/Creek

OLYMPIC
NATIONAL PARK

# THE QUILLAYUTE SYSTEM
## (including the Sol Duc, Bogachiel, and Calawah Rivers)

When driving through Forks, Washington, I get a sense that time has passed the area by and that maybe this long, narrow slice of damp, forested country is just an undiscovered extension of southeast Alaska.

Its towns are dominated by loggers, and its forests are either old-growth, intact gems or are cut down to the dirt, like many of Alaska's. The residents' cars grow mold and rust as they do in Alaska. Ferns, blackberry bushes, and alder trees try to devour every house in their path, as they do in Alaska. And the area offers fish—big king salmon, steelhead, and even sea-run cutthroat trout—like Alaska. But this isn't Alaska. It is, however, as close as you're going to get to Alaska while residing in Washington state.

And that's not so bad. The western Olympic Peninsula and the rivers that spill out of Olympic National Park and meet the Pacific Ocean several miles later offer some of the largest steelhead in the Northwest. In most places, these are beautiful stretches of water, slicing around the base of rock cliffs or mud banks or stands of giant spruce or evergreen trees.

Flyfishers travel from around the Northwest, the brunt arriving from Seattle, to fish these streams. Each angler, at least in the back of his mind, is looking for a 20-pound steelhead. Most anglers spend a few days on the water, then retreat to the cities without reaching that goal, but a few are successful, and that keeps the rest of us dreaming. On the Olympic Peninsula streams, including the Quillayute system, which is comprised of the Sol Duc, Calawah, and Bogachiel Rivers, an average winter steelhead runs 8 to 15 pounds. Yet dozens of fish over 20 pounds are landed each season, and almost all of the fish are wild, produced from millions of years of genetic perfection. These are the fish that most anglers target, but their numbers are supplemented heavily by hatchery stock.

Both wild fish and their hatchery impostors exit the Pacific Ocean and push their snouts into the mouth of the Quillayute beginning in December. During December and January, the bulk of the fish are hatchery-origin steelhead that move through the system quickly, all headed for upstream hatcheries or rearing ponds.

By mid-January, but especially in March and April, big, native fish comprise most of the returnees, making it the prime time to fish the system. Steelhead fishing closes at the end of April, but anglers can continue to fish the river, searching for spring-run king salmon.

When the system reopens in June, steelheaders can work the water for summer-run steelhead and sea-run cutthroat trout. Midsummer flyfishing is accurately labeled "difficult," but the first rains of fall, which can arrive in September or not until October or even November, pump fresh, willing steelhead, fall king salmon, and thousands of sea-run cutthroat into the Quillayute and its tributaries. Summer steelhead remain in the system through November, when the early returning hatchery winter-runs and a few wild winter fish again push in.

*The Olympic Peninsula offers some giant, native steelhead. This 42-inch buck, caught by the author and held here by Chris Cenis, took a green butt skunk on the Sol Duc River.*

The Quillayute River itself does offer some opportunity to catch steelhead on a fly, but there are several factors that influence the quality of the experience.

First, as noted, steelhead move through the Quillayute quickly, all engaged in a search for their natal grounds. Second, Indian tribal netting activity is severe on the Quillayute, and an angler might be pushed from a prime location by the presence of tribal members and their nets. However, there are some points that jut into the river, offering an angler the opportunity to cast a fly. The best time to do so is just after a major high tide, as the tide water recedes and a visible current regains itself in the river.

As steelhead push farther up the Quillayute, they face a major decision at mile 6— do they fire up the Sol Duc or continue through the Quillayute and Bogachiel Rivers, possibly diverting into the Calawah? Wherever they choose to go, the fish offer prime options for flyfishers. If, that is, Mother Nature allows an angler near the stream. These coastal waters can blow out for days or even weeks at a time, depending on the amount of rain and snow that carpets the country during winter months. The worst conditions occur when snow falls at sea level, followed by warm temperatures and

*A prime winter steelhead taken on the Sol Duc River during typical western Washington weather. To catch a fish like this in such conditions, hard-cores only need apply. (Photo by Bob Pigott)*

heavy rain. If you hear Steve Pool or one of the other local weather forecasters describe that situation, seriously consider canceling your coastal fishing plans.

Many flyfishers consider the Sol Duc the premier Olympic Peninsula steelhead stream. It originates from snowmelt high in the Olympic Mountains rather than from the glacier melt that sustains many of the Peninsula's large streams. It receives less rainfall than its southern neighbors, including the Calawah, Bogachiel, Quillayute, and Hoh, and most of its watershed is in good shape, much of it resting in Olympic National Park. Sage anglers know that the Sol Duc is fishable for some time after a rainstorm begins and that it clears faster than most Peninsula waters. For these reasons, Bob Pigott, a year-round guide who specializes in flyfishing, considers the Sol Duc the top Peninsula stream and calls it his home water.

Pigott has fished the Sol Duc for more than 20 years, owns a home on its banks, and is well tuned to its nuances. For Pigott, there really isn't a bad day to fish the Sol Duc. That includes the wind-blasted, rain-soaked occasions when the river runs high and roily and every other flyfisher in the universe is prone on a couch, wrapped up in a blanket, staring into a fire, sipping something warm, and waiting for the storm to break.

"Generally speaking, the best flyfishing on the Sol Duc occurs in March and April," Pigott says. "In fact, if I could only fish the Sol Duc for a short time each year, I'd come in March and April, because that's when the weather is most predictable, and the river is less likely to go out of shape than in January and February."

Another reason that April is a prime time to fish the Sol Duc is a lack of Indian netting at the mouth of the river. That means all Sol Duc steelhead, pushing in from the ocean and the Quillayute, will make it into the river, and they can set up residence for as long as they like. Earlier in the year, fishing can be inconsistent due to netting.

"If there weren't nets at the mouth of the river, we'd have real consistent numbers of fish pushing into the Sol Duc," Pigott says. "But the tribes start on a netting schedule in December, and it doesn't let up until April. It's simple: If the nets are out of the water the fish come in. If the nets are in the water, the fish don't get past them.

"When the nets are in the water, you have to try to figure out how far upstream the last batch of successful steelhead have moved," Pigott adds. "If there is good flow in the river, the fish may move 15 or 20 miles a day. If the water is low and clear, they might limit their movement to the night hours only. It all depends on where they are headed. Some spawn low and some spawn way high, all the way into the (Olympic National) Park. So it can really be a guessing game."

For this reason, local fishing knowledge is key to success. Flyfishers who do well on the Sol Duc are anglers who know what runs hold fish all season and what runs may be vacant. For the visiting, firsttime flyfisher, the services of a guide are essential. Spend a day or two with a guide and get to know a section of the river. Then, if you have time, return and fish the area on your own. Your investment will be well worth it.

"Finding fish is especially tough for a guy who's wading," Pigott says. "Ninety-nine percent of the water looks good, but it doesn't consistently hold fish. If you know the river and can drive to one spot, fish it, then drive to another, you can catch fish. But to just wade blindly around the river isn't too productive. You have to know where to go."

Where to go depends on a variety of factors, including water conditions, access to a boat, and type of water. Typically, steelhead seek a run or hole that offers a moderate flow and depth along with some structure, such as boulders or downed logs. Early in the day, anglers often find steelhead along the inside seams of riffles, near the bank, or at the tailout of runs. During the day, when it's bright, fish move to the meat of the hole. When the water is high, steelhead may be pushed against the banks, trying to stay out of the main flow.

While floating the Sol Duc offers excellent access to a lot of good water, the river is tricky, and novice oarsmen should avoid dropping a boat in here.

"The Sol Duc and Calawah are both technical rivers, and unless a guy is a very good boatman, I'd suggest they stay away from them," Pigott says. "There are some places that, unless you can row expertly, you are going to die. I hate to encourage

*Here's what every winter flyfisher is looking for—a large, native
Sol Duc River steelhead that weighs 20 pounds or more. (Photo by Bob Pigott)*

people to float these rivers, because I see too many guys go to the sportsman's shows, buy a new boat, and sink it the first time they try it on the Sol Duc or Calawah. But people keep trying because access for wade fishers is limited on these rivers."

Whether you choose to float or wade, don't be too concerned about fly type and color when casting a line on the Sol Duc. Basic patterns, such as skunks, comets, and even woolly buggers and muddler minnows, draw takes. Pigott rarely veers from the venerable marabou spider.

"I fish a lot of big marabou spiders and egg-sucking leeches," he says. "If the water is clear, I might go with a size 6 or 8. If the water is up and has some color to it I go with a size 0/2, 2, or 4. I don't have any set rules about flies—like dark flies on a bright day or bright flies on a dark day—but I do like the egg-sucking leech because it offers a contrast of dark body and bright head. You've pretty much got it covered with this pattern. When I fish marabous, I go with black or purple with a little bright contrast at the tip of the feather."

While anglers occasionally take Sol Duc steelhead on the surface, most fish strike when the fly is presented in a classic downstream swing. A typical 13-foot, Type 5 sinktip line works well for single-handed rods. With a two-handed rod, a variety of shooting heads can be used.

*The upper Bogachiel.*

Speaking of two-handed rods, they are advantageous when fishing the Sol Duc, Calawah or Bogachiel, but they are by no means a requirement. "You don't need a two-handed rod, but I believe it outfishes a single-handed rod," Pigott says. "With the two-handed rod, you get better line control, and it takes less time to retrieve and shoot a line back out on the water. There is also a definite advantage when your back is up against the alders and you need to cast 80 feet—with a two-handed rod you don't need to backcast."

While winter fishing on the Sol Duc draws the most attention from fly rodders, there are also decent opportunities in the summer and fall months.

Summer steelhead spread themselves throughout the river and are fairly eager to take flies during June, before runoff subsides and the water drops and clears. July, August, and even September often provide tremendously challenging situations.

However, when the first fall rains arrive in September or October or even early November, fresh fish push into the system, including more summer-run steelhead, fall-run king salmon, and sea-run cutthroat.

"I've never had much success fishing for king salmon during spring, but during fall there are a lot more fish in the river, and they seem to like the added color in the water," Pigott says. "When they lie in the clear pools during summer, you could cast to them for hours and not draw a strike. But during fall they seem more willing. I

*Looking downstream from the confluence of the north and south forks of the Calawah.*

would hold off on the kings until the Sol Duc gets a little color, then you can get them. I use the same flies I cast to steelhead, possibly with a little added crystal flash."

Sea-run cutthroat are an overlooked fish species in Washington, yet they provide some of the finest fishing you'll find anywhere. Sea-runs are eager to take flies, including large, surface offerings. They fight hard, and they are absolutely beautiful specimens.

Sea-runs are present in the Sol Duc, Calawah, and Bogachiel throughout the year, but the late spring and summer seasons are not the best times to pursue them. Instead, an angler should hold off until fall.

"There are quite a few sea-runs around in early summer," Pigott says. "But about the time school gets out, you begin fishing a dwindling stock—all the school kids go down to the river and soak worms.

"When the river comes up, even just an inch, during fall, a bunch of fresh sea-runs move in. On cool, overcast days, cutthroat move from the fast riffles to the slow, dark, slack spots that we call 'frog water.' When they are in the dark water, it's easy to pull them off the banks with stimulators and muddler minnows. I've caught them to 22 or 23 inches, but any time they get up to 16 inches, you've got a heck of a cutthroat. During the summer and early fall, I spend more time fishing cutthroat than anything else. They're really a good fish and seem to like a large meal, so they'll take big dry flies."

While you can find excellent sea-run fishing on the Sol Duc and Bogachiel, the Calawah may host the best run. One October day, Pigott and his clients hit the river just right, and they lost count of netted cutts at 125. When the water is clear, Pigott goes with a size 8 or 10 dry fly. When water colors up and rises, he may go with a size 4 muddler and, if needed, sink the fly just under the surface film.

While the Sol Duc can challenge anglers, both for access and finding fish, it is a gorgeous river that offers excellent options on large steelhead, sea-run cutthroat trout, and massive king salmon. For these reasons, the Sol Duc ranks high on Washington flyfishers' hit list. If you choose to visit this river, realize that you will start an addiction. Your memories will draw you back to this place year after year.

The Calawah also sees good numbers of steelhead shooting up its currents during the winter season, but many of these fish stall out at the hatchery rearing ponds, just a half-mile upstream from the river's confluence with the Bogachiel. There, just below the rearing ponds, massive packs of tight-jawed steelhead congregate each winter. At times, 300 or more fish may occupy a long glide below the ponds.

Like the Bogachiel, the Calawah sees most of its hatchery returnees in December, January, and February, highlighted by the occasional wild fish.

In late February, March and April, plenty of native steelhead fin up the system, but they do so rather quickly, posing a problem for fly casters.

Due to restrictions on the North Fork Calawah (closed to fishing) and on the South Fork Calawah (closed from February 28 through June 1), steelhead are afforded safe havens. And the fish seem to know it—they fire through the mainstem Calawah offering only brief shots at them. However, if anglers can time their visits just right, some excellent action can be had.

The Calawah is a beautiful river that can be effectively wade-fished. It can also be floated, but as mentioned, only by experts. Wade access is available at bridge crossings, and there are plenty of old logging roads that lead out to the edge of the Calawah's canyon section. Anglers brave enough to hike down the banks can fish the river just about anywhere they like.

Similar to the Sol Duc, the Calawah's fish aren't too picky about fly pattern—throw a skunk, comet, marabou, or egg-sucking leech, and you are likely to draw strikes.

"The Calawah is a funny river because most of its steelhead go into the forks and you can't fish there," Pigott says. "So the Calawah fishes pretty well when it's high and fresh fish push in, but when it drops and clears, fish are in the forks and you can't get to them. Even with the forks closed, most guys don't fish the river until late February, March, or April. That's when most of the wild fish are in the river."

The Bogachiel, which is fed on its lower end by the Calawah, remains one of Washington's most popular steelhead streams. However, its native stocks have declined in past years due to Indian gillnetting and illegal harvest by anglers. Steelhead that return today are mostly taken by the spin and baitcasting crew.

"The Bogachiel fishery has mostly turned into a hatchery fishery," Pigott says. "There are some native fish remaining, but they have steadily decreased over the

*The South Fork Calawah is managed under special restrictions and provides only a short season. However, with proper timing, it fishes well for winter-run steelhead.*

years. You'll see lots of hatchery fish in December and January. The wild fish mostly show in March and April. I've had my best luck on the Bogachiel in mid-April."

While most anglers target the lower Bogachiel, the upper reaches do see some native steelhead. In March and April, extending to the April 30 season closure, anglers can hike up the Bogachiel Trail into Olympic National Park and may find decent numbers of steelhead. Some fish remain in the upper reaches as runoff subsides in June.

The Bogachiel also offers good numbers of sea-run cutthroat that may be found throughout the system. On the Bogachiel, sea-runs are prone to school in certain holes. An angler may need to cover a mile or more of unproductive water before finding a hole that holds lots of fish. When encountered, a school full of sea-runs can't be beat.

While it's not quite as pristine as southeast Alaska, Washington's western Olympic Peninsula is beautiful country that offers good steelhead, sea-run cutthroat, and king salmon fishing. With many of its streams originating in Olympic National Park, the future of these fisheries is somewhat encouraging. Spend a few soggy days in this remote part of the state, and you may fall in love with the place. You would be surprised how many gray days and week-long rain storms an angler can put up with when steelhead continually dance on the end of his line.

# Stream Facts: Quillayute System

### Seasons and special regulations

- Quillayute: From mouth to confluence of Sol Duc and Bogachiel Rivers: Trout and steelhead June 1 through April 30. Salmon open May 1 through November 30
- Sol Duc: From mouth to Sol Duc Hatchery: Trout and steelhead open June 1 through April 30. Salmon open March 1 through November 30. From Sol Duc Hatchery to Highway 101 bridge downstream of Snider Creek, trout and steelhead open June 1 through April 30. From Highway 101 bridge downstream of Snider Creek to Olympic National Park boundary, trout ad other game fish open June 1 through February 28. Check Olympic National Park regulations for park seasons.
- Bogachiel: From mouth to Highway 101 bridge: Trout and steelhead June 1 through April 30. Salmon open July 1 through November 30. From Highway 101 bridge to Olympic National Park boundary, trout and steelhead open June 1 through April 30. Check Olympic National Park regulations for park seasons
- Calawah: From mouth to Highway 101 bridge, trout and steelhead open June 1 through April 30. Salmon open July 1 through November 30. From Highay 101 bridge to forks, trout and steelhead open June 1 through April 30. South Fork, extending to Nationl Park boundary, open June 1 through Februaury 28.

### Species

- Steelhead
- Sea-run cutthroat
- Coho and king salmon

### Stream Characteristics

- This system is vulnerable to flooding, but when in shape, each stream provides miles of excellent steelhead water. The lower ends of these streams are large and best fished by boat. But the upper reaches are fairly narrow and very conducive to wade angling.

### Access

- Boat anglers gain the best access to these streams; however, there are excellent options to be had by wade fishers. If you have a boat or raft, bring it, but remember: these rivers are powerful and tricky for novice rowers. If you are not confident in your rowing ability, don't push your luck.

# Hoh River

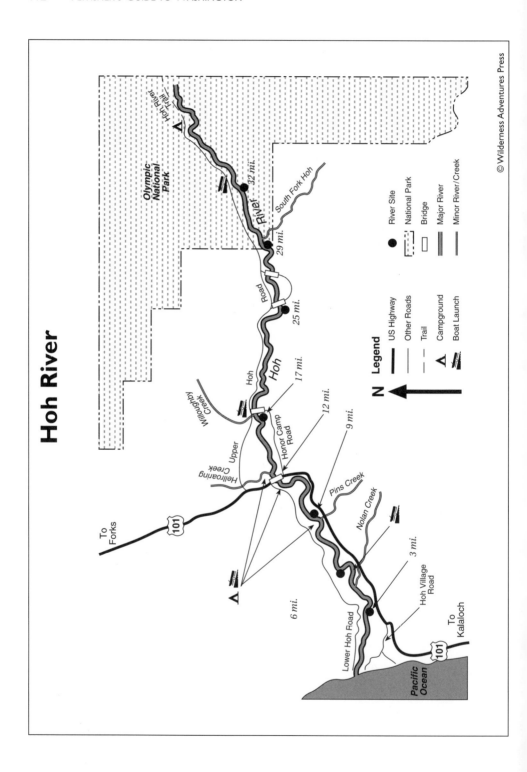

© Wilderness Adventures Press

# HOH RIVER

The Hoh River, which is not part of the Quillayute system but is similar in nature to the Sol Duc, Calawah, and Bogachiel, rests just south of these streams and offers excellent options for winter steelhead.

The Hoh is a large river that shows its muscle during winter storms and spring runoff. When anglers approach the river, they marvel at massive logjams and the disappearance of many familiar gravel bars, their location having changed since the last visit.

Despite its violent flow, the Hoh is a very approachable river for wade and boat anglers and offers winter- and summer-run steelhead. Sea-run cutthroat, Dolly Varden, and spring and fall runs of king salmon round out the smorgasbord.

Most of the Hoh's steelhead are hatchery origin, but some stubborn native fish remain that run to good size—up to 28 pounds or more. It's not uncommon to catch a Hoh River steelhead that weighs between 15 and 20 pounds. The size and determined flow of this river breeds strong, large fish.

Hatchery fish are present beginning in December, along with a few native steelhead. January and February provide decent steelhead catches when the water is in shape (a rainstorm turns the water extremely murky), but March and April are considered the prime times to cast a fly on this stream.

The typical steelhead swing works fine on the Hoh, but a flyfisher needs to offer a pattern that catches a steelhead's attention, especially when the water is off-color, which it typically is. Size 0/2, 2, and 4 marabou patterns work well, as do large egg-sucking leeches and bright red, beadhead flies. Sinktip lines, in varying classes, are needed on the Hoh. An angler must get his fly down to take fish. During summer, the river clears and smaller flies work fine.

For those seeking king salmon, spring does offer the possibility for fish (the season opens in May), but fall is the best time to pursue these brutes. Fish to 40 pounds may be encountered, but the average king runs 15 to 25 pounds. A return of immature "jack" kings also pushes into the river, averaging about 8 pounds—certainly not a trophy fish but one hell of a fight on a 6- or 7-weight fly rod.

Access to the Hoh is excellent via the 18-mile road that leads from Hwy 101 to the Hoh River Ranger Station at the edge of Olympic National Park. Floating the river is the best way to work the river's tempting water, but wade fishing is productive, too. There are several good put-in and take-out sites located along the river, below the Olympic National Park boundary.

# Stream Facts: Hoh River

### Seasons and special regulations
- From mouth to Olympic National Park boundary: Trout and steelhead are open from June 1 through April 15. Salmon are open May 16 through August 31. Salmon are also open from September 1 through November 30 from mouth to Highway 101 bridge. Check Olympic National Park regulations for park rules.

### Species
- Steelhead, sea-run cutthroat, coho and king salmon

### Stream Charactoristics
- A typical coastal river, the Hoh is prone to flooding, but it offers excellent opportunities for large steelhead. Ten-pound steelhead are commonly caught here and 20-pounders are not too uncommon.

### Access
- Boat anglers gain the best access to these streams; however, there are excellent options to be had by wade fishers. If you have a boat or raft, bring it, but remember, these rivers are powerful and tricky for novice rowers. Sweepers and whirlpools are unforgiving.

*The beautiful Hoh River winds out of Olympic National Park.*

# QUEETS RIVER

One of Washington's best options for large, native steelhead, the Olympic Peninsula's Queets River is often overlooked by flycasters due to its deep water nature and turbidity.

Cloudy water conditions start at the river's origin—the Queets flows straight off the flanks of Mount Olympus, which is located in the heart of Olympic National Park and is fed heavily by glacial runoff. Queets Glacier, Humes Glacier, and Jeffers Glacier all offer milky contributions to the Queets.

On a good winter day, which usually arrives after a couple of cold, clear evenings, glacial flow decreases, and the Queets might offer 2, 3, or even 4 feet of visibility. Fortunately, even this limited clarity is enough for flyfishers to place a streamer pattern in front of a steelhead and draw a take.

When that happens, a flyfisher could tie into a fish ranging from 6 to 26 pounds or larger. You just never know. For that reason, most flyfishers arm themselves with stout 8- and 9-weight rods, loaded with sinktip and high-density sinking lines, when fishing this river. A 4- or 5-foot section of 10- to 15-pound Maxima serves well as the leader.

Another option is to go with a floating line, a long leader, and a heavily weighted fly that ticks along the bottom. Some guys just use a leadhead jig under a strike indicator, but I try to doctor my fly so it at least looks like a minnow, leech, or crustacean. It's just personal preference. I mean, hey, if you're going to use a leadhead jig, why not just pick up a spinning rod?

Another beneficial item when fishing the Queets is a drift boat or quality inflatable raft. The Queets does offer lots of wade-fishing opportunity, but to fully appreciate its water, an angler should float the river, drifting between one prime run after the other, hopping out on all the likely looking gravel bars and middepth runs to work the river meticulously.

As mentioned, the Queets begins on the southern flanks of Mount Olympus and flows unimpeded about 55 miles to the Pacific Ocean just north of the Jefferson and Grays Harbor county line.

Throughout its reaches, the Queets offers steelhead, but timing plays a huge role in an angler's chances of tying into a big fish.

Hatchery steelhead begin pushing into the Queets in December, all headed for the hatchery on Salmon River, which enters the Queets from the south, about 6 or 7 miles from the ocean. Most hatchery-origin fish are in the Queets by mid-January, when metalheads are joined by an influx of native, wild fish. These are the big dogs that every avid flyfisher dreams about.

If you chase hatchery fish early in the year, be aware that much of the Salmon River, as well as a section of the lower Queets just above Queets/Clearwater Bridge, flows through the Quinault Indian Reservation. To fish these waters, an angler must hire an Indian guide and purchase a tribal license. Fortunately for flyfishers, there are plenty of steelhead in open water where a guide is not required.

# Queets River

N

## Legend

— US Highway

-- Other Paved Roads

···· Gravel/Dirt Road

-- Trail

▲ Campground

🔱 Boat Launch

● River Site

▢ Bridge

▬ Major River

│ Minor River/Creek

MOUNT OLYMPUS

MOUNT QUEETS

Service Falls

Queets River Trail

Queets River

Douglas Fir Natural Feature

Sams Rapids

Queets Campground

Streater Creek

OLYMPIC NATIONAL PARK

Lyman Rapids

Hartzell Creek

Queets River

Road

Salmon River

To Hoquiam

101

Clearwater Road

Clearwater/ Queets Bridge

Fisher Rapids

QUINAULT INDIAN RESERVATION

To Forks

101

Pacific Ocean

© Wilderness Adventures Press

Early in the year, flyfishers should concentrate on the open section of the Salmon River outside the Indian reservation and downstream sections of the Queets. An excellent early season float extends from the Hartzell Creek put-in, just upstream of the Salmon's mouth, downstream to the Clearwater/Queets Bridge. The take-out is on the south side of the river (river left).

When native fish show in mid- to late January and February, upstream drifts often hold lots of fish. Prime floats during the late winter and early spring months include Streater Crossing to Hartzell and the campground access at the end of the 13-mile Queets River Road downstream to Streater. Each float is about 5 or 6 miles and offers plenty of killer water.

There are also decent opportunities to take steelhead above the campground, but prospective anglers are required to use foot power to reach them. A trail parallels the river to its headwaters, but bushwhacking through the brush to reach the stream may not be ideal for everyone.

In fact, when fishing the Queets, an angler's determination plays a huge role in success. When drifting the river, flyfishers need to concentrate their efforts on a particular run and fish it from top to bottom thoroughly. That can be difficult when wind-blown sleet and rain slaps you across the face and drips down the nape of your neck. When wade-fishing, you'll need to pound through the brush to reach some of the best water, and then you might have to stand in the river for hours on end before hooking up, if you hook up at all. Winter steelhead fishing is not a sissy sport. If you are not cut out for it, don't feel bad. Just don't go through the motions and crowd the river.

Whether fishing from a boat or wade-fishing, look for water that offers steelhead a respite from the river's flow. Yes, it's true that steelhead hold in deep slots next to cutbanks and in the deepest pools, but such water is mostly out of reach of the flyfisher. Let it go and concentrate on middepth runs, shallow pools, behind obstructions such as logs and midstream boulders, and don't pass up on gravel bars that offer a mild slope into the river. Inside corners of riffles and pools also hold steelhead.

Because of limited visibility, it's best to use bright steelhead flies in the Queets. Red, pink, yellow, and chartreuse marabou flies work well. Egg-sucking leeches, egg patterns, and the standard winter flies, such as a polar shrimp, green butt skunk, Skykomish sunrise, and the winter's hope draw takes. Make sure you work these flies just off the bottom rocks—I mean inches above them. By doing so, you will likely lose a pile of flies to the bottom, but you also stand the chance to catch a monster sea-run rainbow.

Because the Queets runs through a temperate rainforest, conditions are variable. One day the river might be in good shape and the next, after a monsoon-type deluge, it might blow out. Such conditions can last for several days, if not a week or more. It always pays to call Olympic National Park or a Forks area fishing shop for up-to-date information. Then glue yourself to the couch and watch the evening news. If it calls for a lot of rain on the Peninsula, you may want to forego your expedition. However, if the river has been in good condition and gets hit by a moderate rain, a pile of fresh steelhead may move into the system and fishing might turn on.

*The Queets offers large winter steelhead, and it can be wade-fished or floated.*

No matter what the weather offers, the river will run cold due to its glacial nature. Five-millimeter neoprene waders, preferably a bootfoot model, should keep your feet and legs warm the longest. Lightweight waders will send you home singing the high-pitched, cold-water blues.

When considering the Queets, it makes no sense to look at the Washington Department of Fish and Wildlife's regulations—they don't even list the Queets in the regulation booklet. Instead, contact Olympic National Park, which manages the river, and get an update on seasons, emergency closures, harvest limits, and tackle restrictions. Generally, anglers can hit the Queets from December through April with good opportunities for steelhead. During summer, summer-run steelhead can be encountered throughout the river, including upstream from the Queets River Campground where some large Dolly Varden add to the mix. Look for Dollies in the

deeper pools. They'll smack a variety of streamer patterns, including muddler minnows and woolly buggers.

The Queets doesn't seem to get the notoriety that its Peninsula neighbors do, but
it can pump out some monster steelhead in good numbers. Because of its wonderful scenery and large steelhead, plus nearly pristine habitat, it ranks high on my
yearly hit list. Give this beautiful broad river a try, and you'll likely be impressed, too.
Especially if a fresh 15-pound buck hammers your offering and takes you on a wild,
downstream ride.

To reach the Queets, follow Hwy 101 north from Hoquiam or south from Forks.
If arriving from the south, turn right on Queets River Road. If driving down from
Forks, cross the Highway 101 bridge over the Queets and follow to Queets River
Road. Turn left and follow upstream. It's 13.6 miles to the end of the road at the
campground. The lower boat take-out, just below the Queets/Clearwater Bridge, is
accessible via Clearwater Road, which connects with Hwy 101 just a couple of miles
west of Queets River Road.

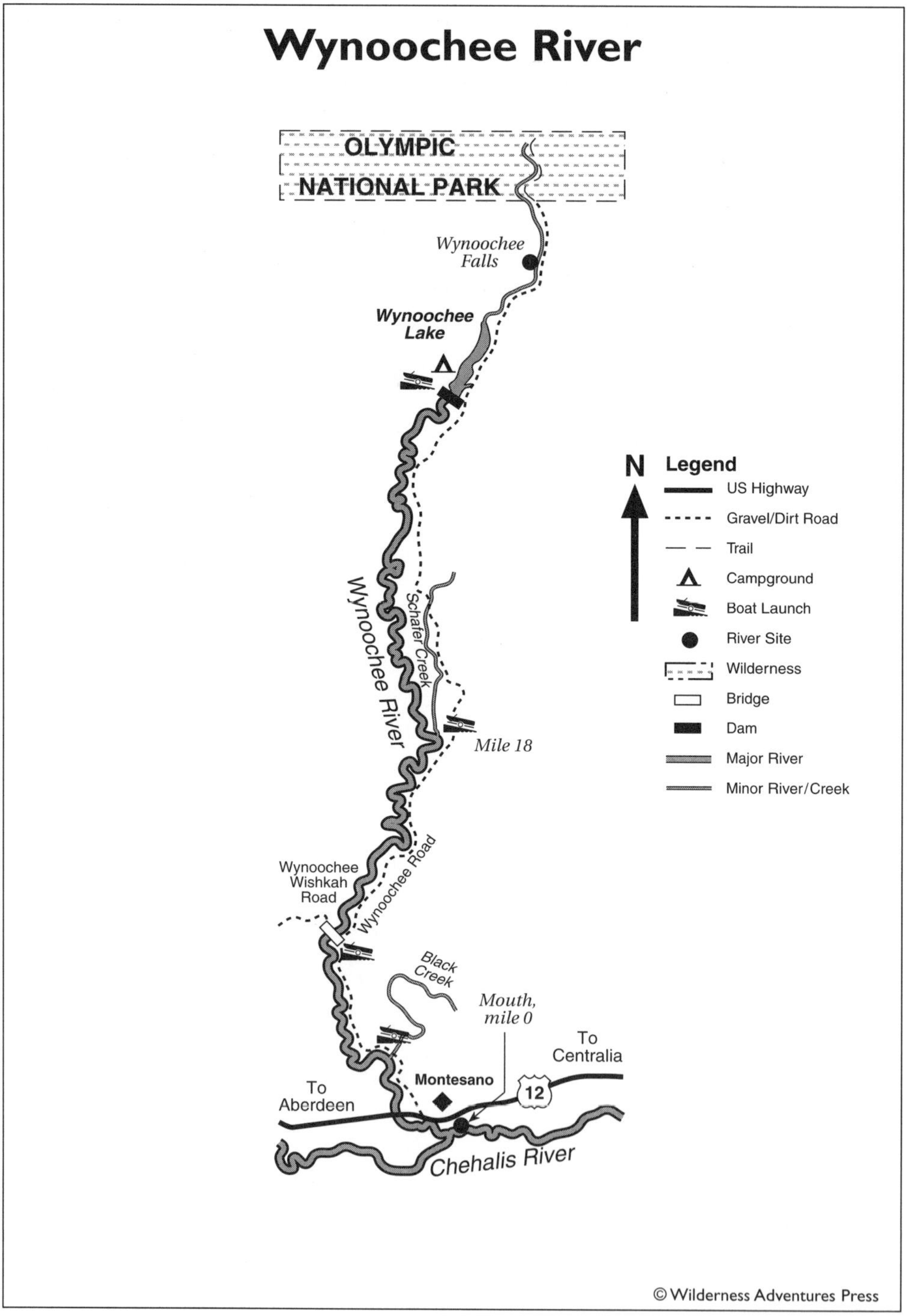

# Wynoochee River

OLYMPIC
NATIONAL PARK

*Wynoochee Falls*

**Wynoochee Lake**

*Wynoochee River*

*Schafer Creek*

*Mile 18*

Wynoochee Wishkah Road

Wynoochee Road

*Black Creek*

*Mouth, mile 0*

To Centralia

To Aberdeen

**Montesano**

12

*Chehalis River*

**N**

**Legend**

| | |
|---|---|
| ——— | US Highway |
| - - - - | Gravel/Dirt Road |
| — — | Trail |
| △ | Campground |
| | Boat Launch |
| ● | River Site |
| | Wilderness |
| ▭ | Bridge |
| ▬ | Dam |
| | Major River |
| | Minor River/Creek |

© Wilderness Adventures Press

# WYNOOCHEE RIVER

Less loved than the big-name Olympic Peninsula steelhead streams like the Sol Duc, Calawah, and Bogachiel, the Wynoochee River has nevertheless developed a faithful following for good reason.

The Wynoochee, which winds out of the Olympic National Forest and flows into the Chehalis River at Montesano, kicks out lots of winter-run hatchery steelhead, as well as summer-runs, and a fair amount of its water tempts flyfishers. On a very good day, the Wynoochee might offer a double on winter- or summer-runs for the flyfisher.

One thing that differentiates this river from most is the origin of half of its hatchery fish—90,000 Chambers Creek smolt are planted each year and are supplemented by 90,000 Wynoochee River stock, which are fully adapted to run their home river.

Flyfishers should look for the Chambers Creek stock in December and January. By February, the Wynoochee stock return and keep pushing into the river through March. They are joined by native, wild fish during that same time frame.

Fishing can be very productive in December and January on the lower river, but water conditions could push anglers off the Wynoochee. The river has been severely degraded along its banks due to logging, which causes silt and sediment to flush into the system after a good rain. The same can be said for fishing in February and March, but the Wynoochee usually offers fewer "unfishable" days during that time.

Probably the best time for flyfishers to hit the river is during the late season, between mid-February and the end of the season, which arrives March 31. During that time, flyfishers can avoid the lower river, where fishing from a boat is the norm, and concentrate on upstream stretches that offer solid banks and gravel bars and access to some prime water. A boat definitely helps a flyfisher access all of the good water, but those restricted to wade fishing can find decent runs, especially if they aren't afraid to bushwhack off the Wynoochee River Road, which parallels the river.

If you are going to float the river, you'll want to dump in at White Bridge and float to Black Creek, about 8 miles. Another option is to launch at Schafer Creek and float down to White Bridge, which is a long, 12-mile float. However, there are several factors that make the Schafer Creek to White Bridge section favorable for flyfishers.

First, this section doesn't receive as much pressure as downstream portions. Second, there are some excellent runs to be probed. Third, by late February extending through March, many wild fish and Wynoochee-origin hatchery stock set up camp in this section. It's a matter of personal preference, but I would much rather catch a wild steelhead than a hatchery fish any day. If it has to be a hatchery fish, I'll take one that originated from the river.

One problem with the Schafer Creek to White Bridge float is the amount of time a shuttle takes—it's an hour or more over dirt road to dump a boat in at Schafer Creek and shuttle vehicles.

"I'd say that the Wynoochee is the best steelhead stream in the [Grays] Harbor area," says Washington Department of Fish and Wildlife biologist Rick Brix. "It gets a

*The Wynoochee River offers good options on winter- and summer-run steelhead.*

fair amount of pressure, but people do well as long as the water clarity is alright. When we get a freshet, the water can go out of shape, and it becomes unfishable.

"For flyfishing, you have to watch the water closely," Brix adds. "If the clarity is decent, you probably have a good chance during winter. There are not a lot of access points, especially on the upper river, but if a guy is adventurous, he'll find some good water."

A typical Wynoochee winter steelhead runs about 6 or 8 pounds, with fish to 12 or 13 pounds fairly common. Wynoochee's summer-run steelhead, which run slightly smaller on average, return in July and August.

"We see steelhead as early as June, but July and early August are the best times to go for summer-runs," Brix says. "The water is low and clear, and you can find fish throughout the system."

If pursuing winter-run steelhead, flyfishers should take sinktip lines, accompanied by short, 3- or 4-foot leaders and large, bright marabou flies. For summer-run steelhead, flyfishers can go with a sinktip or a floating line and less gaudy flies—a Knudson's spider, fall favorite, or muddler minnow should draw strikes.

The Wynoochee also hosts chinook and coho salmon and sea-run cutthroat. Look for kings and cohos in October. The salmon season runs September 16 through October 31 (check current regulations for amendments). Sea-run cutthroat push into the Wynoochee in late August and September. Fishing can be decent for them through fall. All wild cutthroat must be released.

To reach the Wynoochee, follow Hwy 12 out of Olympia and turn north at Montesano onto Wynoochee River Road. Note that the river is closed during April and May. The portion of the Wynoochee above Schafer Creek is closed from October 31 through June 1.

## Stream Facts: Wynoochee River

### Seasons and Special Regulations
- From mouth to bridge above mouth of Schafer Creek: Open for trout and other game fish June 1 through March 31 and for salmon September 16 through October 31. Single point barbless hooks only from September 16 through October 31. Release all wild cutthroat, wild coho, and all chum.
- From bridge above mouth of Schafer Creek upstream: Open for trout and other game fish from June 1 through October 31.

### Species
- Steelhead
- Coho, chinook, and chum salmon
- Sea-run cutthroat trout

### River Characteristics
- This is a less publicized but worthwhile steelhead river with the average fish running 6 to 8 pounds
- Fishing can be good for much of the year, but the best time to visit is in late February through the end of the season, depending on water clarity.
- Fishing is primarily for hatchery-run steelhead, but some opportunities exist for wild fish, as well.

### Access
- A boat definitely allows more access to good water, but wading anglers can access the river from the Wynoochee River Road that parallels the river if they are willing to bushwhack.
- The best floats for flyfishers may be the 12-mile stretch from Schafer Creek to White Bridge and the 8-mile run from White Bridge down to Black Creek.

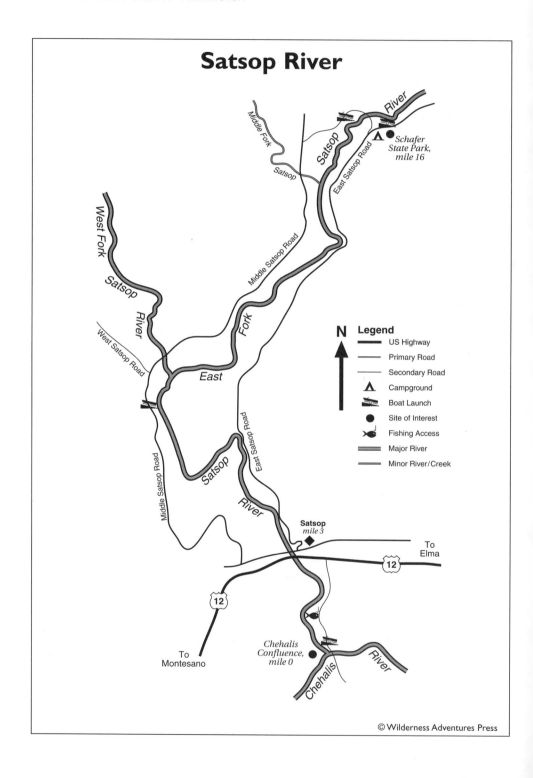

# Satsop River

**Legend**

| | |
|---|---|
| | US Highway |
| | Primary Road |
| | Secondary Road |
| ▲ | Campground |
| | Boat Launch |
| ● | Site of Interest |
| | Fishing Access |
| | Major River |
| | Minor River/Creek |

© Wilderness Adventures Press

# SATSOP RIVER

A tremendous salmon and steelhead stream earlier this century, the Satsop River has been rendered a skeleton of its former self insofar as its wild fish runs and the opportunity they once provided anglers.

That shouldn't come as any surprise to those who follow the history of anadromous fish runs in Washington—the depression of wild runs occurs on almost every viable stream in the state. However, the Satsop still provides some decent opportunities for flyfishers, and the best of the lot is a chance to hook big, wild, strong chum salmon that ascend the Chehalis River system, including the Satsop and its forks, in late October and November.

While some river systems may host more chum salmon than the Satsop, it would be difficult to locate an area to catch larger "dog" salmon. The Satsop's chums are all wild and very large on average. In fact, in 1997, a 26-pound male chum salmon was landed on the Satsop, and it holds the title of "state record."

According to Rick Brix, a biologist for Washington Department of Fish and Wildlife in Montesano, the Satsop does provide huge chum salmon, but the number of large fish entering the system varies from year to year.

"It's all dependent on the size of the run and the strength of each age class," Brix says. "We see 3-, 4-, and 5-year-old fish returning each season. Some years we get a 60 percent return of 3-year-old fish that average 9 or 10 pounds. Some years we get 80 percent 4-year-old fish averaging 12 to 14 pounds. And then sometimes we get a high percentage of 5-year-old fish that average 15 to 20 pounds."

Like all chum salmon, the Satsop's fish are not picky about fly patterns and aren't shy about attacking them, either. Strip a streamer, such as a chartreuse chum candy or a double egg fly, through a prime run or let it dead-drift through a medium-depth riffle, and you are likely to get a take if the fish are there.

Chum salmon enter the Satsop in late October, and anglers find a fairly steady stream of them through the first week of December, but they don't live long once they reach the river.

"I think all of the fish are pretty much spawned, dead and gone by the end of that first week in December," Brix says. "Their life expectancy in freshwater is only about 10 days. In fact, they die so quickly that we have to monitor their numbers by doing live counts and dead counts. We have a really short season here, but it can be pretty good when the fish are in."

Chum salmon ascend all of the Satsop's forks, but angling is only allowed in the mainstem and east fork Satsop. Chums can be found as high on the east fork as the Bingham Creek Hatchery at mile 17.5, but angling is only allowed upstream to Schafer State Park at mile 12.4.

The east fork can be packed with anglers, hardware guys and flyfishers alike, when the fish are in. If you are looking for a solitary experience, you won't find it here. However, by engaging the option of a drift boat or raft, flyfishers can duck the crowds and find some relatively undisturbed water.

"When chums are in, there are about 40 'bajillion' guys fishing the river," Brix says. "There is enough room for everybody, but wade anglers can be severely limited, depending on the condition of the river.

"Usually in late October and November we get heavy rains—that can be both good and bad," Brix adds. "On one hand, rain brings fish into the Chehalis system and the Satsop River. On the other hand, water conditions become poor, and there is very little bank access. In that case, you almost have to have a boat to get around. But if we have a mild, dry fall, conditions can be good for wading. It all depends on the weather."

If you choose to float the river in a boat or raft, don't worry about any dangerous rapids or waterfalls—the Satsop is a medium-sized, relatively gentle river that offers little in the way of dangerous obstruction. Just watch out for logjams and downfalls and don't run your boat close to wade-fishers. Try to drift down the opposite side of the river if possible.

Although access is not abundant on the Satsop, boats may be launched on the lower river at the Hwy 12 boat ramp near Satsop and may be taken out on the Chehalis. A boat launch is also located on the east fork below Schafer State Park that affords a nice drift downstream to the Hwy 12 boat ramp. Wade anglers may gain access at bridge crossings along the mainstem and east fork or at Schafer State Park.

While the Satsop currently offers decent chum salmon runs, its fish are in peril, and anglers should consult regulations before visiting the river. Regulations could change from year to year depending on the size of annual runs, which vary with the nuances of ocean and freshwater conditions.

While chum salmon offer the most consistent angling opportunity on the Satsop, the river also hosts fall-run silver and chinook salmon along with a modest run of winter steelhead.

The chinook run consists of salmon that range from 10 to 35 pounds, with numbers peaking in mid-October. Some chinook are wild, native fish, but most of them are headed back to the Bingham Creek Hatchery. Catch-and-keep seasons are dependent on the strength of hatchery runs. Any decrease in native chinook populations could close the fishery.

Silver salmon, also called cohos, return in late October and can show up in fairly decent numbers, affording fly casters fair action. However, when the first cohos arrive, anglers need to hit the river immediately. They don't hang around very long.

"Cohos hold out in Grays Harbor or in the Chehalis waiting for the right conditions," Brix says. "When we get a good rain, fish push into the system and cruise right on through. There is only a short period to intercept them, but often it overlaps with the chum run, so guys have some pretty good options."

Satsop steelhead, a mix of hatchery and wild fish, begin showing in December and remain in the system until the season closes March 31. The Turnow Branch and the west fork are open from November 1 through January 31.

Satsop steelhead are not a big draw for western Washington steelheaders—there are plenty of places nearby that offer far greater runs—but they are present in

*The Satsop River offers a few winter-steelhead
and plenty of fall-run chum salmon.*

small numbers, and a flyfisher may encounter them on any given cast. Wild fish
must be released. January and February are the prime months for steelhead.

While the Satsop doesn't provide the killer steelhead and salmon runs that it
once did, it remains an excellent option for flyfishers who want to chase some big
chum salmon. Given the opportunity to fish for state-record class chums (even some
cohos, kings and steelhead), surrounded by excellent southern Olympic Peninsula
scenery, flyfishers should walk away from the Satsop refreshed.

Note: Flyfishers may encounter a few sea-run cutthroat trout in the Satsop.
Don't be surprised if they hammer steelhead patterns. They might even dart out
from beneath a log to inhale an egg fly or a streamer. Only fin-clipped, hatchery-
origin cuts may be kept. All wild fish must be released immediately. Treat them
well; a sea-run cutthroat is a beautiful fish that needs all the help it can get.

To reach the Satsop, take U.S. Hwy 12 west from Olympia to Satsop. Turn north
onto East Satsop Road and follow it upriver.

# Stream Facts: Satsop River

### Seasons & Special Regulations, Satsop River and East Fork

- From mouth to bridge at Schafer State Park: Open for trout and other game fish: June 1–March 31 and for salmon September 16–October 31.
- From bridge at Schafer State Park upstream: Open for trout and other game fish June 1–October 31.
- Release all wild cutthroat, wild coho, and all chum. Single point barbless hooks only from September 16–October 31. Selective gear rules for all species from Bingham Creek upstream.

### Species

- Steelhead
- Coho, chinook, and chum salmon
- Sea-run cutthroat trout

### River Characteristics

- This is a medium-sized river with a gentle current.
- Large chum salmon are available in the mainstem and east fork and offer the best shot at large fish.
- Runs of coho, chinook, and winter steelhead add to catch in fall and winter, as well.

### Access

- Wade anglers are limited to bridge crossings along the mainstem and east fork and at Schafer State Park. Floaters can put in at the Hwy 12 boat ramp near Satsop and take out on the Chehalis or from the east fork below Schafer State Park, down to the Hwy 12 ramp.

# HOODSPORT AND HOOD CANAL'S CHUM SALMON STREAMS

Each October and November, just as nasty winter winds and pounding rains push in from the Pacific Ocean and spread over western Washington, hordes of chum salmon enter Puget Sound, many of them pointing their snouts at a single destination—the Hoodsport fish hatchery.

In their marine environment, these fish follow the beaches, testing any freshwater tributary that arrives in their path. By mid-November, most chums, also called dog salmon or calico salmon, reach Hoodsport. It is there that they are met by one giant horde of anglers, some casting flies, others chucking spoons and spinners. It's not a pretty sight, and often it's dangerous.

In fact, if you're looking for a fight, Hoodsport is the place to go. Overzealous anglers wage little miniature wars for casting space in front of the Hoodsport Hatchery and surrounding terrain. If you must wade in and brave the crowds, try throwing chartreuse streamers. Chum salmon love chartreuse, and any number of patterns, such as marabou streamers, should draw strikes.

Troy Denton, who works at Northwest Angler Fly Shop in Poulsbo and fishes Hood Canal extensively, says chum salmon are not picky about their meal. In fact, Denton believes they strike more out of aggression than the need to eat.

"They are really aggressive," Denton says. "Usually, a chartreuse streamer will work, but if they don't take that, I switch to a blood red and then a turquoise. They see a lot of chartreuse, and sometimes they turn off of it. When that happens, I'll go with something else, and it normally works."

Because Hoodsport is so cluttered with anglers, Denton and many other flyfishers try to intercept Hood Canal's chum salmon before they reach Hoodsport. One such place is a small tributary stream, located 6 miles north of Hoodsport, called Eagle Creek.

"It's just a small creek, but it has a large clam bed that spreads out like an alluvial fan in front of its mouth," Denton says. "The fish smell fresh water and push over to it to take a look. Sometimes they are really plentiful, and when they get out over the shallow clam bed, you can see them pushing water out in front. It's like casting to bonefish on the flats."

Another good saltwater stream mouth option is Kennedy Creek, located off Hwy 101 south of Shelton and the Thurston/Mason county line. From Highway 101, the Old Olympic Road follows the creek toward the saltwater. Upstream sections can be accessed at bridge crossings, but only the section of creek downstream from Highway 101 is open for salmon fishing.

Kennedy Creek, a tiny little salmon and steelhead stream, has a pretty big reputation. However, fishing the creek itself for steelhead with a fly rod invites frustration. The creek is choked with a tangle of alder and blackberry bushes, and the clutter eats flies like candy.

# Hood Canal

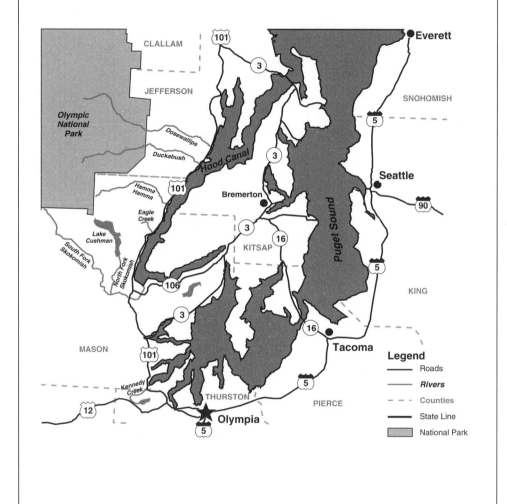

CLALLAM

JEFFERSON

Olympic
National
Park

Dosewallips

Duckabush

Hood Canal

Hamma
Hamma

Eagle
Creek

Lake
Cushman

South Fork
Skokomish

North Fork
Skokomish

Bremerton

KITSAP

Puget Sound

SNOHOMISH

Everett

Seattle

Tacoma

MASON

Kennedy
Creek

THURSTON

PIERCE

KING

Olympia

## Legend

— Roads

~~~ *Rivers*

- - - Counties

— State Line

National Park

© Wilderness Adventures Press

# Eagle Creek

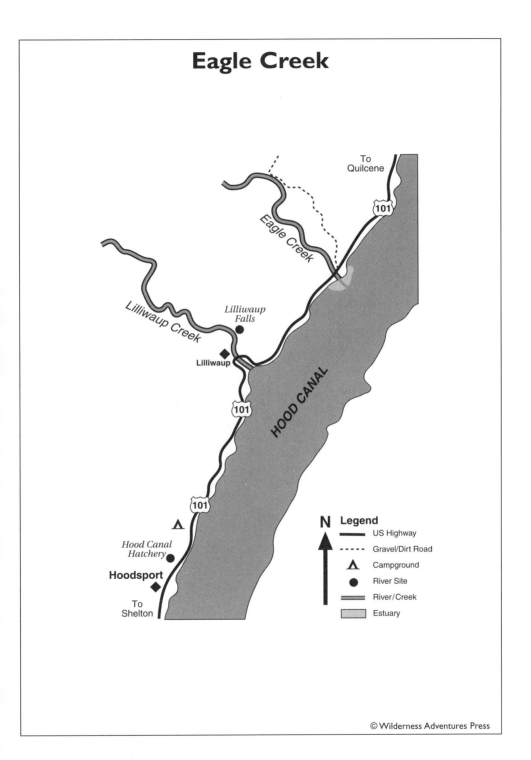

© Wilderness Adventures Press

# Kennedy Creek

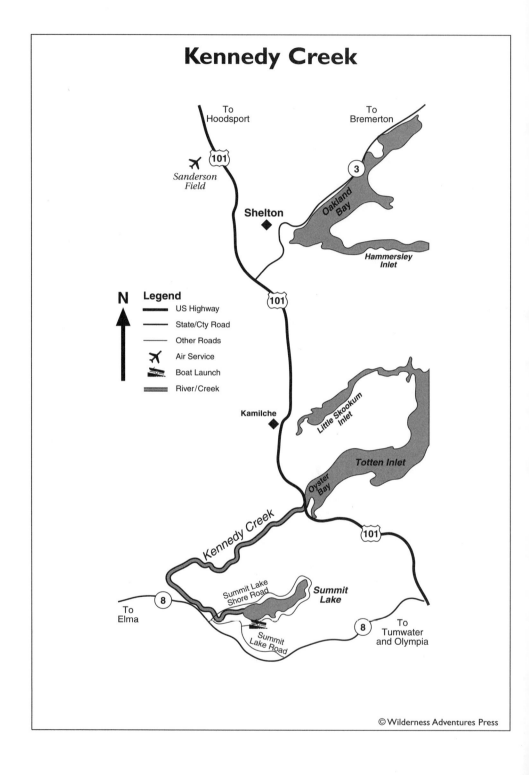

To
Hoodsport

To
Bremerton

101

3

✈
Sanderson
Field

Oakland
Bay

**Shelton** ◆

Hammersley
Inlet

101

**N**

**Legend**
— US Highway
— State/Cty Road
— Other Roads
✈ Air Service
🚤 Boat Launch
▦ River/Creek

Little Skookum
Inlet

**Kamilche** ◆

Totten Inlet

Oyster
Bay

Kennedy Creek

101

Summit Lake
Shore Road

**Summit
Lake**

8

To
Elma

Summit
Lake Road

8

To
Tumwater
and Olympia

© Wilderness Adventures Press

*The mouth of Kennedy Creek invites winter steelhead and fall chum salmon.*

Fortunately, both chum salmon and steelhead can be pursued at the mouth of the creek, where it twists through mudflats with plenty of backcast room. Most anglers concentrate efforts on the incoming tide when "chromer" steelhead push toward freshwater, but it pays to hit it just after high tide, too.

Due to its size, anglers won't hear a lot about Kennedy Creek. In fact, you can drive right over it on Hwy 101, and if you are not extremely observant, you'll have to turn around to find it. But if you snoop around Hood Canal for very long, the creek will be brought up in conversation. Hook a steelhead, chum salmon, or even a sea-run cutthroat in this small water, and you're bound to push it toward the top of your priority list.

But don't get me wrong. Kennedy Creek is not the steelhead fishery it was 20 years ago. You'll still find fish pushing in from December through the end of February, when the season closes, but it's not a factory.

At Hoodsport, Eagle Creek, Kennedy Creek, and any other location where chums congregate in good numbers, a flyfisher's challenge often is not to induce a strike but rather not to foul hook a fish. To alleviate this problem or at least to lessen the potential, Denton uses a floating line or a Scientific Angler Mastery intermediate stillwater line rather than a full-sink line. When his fly is in the water, Denton retrieves in quick strips.

"I usually give it two quick strips and then one, long, slow pull," he says. "I think the quick strips get the salmons' attention, and they hit it when you give it the long pull. It helps to keep from snagging them."

When fishing the mouths of Hood Canal's streams for chum salmon, flyfisher's who have a boat (or a float tube) are offered almost unlimited access. For those who do not, wear high-back waders when you plod into the saltwater and don't get stranded by the tide.

If you want to pass on the saltwater option, try one of the Hood Canal streams, such as the Skokomish, Dosewallips, and Duckabush. Here's a look at the options as an angler travels north to south on Hwy 101:

### Duckabush River

A beautiful, freestone stream that originates in Olympic National Park, the Duckabush is a pleasure to fish. Access is excellent along Duckabush Road, and primitive campgrounds can be found along its length. Near the saltwater, where Hwy 101 passes over it, the river slows down a bit and salmon, sea-run cutthroat and steelhead can be pursued in its estuary.

Winter steelhead can be encountered from December through February, and chum salmon make their presence felt in November and December. Sea-run cutthroat, also called harvest trout (don't get the wrong idea—wild sea-runs and steelhead must be released), push into the Duckabush in September and October.

### Dosewallips River

Once an excellent steelhead river, the Dosewallips still manages to kick out a metalhead or two each year, but it's just a ghost of its former self. That doesn't mean that you can't find steelhead in its currents. Some of the best places to look for them are just east of Dosewallips State Park near the mouth of the river. Some deep holes and prime runs hold fish after modest winter rains.

The river isn't very big, so leave your spey rods at home and uncase a 6- or 7-weight single-handed rod. Sinktip lines should allow a fly to reach the bottom, and various patterns draw strikes. Skykomish sunrises, green butt skunks, general practitioners, and polar shrimp are excellent choices.

Chum salmon enter the Dosewallips in late October and early November. Like all chum salmon waters, chartreuse flies seem to draw the most strikes. The action is limited to the short reach of river below the Highway 101 bridge.

### Hamma Hamma River

The Hamma Hamma also receives a fall run of chum salmon, but they are off-limits to anglers—the season is permanently closed.

However, the Hamma Hamma is worth visiting. It's a beautiful stream that rushes out of Olympic National Park and provides all sorts of enticing holes that often hide sea-run cutthroat during August, September, and October, as well as a few

# Duckabush River

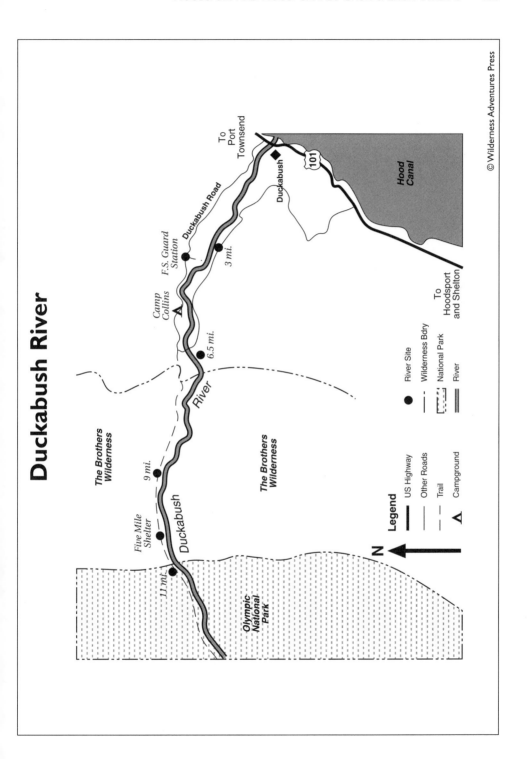

**Legend**

| | |
|---|---|
| US Highway | River Site |
| Other Roads | Wilderness Bdry |
| Trail | National Park |
| Campground | River |

N

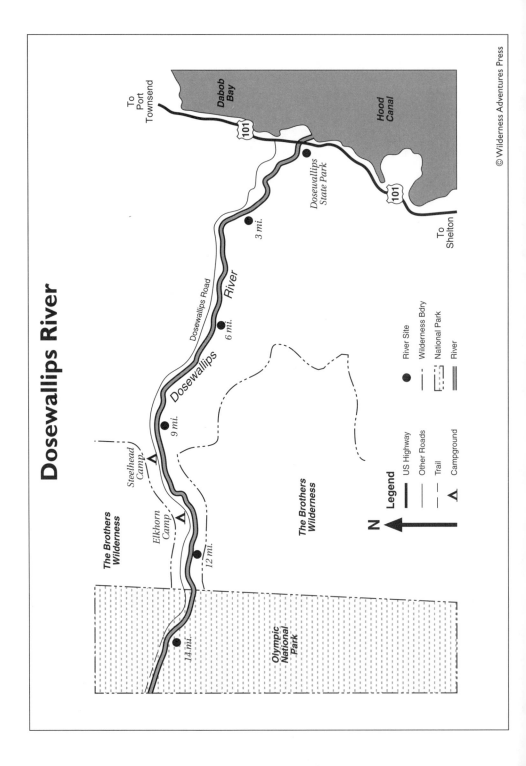

# Dosewallips River

# Hamma Hamma River

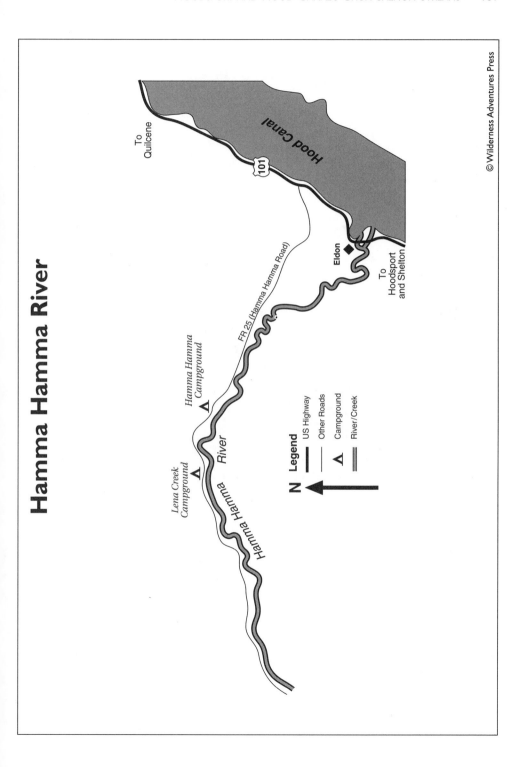

© Wilderness Adventures Press

*The Dosewallips offers a few winter steelhead and fall chum salmon.*

steelhead during the winter season. Only wild fish return to the river, so it's strictly catch and release on metalheads.

Because the river often runs crystal clear, it pays to follow the Hamma Hamma Road upstream 6 miles to where it reaches the river, then peer into the holes to spot steelhead and sea-runs. For those looking for a place to stay, the Hamma Hamma Campground, located next to the river, is a nice spot.

### Skokomish River

Larger than its northern counterparts, the Skokomish River is an enticing stream. And, fortunately, it provides a good run of chum salmon. Its steelhead fishery, however, is less appealing.

If you're into salmon fishing for the meat, this is the wrong place to be. The Skokomish offers good numbers of chums, but it's all catch and release on salmon. So

*The Hamma Hamma flows through beautiful forests*
*on the west side of the Olympic Peninsula.*

much for the barbecue, right? Coho salmon, which may also be encountered during fall on the Skokomish, must also be released.

Chums enter the lower river during November and early December, and the fishing can be quite good at times. Look for them to stack up in the deep pools, and use a sinktip or full-sink line to reach them. For this river, a 7- or 8-weight rod is ideal.

During fall, sea-run cutthroat ascend the river. They provide decent action, and every one landed should be considered a treasure. Remember, it's strictly catch and release.

## Other Options

There are other streams on the east flanks of the Olympic Mountains that attract chums, but the Dosewallips, Duckabush, and Skokomish offer the best public access and solid fish runs. Many other waters have very restrictive regulations, or they are simply closed.

"Typically, all of our streams get pretty good returns," says Tim Flint, region 7 fisheries manager for Washington Department of Fish and Game. "The Skokomish probably gets the most fish, but the Duckabush and Dosewallips get good runs, too.

# Skokomish River

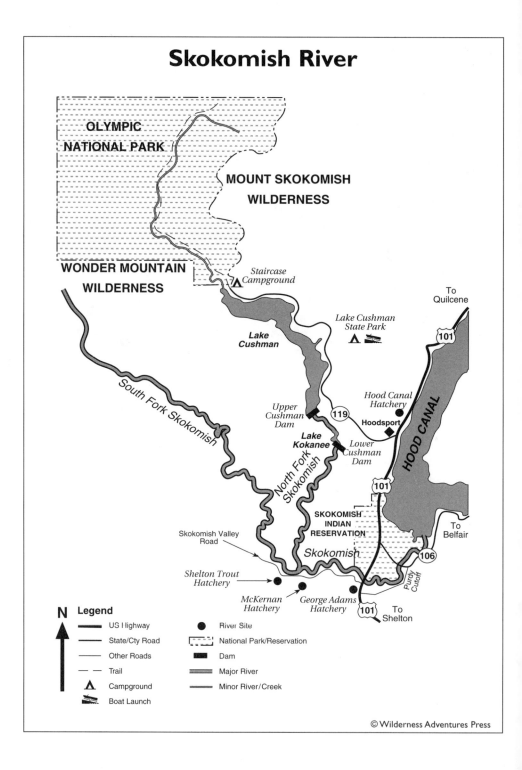

*The Skokomish produces excellent chum salmon runs; these fish can be taken on chartreuse streamers during late fall and early winter.*

"Chums don't tend to travel way up a system because they don't like to jump over falls, so the best opportunities are on the lower ends of these systems. There is quite a bit of private property on these streams, so you need to remain in the stream or ask a landowner for permission to fish."

The Skokomish, Dosewallips, and Duckabush all offer a nice run of chums in November and December, and anglers can easily find chum salmon at the Hwy 101 bridges that cross these rivers. Hike upstream, where allowed, or downstream and look for chums in the slow runs.

"You can find chums in about any type of water, but they tend to hold in the slower runs," Flint says. "Look closely at the lower ends of holes and pools. They might hold in a foot of water or a place where it's 10-feet deep, but they do seek out slow water. Usually, they like a little cover nearby, such as a log or overhanging brush."

When fishing any of the Hood Canal streams, be aware that your chance to cast a fly for chums may be fleeting.

"There are two different chum salmon stocks that we get in Hood Canal," Flint says. "One is the summer chum, which is recommended for listing under the Endangered Species Act. They go into a number of streams in September, and spawning is usually complete by mid- to late October.

"The other group we see is the fall-run, which generally enters the rivers in mid-October to early November," Flint adds. "To protect the summer fish, we have significant restrictions on chum salmon fishing in marine waters from July 1 through mid-October. After October 16, we allow retention of chums in the marine waters. On the streams, we usually open them up for chums November 1. This gives the summer chum enough time to spawn."

No matter where you encounter chum salmon, whether in saltwater or their natal freshwater streams, take a stout rod and leaders rating 10-pound test or better. Fifteen-pound tippet is ideal, and 20-pound test isn't going to turn fish away—chums are not leader shy.

When you hook a fish, try to fight it quickly. Make it work against the bend of your rod by twisting the rod from side to side, depending on which way the fish decides to cruise. Don't let it just plod downstream.

After taking a backseat throughout flyfishing history to their more popular cousins, the coho, sockeye, and Chinook salmon, the chum salmon is gaining recognition for what it offers. Unfortunately, its popularity is the result of a decline in the other species.

Go astream with your fly rod in November and December, and you, too, will find a fish that displays an aggressive attitude and a reel-sizzling fight. When you land a chum, enjoy looking at its calico body and release it to fight again.

# OLYMPIC PENINSULA HUB CITIES
# Bremerton
### Elevation–0 • Population–37,760

## ACCOMMODATIONS
Best Western Bayview Inn, 5640 Kitsap Way / 360-373-9900
Flagship Inn, 4320 Kitsap Way / 360-479-6566
Oyster Bay Inn & Restaurant, 4412 Kitsap Way / 360-377-5510
Howard Johnson Plaza Hotel, 5640 Kitsap Way / 360-373-9900
Super 8 Motel, 5068 Kitsap Way / 360-377-8881

## RESTAURANTS
Boat Shed Restaurant, 101 Shore Drive / 360-377-3943
Denny's Restaurants, 5004 Kitsap Way / 360-479-8941
                  3621 Wheaton Way / 360-479-4144
Gold Mountain Bar & Grill, 7263 West Belfair Valley Road / 360-674-2001
International House of Pancakes, 4080 Wheaton Way / 360-479-1059
Ivar's Seafood Bar, 1550 Neriddell Road / 360-479-2526
The Keg Restaurant, 2620 Wheaton Way / 360-373-8088
Northlake Steak House Restaurant, 3050 Northlake Way Northwest /
    360-377-8861
Oh Gallagher's Sports Pub & Grill, 1550 Northeast Riddell Road / 360-377-7126
Oyster Bay Inn & Restaurant, 4412 Kitsap Way / 360-377-5510
Popeye's Pub & Eatery, 209 1st Street / 360-479-4406
Waterfront Cafe, 112 Washington Avenue / 360-792-1603

## VETERINARIANS
Bayview Veterinary Hospital, 4214 Kitsap Way / 360-373-1465
Tender Care Animal Hospital, 32 Northeast Silver Pine Drive / 360-692-7387
Wheaton Way Veterinary Clinic, 1220 Sheridan Road / 360-377-0078

## FLY SHOPS AND SPORTING GOODS
Norhwest Angler Fly Shop, 18830 Front Street, Poulsbo / 360-697-7100
Kitsap Sports, 10516 Silverdale Way Northwest, Silverdale / 360-698-4808
Tom's Guns Bremerton, 318 Callow Avenue North / 360-479-4901
K-mart, 1353 Olney Southeast (Port Orchard) / 360-876-7761
Wal-Mart, 6797 State Hwy 303 Northeast / 360-698-2889

## AUTO REPAIR
Firestone Tire & Service, 3957 Wheaton Way / 360-479-1775
Juneau's Auto Service, 115 National Avenue South / 360-377-8366
L & R Automotive, 1112 Pearl Street / 360-377-2220
Mike's Auto Repair, 934 North Wycoff Avenue / 360-377-5032
Penske Auto Center, 4210 Wheaton Way / 360-377-4464

## AUTO RENTAL

**Budget Rent-A-Car,** 2114 6th Street / 360-479-4500
**Enterprise Rent-A-Car,** 280 Wilkes Avenue / 360-377-1900
**National Car Rental,** 501 West Hills Boulevard / 360-479-4910

## MEDICAL

**Harrison Memorial Hospital,** 2520 Cherry Avenue / 360-377-3911
**Kitsap Community Clinic,** 423 Pacific Avenue / 360-478-2366

## FOR MORE INFORMATION

Bremerton Area Chamber of Commerce
120 Washington Avenue
Bremerton, WA 98337
360-479-3579

# Port Angeles
### Elevation–0 • Population–17,710

## Accommodations
Bayshore Inn, 221 North Lincoln Street / 360-452-9215
Best Western Olympic Lodge, 140 Del Guzzi Drive / 360-452-2993
Four Seasons Ranch, 673 Strait View Drive / 360-457-5211
Hill Haus Motel, 111 East 2nd Street / 360-452-9285
Klahhane Bed & Breakfast, 1203 East 7th Street / 360-417-0260
Red Lion Bayshore Inn, 221 North Lincoln Street / 360-452-9215
Royal Victorian Motel, 521 East 1st Street / 360-452-2316
Super 8 Motel, 2104 East 1st Street / 360-452-8401

## Campgrounds and RV Parks
Al's RV Park, 521 North Lees Creek Road / 360-457-9844
Carol's Crescent Beach RV Park, 2860 Crescent Beach Road / 360-928-3344
KOA Kampgrounds, 80 O'Brien Road / 360-457-5916
Whiskey Creek Beach, 1392 Whiskey Creek Beach Road / 360-928-3489

## Restaurants
Bella Italia, 1178 East 1st Street / 360-457-5442
Bushwhacker Restaurant, 1527 East 1st Street / 360-457-4113
C'est Si Bon, 2300 East Highway 101 / 360-452-8888
Destiny Seafood & Grill, 1213 Marine Drive / 360-452-4665
El Amigo Mexican Food, 1017 East 1st Street / 360-457-6477
Fisherman's Wharf, 826 Boat Haven Drive / 360-457-4274
Granny's Cafe, 235441 Highway 101 / 360-928-3266
The Landing Fish and Burger Bar, 115 East Railroad Avenue / 360-457-6768
Oh Gallagher's Sports Pub & Grill, 1605 East Front Street / 360-452-0873
Pete's Pancake House, 110 East Railroad Avenue / 360-452-1948

## Veterinarians
All Animal Veterinary Hospital, 1811 West Highway 101 / 360-452-4551
Blue Mountain Animal Clinic, 2972 Old Olympic Hwy / 360-457-3842
Olympic Veterinary Clinic, 1417 East Front Street / 360-452-8978

## Fly Shops and Sporting Goods
Greywolf Angler, 275953 Highway 101, Gardiner / 360-797-7177
Port Townsend Angler, 940 Water Street, Port Townsend / 360-379-3763
Quality Fly Fishing Shop, 2720 East Highway 101 / 360-452-5942
K-mart, 3471 East Kolonels Way / 360-457-0404
Wal-Mart, 3500 East Highway 101 / 360-452-1244

## Auto Repair
Auto Doctor, 33 Wall Street / 360-452-5278

**Bob Holt's Rescue Repair** / 360-457-4551
**Mark's Mobile Tune,** 934 Marine Drive / 360-452-1704
**Midway Auto Repair,** 51 North Barr Road / 360-452-9644

## MEDICAL

**Virginia Mason Medical Center,** 433 East 8th Street / 360-452-3373
**Olympic Memorial Hospital,** 939 Caroline Street / 360-417-7000

## FOR MORE INFORMATION

Port Angeles Chamber of Commerce
121 East Railroad Avenue
Port Angeles, WA 98362
360-452-2363

# Forks

**Elevation–300 • Population–3,000**

## Accommodations

**Kalaloch Ocean Lodge,** Kalaloch / 360-962-2271
**Pacific Inn Motel,** 352 North Forks Avenue / 360-374-9400
**The Caboose,** Forks Avenue North / 360-374-5530

## Campgrounds and RV Parks

**Forks 101 RV Park,** Hwy 101 850 South / 360-374-5073
**Hoh River Resort and RV Park,** 175443 Hwy 101 South / 360-374-5566

## Restaurants

**Mikey's Fine Mexican Food,** 80 Spartan Avenue / 360-374-9448
**Smoke House Restaurant,** 19316 Hwy 101 / 360-374-6258

## Veterinarian

**All Animal Outwest Veterinary Clinic,** 80 C Street / 360-374-9100

## Fly Shops and Sporting Goods

**Olympic Sporting Goods,** 1905 Forks Avenue / 360-374-6330

## Auto Repair

**B & P Auto Repair,** 382 North Forks Avenue / 360-374-5556

## Auto Rental

**Budget Rent-A-Car,** 65 West E Street / 360-374-4033

## Medical

**Forks Community Hospital,** 530 Bogachiel Way / 360-374-5353

## For More Information

Forks Chamber of Commerce
1411 South Forks Avenue
Forks, WA 98331
360-374-2531

# Aberdeen

## Elevation–0 • Population–16,665

### ACCOMMODATIONS

**Central Park Motel,** 6504 Olympic Highway / 360-533-12109 units, cable TV, kitchenettes / $

**Olympic Inn Motel,** 616 West Heron / 360-533-4200 / 55 units, cable TV, kitchenettes / $$

**Red Lion Motel,** 521 West Wishka/ 360-532-5210 / 67 units, nonsmoking rooms, cable TV, continental breakfast / $$$

### CAMPGROUNDS AND RV PARKS

**Arctic RV (in Cosmopolis),** 893 State Highway 101 / 360-533-4470 / 20 RV sites, full hook-ups, shower, laundry, tent sites, pay phone, pop machine

### RESTAURANTS

**Al's Humdinger,** 104 Lincoln Street / 360-533-2754 / Fast food, take out, coffee shop

**Duffy's,** 1605 Simpson Avenue / 360-538-0606 / Steaks and seafood, pies, 6AM–10PM

**Jack in the Box,** 400 East Heron / 360-532-7243 / Hamburgers, fries

**Rod's Diner,** 413 Ontario / 360-533-7019 / Family dining, seafood, steaks, brunch, salad, 6AM–9PM

### FLY SHOPS AND SPORTING GOODS

**The Backcast Fly Shop,** 720 Simpson Avenue, Hoquiam / 360-532-6867

**Big Mouth John's Tackle Traders,** 521 East 1st Street / 360-533-0143

**Blaine's Tackle,** 416 West Marion Street / 360-532-1297

### AUTO REPAIR

**Advanced Automotive,** 521½ East 1st Street / 360-538-9786

**City Center Automotive,** 115 West Heron Street / 360-532-9512

**Les Schwab Tire Center,** 420 East Heron Street / 360-533-3643
2601 Simpson Avenue / 360-538-0100

### AIR SERVICE

Nearest is Portland International Airport

### MEDICAL

**Grays Harbor Community Hospital,** 1006 North H Street / 360-533-0450

### FOR MORE INFORMATION

Grays Harbor Chamber of Commerce
506 Duffy Street
Aberdeen, WA 98520
360-532-8611

# Olympia
**Elevation–0 • Population–39,070**

## ACCOMMODATIONS
**Best Western Aladdin Motor Inn,** 900 Capitol Way South / 360-352-7200
**Capital Inn Motel,** 120 College Street Southeast / 360-493-1991
**Comfort Inn of Lacey,** 4700 Park Center Avenue Northeast / 360-456-6300
**Days Inn,** 120 College Street Southeast / 360-493-1991
**Harbinger Inn,** 1136 East Bay Drive Northeast / 360-754-0389
**Holiday Inn Express,** 4704 Park Center Avenue Northeast / 360-412-1200
**Holiday Inn Select,** Evergreen Peak Drive Southwest / 360-943-4000
**Ramada Inn Governor House,** 621 Capitol Way South / 360-352-7700

## CAMPGROUNDS AND RV PARKS
**American Heritage Campground,** 9610 Kimmie Street Southwest / 360-943-8778
**Nisqually Plaza RV Park,** 10220 Martin Way East / 360-491-3831
**Olympia Campground,** 1441 83rd Avenue Southwest / 360-352-2551

## RESTAURANTS
**Brewster's Restaurant,** 4611 Tumwater Valley Drive Southeast / 360-357-9020
**Bristol House,** 2401 Bristol Court Southwest / 360-352-9494
**Casa Mia,** 4426 Martin Way East / 360-459-0440
**Ebb Tide Inn,** 1525 Washington Street Northeast / 360-943-7770
**El Sarape,** 4043 Martin Way East / 360-459-5525
**Falls Terrace Restaurant,** 106 Deschutes Way Southwest / 360-943-7830
**Fifth Avenue Bistro,** 209 5th Avenue Southeast / 360-709-0390
**Gardner Seafood & Pasta,** 111 Thurston Avenue Northwest / 360-786-8466
**Hawks Prairie Inn,** 8214 Quinault Drive Northeast / 360-459-0900
**International House of Pancakes,** 3519 Martin Way East / 360-459-5649
**The Keg Restaurant,** 500 Black Lake Boulevard Southwest / 360-754-4434
**O'Blarney's Pub,** 4411 Martin Way East / 360-459-8084
**Olive Garden Italian Restaurant,** 2400 Capitol Mall Drive Southwest / 360-754-6717
**Steamboat Annie's,** 3634 Steamboat Island Road Northwest / 360-866-2274
**Titanic Brewing Company,** 520 4th Avenue / 360-943-7505

## VETERINARIANS
**Animal Medical Hospital,** 2022 4th Avenue / 360-943-8900
**Boulevard Animal Clinic,** 2806 Boulevard Road Southeast / 360-943-1566
**Deschutes Animal Clinic,** 7248 Capitol BoulevardSouth / 360-943-8144
**Olympia Pet Emergency,** 1602 Harrison Avenue Northwest / 360-709-0108

## FLY SHOPS AND SPORTING GOODS
**Streamside Anglers,** 4800 Capitol Boulevard Southeast / 360-709-3337
**The Fly Fisher,** 5622 Pacific Avenue Southeast / 360-491-0181

**Tumwater Sports Center,** 6200 Capitol Boulevard Southeast / 360-352-5161
**Big 5 Sporting Goods,** 909 Cooper Point Road Southwest / 360-786-6529 /
  Some flyfishing equipment

## Auto Repair

**Hawks Prairie Automotive Tune,** 8045 Martin Way East / 360-456-8000
**Rick's Auto Repair,** 3531 Pacific Avenue Southeast / 360-491-6644
**Stop and Go Auto Service,** 600 4th Avenue East / 360-786-8100

## Auto Rental

**Budget Rent-A-Car,** 720 Legion Way Southeast / 360-943-3852
**Enterprise Rent-A-Car,** 2225 Carriage / 360-956-3714
**Hertz Car Rental,** 490 Tyee Drive Southwest / 360-352-0171

## Medical

**St. Peter Hospital,** 413 Lilly Road Northeast / 360-491-9480

## For More Information

Olympia Chamber of Commerce
521 Legion Way Southeast
Olympia, WA 98501
360-357-3362

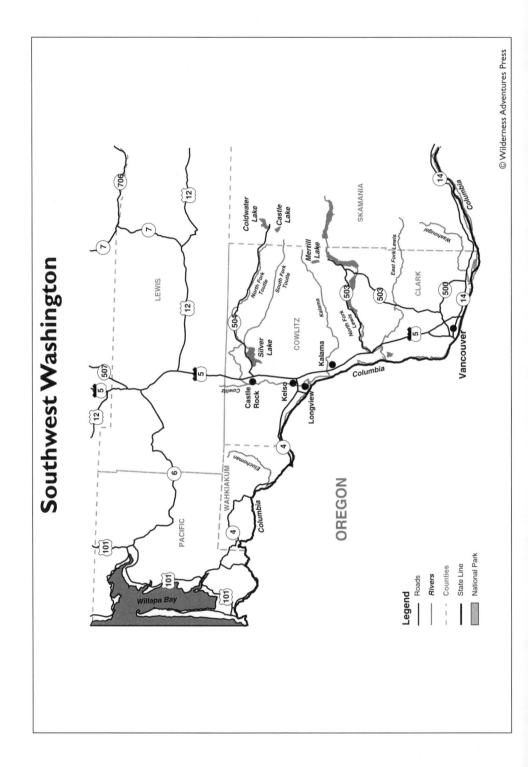

Southwest Washington

# Southwest Washington

In 1980, Mount St. Helens blew its top and thrust southwest Washington into the national spotlight. News crews reported on human tragedies and the loss of giant timber stands; the region's steelhead anglers directed their attention to another misfortune —the destruction of the North and mainstem Toutle River due to pyroclastic mudflows and landslides.

Previously considered one of the better steelhead streams in the state, the Toutle isn't what it used to be, but it has made progress since the eruption. Today, winter- and summer-run steelhead can be pursued in the river, with the South Fork providing the best opportunities.

During the Toutle's downtime, southwest Washington anglers haven't suffered too badly. This region hosts some of the best summer-run steelhead fishing to be found anywhere in the Northwest. Plus, the area hosts king salmon, sea-run cutthroat trout, and even a few coho salmon. The region's rivers, including the Kalama, Lewis, Washougal, and Elochoman, offer year-round opportunities.

But river fishing isn't the only draw here: The lakes surrounding Mount St. Helens, including Merrill, Coldwater, and Castle, host large trout and some excellent aquatic emergences to match. The top hatch is an emergence of huge *Hexagenia* mayflies that thrust Merrill Lake's brown and rainbow trout into feeding frenzies each summer evening.

Throw in a unique opportunity to land hard-fighting American shad on the Columbia River, plus the chance to catch bluegill, crappie, and some sizable largemouth bass at Silver Lake, and you can see why so many area anglers call in sick during the mild summer months.

While southwest Washington's steelhead and salmon fisheries aren't what they were earlier in the century, a flyfisher hooking a fired-up summer-run on the Kalama, a big brown at Merrill Lake, a giant steelhead in the Lewis, or one of the region's enormous king salmon won't soon forget the experience.

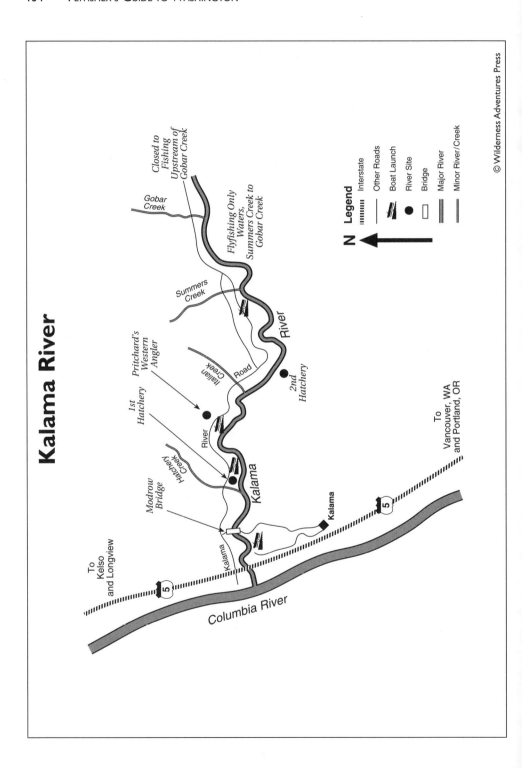

# Kalama River

Closed to Fishing Upstream of Gobar Creek

Gobar Creek

Flyfishing Only Waters, Summers Creek to Gobar Creek

Summers Creek

Pritchard's Western Angler

1st Hatchery

Italian Creek

Road

2nd Hatchery

Modrow Bridge

Hatchery Creek

River

Kalama

Kalama

Kalama River

To Kelso and Longview

5

To Vancouver, WA and Portland, OR

5

Columbia River

N Legend

||||||| Interstate

— Other Roads

Boat Launch

● River Site

□ Bridge

Major River

Minor River/Creek

© Wilderness Adventures Press

# KALAMA RIVER

Unlike most western Washington steelhead and salmon streams, the Kalama River isn't beset with the tribal netting, destructive dams, and large tracts of private property that diminish fishing quality on other rivers. Add spring- and fall-run chinook salmon, a fall run of coho salmon, and the opportunity to catch summer-run steelhead in fly-only water, and you have an angling gem worth visiting, especially if you prefer native fish.

That statement is particularly accurate when considering the Kalama's prime fly-only water, which extends from Summers Creek upstream to the 6420 Bridge at the mouth of Arnold Creek. Upstream from the bridge, the Kalama is closed to protect spawners.

In the fly-only water, anglers can test their prowess on native fish without interruption from spinfishers or hatchery fish—Washington Department of Fish and Wildlife intercepts hatchery fish at Kalama Falls and only allows native steelhead past the natural barrier. A few hatchery steelhead do slip through, and DFW encourages anglers to help the native fish by inviting hatchery impersonators home for dinner, courtesy of a solid bonk to the head.

While the fly-only section offers the best water and guarantees a purist experience, the lower river, from Kalama Falls to its mouth, isn't too shabby, either. Sure, you'll have to pass on a few prime holes due to the presence of spinfishers, but there is enough prime water on the lower river to ensure a good day astream. Through that lower section, including the canyon area, flyfishers may encounter native and hatchery fish. Certainly, a hatchery steelhead is not the special catch that a native is, but I'll take a tight line, whether it's an imitation steelie or not, any day.

As for hatchery steelhead, don't be surprised if you see the same fish twice. Once DFW captures enough steelhead to carry on its hatchery production, excess hatchery fish are trucked downstream and are usually released at the lower boat ramp, a half-mile upstream from the river's mouth. These fish must run the gauntlet again (some fish have returned to the hatchery six times in a season), which is definitely not fair, but it offers one hell of a second chance for anglers.

The Kalama begins in the rugged Cascade Mountains on the southern flank of Mount St. Helens, which is in the Mount St. Helens National Volcanic Monument. The river runs almost directly west through a tight canyon and the gorgeous fly-only section before spilling over Kalama Falls. From there, it descends toward its mouth, flowing through another nice canyon before broadening out and spilling its contents into the Columbia River 2 miles north of Kalama.

While the river offers good salmon and winter-run steelhead options, it has always been noted for its summer-run steelhead fishing. And that is what it continues to be heralded for today.

Hatchery and native summer-runs enter the Kalama in May, and their numbers peak in July. Anglers can still find plenty of fish in August and September, when weather and water conditions are at their prime and an angler doesn't ever know for

*The Kalama River is one of Washington's top summer steelhead streams.*

sure what might inhale his fly. Forty-pound king salmon? Ten-pound coho? Twenty-pound steelie? Uh, I wouldn't complain no matter what fish drilled me.

Steelhead returns fluctuate each year, but the Kalama usually hosts about 2,450 summer-runs. About 1,700 of these fish are hatchery origin, while 750 native fish make the journey to this amazing stream each year.

"The Kalama is a special river," says Rob Orzel a 12-year veteran guide and dedicated flyfisher who works for Pritchard's Western Anglers, which is located about 4 miles up the Kalama River Road. "It's absolutely beautiful, and it runs gin-clear during summer and fall so you actually do as much hunting for fish as fishing itself—it's a spot-and-stalk situation, and surprisingly, the fish let you get pretty damn close to them. In the average day, I'll be looking at steelhead the whole time, figuring out a way to present a fly to them.

*Typical summer-run steelhead water on the upper Kalama,*
*which is restricted to flyfishing only. (Photo by Rob Orzel)*

"And they take a fly real well," Orzel adds. "I feel that if I can see a fish, I can eventually get it to take. Sometimes it can take a while, but it's mostly a matter of putting the fly in the right spot. You almost want to bump them with the fly to make them move slightly and pique their interest. Then it's just a matter of switching fly color and size until you find the right one. On this river, a flyfisher can walk from hole to hole and beat the spinfisher—that's how good the flyfishing can be here."

While dry-fly fishing can also be productive on the Kalama, Orzel warns flyfishers not to spend too much time on the surface unless they enjoy extended doses of pure frustration.

"There's no doubt that these fish can be taken on dry flies, but that's not the most productive way to fish the river," Orzel offers. "Unless you see the fish up top really splashing the water for stuff, you're going to have a tough time. I would rather go underneath and catch a lot of fish than work all day to catch one on a dry fly. When I do try a dry fly, I throw a half-dozen casts, and if a fish doesn't eat it by then, I feel like I'm wasting my time, and I give up."

Because the Kalama is mostly a spot-and-stalk stream, an angler can also waste a lot of time by not wearing polarized glasses when searching for fish. Cheap glasses in the 5- to 10-dollar range aren't going to do it. Invest in a quality pair of glasses, and you will substantially increase your odds of hooking up. I wear Action Optics and Smith sunglasses, which are made in Ketchum, Idaho. They cut through the surface glare wonderfully, allowing me to spot fish easily, even when they hold in deep water amid submerged logs and bottom rocks. According to Orzel, sunglasses are key during the summer-run season.

"A guy with good eyes really benefits," he says. "Polarized glasses are a must, because you have to see into the holes and runs. You don't just fish blind here. You look into a hole, and when you spot five or six fish, you get set up above them and work a fly downstream."

Although there are good numbers of steelhead in the system year-round, flyfishers should find the summer months particularly appealing. It's during summer, specifically May through September, that the Kalama drops into prime shape. Most avid Kalama flyfishers agree—when the river is low and clear and a freshet (a rain) occurs, flyfishing can be tremendous. Orzel agrees.

"If I just wanted to focus on steelhead and I could only fish the river for two weeks of the year, I'd pick the first two weeks of August," he says. "If I also wanted a chance for salmon, I'd take the last two weeks in September."

No matter what time of year you arrive, fly selection is important for Kalama steelhead. If you choose to fish for summer runs, a variety of patterns should be included in your arsenal. Try freight trains, purple perils, green butt skunks, woolly buggers, sculpins and, especially, black-bodied woolly worms with red and green tails. Take these patterns in sizes ranging from 4 to 8. Orzel's most productive pattern, a black woolly worm, is tied on a size 6 hook.

Because the Kalama is a medium-sized river, light fly rods, in the 5- and 6-weight range, can be used. However, 7- to 10-weight rods are best for both flyfisher and native fish. With a heavier rod, flyfishers will not wear their arms out making long casts all day and can fight, land, and release steelhead more quickly than with a lighter rod.

No matter what weight rod you choose to throw, floating lines with sinktips and short, 3- to 6-foot leaders are required. As mentioned, the Kalama's steelhead are prone to strike near bottom, and that is where flyfishers must place their offerings (lead split shot is not allowed on the leader in the fly-only section). Sections of varying sink rates best serve anglers, and the Kalama's premier flyfishers carry a few different sinktips, which they can loop to the end of their floating line (also called running line), depending on the depth of the hole or run they choose to fish. According to Orzel, the best runs rate 2 to 6 feet deep and offer a combination of currents.

"Kalama summer-runs like to hold in water that is fast near the top of a run before fanning out into calm water near its tailout," he says. "You don't want to spend

*A typical
Kalama River steelhead.
(Photo courtesy
of Rob Orzel)*

your time fishing the deep holes. You can see a lot of fish in deep water, but they are extremely difficult to get to bite."

That statement can also be made concerning the Kalama's winter-run steelhead. In fact, due to cold weather, marginal water conditions, and the need to use heavily weighted flies and full-sink lines, most anglers avoid the winter option. But if you are up to the task, try the river in late December or January, when the hatchery winter-run peaks at about 600 fish. The native winter-run peaks in April, when flyfishers typically find about 1,200 wild fish in the river.

While the Kalama can present some difficult conditions when water is up during winter and spring or after a fall rain, it is not an intimidating river. Rather, it beckons to the wade fisher. In most places, the river can be covered, bank to bank, with a cast. Drift boats are not necessary for success, but they do offer the option to cover a lot of water, especially if you are fishing the lower river below the canyon or chasing spring chinook throughout the system.

Spring chinook begin to trickle into the Kalama in April with peak numbers around mid-May. A few fish will remain in the river through June.

While some "springers" are taken by flyfishers, they do not offer an easy proposition, because they congregate in deep pools and are extremely temperamental.

"Spring chinook are a tough deal," Orzel says. "They hold in deep water with current, and it can be tough to get a fly to them. If I find a group of 15 to 30 fish, I'll get out the fly rod and give them a try, but it's not easy. Typically, I'll only catch a dozen spring chinook on a fly each year."

If you are up to the spring king challenge, commandeer a boat or plan on walking large sections of river searching for fish.

"If you have a boat, you can really cover some water," Orzel says. "If you don't, you probably want to walk the bank and cover as much water as possible. I think your best bet would be to walk the entire canyon, looking into all the deep holes until you find salmon. Spring fish hold deep and can be tough to see, but you can find them."

For spring chinook, carry large fly patterns in the size 1 and 2 range and fish them off full-sink lines. Egg sucking leeches should draw strikes.

If you are truly bent on catching a king salmon and you have the freedom of time, try for Kalama chinook during fall, especially in late September and October when the leaves are flaming red, orange, and yellow, and water and weather conditions are excellent. Fall fish are more eager to inhale flies than their spring-spawning cousins, plus they can be found in shallow water if an angler is willing to rise from bed early or stay on the river late.

"They (fall chinook) are really different from the spring fish," Orzel says. "They like to hide in the deeper pools, but they move into shallower runs early and late in the day.

"During fall there are usually fish in every hole from I-5 up to the hatchery, and they splash the water a lot so they are easy to see. If you spot a hole and it looks like it should have a salmon in it, it probably does and you should fish it.

"For fall fish, the standard steelhead fly patterns will work. Usually the fish will take on a dead-drift."

While dead-drifts work well for spring and fall chinook, Kalama's cohos prefer some action.

Cohos show up in August, and their numbers peak in September. They stack up in deep pools, where sinktip and full-sink lines are required to reach them. Cohos seem particularly aggressive when flies are strip retrieved.

"I like to cast my line and let it sink for five or six seconds before retrieving it," Orzel says. "Sometimes short strips work, sometimes long strips, sometimes strips with pauses. You can fool around until you find what the fish want."

One thing for flyfishers to keep in mind when fishing fall salmon is a flyfishing-only section on the lower river that extends from the natural gas pipeline crossing to

*The Kalama hosts king and coho salmon. Here, Kim Thomas hoists a large, fly-caught coho.*

the deadline at the intake to the lower salmon hatchery. That flyfishing only designation runs from September 1 through October 31.

Overall, the Kalama has a lot to offer the dedicated flyfisher. With its fly-only water, beautiful scenery, and year-round angling options, it beckons each day of the year. Fish the river in winter for elusive steelhead, test its tricky currents for spring kings or visit the river during summer and fall for a steelhead and salmon smorgasbord. No matter what season you choose to fish, you won't be disappointed.

To reach the Kalama, take I-5 to the Kalama River Road (Exit 32), which begins about 2.5 miles north of Kalama. Follow the road east. It follows the north side of the river, and access to the water is easy.

# Stream Facts: Kalama River

## Seasons and Special Regulations

- From mouth to Modrow Bridge: May 1 through August 15 and October 16 through April 30—2 trout and steelhead limit with 14-inch minimum size. All wild cutthroat must be released. Open for salmon from January 1 through April 30—all wild coho and all chum salmon must be released. Flyfishing only in that section from natural gas pipeline crossing to the deadline at the intake at the lower salmon hatchery September 1 to October 31.
- From Modrow Bridge to upper salmon hatchery: Open year-round for trout and steelhead, 14-inch minimum size applies with 2-fish limit. All wild cutthroat must be released. Selective gear rules for all species. Statewide rules apply for salmon.
- From upper salmon hatchery to Summers Creek: Open year-round for trout and steelhead, 14-inch minimum size applies. All wild cutthroat must be released. Selective gear rules apply.
- From Summers Creek to Kalama Falls: Flyfishing only. Open June 1 through March 31 for trout and steelhead, 14-inch minimum applies. All wild cutthroat must be released. Closed from 6420 Road to Kalama Falls.

## Species

- Steelhead and cutthroat trout
- Chum, coho, and king salmon

## Stream Characteristics

- A wonderful flyfishing river, the Kalama offers excellent opportunities for steelhead and king salmon.
- Most steelhead average 6 to 10 pounds, and the king salmon go 15 to 25 pounds on average.

## Access

- Excellent boat access via a series of public access sites allows anglers plenty of water to fish.
- Wade fishers also can find plenty of places to pull off Kalama River Road and hike down the bank to the water.

# LEWIS RIVER FORKS

Anglers who drift a fly on this revered southwest Washington salmon and steelhead stream do so with a bit of anxiety.

Those who are familiar with the Lewis River's native steelhead stock realize that on any given cast, a chromer weighing 30 pounds or more could take the fly. That's the extreme case, but Washington's winter-run record, a 32-pound, 12-ounce fish, was landed here. And the river's summer-run steelhead aren't slouches, either.

As with most Northwest steelhead streams, the Lewis doesn't fish as well as it used to, but it does continue to kick out solid catches of hatchery steelhead, with a few natives thrown in on the side in summer and winter. However, the East Fork of the Lewis River, which is highly conducive to flyfishing, is becoming more difficult to access due to private land and a "Keep Off" mentality by local landowners.

Fortunately, there are places where an angler can launch a drift boat on the East Fork and float the river at a leisurely pace, working plenty of prime water. The North Fork also offers excellent float options, with decent chances for a wade-fisher to score. For that reason, the Lewis River forks remain one of the better places in western Washington for a fly-rodder to search for large steelhead. Throw in a spring and fall run of king salmon, and it's easy to see why the Lewis still draws attention.

The North Fork Lewis begins as a small stream flowing off the western flank of Mount Adams. It gains volume from numerous small creeks before flowing into the first of three reservoirs (Swift Creek) that impound the river and prevent upstream migration of anadromous fish. The river then dumps into Yale Reservoir, flows freely several miles, then pours into Merwin Reservoir. From Merwin downstream to its confluence with the Columbia River near Woodland, the Lewis flows strong and unimpeded.

The East Fork Lewis begins in the Gifford Pinchot National Forest east of Battleground. It flows west, running over Sunset, Horseshoe, Moulton, and Lucia Falls. As amazing as it might seem to those who view the falls, steelhead do negotiate those vertical barriers, and they can be found as high as Horseshoe Falls in decent numbers, depending on the time of year.

The East Fork is prime fly water, and it has drawn avid anglers to its banks for many years. One flyfisher who has tested its currents extensively is Jim Teeny who runs Teeny Nymph Company in Gresham, Oregon. Teeny has fished his own line of nymphs as well as standard steelhead flies on the East Fork for more than 35 years. Although private property has limited options on the stream, he rates it as one of his favorite waters.

"The East Fork is a great river to wade," Teeny says. "It runs through canyons, has lots of boulders, and a guy who doesn't mind climbing around the banks can do well there. It's not a roadside river, so once you get on it you can hike a long way. The river has winter- and summer-run steelhead, and they take flies pretty well."

Steelhead can be found in the East Fork almost any day of the year, but the prime time for winter-run fish stretches between mid-December and March 15 when the

# Lewis River Forks

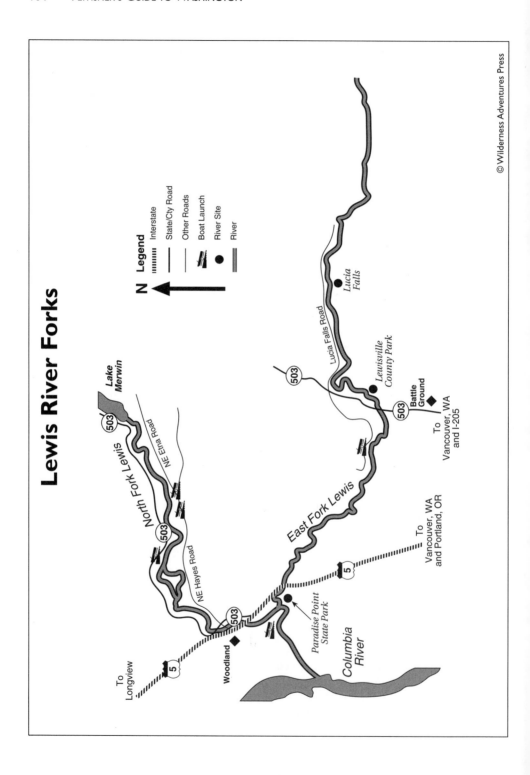

*The East Fork Lewis produces large native steelhead.*
*Here, Jim Schmitz of Seattle hoists a large native.*

upper sections above Lewisville Park close to angling. Below Lewisville Park, the river reopens April 16. The upper river reopens June 1.

"December and January can be really good on the East Fork," Teeny says, "but I like to fish a little later in the winter season. My favorite month is March, and I've taken a lot of fish at that time."

Summer steelhead ascend the East Fork as early as April, but their presence isn't strong until May and June. Flyfishers who try the river during those months are likely to find fairly high water, which tests an angler's skill. However, if the river isn't blown out of shape, the fish respond to flies at that time. Keep in mind that the East Fork may blow out one day and drop into shape the next—it is one of western Washington's fastest rivers to clear.

"The East Fork is a good watershed," Teeny says. "It has no dams, and it hasn't been torn up. It is always the last river to go out and the first to come back into shape. It can clear in a day. So summer-run fishing can be good in May and June."

As summer progresses and the water level drops, the East Fork's steelhead become incredibly wary. Place a fly line over their heads, cast a shadow on the water, or present your silhouette above the river, and fish are likely to spook. During July and August, an angler needs to exercise stealth to hook East Fork fish.

"They are incredibly spooky in July and August," Teeny says. "You just cannot believe where those fish see you coming from. I've never seen more spooky fish than on the East Fork. You have to be sneaky to catch them—wear dark clothing, cast gently and use long leaders, crawl along the banks, and don't throw big flies at that time. It's tough, but fishing the East Fork in July and August can be fun."

The East Fork can be divided into two sections—the upper and lower river. The upper river begins at Lucia Falls. The lower river runs west of Lucia to its confluence with the North Fork near Woodland.

The upper river is not floatable unless you have a death wish. The lower river can be effectively floated, and the most popular drift runs from Lewisville County Park downstream to Daybreak Bridge, which covers about four or five miles of river. Boaters can drift farther than Daybreak; however, access sites are crude and you have to hunt for them. There is one improved boat takeout near the river's confluence with the North Fork, just off Northwest Pacific Hwy near I-5.

The North Fork Lewis runs broader and stronger than the East Fork, and it hosts big steelhead as well as king salmon.

Spring kings show in the North Fork in April and May while fall-run chinook are most pronounced in September and October. For the flyfisher, the North Fork's kings can be a blast.

"The river gets an especially good run of fall chinook," Teeny says. "You may see them in late August, but September is the best month. They take black flies really well, and we fish them in sizes 2 and 4. They also like combinations of ginger and flame orange or hot green and purple. If fish have been on one color and stop taking it, we change to another color. Two-tone flies also work well. Black and hot green or orange work well."

The Lewis River's chinook are like king salmon everywhere: they favor deep water. Flyfishers should pay particular attention to deep pools and heavy, deep runs. When kings are located, flyfishers should make a quartering cast upstream and allow a fly to dead-drift through the hole. Follow the fly and line with your rod and keep your line taut without dragging the fly. Takes can be severe, or they may be subtle. Be ready in either case.

For kings, flyfishers should carry medium and fast sinktip lines to reach fish that hold at varying depths.

The North Fork also offers excellent opportunities for winter and summer steelhead, and although it is a larger river than the East Fork, the North Fork supplies prime flywater extending from Merwin Dam to its confluence with the East Fork.

"The North Fork also gets some nice winter steelhead," Teeny says, "and I like to fish those with a 400- or 500-grain sinktip. You'll find the fish holding in the deeper running water and in the tailouts. There can be a heavy flow during winter, but it can still be waded in many places. If you have a boat and can drift the river, that's even better."

While winter steelheading can be productive on the North Fork, it's the summer-run fish that offer the greatest opportunity for the fly-rodder.

A few summer-runs show up as early as April, but prime fishing doesn't occur until the summer months arrive. June, July, and August offer excellent, stable river conditions and aggressive fish.

According to Teeny, summer is the time for a minitip line and small black or green nymphs or leeches. "During summer you'll find the North Fork's steelhead in the riffles and runs and tailouts," he says. "It's classic water, and at times you can get some big summer-runs in there—we see fish that go from 6 pounds all the way to 20 pounds, which is big for a summer-run.

"I like to use the minitip, which is a 5-foot sinktip," Teeny added. "It just depends on the speed and depth of the water. If the fish are in some bigger water, I go with a 300- or 400-grain sinktip. During summer I like to use size 2, 4, and 6 black Teeny nymphs or leeches. Usually, a size 4 works best, but if we were searching for fish, I'd go with a size 2."

While wade fishing is productive on the North Fork, especially below the Lewis River Hatchery or off the golf course, a boat angler has the best opportunity for success. There are many excellent drifts on the North Fork and boat ramps are located in these areas: the mouth of Cedar Creek, a rough launch at the end of Haapa Road, a launch off of Dike Road, an unimproved launch at the golf course, and several downstream accesses near Woodland. Because the North Fork is subject to major change in stream course each year, anglers should inspect take-out sites before launching a boat.

While the Lewis doesn't offer as many big, native fish as it once did, the river still offers the opportunity to hook a large steelhead on any given cast. And with spring and fall chinook often exceeding 30 pounds, you can see why flyfishers still consider the Lewis worthy of their time.

# Stream Facts: Lewis River

## Seasons and Special Regulations
- From mouth to mouth of East Fork: Open year-round. Wild cutthroat and steelhead must be released. Salmon regulations may vary from year to year.
- East Fork:
  - From mouth to top of boat ramp at Lewisville Park: Closed for trout from March 16 through April 15. Salmon open April 16 through July 31.
  - From Lewisville Park to 100 feet upstream of Lucia Falls: Closed for trout, steelhead, and salmon from March 15 through May 31.
  - From 100 feet upstream of Lucia Falls to 100 feet upstream of Sunset Falls: Closed for trout, steelhead, and salmon from March 15 through May 31. Wild steelhead must be released.
  - From 100 feet upstream of Sunset Falls upstream: Closed for trout, steelhead, and salmon from January 1 through May 31.
- North Fork:
  - From mouth to Johnson Creek: Trout, steelhead, and salmon open year-round. Wild steelhead and cutthroat must be released.
  - From Johnson Creek to Colvin Creek: Trout, steelhead, and salmon closed May 1 through June 15.
  - From Colvin Creek to Merwin Dam: Trout and steelhead closed November 1 through December 15. Salmon open August 1 through September 30 and January 1 through April 30.
- Please check all Lewis River regulations before fishing this stream; more restrictions apply, and they may differ each season.

## Species
- Large steelhead are the main attraction
- Decent numbers of sea-run cutthroat trout also ascend the river
- Chinook salmon
- Dolly Varden

## Stream Characteristics
- Take your pick—the Lewis River offers all water types.
- The lower river is wide and slow, best suited to the spinfisher.
- The North Fork is large, but it offers the flyfisher a crack at large steelhead and sea-run cutthroat. Its upper portions, above the reservoirs, offer large bull trout.
- The East Fork offers excellent steelhead fly water.

## Access
- Boat anglers have the best access, but wade fishers can ply the stream when the water is down.
- Private property limits options on the East Fork, however, an angler who picks his spots can find plenty of water.

# ELOCHOMAN RIVER

Two of the shortest rivers to be found on the lower Columbia River system, the Elochoman and Washougal Rivers shouldn't be judged by their lengths.

Instead, the avid flyfisher should consider the good numbers of steelhead that these rivers boot out each year. Elochoman, for instance, offers winter- and summer-run steelhead, and, at times, flyfishing for them can be good. Elochoman is a relatively small river that can be covered in a cast, but finding a place to backcast without hooking a spinfisher during the winter season can be a challenge.

If you can hit the river midweek, pressure is sure to be less. Also, if you walk a distance away from access points, you can usually find a run to fish.

Elochoman mostly offers hatchery steelhead, and they return to Beaver Creek Hatchery, which is located about 6 miles upstream from the mouth, in December and January, with a few stragglers running the river in February or March.

Summer-run steelhead show up in June, and fishing for them is productive through July, before water drops to a critical level. At that time, putting a line near a fish, let alone dropping a fly into its view, can be maddening.

During fall, sea-run cutthroat invade Elochoman, and fishing can be decent for them. Chinook and coho salmon also show up in the fall. Regulations change from season to season, so check the pamphlet thoroughly.

To reach Elochoman, which is open from June 1 through March 15, follow Hwy 4 west from Kelso. Turn north at Cathlamet. The road parallels the river, and access can be found throughout. Don't bother dragging your drift boat along—this river is best waded.

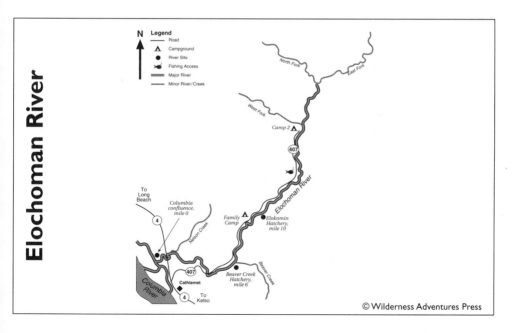

© Wilderness Adventures Press

# Washougal River

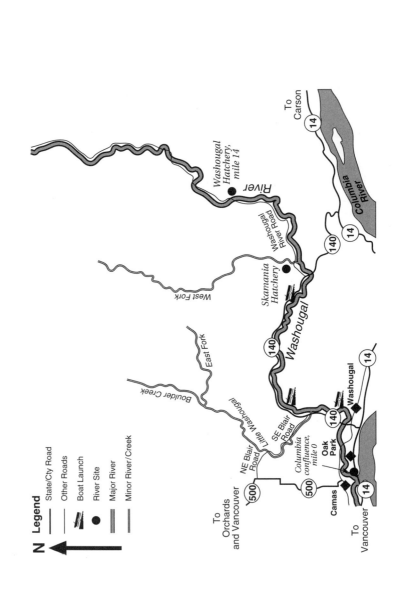

# WASHOUGAL RIVER

Washougal River begins in the Gifford Pinchot National Forest and flows southeast before dumping into the lower Columbia River at Washougal.

Comprised mostly of hatchery stock, Washougal offers summer- and winter-run steelhead, and it can fish very well for flyfishers when conditions are right.

Those chasing winter-run fish in this medium-sized stream should focus efforts during December, January, and February. Summer-runs start showing in late May or early June, and fishing can be outstanding through summer. During wet years, when the river holds a little more water and the fish are easier to approach, August can provide decent chances. During low-water years, casting to steelhead in August can be trying at best.

Typically, steelhead fishing on the Washougal is open from June 1 through March 15. The lower river reopens, strictly for steelhead, on April 16. Other restrictions apply, so check regulations thoroughly.

During fall, Washougal gets a nice run of sea-run cutthroat as well as king and coho salmon. Sea-runs can show up in good numbers depending on the year, and they provide excellent sport. Release of wild cutthroat is mandatory. King and coho runs are in jeopardy, and regulations change often. Consult the regulations booklet before you head for the river, let alone cast a line. Chum salmon also invade the river, and they can be pursued from January 1 through March 15.

To fish Washougal River, follow State Route 140 north out of Washougal. The road parallels the river for 10 miles. Turn north on Skye Road, then turn east on Washougal River Road.

Like Elochoman, Washougal is best waded, but there are boat accesses on the lower river that allow drift fishing.

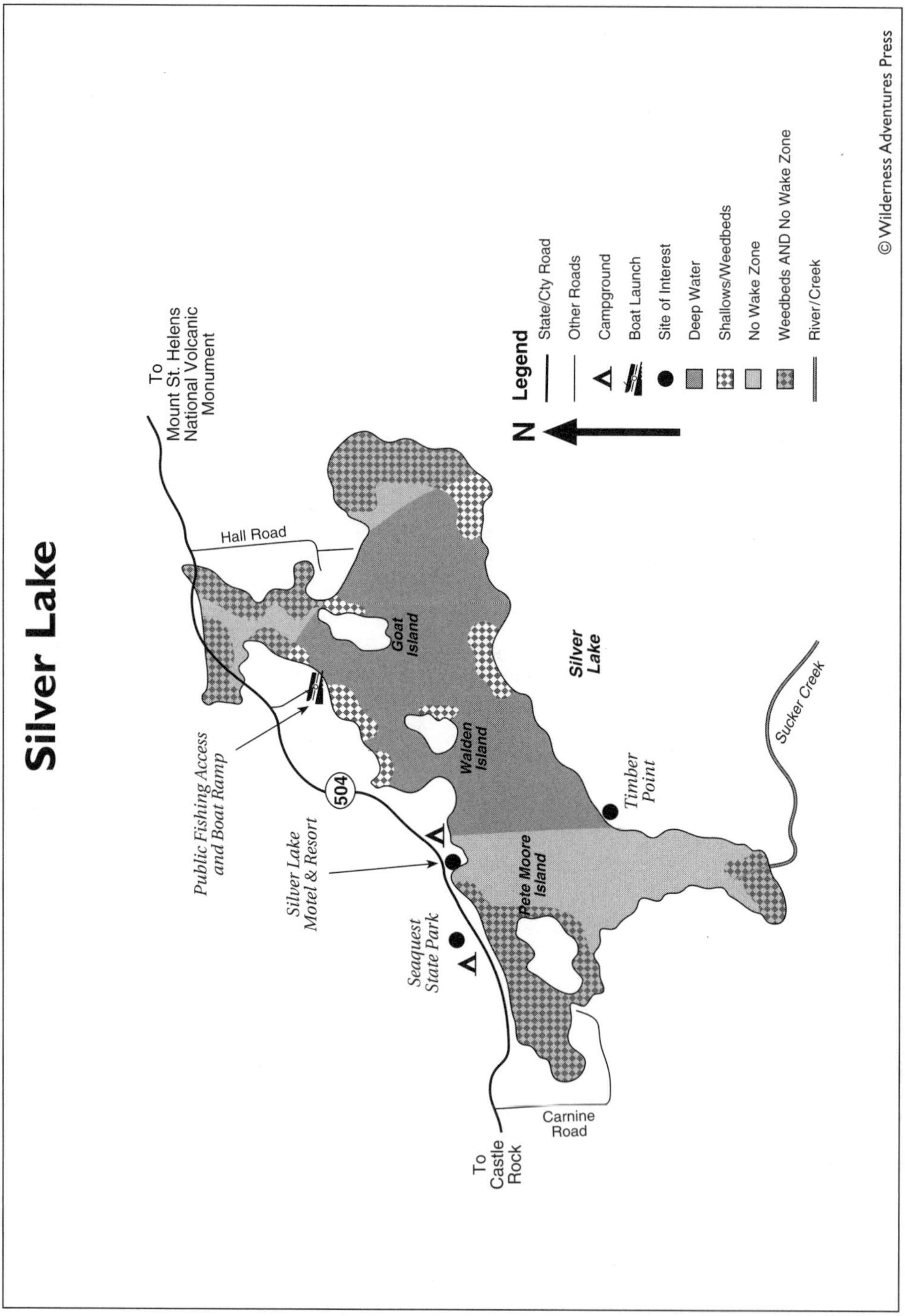

# Silver Lake

To
Mount St. Helens
National Volcanic
Monument

Hall Road

Public Fishing Access
and Boat Ramp

504

Silver Lake
Motel & Resort

Seaquest
State Park

Goat
Island

Walden
Island

Pete Moore Island

Silver
Lake

Timber
Point

Sucker Creek

To
Castle
Rock

Carnine
Road

**N**

**Legend**

| | |
|---|---|
| State/Cty Road | |
| Other Roads | |
| Campground | |
| Boat Launch | |
| Site of Interest | |
| Deep Water | |
| Shallows/Weedbeds | |
| No Wake Zone | |
| Weedbeds AND No Wake Zone | |
| River/Creek | |

© Wilderness Adventures Press

# SILVER LAKE

You could probably find several dozen Silver Lakes in Washington if you really got down and dirty with a detailed map, but possibly the best lake recognized by that name rests just east of Castle Rock and offers some big, hard-fighting largemouth bass.

Well-known among the western Washington warmwater circles, Silver Lake has always drawn lots of anglers to its banks. And for good reason: Silver commonly kicks out largemouths to 5 pounds, with a 1.5- to 2-pound fish being the average. On a good day, Silver might place a half-dozen or more solid bass in your grasp.

While it's pretty cool to be seen skimming across Silver Lake at 60 miles an hour in a bass boat (don't do it in the no-wake zones), you don't have to own a big boat to fish here. In fact, a float tube offers some access, and a 12-foot aluminum skiff with a 10- or 15-horse outboard motor gives access to the entire lake. Note: there is almost no shore access for those limited to wade fishing.

Silver Lake's fishing season extends year-round, but the best time to hit it with a fly rod extends from mid-April through mid-October. During that time, largemouth bass are receptive to surface offerings, and for a flyfisher, that is a bass' greatest attribute.

Monte Martinsen, who lives in Castle Rock, owns an impressive collection of classic bass lures and flies and fishes Silver Lake extensively, says, "I've lived within 7 miles of the lake all of my life, and I've seen a lot of changes here. I don't think it fishes as well as it used to, but you can still go out there with a fly rod any day of spring, summer, or early fall and catch lots of 10-inchers with a couple large fish thrown in on the side. It's a real nice lake."

Silver Lake's problems may have stemmed from an introduction in the early 1990s of grass carp that were expected to control a moss and weed problem—which they did, to Martinsen's dismay.

"I think they put twice as many carp in here as they needed," Martinsen says. "They obliterated the small weed growth next to shore. That's where the bass used to hang out, between the lily pads and shore in the open pockets, in 3 or 4 feet of water. But now they have no cover, so they are tucked back in the brush, and you can't get to them."

However, Martinsen admits, if you can get a popper into the brush or cover a bass in the shallow pockets near shore, it will likely take.

"I've never needed to get involved with fishing bass underneath the surface," he says. "They love floating poppers and deer hair bugs. I like to cast a popper, let it land, let the ripples die down, then twitch it three or four times. Then I cast again. You are only fishing open areas between the weeds that are maybe 4 or 5 feet in diameter, so it doesn't make sense to fish a cast back to the boat. Just work the popper a couple times, and if nothing takes it, move on to the next open area."

Because you may be required to pop a cast into the brush or haul a big bass out of the weeds, most fly-rodders go with a 7- or 8-weight rod, spooled with a floating, weight-forward taper fly line. A heavier rod facilitates casting against a heavy wind, which can crop up any day on Silver Lake.

During spring expect to find bass spawning in the shallows. They may be actively spawning by mid-April or not until sometime in May, depending on the weather. During cool years, the spawn occurs later.

"During the spawn, I try to hit the weedbeds in about 3 feet of water," Martinsen says. "That's when I catch most of the big fish. As the water warms up and we go into the summer season, the fish are less active during the day, so you have to hit them in the morning or evening. The last hour of light seems best. When the water cools down in the fall, fishing is good all day, and you can take some nice-sized fish at that time, too. I really don't vary my flies; I like black deer hair poppers best, and I use them all year. I also like frog-colored poppers. I've had some luck on yellow, too. Cork-body minnows, about 3 inches long, are also a good bet. They wiggle from side to side, and they catch fish like crazy. I like those with a green or black body and orange feathers. That's an old-time lure that is still effective."

Although anglers can find largemouths throughout Silver Lake, over the years, Martinsen has developed a liking for the south and west shores.

"I think it's just a personal preference, but I do seem to catch more fish from those areas than anywhere else," he says. "Maybe there's just less pressure on those shores."

Pressure is something that a fly-rodder may have to put up with at Silver Lake. However, just keep in mind that there is plenty of water to work. If you see someone working down the shore toward you, head for another area or swing outside of that angler when he passes by. You can work up the bank and cover water that he may have missed or find another area. However, pay attention to what other anglers are fishing with—if it's spinnerbait, clear out.

"I really don't like to follow a guy who's throwing spinnerbait or diving plug," Martinsen says. "If a guy is fishing popper or fly, that's OK, I'll follow him. But, spinnerbait seems to really spook bass, and you might have to wait an hour or so for the fish to settle down."

Whether you fish Silver Lake during spring, summer, or fall, release your bass—the lake gets hammered, and the bass deserve a break.

"Over the years I've caught hundreds if not thousands of bass from Silver Lake," Martinsen says. "I haven't kept one in 15 years. I like to eat fish, but this lake gets too much pressure. Often, you'll catch a fish here that has hook scars, and you realize why catch-and-release is such a good thing."

When fishing Silver Lake for bass, you may encounter bluegill and crappie. Those are the fish you want for dinner. They can be taken on small woolly buggers, hare's ear nymphs, and leeches.

While Silver Lake's bass fishing may not stack up to what it was several years back, it still offers a great shot at a big largemouth bass in western Washington. For that reason alone, Silver is worth a visit.

To reach Silver Lake, follow Hwy 504 east out of Castle Rock. The lake rests on the south side of the highway. Boats can be launched at the public fishing access on the northwest side or at Silver Lake, Streeter, or Anderson's resorts.

# Lake Facts: Silver Lake

### Seasons
- Open year-round.

### Special Regulations
- Daily limit is 5 bass, none under 14 inches.

### Species
- Largemouth bass to 6 pounds or more. Most fish average 1.5 to 2 pounds.
- Crappie and bluegill are also available.

### Lake Characteristics
- Best fishing occurs in the spring, specifically late April through early June.
- Summer evenings are also good.
- Fall triggers heavy feeding, and action can be good.

### Access
- Two private launches and one public access.
- Must have a boat, canoe, or float tube to fish the lake effectively.

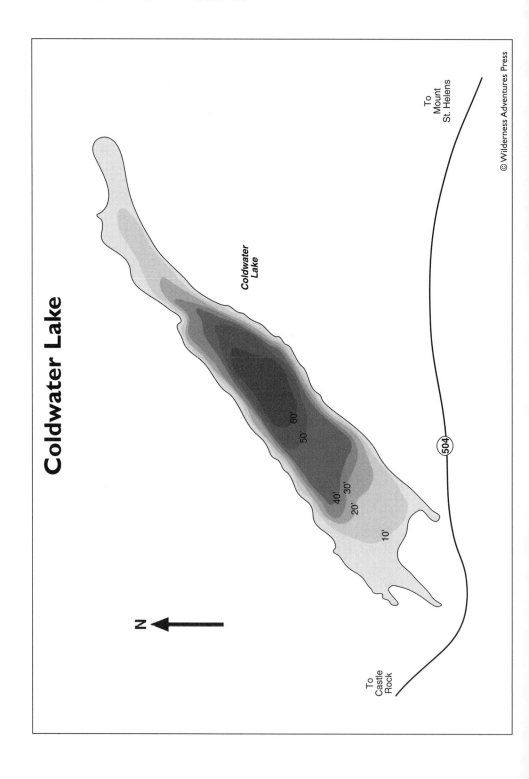

Coldwater Lake

Coldwater Lake

N

To Mount St. Helens

To Castle Rock

504

© Wilderness Adventures Press

# THE MOUNT ST. HELENS LAKES

### Coldwater Lake

Formed by the eruption of Mount St. Helens in 1980, Coldwater Lake quickly turned into one of the most intriguing large trout options in the state, thanks to Washington Department of Fish and Wildlife.

The department stocked the lake with rainbow and cutthroat trout nine years after the blast, and today those fish are self-sustaining, meaning they spawn successfully. Many of Coldwater's trout are mature fish that measure between 16 and 20 inches and really put a bend in a fly rod. That large average size, coupled with unique volcanic scenery surrounding the lake, is Coldwater's biggest draw—maybe nowhere in western Washington, other than Pass Lake, is there a better place to catch big rainbows on a fly rod.

For those who are familiar with the nuances of this lake, it's not uncommon for a competent flyfisher to land several fish between 16 and 20 inches in an afternoon. On a really good day, maybe five or six fish, with one or two stretching to 20 inches or slightly better, may come to net. However, Coldwater is also one of the most temperamental waters you may ever visit—if you have little patience and must keep a bend in your rod to be happy, reconsider your options.

Coldwater, a 766-acre lake that reaches 203 feet deep, was originally opened to fishing on a limited permit basis in 1993.

Today, Coldwater is open year-round, and a permit is not needed. However, there is a one fish over 16 inches limit and a single, barbless hook restriction that helps protect the fishery. Also limiting anglers is a no-gas engine restriction. Conditions can become ferocious at the lake, and trying to row a boat or kick a float tube from one end of the lake to the other in a windstorm is not for the faint of heart. Electric motors are allowed, and many anglers navigate a small boat with an electric motor while towing a float tube behind. Once they reach their desired spot, they anchor the boat and climb into the float tube, which saves the battery on the electric motor for the return trip.

You do need a boat or float tube to fish Coldwater effectively. There are only three shore accesses, and you can't fish from or even launch a float tube from other areas —that is against the regulations of the Mount St. Helens National Volcanic Monument, which operates a visitor's center near the lake. To visit the monument, which includes fishing the lake, a National Forest pass is required, and that will tax your wallet slightly. In 1998, the cost for a three-day permit was $8.

When fishing Coldwater, anglers may catch the aforementioned rainbow or two species of cutthroat—the coastal and the Twin Lake.

Coastal cutthroat can be identified by small black spots extending from the head all the way to the tail. Twin Lake cutthroat display large spots extending from behind the dorsal fin through the tail.

*A rainbow trout caught in Coldwater Lake.*

In a 1997 survey, it was determined that 58 percent of Coldwater's trout are rainbow, 11 percent coastal cutthroat, and 27 percent Twin Lake cutthroat. Four percent were rainbow/cutthroat hybrids.

While anglers could feasibly catch trout in Coldwater any day of the year (provided they can reach the boat launch via a mountain road that could be covered with snow), the most productive times to fish the lake extend from late spring through summer and fall.

Gary Brault, who runs Toutle River Fly and Tackle and fishes Coldwater regularly, suggests that fly-rodders hold off on the lake until June 15. Coldwater lies at 2,500 feet, and even spring storms can bring a taste of snow and frigid temperatures.

"Coldwater Lake is a mean spot to fish," he says. "It really gets hit by the wind worse than any surrounding lake, and it's a cold area. We get some ant hatches prior to June 15, but that's just a tough time to fish. I like to wait until all of the snow is melted and things warm up.

"If you are going to fish during spring, you should work the north end of the lake, where Coldwater Creek dumps in with Chironomid or streamer patterns. That's where the fish spawn and congregate. (Note: the inlet and outlet areas of the lake are closed to fishing.)

"After that, the weather gets better, and you will definitely see terrestrial insects, but the hatches are totally unpredictable. Any fluctuation in weather changes things. There's no consistency. You just have to be prepared and take what the lake gives you."

Typically, Coldwater Lake offers more to the subsurface fly than the dry fly. In fact, the nature of the lake demands that anglers fish subsurface. Only occasionally is the dry fly or an emerger a good option. Coldwater contains very little aquatic vegetation so typical lake hatches, such as Callibaetis mayflies, damselflies, caddisflies, and dragonflies, are an anomaly here.

"I tell people if you live by the dry fly, you die by the dry fly," Brault says. "This is a very deep lake with steep shores and little in the way of vegetation. I fish deep all the time with a full-sink line about 30 feet deep and 30 feet off the shore. I use a fishfinder and I see schools of fish at that depth. Typically, I strip about 90 feet of line off my reel and troll at different speeds until I find what the fish like."

If forced to fish the lake for only one week of the year, Brault says he would choose September, because August can be too hot and October can be too cold. In fact, by October early snowstorms may blanket the area.

"September is a great time to be on the lake," Brault says. "You can get ant hatches, the weather is beautiful, and the fish are in real nice shape—they're strong. At that time of the year, it's not uncommon to catch one that goes between 22 and 24 inches. They've fed hard all summer and they are heavy fish."

Because he does most of his fishing subsurface, Brault's favorite fly is the egg-sucking leech. Other patterns work well at Coldwater, such as woolly buggers, zonkers, and sculpins, but the egg-sucking leech is a standby.

"It's my favorite pattern," Brault says. "I like to tie them in size 8 rather than larger sizes, because I get better hookups that way. My preference for color is olive, black, then purple. I fish leeches off a 6-foot long leader tapered to 3X."

While streamers are your best bet at Coldwater, there is the occasional opportunity for a floating line and small fly. Midges hatch throughout the season, and typical Chironomid tactics work here. Emergent midge patterns, in size 16 and 18, draw strikes when those insects hatch.

While Coldwater can be classified as a quirky lake, it offers large trout and interesting scenery. On a good day, it can put a lot of pounds of trout in your net. On a bad day you can console yourself by peering at Mount St. Helens. Go ahead, ponder the cataclysmic forces that dismantled the mountain that infamous May day in 1980. At least your weren't stuck on the mountain when it blew.

# Lake Facts: Coldwater Lake

## Seasons
- Year-round.

## Special Regulations
- One fish over 16 inches a day. Selective gear rules apply. No internal combustion engines.

## Species
- Rainbow and cutthroat to good size. Average fish stretches 16 inches, plenty available over 20 inches.

## Lake Characteristics
- Formed by the eruption of Mount St. Helens, this lake is known to be cold and windy due to lack of surrounding vegetation, including trees.
- Fishing can be good from ice-out through fall.

## Access
- A boat or float tube is required to fish the lake.
- Shore access is severely limited by the Mount St. Helens Volcanic Monument.
- A fee must be paid to the Monument to fish the lake.

## Merrill Lake

Each year, as early summer gives way to the hot days of July and August, Washington's hard-core flyfishers turn their attention toward the Mount St. Helens area and Merrill Lake.

At that time, massive emergences of *Hexagenia limbata*, the largest of mayflies, emerge from this 344-acre, flyfishing-only lake, and Merrill's inhabitants, including some hefty brown trout, key on them. You really can't blame the trout. After surviving on smallish mayflies, midges, and caddis all year, big, 1- to 2-inch long mayflies represent a smorgasbord.

As the insects emerge—trying desperately to shed their nymphal shuck, dry their huge wings, and take flight before death fins their way—the trout are locked into them. Fortunately, the lake's wary browns lose caution when feeding on the big insects, in no small part due to fading light.

As mentioned, *Hexagenia* emerge in July and August, and they do so in the evening, extending from an hour before dusk through several hours of darkness. Each summer evening around 7pm, the flyfishing faithful show up, take their time rigging rods, then hit the water an hour later, just as the first flies begin showing on the surface.

"The hatch starts around July 1 and ends the middle of August," Brault says. "They come off like clockwork around 8:30pm, and the water just goes alive with them. It's crazy.

"You'll see a lot of guys on the water in the evening with their flashlights," Brault adds. "Everyone fishes until about 10pm and quits when the hatch dies. It's really a spectacle, because the fishing can be so good."

To imitate *Hexagenia*, which match a size 4 hook and include a lot of yellow in their coloration, try large sparkle duns, cripples, and Adams style flies, tied with yellow dubbing.

"The flies are very bright," Brault says. "They have yellow in their bodies and a yellow tint to their wings. I've caught fish on a big yellow humpy but only in a pinch. The specific mayfly imitations work best."

One of the best areas to fish the *Hex* hatch is off the east shore, no more than 50 feet off the bank, where lots of brush and aquatic vegetation provide excellent habitat for *Hexagenia*. On a good night, you'll find big mayflies popping out of the water along the entire bank, and, of course, you'll see trout sucking them down.

Although *Hexagenia* are Merrill's big draw, this lake does offer other attributes. In fact, during spring and summer expect to see midges, damselflies, dragonflies, and caddisflies. All can be matched with standard patterns, and anglers often overlook these insects. The trout, on the other hand, take advantage of what they are offered.

Streamers are also effective patterns at Merrill, and standards such as egg-sucking leeches, woolly buggers, and zonkers draw strikes. Those offerings should be fished off a sinktip or full-sink lines with a short, 3- or 4-foot leader that tapers to 3X.

"When nothing is happening, I tie on an egg-sucking leech and work the deeper areas and dropoffs," Brault says. "I catch a lot of browns that way but also rainbows

# Merrill Lake

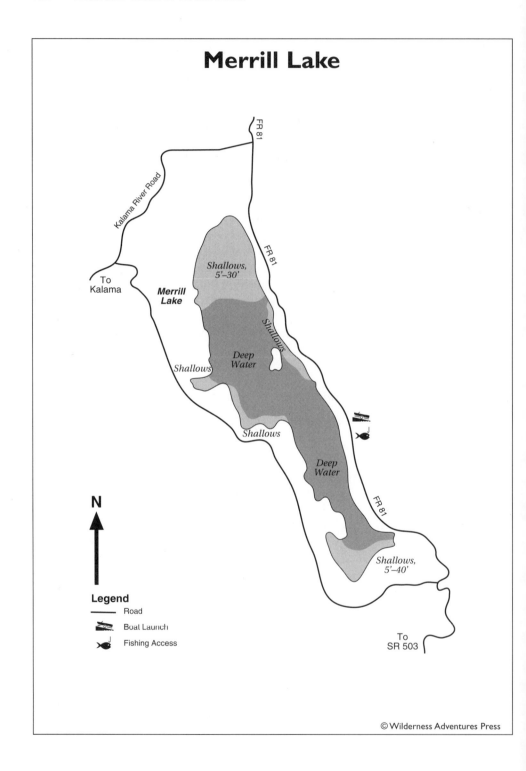

FR 81

Kalama River Road

Shallows,
5'–30'

FR 81

To
Kalama

**Merrill
Lake**

Shallows

Shallows

Deep
Water

Shallows

Deep
Water

FR 81

Shallows,
5'–40'

**N**

**Legend**
—— Road
Boat Launch
Fishing Access

To
SR 503

© Wilderness Adventures Press

*A healthy brown trout taken on a fly in Merrill Lake.*

and cutthroat. Sometimes I'll tie on a large (size 4, 6, or 8) *Hexagenia* nymph, such as a giant hare's ear with a yellow body and lots of plumage on its back, and work that very slowly. You can pick some fish up in the middle of the day or late afternoon doing that."

Streamers are especially effective during fall, when the lake's brown trout feel the inherent need to spawn and move into the shallows. They'll cruise Merrill, searching for inlets and suitable spawning beds. If you can place a woolly bugger or zonker in front of a fish in September, October, and November, it's likely to take.

Unlike Coldwater Lake, where the volcanic blast's severity rendered the area desolate, Merrill Lake is scenic and offers some old-growth and new growth timber that is ideal for camping. A public campground rests on the east shore. If you want to escape the masses, paddle over to the west shore and pitch a tent.

# Lake Facts: Merrill Lake

## Seasons
- Year-round.

## Special Regulations
- Two trout, none larger than 12 inches.
- Flyfishing only.
- No internal combustion engines.

## Species
- Brown and rainbow trout to 16 inches with an occasional large brown stretching past 20 inches.

## Lake Characteristics
- Best known for its lengthy summer emergence of *Hexagenia* mayflies. Anglers show up *en masse* for this event. Brown trout and rainbows feed heavily on the big mayflies, especially from 8PM to dark. It's the only time of year that the fish throw caution to the wind and inhale dry flies like candy. Definitely one of western Washington's best hatches.

## Access
- The east side of the lake offers a boat ramp.
- Shore access is plentiful.
- Lake may not be accessible until May due to snow on Forest Service access roads.

## Castle Lake

If you are looking for a truly monster-size rainbow trout and aren't afraid to put a couple dozen harrowing miles on your pickup truck or Jeep, not to mention your own legs when hiking down a steep hill (cliff?) to the water, give Castle a try—it's worth the effort.

Castle is located in the Mount St. Helens National Volcanic Monument off of Forest Road 3000. Landslides and mudflows periodically close roads into the lake, so check with the Forest Service or Volcanic Monument folks before you plan a trip there. The Mount St. Helens West hunting map gives detailed directions to the lake. Also, Castle is open year-round, but snow generally blocks the entrance until sometime in May. That's OK—the best fishing arrives in late May, June, and July and returns during fall.

"I think Castle is probably the best trout lake in Washington," Brault says. "It's full of rainbows, and they love a fly. Anything that hits the top they'll take, and if it happens to be your fly, they'll nearly pull the rod right out of your hand. The whole scene reminds me of fishing in Alaska."

Castle is a lucky lake—when St. Helens blew up, Castle received a modest side blast and wasn't inundated by ash. Due to that good fortune, it offers excellent aquatic vegetation patches that facilitate robust insect populations. Caddisflies, damselflies, Callibaetis mayflies, midges, dragonflies—they're all present in decent numbers, and the trout certainly key on those bugs.

Basic imitations, such as an Adams, Wulff, elk hair caddis, renegade, marabou damsel, or Trude, will take fish at Castle, but, as always, specific imitations draw more strikes. If Callibaetis are emerging, go with a gray sparkle dun or cripple or a Stalcup's CDC biot Callibaetis. For damsels, marabou nymphs work well underneath; up top use a braided butt damsel. If caddis come off, tie on a LaFontaine sparkle emerger or an X-caddis. For midges, try emergent patterns that rest in the surface film. If you don't have those specific patterns, don't fret—you'll still catch fish with attractor patterns, not to mention nymphs and streamers.

"You don't have to match the hatch," Brault says. "If I see mayflies, I use a size 14 pink lady. An Adams also works well. If caddis are around, I'll use an elk hair caddis. If nothing is hatching, I'll use an egg-sucking leech or woolly bugger. One day in October, three of us caught 67 fish at Castle. I caught 25 of those on an egg-sucking leech."

To fish Castle Lake, you'll want to pack in a float tube or small pontoon boat, plus camping gear. The banks of Castle are heavily timbered and very steep. And due to a rapid dropoff, shore fishing is a bust. With a float tube or pontoon boat, an angler can cruise the lake and fish all of the prime water. Pay particular attention to the shallow bays, where insect populations are most dense.

The hike into Castle measures about a half-mile, but as mentioned, it's quite a steep descent. What's worse is the hike back out—bring some stout hiking boots and all the lung capacity you can muster.

Most of Castle's trout run 14 to 17 inches, but some fish stretch to 6 pounds or more. The trout population is self-sustaining and protected by a 1-fish, 16-inch minimum length limit. Most flyfishers, whether they are camping along its shores, firing up the Coleman stove or not, release their catch at Castle.

# Lake Facts: Castle Lake

## Seasons
• Year-round.

## Special Regulations
• Only 1 fish over 16 inches a day.
• Selective gear rules in effective.

## Species
• Rainbow and cutthroat trout to trophy size.

## Lake Characteristics
• A beautiful, mountain lake that offers excellent insect hatches. Dry-fly fishing can be outstanding at times.

## Access
• Difficult over many miles of logging roads.
• A trailhead leads down some steep terrain for about a half-mile to the lake. The climb back out is difficult.
• Flyfishers need to pack in a float tube, and they may want to bring camping gear for an overnight stay.

# COLUMBIA RIVER SHAD

Often overlooked by Washington's flyfishers, the American shad ascends the Columbia River each spring and early summer, providing decent opportunities to catch one of the world's best-fighting fish on light tackle.

First given sportfish accolades in 1849, shad was immediately embraced by fly-fishers and was often called "the poor man's salmon."

Originally an East Coast fish, the American shad was introduced to Washington and the Columbia River between 1870 and 1880, where it immediately took hold. Today, a million to two million or more fish ascend the Columbia each year.

American shad, a member of the herring family, begin their life in freshwater, and just like salmon, migrate to sea, then return to freshwater as mature adults to spawn. As adults, shad average 3 to 5 pounds, but specimens to 12 pounds have been observed. Shad make their first spawning run when they are 4- or 5-years-old and can be repeat spawners if they survive the gauntlet they face in fresh and saltwater.

Shad begin moving up the Columbia in May, with their numbers peaking in late June and early July. Most fishing action takes place below Bonneville Dam, which is open for shad on May 16. Prime places to cast flies include the top end of Lady Island, Cascade Island, Bradford Island, and Robins Island. Shad are encountered below Bonneville Dam in many places, including the very productive mouth of the Washougal River, but the hot spot is just below the tailrace of Bonneville Dam. However, the spoon- and spinner-chucking masses congregate there, and flyfishing cannot only be difficult in proximity to thm, it's also a little dangerous—not good to hook someone in the head with a white streamer.

Speaking of white streamers, white marabou patterns, tied to size 6, 8, and 10 hooks, are possibly the most productive shad flies, although bucktail streamers and even the simple woolly bugger will work. Shad can be quite picky about fly patterns, so it pays to change if you are not getting strikes. Popular steelhead flies don't work too well, but small baitfish patterns with a silver flash often draw strikes. Patterns with a hint of red are top choices, as well. Patterns should be weighted and fished off high-density sinking lines.

Shad are notorious for holding deep and in the Columbia they can go way down. However, most are taken in the 8- to 12-foot deep range in fairly heavy current. Finding the holding level of fish is extremely important. If you fish a fly above the holding level or below it, you may not touch a fish. If you find the proper level, you may not be able to keep them off your line. And when shad fishing is good, you might hook 15 to 35, or even 40, fish in a day.

To reach fish, anglers must cast from shore or from a boat. Wading in the Columbia is not only difficult, it's dangerous. Although a 4- or 5-weight fly rod would be ideal for fighting shad, a 7- or 8-weight stick allows long casts from shore, which are almost always necessary. As mentioned, high-density sinking lines work best, and short, 3- or 4-foot leaders should be attached to them. If fishing from a boat, flyfish-ers may want to cruise the line between current and slackwater, dragging a fly behind the boat, and varying depth until the fish are found.

If fishing from shore with high-density lines, cast upstream and allow the fly and line to sink while keeping slight tension on the line so you can feel a strike when it occurs. Shad will take on a dead-drift and may pound on a fly as it swings downstream from an angler. They can also strike subtly. Whether they pound a fly or simply mouth it, don't set the hook too hard. Again, shad are members of the herring family, and their mouths are small and soft—easy to tear if you horse them.

While shad fishing opens May 16, most anglers wait until June to begin casting. Daily tallies of fish passing over Bonneville Dam can be found in the larger newspapers, such as the *Seattle Times*. A tally of 20,000 is cause for a trip to the Columbia, although on the best days, somewhere in the neighborhood of 40,000 to 70,000 fish will pass by the dam.

Columbia River shad are truly an overlooked game fish in Washington and Oregon, but they can be taken on a fly rod with good success. Anglers who complain about a lack of steelhead and salmon are doing themselves a disservice if they do not visit the Columbia and challenge this fish. It's true that there are a lot of variables to keep in mind, including the number of shad in the river and the amount of water being released from upstream dams, but there is no catch limit on this fish. When you get into them, the action can be hot. Shad are no sissies when it comes to a fight, and once you hook one, you'll be back to the Columbia for more. Remember, there is no limit on shad, but don't take more than you plan to smoke, can, or slowly bake. Shad are bony creatures, but their flesh has a delicate flavor, and their eggs are said to be excellent. No comment from the author on that boast.

# SOUTHWEST HUB CITIES
# Vancouver
### Elevation–300 • Population–132,000

## ACCOMMODATIONS
Best Western Ferryman Inn, 7901 Northeast 6th Avenue / 360-574-2151
Comfort Inn, 13207 Northeast 20th Avenue / 360-574-6000
Guest House Motel, 11504 Northeast 2nd Street / 360-254-4511
Holiday Inn Express, 9107 Northeast Vancouver Mall Drive / 360-253-5000
Residence Inn by Marriott, 8005 Northeast Parkway Drive / 360-253-4800
Salmon Creek Motel, 11901 Northeast Highway 99 / 360-573-0751

## FLY SHOPS AND SPORTING GOODS
GI Joe's, 13215 Southeast Mill Plain Boulevard / 360-253-2420
The Greased Line Fly Shoppe, 5802 Northeast 88th Street / 360-573-9383

## AUTO REPAIR
Caldwell's Auto Repair, 8616 Northeast 55th Avenue / 360-573-3709
Larkin's Garage, 1708 Washington Street / 360-693-4881
Swanson's Automotive Service, 9012 Northeast 117th Avenue / 360-254-4447

## AUTO RENTAL
Agency Rent-A-Car, 6202 Northeast Highway 99 / 360-694-1947
Enterprise Rent-A-Car, 8724 Northeast Highway 99 / 360-576-9999
Practical Rent-A-Car, 7831 Northeast Highway 99 / 360-576-9145

## AIRPORT
Canica Airport Operations, 101 East Reserve Street / 360-695-0656

## MEDICAL
Southwest Washington Medical Center, 3400 Main / 360-256-2000

## FOR MORE INFORMATION
Greater Vancouver Chamber of Commerce
404 East 15th Street, Suite 11
Vancouver, WA 98663
360-694-2588

# Kalama

## ACCOMMODATIONS

Motel 7 West, 864 Walsh Avenue Northeast / 360-274-7526
Mt. St. Helens Motel, 1340 Mt. St. Helens Way Northeast / 360-274-7721
Timberland Motor Inn, 1271 Mt. St. Helens Way Northeast / 360-274-6002

## CAMPGROUNDS AND RV PARKS

Camp Kalama RV Park, Interstate 5 / 360-673-2456
Mahaffey's Campground, 1134 Kalama River Road / 360-673-3867
Louis H. Rasmussen RV Park, 268 Hendrickson Drive / 360-673-2626

## RESTAURANTS

The Cache, 4858 Westside Hwy / 360-274-7971
Castle Rock Barbecue, 103 Huntington Avenue North / 360-274-8371
Mt. St. Helens Restaurant, 15000 Spirit Lake Memorial Hwy / 360-274-7750
Pepers 49er Restaurant, 916 Walsh Avenue Northeast / 360-274-7957
Waldo's, 51 Cowlitz Street West / 360-274-7486

## FLY SHOPS AND SPORTING GOODS

Prichard's Western Anglers, 2106 Kalama River Road / 360-673-4690

## AUTO REPAIR

Kalama Auto Supply, 498 Northeast Frontage Road / 360-673-2445

## MEDICAL

Castle Rock Medical Clinic, 606 Roake Avenue Southeast / 360-274-4179

# Longview/Kelso

### Elevation–120 • Population–33,480

Gateway to the Cowlitz and Lewis Rivers. Close to Mount St. Helens.

## ACCOMMODATIONS

**Super 8,** 250 Kelso Drive / 360-423-8880 / Indoor pool and Spa
**Motel 6,** 106 Minor Road / 360-425-3229 / 63 units, pool
**Red Lion Inn,** 510 Kelso Drive / 360-636-4400 / 162 units, pool, sauna

## CAMPGROUNDS AND RV PARKS

**Brookhollow RV Park,** 2506 Allen Street / 360-577-6474 / Full hook-ups
**Fisher Island RV Park,** 5558 Willow Grove Road / 360-425-9198 / Full hook-ups,
tent sites

## RESTAURANTS

**Judy's,** 1036 Washington Way / 360-423-9262 / Lunch and dinner, pasta, steaks
burgers, seafood, soups, smoke-free
**Hilander Family Restaurant,** 1509 Allen Street / 360-423-1500 / 18-foot salad bar,
cocktail lounge, steaks, seafood, burgers, Sunday brunch, open 6:30AM
**Burger King,** 3003 Ocean Beach Highway / 360-577-5464

## FLY SHOPS AND SPORTING GOODS

**Baker's Corner Store,** 5601 Ocean Beach Hwy / 360-423-3636
**Bob's Merchandise,** 1111 Hudson Street / 360-425-3870
**Wal-Mart,** 3715 Ocean Beach Hwy / 360-414-8482

## AUTO REPAIR

**Longview RV,** 915 Tennant Way / 360-577-1919 / RV care and service
**Brent's Quality Auto Repair,** 965 15th Ave / 360-577-1838

## AUTO RENTAL

**Enterprise Rent-A-Car,** 1210 Vandercook Way / 360-423-9999

## AIR SERVICE

**Kelso/Longview Regional Airport,** P.O. Box 1253, Longview / 360-425-3688 / Small
airplanes / Closest commercial service in Portland

## MEDICAL

**St. John Medical Center,** 1614 East Kessler Boulevard / 360-423-1530
**Northwest Continuum Care Center,** 128 Beacon Hill Drive, Longview / 360-423-
4060

## FOR MORE INFORMATION

Longview Area Chamber of Commerce
1563 Olympia Way
Longview, WA 98632
360-423-8400

Kelso Area Chamber of Commerce
105 Minor Road
Kelso, WA 98626
360-414-8442

# Castle Rock

## ACCOMMODATIONS
Motel 7 West, 864 Walsh Avenue Northeast / 360-274-7526
Mt . St. Helens Motel, 1340 Mt. St. Helens Way Northeast / 360-274-7721
Timberland Motor Inn, 1271 Mt. St. Helens Way Northeast / 360-274-6002

## CAMPGROUNDS
Mt. St. Helens RV Park, I-5 Exit 49, go east on Hwy 504, then northeast on Tower, 1 block east on Schaffran Road / 360-274-8522

## RESTAURANTS
The Cache, 4858 Westside Hwy / 360-274-7971
Castle Rock Barbecue, 103 Huntington Avenue North / 360-274-8371
Mt. St. Helens Restaurant, 15000 Spirit Lake Memorial Hwy / 360-274-7750
Pepers 49er Restaurant, 916 Walsh Avenue Northeast / 360-274-7957
Waldo's, 51 Cowlitz Street West / 360-274-7486

## FLY SHOPS AND SPORTING GOODS
Fish Country Sports Shop, 2210 US Hwy 12, Ethel
Wal-Mart, 3715 Ocean Beach Hwy (Longview) / 360-414-9956

## AUTO REPAIR
Ken's Carquest, Huntington at Cowlitz / 360-274-7727

## MEDICAL
Castle Rock Medical Clinic, 606 Roake Avenue Southeast / 360-274-4179

# Columbia Basin Lakes

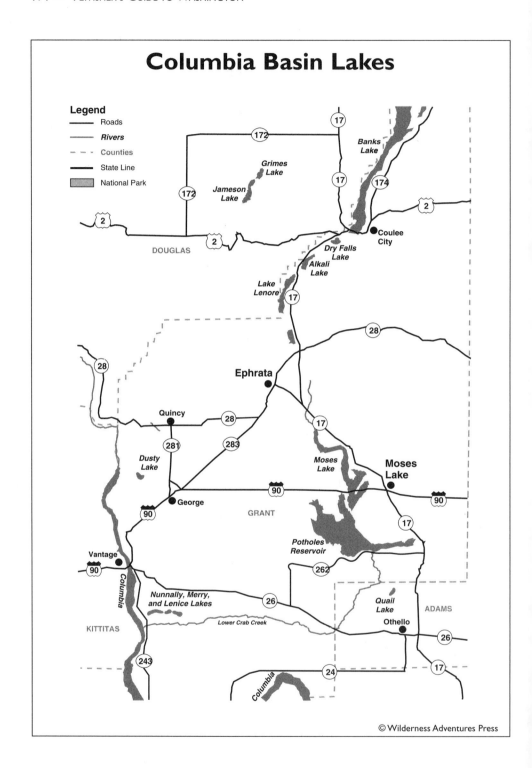

**Legend**
— Roads
— *Rivers*
—·—· Counties
— State Line
▨ National Park

© Wilderness Adventures Press

# Columbia Basin Lakes

Washington's Columbia Basin offers some of the finest lake fishing to be found anywhere in the country. Within an hour's drive of each other rest a couple dozen lakes, all holding the potential to bend your 4- or 5-weight fly rod with a trout exceeding 4, maybe even 5, pounds. On a really good day, any of the Basin lakes could place 20 or more mature trout in a flyfisher's net.

These lakes are fertile environments that offer tremendous weed growth, which facilitates massive aquatic insect hatches. Midges (Chironomids), damselflies, caddisflies, dragonflies, Callibaetis, Baetis, and pale morning dun mayflies are all present in good numbers, and don't think for a second that the fish don't know it.

While most of Washington's lakes open in late April, many Columbia Basin fisheries, such as Dusty Lake, Lake Lenore, Lake Lenice, Nunnally Lake, Merry Lake, and Quail Lake, offer relief on March 1 for flyfishers who just can't wait until late April to throw a line. Plus these lakes, with the exception of Dusty, are managed under special regulations that keep the harvest down and overall size of the trout up.

For instance, Lake Lenore commonly kicks out two or three Lahontan cutthroat of 4 pounds or more a day to an angler. Lake Lenice offers rainbow trout that average 14 inches, with fish to 20 inches regularly caught and released. Dry Falls Lake also offers large rainbows, plus a fairly healthy supply of large brown trout that may stretch to 26 inches or more. They are especially fond of streamer patterns and commonly gather around the dinner table at night. A large brown hooked at night offers some surreal moments in a flyfisher's life.

Fishing at most of the Basin lakes really picks up in April, May, and June, then diminishes as the summer sun warms the water and sends trout diving for the bottom. By mid-September, the water cools down and fish become active, right in time to meet the fall mayfly hatches.

To fish the Basin lakes, flyfishers should take a small pram or a float tube. Several lakes, such as Dusty, Quail, and Lenice, require a short hike to reach. If you don't want to roll a pram into those waters, you definitely should opt for a float tube.

# Lake Lenore

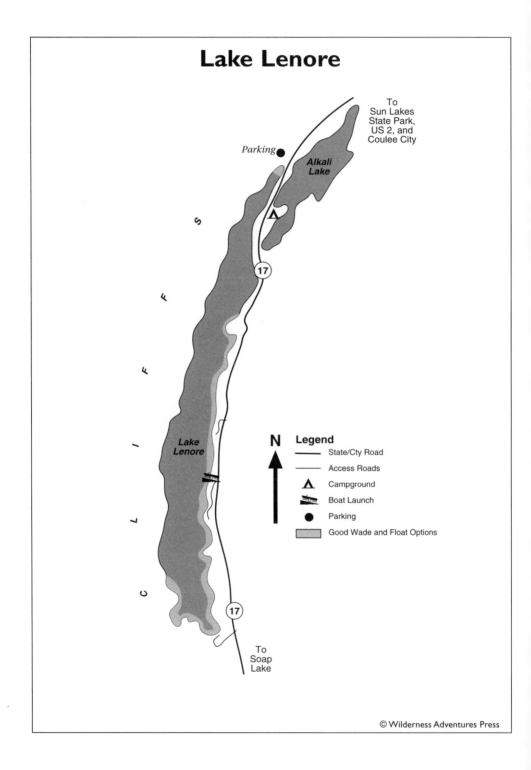

To
Sun Lakes
State Park,
US 2, and
Coulee City

Parking

*Alkali
Lake*

S

17

F
F
L
I
C

*Lake
Lenore*

**N**

**Legend**

State/Cty Road

Access Roads

Δ Campground

Boat Launch

● Parking

Good Wade and Float Options

17

To
Soap
Lake

© Wilderness Adventures Press

# Lake Lenore

Stingy at times, generous at others, the potential to land one trout that makes all others pale in comparison is an attraction that places Lake Lenore on the destination map of Northwest flyfishers.

Lake Lenore is a highly alkaline water located in the scabrock country of eastern Washington, and it is commonly referred to, with good reason, as Washington's most productive trophy cutthroat trout lake.

There's no doubt that Lenore kicks out more 4-pound-plus fish than any other trout lake in the state. However, part of the reason for that tally is that so many people cast flies here. I'm one of those culprits who make Lenore quite crowded at times. I don't like crowded fishing conditions any more than the next guy in line, but flyfishers as a lot are a pretty good group of people, and I enjoy the company of fellow anglers. Good stories and a few new fly patterns are often exchanged when fishing Lenore. However, there are those times, for whatever reason, when the lake is nearly devoid of anglers and the cutthroat are feeling hungry.

That was the case when Jeff Bobin and I rose early one morning in April and drove three anticipation-filled hours from the cluttered confusion of Seattle to that desolate chunk of country just north of Ephrata and Soap Lake, where enormous Lahontan cutthroat trout were congregated in the shallows.

I spent the prior night feasting on rekindled flames and was rather shocked when I looked at the clock and realized it was already 4:45AM—and I hadn't caught a wink of sleep. I slipped out from the covers and threw the truck into overdrive. I was supposed to meet Jeff at my parents' house at 5AM.

When I arrived, my father and Jeff were sitting in the living room waiting for me. Jeff was eating a bowl of cereal. He looked me in the eyes and tapped his wristwatch. I wiped the cobwebs from my eyes and said, "Come on, let's go."

During our drive to Lenore, Jeff told me he found the front door of my parents' house locked. Instead of knocking on the door, possibly waking my parents in the process, he threw rocks at my bedroom window.

Dad opened his window and said, "Jeff, come on inside. If Greg said he'd be here at five to fish Lenore, he'll be here soon."

Jeff replied, "Sorry, Fred."

Despite my self-induced sleep deprivation, I was fired up during our drive, thanks to Lenore's promise and several industrial-strength cups of coffee.

When we arrived at the lake, we saw few anglers but plenty of wicked whitecaps that had the lake whipped into a froth. That's nothing out of the ordinary for Lenore —it covers 1,700 surface acres and rests at the lower end of Grand Coulee, a natural wind funnel.

The largest Lahontan cutthroat recorded from Lake Lenore weighed nearly 11 pounds and was landed in 1987. Today, fish ranging from 3 to 5 pounds are not uncommon, and it's believed that a new state record may be cruising under the surface of Lenore, waiting for some lucky angler's offering.

"The average Lenore cutthroat is young and weighs about three pounds," says Joe Foster, a Washington Department of Fish and Wildlife biologist working out of Ephrata. "But we do see a number of fish in the 5- to 9-pound range, and we've had some pretty incredible reports about fish that weigh over 11 pounds. I think it's very possible that those reports are true."

There are several good times to fish Lake Lenore, but it's tough to beat spring. At that time, cutthroat concentrate in pods, often numbering in the hundreds, while trying to satisfy an instinctual urge to spawn. The spawn begins sometime in April and lasts through May. The cutthroat's spawning effort in the lake is mostly futile. But biologists secure about 75,000 prime eggs from 250 female trout (hens) that they trap in a small inlet stream. Those eggs assure Lenore's future.

Originally believed to be too alkaline for the survival of trout, Lenore received a plant of 30 cutthroat in 1977. The fish, which were acquired from a hatchery in Nevada and contained in submerged boxes, remained alive in Lenore—a few began to grow and put on weight. Later, the fish were released from their confinement and in October 1980 an angler caught one of the original 30 trout—it measured 25 inches, weighed 6.5 pounds, and effectively established the lake as one of the Northwest's destination fly waters.

Today, many years after that first cutthroat was caught, Lenore's trout number in the hundreds of thousands and, on occasion, anglers may land 20 or more fish a day. Emphasis should be placed with "on occasion," because when my father and I visited Lenore one summer day, it was nearly a fishless occasion.

In fact, during our brief three-hour visit, we witnessed the landing of only three fish. Luckily, one was a 24-inch beauty that engulfed my black woolly bugger and offered a strong fight. Dad photographed the fish before I released it. Catch and release is required on Lenore between March 1 and May 31. Only boats driven by electric motors and float tubes are allowed on the water. Those regulations keep the spin-dog masses off the water and provide float-tubers with a measure of safety—nobody likes to ride the wake of a Bayliner flying by at Mach III.

As mentioned, when Jeff and I visited Lenore that groggy morning in April, we were greeted by wind gusts traveling faster than the highway speed limit. Positioned in float tubes, Jeff and I bounced and lurched in the whitecaps, showers of white spray flying past our sides and over our heads. We tried to launch our craft, but waves broke over our backs and threatened quick death if we progressed any farther. Float tubes are not really safe watercraft, and Mother Nature should not be challenged with them. If the wind is up or has the potential to blow you off the water, stay close to shore and exit the water if needed.

Returning to the relative safety of shore, Jeff and I worked out casts, between wind gusts, to a pod of maybe a hundred cutthroat trout.

Lahontans are notorious for losing their appetite—fasting—during windstorms, and that pod of fish proved no different. Despite their reticence, one trout found my partner's lime green soft hackle fly too enticing.

*Brooke Wight working Lake Lenore for giant cutthroat trout
as the sun lights up the surrounding country.*

With the fly firmly imbedded in the corner of its mouth, the Lahontan took off for the Columbia River, changed her mind, dove back into the pod, scattering trout quicker than an osprey's shadow, then rolled on her side and slid into Jeff's net. She measured 25 inches and, with her belly full of eggs, weighed maybe 7 pounds—the best trout of Jeff's life. He was ecstatic, his eyes wide. It was a good sight to see.

Some purist flyfishers (and you will meet them at Lenore) frown at fishing for spawning trout, believing that it is unethical to disrupt natural processes.

To counter, Jeff and I decided that if trout are somewhat handicapped by their willingness to congregate and spawn, anglers have been handicapped even more by the wind and whitecaps. Such conditions are not ideal for a flyfisher, and we feel that taking fish under difficult conditions is the true appeal of angling. Biologists certainly agree.

"We considered closing the lake during spring," says Foster, "but we thought about the tremendous recreation we would deny sportsmen. The Lahontan cutthroat is a very hardy—a very tough fish. It takes a lot to hurt them and rarely does a fish die because an angler fought and released it. Therefore, we decided to leave the lake open for fishing during spring."

Remember, barbless artificial flies and lures are required at Lenore (no bait). It is catch-and-release only until June 1 when a one-fish-limit goes into effect. The lake closes November 30.

When Lake Lenore opens March 1, expect decent midge hatches—if the lake isn't covered in ice. During mild years, the ice may be off by the opener. If winter holds its grip on eastern Washington into March, the ice will delay fishing for a couple of weeks to a month.

When the ice comes off, flyfishers can do well casting Chironomid imitations into the shallows at the north and south ends of the lake, as well as most of the east shoreline. The west shore is composed of steep cliffs, and fishing options are virtually nonexistent unless you feel like rowing a boat or kicking a float tube to that far shore.

Typical Chironomid fishing consists of working a fly under a strike indicator. It's not the most exciting way to fish, but it's a tactic that does take fish, and it allows one hand to remain in a warm pocket while the other braves the elements.

When fishing Chironomids, try different patterns. The TDC (Thompson's Delectable Chironomid), Chan's Chironomid, Ross Chironomid, Swannundaze midges, brassies, basic Chironomid pupa with a grizzly hen hackle wing, disco midges, and palomino midges work well. Try them in a variety of sizes and colors. The standard size is a 16 or 18, and black, olive, and red are good colors.

When working these patterns, cast out as much line as you can, then let the fly sit and sink for 15 or 20 seconds. Watch your strike indicator for any movement. If you see it dive under the water, strike quickly.

An extremely slow retrieve works best when fishing Chironomids. Don't let the temptation to strip the pupa in overwhelm you. Cutthroat want it moving slowly. Believe me, they'll see it. Chironomid patterns are most effective when fished off of 5X tippets.

If you don't want to fish small flies, you don't have to. Cutthroat will eat woolly buggers, muddler minnows and zonkers every day of the year. Here's where a quick, active strip works well. You can work these patterns off of floating or sinking lines, depending on where the trout are cruising. Play around at different depths until you find the fish.

By late April and May, Lenore's cutthroat can be found in shallow water, cruising the banks, searching for a place to spawn. At that time, flyfishers congregate at the north end of the lake like flies. In fact, an angler may often be required to muscle his way in among other flyfishers, ducking backcast lines and ear-piercing flies, while earning a position at the popular north end. If an angler launches a boat or float tube, he must frequently turn his head swivel fashion to locate nearby craft. Encroaching backcasts are frequently encountered.

It doesn't have to be that way. Lenore is about 5 miles long, and much of the west shore remains unexplored during the spring spawn. Backcast room is endless on the west shore, and the whole area is excellent for float tubes and boats.

*Crowded spring conditions at Lake Lenore. Why not prowl
the east shore instead?*

The only factor that really throws the fishing off during spring is muddy water conditions. If that occurs, expect slow fishing and shy away from midge imitations. Stick with big, ugly, black woolly buggers.

After the spawn in June, Lenore's cutthroat are ready to put weight back on, and that means they'll be looking for minnows and larger aquatic insects, such as damselflies, Callibaetis mayflies, and dragonflies.

If damselfly nymphs are present, try a marabou damsel or Nyergess nymph. To match Callibaetis, offer a parachute Adams or gray sparkle dun on the surface. Underneath, try a gray hare's ear or pheasant tail nymph.

Fishing slows during the summer months when the surface temperature rises and big cutthroat dive for the bottom. Trout can still be taken when stripping streamers off of full-sink lines, but it's not the most productive fishing. Mornings and evenings are the times to hit the lake during July and August.

In September, the water temperature cools and fish move back into shallow water. At that time, streamers are your top option, but scuds, soft hackles, and Chironomids will also take fish.

*The author examines a typical Lake Lenore Lahontan cutthroat before release.*

Lenore is a favorite among Washington's trout bums because it offers really large fish. People arrive with the thought of taking a trout over 5 pounds, and when they hook a large trout, the last thing they want to do is lose it. However, some cutthroat die an early death because anglers play them gingerly. When fishing Lenore, bring a 5-, 6-, or 7-weight rod and try to work a fish quickly to net.

Although some anglers complain about Lake Lenore's crowded conditions, the masses can be avoided by fishing during the middle of the week and avoiding the lake's north end. In the realm of northwest trout angling, catching numerous 4-pound-plus fish is a tough option to find. It exists at Lenore, and you should give it a try—crowds or no crowds.

To reach Lake Lenore, follow Hwy 17 north past Soap Lake. Lake Lenore is visible on the left side of the highway.

# Lake Facts: Lake Lenore

### Seasons
• March 1 through November 30.

### Special Regulations
• Catch and release only from March 1 through May 31.
• One trout limit from June 1 through November 30.
• Selective gear rules apply.
• No internal combustion engines.
• Consult regulations booklet for closed water areas.

### Species
• Lahontan cutthroat trout to large size. Most fish run 3 or 4 pounds, but fish to 10 pounds or more are a possibility.

### Lake Characteristics
• Fishes best in March, April, May, and June. Action tails off in July and August but rebounds by September 15.
• Excellent midge emergences, plus damselfly and Callibaetis hatches.
• Streamers, such as woolly buggers, work well here, too.

### Access
• Easy access at north and south ends of the lake, plus several eastside pullouts off Hwy 17.
• Boats can be launched at the south end and on the east side.
• A float tube or boat helps anglers, but there is decent shore fishing located around the lake, excluding the west side, where massive cliffs drop into the lake.

## LAKE LENORE MAJOR HATCHES

| Insect | J | F | M | A | M | J | J | A | S | O | N | D | Flies |
|---|---|---|---|---|---|---|---|---|---|---|---|---|---|
| Chironomid |  |  | █ | █ | █ | █ | █ | █ | █ | █ | █ |  | Midge Emerger #14–18; Chan's Chironomid #12–16; Palomino Midge #14–18; Griffith's gnat #14–18; Disco Midge #14–18; Black Biot Midge #14–18; Thompson's Delectable Chironomid #14–18; Ross' Susperder Midge #12–18 |
| Streamers |  |  | █ | █ | █ | █ | █ | █ | █ | █ | █ |  | Zonker #2–6; Woolly Bugger #2–6; Woolhead Sculpin #4–6; Rubberleg Woolly Bugger #2–6 |
| Damselfly |  |  |  |  |  | █ | █ |  |  |  |  |  | Nyergess Nymph #4–10; Marabou Damsel #6–12; Six-pack #4–8; Braided Butt Damsel #2–6; Sheep Creek Special #6–10 |
| Callibaetis |  |  |  | █ | █ | █ |  | █ | █ |  |  |  | CB Cripple #14–18; Sparkle Dun #16–18; Parachute Adams #14–18; Hare's Ear Nymph #12–16; Spinner #14–18 |
| Caddis |  |  |  | █ | █ | █ | █ | █ | █ |  |  |  | Traveling Sedge #4–8; LaFontaine Emergent Sparkle Pupa #14–16; X-Caddis #12–16; Diving Caddis #12–16; Prince Nymph #12–16 |
| Scud |  |  |  |  |  |  |  | █ | █ | █ |  |  | Bighorn Scud #10–16 |
| Leeches |  |  | █ | █ | █ | █ | █ | █ | █ | █ | █ | █ | Canadian Mohair Leech #6–8; Kaufmann's Mini Leech #6–8; Marabou Leech #4–8 |

# GRIMES LAKE

With its basalt cliffs, giant Lahontan cutthroat trout and fertile, highly alkaline water, Grimes Lake differs little from Lake Lenore, Washington's big cutthroat draw that entices thousands of anglers to its banks.

However, Grimes hosts far fewer anglers than Lenore, and it just isn't talked about very much. That's fine for those of us who know what Grimes offers and are not afraid to stick an extra 100 miles (round trip) on our vehicles to pass on Lenore and fish Grimes.

I think it's those extra miles, plus no place to camp at Grimes, that deter most anglers from casting a fly there. First of all, if arriving via Ephrata, anglers must steer their vehicles right past Lake Lenore and Dry Falls Lake—two super enticing fisheries—to reach Grimes. And during that drive, especially when following Hwy 17 north toward Canada, Hwy 172 west toward Mansfield, then Mansfield Road south to the lake, it's easy to strike up a serious case of the "lonelies."

The country surrounding Grimes is relatively desolate, and it offers very few amenities, including gasoline and ammunition (you always feel like you might need it out there). For an angler who's used to the big cities in western Washington, or even those who venture over from Spokane, the wide-open spaces around Grimes can be a little disconcerting.

I think my affinity for Grimes Lake and the country surrounding it stems from my years spent in the Rocky Mountains, tooling around western Wyoming, central and eastern Idaho, and all of Montana with two Labradors in the back of my pickup truck, an assortment of fly rods, plus fly-tying material tucked behind the seat and a pair of musty waders pinched between the canopy lid and tailgate, drying out in the wind.

I really had no home, no place to be, and nobody wanting me back at a certain time in the evening, let alone any particular month. So when I visit Grimes and drive over those long, straight roads and pass through that open country, mountain peaks rising from the earth in the distance, I get that feeling of freedom. Of course, it doesn't hurt matters that Grimes is full of big Lahontan cutthroat that seem quite willing to swallow a variety of flies, most notably, Chironomid, Callibaetis, damselfly, and minnow patterns.

The first time I visited Grimes, I got a weird feeling when passing through Mansfield. Maybe it's that name itself, Mansfield. When it rolls off the tongue it makes me think of Manson. And we know the demented history behind that title.

It didn't help matters that the local schoolhouse or church (I didn't stop to ask questions) was engulfed in flames, burning itself into little piles of rubble. I pulled the truck over, snapped a photo and took off, thinking, "I don't believe I'll be visiting the local watering hole this evening."

Fortunately, the lake itself, located in a low swale out of sight of the road, was perfectly beautiful. The surrounding cliffs lit up in the late afternoon sun, Callibaetis mayflies sprinkled themselves on the water and, yes, a few big Lahontans swirled on the surface to devour them. Hot damn!

# Grimes Lake

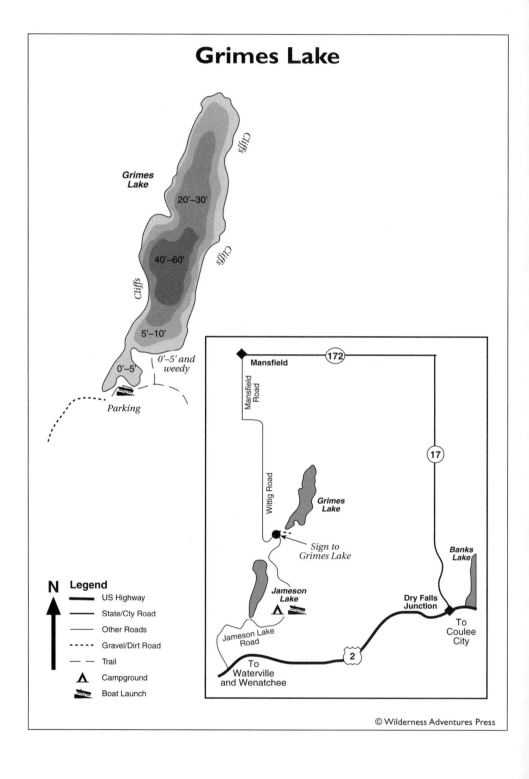

Grimes Lake

Cliffs

20'–30'

40'–60'

Cliffs

Cliffs

5'–10'

0'–5' and weedy

0'–5'

Parking

Mansfield

172

Mansfield Road

Wittig Road

Grimes Lake

Sign to Grimes Lake

17

Banks Lake

Jameson Lake

Jameson Lake Road

Dry Falls Junction

To Coulee City

2

To Waterville and Wenatchee

N

Legend
- ——— US Highway
- ——— State/Cty Road
- ——— Other Roads
- - - - - Gravel/Dirt Road
- — — Trail
- ▲ Campground
- ⛴ Boat Launch

© Wilderness Adventures Press

I launched my float tube, paddled monotonously through the shallows and started working a Callibaetis spinner over the water. Unfortunately, my offering was rejected. I quickly switched to (what else?) a brown woolly bugger and promptly hooked a heavy fish off the steep, rocky east shore, just outside the weedline. Several more fish followed that evening.

That's Grimes at its best: relatively deserted, a decent insect emergence coming off, the temperature (both air and water) relatively mild, and the fish willing to eat. When those events align themselves, Grimes could accurately be called Washington's best Lahontan cutthroat lake.

However, there are several problems with Grimes that severely limit flyfishing options. The lake doesn't open until June 1, and it closes August 31, just before the water temperature cools and fishing—if we could get at it—would become awesome.

That's OK. Feel fortunate that anglers get any kind of shot at Grimes—the lake is located on private land, and the landowner doesn't necessarily have to allow access.

When Grimes opens, expect plenty of company on this 180-acre lake. Some years, you might find 60 to 100 vehicles parked near the lake on opening day. Other years, perhaps 40 vehicles arrive. The rush to fish the lake stems from Grimes' short, three-month season. In fact, if you want to look at Grimes' productive time, it only extends from June 1 to July 1. July and August are typically a bust due to algae blooms and severe weed problems.

During a cold year, the lake may remain productive through mid-July, but that is the rare occasion. So, essentially, Grimes is worth fishing in June and that's it. In fact, during a hot year, the lake may be unproductive by mid-June. Fortunately, if you fish the lake on a weekday—you do have that option, don't you?—fishing pressure is light. And, because there are no areas of the lake that really concentrate fish, anglers spread out—it's not the north end of Lenore situation where anglers rub shoulders and cross lines with some regularity.

When you get down to it, Grimes is really worth fishing. It receives a plant of young 3- or 4-inch trout each year, and they grow to 12 or 14 inches in their first year. By the second year, they measure 18 or 19 inches long. By year three, they weigh 4 or 5 pounds and can really put a bend in a light fly rod. The largest fish in Grimes may weigh 7 or 8 pounds.

There's a good reason for the fast growth rate of Grimes' fish. There are dense aquatic insect populations in the lake, and the fish feed readily on them.

The most important insect is the Chironomid (also called midge). Grimes' cutthroat feed heavily on midge pupa as soon as the ice goes off the lake in March or April, and they continue to do so through the open fishing season. Summer mornings are particularly productive when fishing midge imitations. Most anglers fish a midge emerger or pupa just under the surface. A strike indicator is placed about 3 or 4 feet above the fly. Prime places to work these offerings are just off the weedbeds, where cruising fish are likely to spot them as they pass by.

When fishing midges, let them dead-drift or use an extremely slow retrieve. When the indicator goes under, set the hook, but not too hard. When fishing midges,

*Grimes Lake rests in a beautiful, placid setting and offers*
*large Lahontan cutthroat trout.*

a 5X tippet is required, and a big Lahontan can quickly bid adieu if you set the hook too hard.

Callibaetis mayflies also gain the attention of Grimes' cutthroat. Best hatches occur in April and May, before the season opens, but decent emergences and spinnerfalls occur in June. Callibaetis can be matched with basic patterns, such as a size 16 Adams, but specific patterns like a Callibaetis cripple draw more strikes. Those patterns should be fished off a 5X tippet.

Damselflies are also present at Grimes, and don't think for a second that cutthroat don't key on the big olive nymphs. During June, fish olive or drab brown nymph patterns off a sinktip or full-sink line and a 3- or 4-foot leader that tapers to 4X. If adult damsels are present around the lake's edge and you see fish rising violently for them, change to a floating line and a braided butt damsel, which floats on the surface. Strikes on these patterns can be jarring. And there's nothing better than seeing a 5-pound trout roll on a dry fly!

During summer evenings at Grimes, anglers may encounter a few caddisflies, their numbers growing as overall fishing conditions deteriorate in July and August. However, caddis do draw a cutthroat's attention, and an angler who sees fish working caddis should quickly tie on a size 14 or 16 LaFontaine sparkle emerger, an X-caddis or even a standard elk-hair caddis.

As with Lahontan cutthroat trout wherever they are found, Grimes' fish dig large nymphs and streamers. Standard mayfly patterns, such as a hare's ear nymph or pheasant tail nymph, work well. Leeches, woolly buggers, zonkers, and sculpin patterns draw strikes, too.

Whether fishing dry fly emergers, nymphs, or streamers, flyfishers are severely limited if they are stuck on the shore. For that reason, most anglers ply the lake by float tube or small boat—motors are not allowed. Prams and johnboats can be rented from Jameson Lake Resort.

Although Grimes offers a short season, it is well worth an angler's extra effort to get there. The lake's cutthroat are strong and eager to feed. The lake itself sits in a beautiful desert coulee where wildlife is abundant. For these reasons, I make at least one trip a year to Grimes, and it has always been worth the effort.

To reach Grimes, follow Hwy 17 north to its junction with Hwy 172. Turn west on 172 and follow it to Mansfield. Follow Mansfield Road south out of town toward Jameson Lake. A sign and a gravel road leading to Grimes can be found 8 miles down the road on the left. Follow the gravel road a short distance to the lake. Remember, no camping is allowed at Grimes or the surrounding area. There are campsites available at Jameson Lake Resort, but it will cost you.

# Lake Facts: Grimes Lake

### Seasons
- June 1 through August 30.

### Special Regulations
- One fish limit. No size restriction.
- Selective gear rules apply.

### Species
- Lahontan cutthroat trout to good size. Most fish go a couple pounds. A good one weighs 5 pounds or more.

### Lake Characteristics
- Excellent aquatic insect populations. Solid damselfly and Callibaetis emergences. Midges each day of the summer.

### Access
- A dirt road delivers anglers to the south end of the lake.
- A boat, canoe, or float tube is needed to adequately probe the lake.
- Boats can be rented from nearby Jameson Lake Resort.

## GRIMES LAKE MAJOR HATCHES

| Insect | J | F | M | A | M | J | J | A | S | O | N | D | Flies |
|---|---|---|---|---|---|---|---|---|---|---|---|---|---|
| Chironomid | | | ▓ | ▓ | ▓ | ▓ | ▓ | ▓ | ▓ | ▓ | ▓ | | Midge Emerger #14–18; Chan's Chironomid #12–16; Palomino Midge #14–18; Griffith's gnat #14–18; Disco Midge #14–18; Black Biot Midge #14–18; Thompson's Delectable Chironomid #14–18; Ross' Susperder Midge #12–18 |
| Streamers | | | | | | | | | | | | | Zonker #2–6; Woolly Bugger #2–6; Woolhead Sculpin #4–6; Rubberleg Woolly Bugger #2–6 |
| Damselfly | | | | | | ▓ | ▓ | | | | | | Nyergess Nymph #4–10; Marabou Damsel #6–12; Six-pack #4–8; Braided Butt Damsel #2–6; Sheep Creek Special #6–10 |
| Callibaetis | | | | | | ▓ | ▓ | ▓ | ▓ | | | | CB Cripple #14–18; Sparkle Dun #16–18; Parachute Adams #14–18; Hare's Ear Nymph #12–16; Spinner #14–18 |
| Caddis | | | | | ▓ | ▓ | | ▓ | ▓ | | | | Traveling Sedge #4–8; LaFontaine Emergent Sparkle Pupa #14–16; X-Caddis #12–16; Diving Caddis #12–16; Prince Nymph #12–16 |
| Scud | | | ▓ | ▓ | ▓ | ▓ | ▓ | ▓ | ▓ | ▓ | ▓ | | Bighorn Scud #10–16 |
| Leeches | | | ▓ | ▓ | ▓ | ▓ | ▓ | ▓ | ▓ | ▓ | ▓ | | Canadian Mohair Leech #6–8; Kaufmann's Mini Leech #6–8; Marabou Leech #4–8 |

*Note: The legal season for Grimes Lake is July 1–August 31.*

# Dry Falls Lake

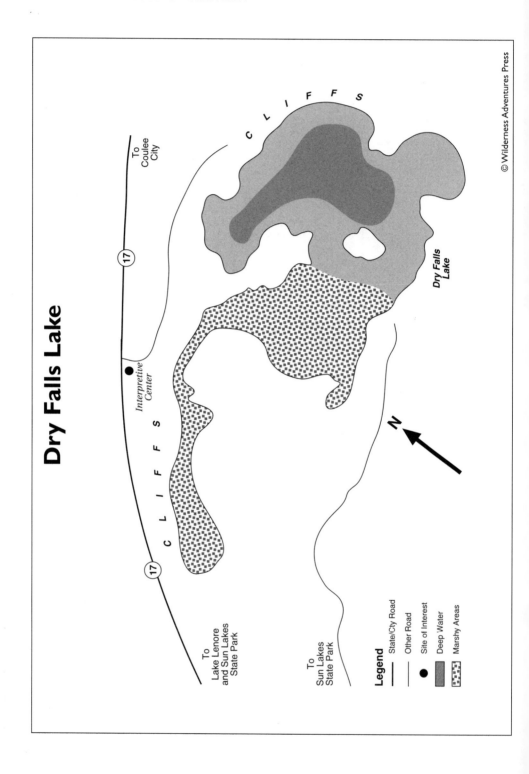

To Coulee City

To Lake Lenore and Sun Lakes State Park

Interpretive Center

C L I F F S

C L I F F S

Dry Falls Lake

To Sun Lakes State Park

N

**Legend**

| | State/Cty Road |
| | Other Road |
| ● | Site of Interest |
| | Deep Water |
| | Marshy Areas |

© Wilderness Adventures Press

# Dry Falls Lake

When fishing Dry Falls Lake, I always get the sensation that somebody is about to unload a 7mm deer-hunting rifle from the highway overlook.

That overlook is several hundred feet above the lake and at almost any hour of the day somebody is present, watching float tubes bob on the lake's surface. Unfortunately, we're perfect targets for psychopaths.

If PETA (People For the Ethical Treatment of Animals) ever goes ballistic, my days at Dry Falls may be over. That would be a shame—Dry Falls is the Columbia Basin's most popular flyfishery. And for good reason: The lake rests in a unique geological setting and offers some sizable brown and rainbow trout that can really bend a fly rod.

Maybe my fear of getting shot stems from reading the newspapers too much. Or maybe it's Tom Brokaw's frightening evening newscasts that fuel my fear. In any case, I usually fish Dry Falls early in the morning, before tourists and freaks are typically out of bed, or in the evening when my presence on the lake is shrouded in darkness. Fortunately, those two times of the day offer some of the best fishing Dry Falls has to offer.

Dry Falls, which is located just east of Hwy 17 and north of Soap Lake, is managed under special regulations. It's strictly artificial lures and flies only with a 1-fish limit. With that limit and its uncommon fertility, Dry Falls produces really nice fish.

According to Joe Foster, a biologist for Washington Department of Fish and Wildlife in Ephrata, the lake's rainbow and brown trout are stocked during spring when they are 3 or 4 inches long. By the following spring, they measure 11 to 14 inches. Two- and three-year-old fish run 15 to 19 inches long. There are a few fish in the lake that stretch 20 inches or more. However, the lake's rainbows rarely live past two or three years old, so they don't commonly reach gigantic size.

A Dry Falls brown trout lives slightly longer, and a good one goes 22 to 24 inches. Foster has caught browns to 22 inches, and he heard a report of a 26-incher. Whether that report is true or not is for you to find out. Go fish the lake hard at night and see what you come up with.

Rainbow trout vastly outnumber browns in Dry Falls, and that makes perfect sense since about 11,000 rainbows and just 2,000 browns are stocked into the lake each year.

Dry Falls opens for fishing the last Saturday in April and closes November 30. Early in the season, some of the best patterns to use, especially for brown trout, are minnow imitations. There is no doubt that a substantial number of rainbow and brown trout fry end up in the bellies of their larger brothers. Fished near the rock ledge dropoffs or in the shallow bays at night, patterns, such as woolly buggers, epoxy minnows, white zonkers, and sculpins, draw hearty takes.

"I'm sure the browns, especially, make use of the young rainbows we plant," Foster says. "In general, browns hold in deep water. But the best time to fish for them is at night when they get in the long, narrow bay that extends down the west side of the lake. During the day, the deep dropoffs near the island are good for browns. My best luck during the day has been with a damselfly nymph, size 10 or 12, on a long-shank hook. I fish damsels off a sinktip line with a 10- or 12-foot leader. I also place weight on the fly so it really sinks."

If you visit Dry Falls in May or June, you'll notice a bunch of swallow nests on the cliffs surrounding the lake, especially on the island cliffs. Whenever I fish Dry Falls at that time, I can't help but picture huge brown trout cruising under the cliffs, hammering every unfortunate swallow chick that falls from its nest. Casting a very large woolly bugger at that time makes good sense.

There are some flyfishers (you know who you are) who wouldn't tie a woolly bugger to the end of a line if it was the last fly in their box. And they wouldn't drop below a 5X tippet or spool a sinktip line to their reel if their spouse was held for ransom and they were required to do so for immediate release. I'm talking purists, and you'll meet them at Dry Falls. Fortunately for them and the rest of us who are more of the "what the hell, it works" persuasion, there are some excellent surface options at Dry Falls existing throughout the season.

The best insect emergences begin with the Callibaetis mayfly hatch in May and June. That hatch, which can be heavy at times, really brings fish to the top, and if an angler correctly matches the proper stage of the hatch, some healthy trout tallies can be garnered in a day. Twenty fish. Thirty fish. It happens at Dry Falls.

Anglers need to pay attention to the actual insect resting on the surface. What you will find is an emerging Callibaetis dun or a Callibaetis spinner.

Duns are easily identified by a trailing nymphal shuck. If they've successfully exited their shuck, they'll rest on the surface momentarily while their wings dry. They rate about a size 12 or 14 early in the season, but by August or September, they'll match a size 16 or 18 hook. Duns have two tails, and the body is gray or close to black. The body is light gray on the underside. Wings are opaque, tan, or brown, and they offer a distinct black mottling on the forward side of the wing.

Spinners closely resemble duns, but they can be identified by a specific trait: most land on the water and die, wings laid out to the side. Downwing patterns that match that trait are extremely effective. One thing to be careful of is identifying a spinner as a dun. Spinners can be found on the water with their wings upright. Just look for a lack of a trailing shuck and nearly clear wings with a slightly mottled section—that signifies spinner.

The standard Callibaetis dun and spinner patterns work well at Dry Falls, but remember, this is the Columbia Basin's most heavily fished fly water. These trout do get picky, and specific patterns draw more strikes. Don't dump your tube into Dry Falls without several of these patterns: Callibaetis cripple, Stalcup's CDC biot Callibaetis, and AK Best's Callibaetis spinner.

Damselflies are also a very important insect at Dry Falls, and trout chew them up like tiny gumballs. You can take rainbows and, possibly, a brown or two on adult damsel patterns worked along the edge of reeds and weedbeds. But a damsel nymph, fished off a sinktip or full-sink line, is the ticket. When the hatch is on and damsels can be found swimming through every available inch of water and dozens are crawl-

*A view of Dry Falls Lake from the highway overlook.*

ing out on your float tube to discard their nymphal shuck and sunbathe, some incredible fishing can be had.

Marabou damsels, six-packs, Nyergess nymphs, and even olive woolly buggers, all rating size 8 or 10, work well at Dry Falls. Fish these patterns off a sinktip or full-sink line with a short 4- or 5-foot leader that tapers to 5X.

Damsels are present at Dry Falls through summer, but the bulk of those flies hatch in May. On a calm May day at Dry Falls, with damsel nymphs swimming through the water and Callibaetis spinners dropping to the water like snowflakes, you may consider a change of zip code.

If you arrive at Dry Falls and find a lack of those insects, don't fret—Chironomids are almost always present, and a midge pupa or emerger can draw takes when nothing else works.

As with all of the Columbia Basin lakes, the preferred method to fish Chironomids is under a strike indicator, using a terrifically slow twist retrieve. It's not the most heart-wrenching type of fishing, but nobody can argue with the Chironomid's effectiveness.

One thing to keep in mind is the size of Dry Falls' Chironomids: they're large, up to three-quarters of an inch long, and they can be matched with inch-long midge imitations. A pattern that size is larger than the actual insect, but the trout don't mind. In fact, they seem to prefer the oversized fly to one that matches the true proportions of the insect.

*The author and a prime Dry Falls rainbow.*

As summer winds down and fall approaches, flyfishers may encounter tiny Trico mayflies on the surface each morning. Trout eagerly scarf on these little bugs, so you'll want to carry a couple size 20 or 22 black comparaduns or sparkle duns. A downwing Trico spinner is also a good pattern.

When Dry Falls' trout get on Tricos, they'll align themselves with a wind line where Tricos congregate, and they'll suck them down every couple feet. An angler simply needs to place a fly in the path of a trout and drawing a strike is likely.

Caddis are also present during fall, their numbers building as the afternoon turns to evening and shadows creep across the water. Standard patterns, such as an elk-hair caddis work fine, but size 14 and 16 sparkle emergers and X-caddis work best.

Mayfly nymphs, such as hare's ear or pheasant tail, always draw takes when the fish are not feeding off the surface. Gamerus scuds are also present in the lake in heavy numbers and it pays to tie one to the end of your leader when the surface activity slows. Fish scuds in the shallow bays.

Because shore access is poor, when fishing Dry Falls you'll want to bring a float tube, pontoon boat, or small aluminum skiff. Anglers can cover the entire lake in a float tube. However, if the wind comes up, which it does almost every day of the season, kicking back to your rig is no easy proposition.

Once you've fished Dry Falls, it will be easy to see why this is one of Washington's most popular fisheries. The area surrounding the lake, complete with lava flows and 400-foot basalt cliffs, is spectacular. The trout—really healthy, hard-fighting fish that can strip a lot of line, not to mention some backing, off your reel—are frosting on the cake.

One June morning I dumped my tube into the lake and was greeted with a moderate Callibaetis spinnerfall. I tied on a Stalcup's CDC biot Callibaetis comparadun and proceeded to slay. I caught a couple dozen fish before noon and had the lake to myself—not another boat or tube on the water, and no psychopaths firing rounds from the highway overlook. The wind was down, the lake's surface only disturbed by rising rainbows. One fish hauled ass across the lake and took me into my backing. Life, I quickly determined, was good. Later in the day, when the wind kicked up, I tossed my float tube in the truck, threw sticks for my Labradors, Moose and Shadow, until they tired, then packed up and headed out for a four-day stint at Chopaka. Driving out of the area through Dry Falls State Park I thought to myself, "Every flyfisher in the state owes himself a trip to this wonderful fishery."

Hey, that flyrod is right there in the closet, isn't it? The tube has air in it, doesn't it? You've got your license, don't you? You can grab ice, beverage, and Callibaetis patterns on your way out of town. The spouse will understand. That's why you married, right? The yard can wait. Giddy-up!

# Lake Facts: Dry Falls Lake

## Seasons
• Last Saturday in April through November 30.

## Special Regulations
• One trout limit. No size restriction.
• Selective gear rules apply.
• No internal combustion engines.

## Species
• Rainbow and brown trout that average 14 to 17 inches. Brown trout have been caught to 26 inches, mostly at night.

## Lake Characteristics
• Very fertile, Dry Falls offers excellent insect emergences.
• Callibaetis and damselfly hatches in late April, May, and June draw the most attention.
• Brown trout are commonly caught after dark on large streamers.

## Access
• Easy access to the lake, via Dry Falls State Park.
• A float tube or boat is needed to fish the lake, due to cliffs and extensive reeds that surround the shoreline.

## DRY FALLS LAKE MAJOR HATCHES

| Insect | J | F | M | A | M | J | J | A | S | O | N | D | Flies |
|---|---|---|---|---|---|---|---|---|---|---|---|---|---|
| Callibaetis | | | | | | | | █ | █ | | | | CB Spinner #14–18; CDC Biot Callibaetis #14–18; AK's CB Spinner #14–18; Hare's Ear #12–18; CB Cripple #14–16 |
| Damselfly | | | | | | | | | █ | | | | Nyergess Nymph #6–12; Six-pack #6–10; Burk's Olive Damsel #8–12; Braided Butt Damsel #4–10; Sheep Creek Special #6–10 |
| Streamers | | | | █ | █ | █ | █ | █ | █ | █ | █ | | Woolly Bugger #4–6; Zonker #2–4; Woolhead Sculpin #2–4 |
| Chironomids | | | | █ | █ | █ | █ | █ | █ | █ | █ | | Chan's Chironomid #12–16; Brassie #12–18; Palomino Midge #12–18; Midge Pupa #12–18; Griffith's Gnat #14–18; Biot Midge #14–18; Beadhead Serendipity #16–18; Gulper Special #14–18 |
| Scuds | | | | | | █ | █ | | | | | | Bighorn Scud #10–12; Epoxy Scud #8–14 |
| Leeches | | | | █ | █ | █ | █ | █ | █ | █ | █ | | Canadian Mohair Leech #6–8; Kaufmann's Mini Leech #6–8; Marabou Leech #4–8 |

# Dusty Lake

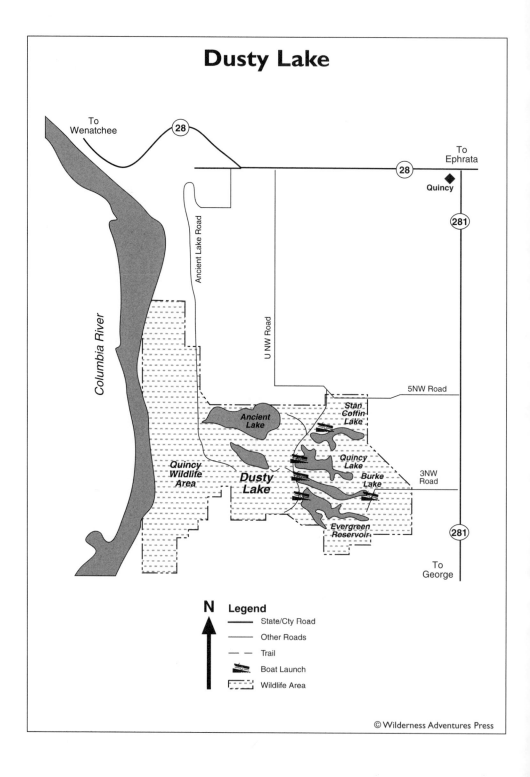

To Wenatchee

28

To Ephrata

28

Quincy

281

Ancient Lake Road

U NW Road

5NW Road

Columbia River

Stan Coffin Lake

Ancient Lake

Quincy Lake

Quincy Wildlife Area

Dusty Lake

Burke Lake

3NW Road

Evergreen Reservoir

281

To George

N

## Legend

—— State/Cty Road

—— Other Roads

– – Trail

Boat Launch

Wildlife Area

© Wilderness Adventures Press

# DUSTY LAKE

Here's a lake that many flyfishers drive past on their way to Washington's more noted trout fisheries, and that's a shame. Dusty Lake, which is located south of Quincy, offers some of the largest trout in the state.

Part of the reason this lake lacks appeal is its regulations. Unfortunately, it is managed under statewide rules, so it gets some serious bait-chucking pressure. Nevertheless, Dusty is worth hitting whether you encounter other types of anglers or not. The only thing that saves this lake is the fact that you have to hike a mile in on a closed road to reach it. The other option is to follow a trail for a half-mile past steep basalt cliffs to the lake.

According to Joe Foster, a regional biologist for Washington Department of Fish and Wildlife, there are no regulation changes planned for Dusty. Fortunately, there are still some fish to be had.

"Dusty is well worth the hike in for flyfishers," Foster says. "Even when the lake opens March 1, it's not really a zoo. You might find 20 or 30 people fishing from shore, but you can get away from them with a float tube. And it's remote enough that guys can't really haul in a boat. So it gets pressure on opening day, but after that it's not too bad."

Dusty follows the typical Columbia Basin insect emergence schedule: Chironomids from March through the July 31 closing date; Callibaetis in April, May, and June; damselflies and dragonflies in May and early June; caddis on warm summer evenings.

Dusty's trout are a mix of brown and rainbows, and they really grow large. A typical rainbow might stretch 17 inches. An average brown measures 15 to 20 inches. However, there are plenty of monster 5-pound browns and rainbows to catch and release.

Unlike many other Columbia Basin lakes, Dusty remains productive through its short season. Even in late July, the lake isn't too weedy or choked with algae to fish.

One good tactic in June and July is to fish streamers at night for big browns. Brown trout hide in the depths during the day, but they move into the shallows at night to wreak havoc on any unsuspecting baitfish. Weighted woolly buggers, zonkers, epoxy minnows, and sculpins, cast into the shallows and strip-retrieved, draw solid takes. When fishing at night with large patterns, go with a sinktip line and a 4- or 5-foot leader that tapers to 2X or 3X. No reason to lose a big fish after you've hooked it.

"Dusty isn't your typical Columbia Basin lake," Foster says. "The catch rate doesn't begin to compare with Dry Falls or Lenice or some of the other lakes, but the size of these fish in Dusty is impressive. It's really one of the best places in the state to fish for large trout. Because of the hike in, most guys take camping equipment and spend a day or two on the lake. That's a good idea because you can fish for brown trout at night."

When you fish Dusty, bring plenty of aquatic insect imitations, as well as streamer and leech patterns. Also bring some patience and understanding. You will be in close proximity to the fish-whacking hordes, but everybody needs a place to cast a line. With the proper mindset, Dusty is a treat to fish.

# Lake Facts: Dusty Lake

### Seasons
- March 1 through July 31.

### Special Regulations
- Statewide rules apply.

### Species
- Rainbow and brown trout to large size. Fish to 5 pounds or more are not uncommon.

### Lake Characteristics
- Open to general regulations, this lake draws spinfishers and baitchuckers. However, it is a fertile environment, and it does offer large fish—tradeoffs.

### Access
- To reach Dusty, anglers must hike in a mile on a closed road or via a steep trail for a half-mile.
- A float tube allows flyfishers to move away from spinfishers who mostly toss marshmallows and worms from the bank.

# POTHOLES RESERVOIR

Although less loved than the highly heralded salmonids, the largemouth bass is a prime flyfishing adversary, and fortunately for anglers, there are good numbers of sizable largemouths in many eastern Washington lakes.

Heading that list is Potholes Reservoir, where largemouth bass to 6, 7, even 8 pounds are possible. Most Potholes bass weigh a solid 1.5 to 3 pounds, and they seem quite fond of flies. For those who understand the reservoir, such as Skip Davis, who lives in Warden and has guided on the reservoir for 20 years, it's not uncommon to catch fish in the 5-pound range.

Prime bass fishing at Potholes Reservoir begins in mid-June and extends into October. Flyfishers catch bass prior to June, but it's not an easy proposition.

"The bass spawn during spring, when the water temperature reaches 65 to 75 degrees," Davis says. "That can occur any time between mid-April through June. Bass are active at that time, but flyfishing for them is difficult, because the fish are in the brush, and you have to drag a leech through that stuff off a sinking line. Tangles and snags galore."

In contrast, those same bass can be taken outside of brush on floating and sinking flies after the spawn. That's when Davis really likes to hit them hard with poppers.

"Right after the spawn, fish move to shallow water, and you can get them on Dahlberg divers, poppers, and leech patterns," Davis days. "At that time, they really feed heavy. I concentrate on the shallow flats, points, and dropoffs in several inches to 5 feet of water. You won't be able to see the bass, but they hear the noise from a popper, and they'll come to it."

Another sure bet is probing the entrance to "beaver huts," as Davis calls them. He estimates nearly 400 huts are sprinkled around Potholes Reservoir, and each holds bass when they are exposed to the water.

"The reservoir level can fluctuate as much as 18 feet each year, so beavers build a high water hut, a medium water hut, and a low water hut," Davis says. "The huts attract minnows, and the bass move right in. The best fishing near the huts occurs on overcast days. When the sun is off the water, bass come out of the huts, reeds, and undercut banks to feet. When you encounter that situation, you can really get them. On a good topwater day, you'll catch 6 to 10 nice fish. On an average day, you'll land 2 or 3 good bass."

If presented with a bright, hot summer day (the norm in eastern Washington), expect the best fishing to occur from 5:30AM to 11AM. Afternoons can be a bust. However, by September, you can sleep in until 7AM and expect active fish all day long.

An option during the dog days of summer is to fish at night with large, black poppers. At that time, even the reservoir's largest bass come out of hiding, searching for a meal that consists of anything that moves. They aren't picky when it's dark.

"At night you want to use a big, size 1 or 2 cork popper," Davis says. "The fish may see a dark popper's silhouette, but they are more likely to hear it. You can really catch some large fish doing that."

# Potholes Reservoir

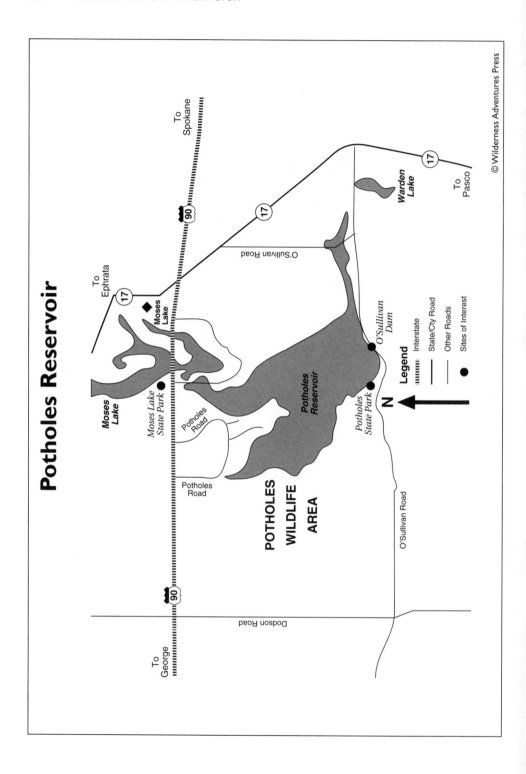

*Potholes Reservoir kicks out lots of largemouth bass to 5 pounds.
This fish, perhaps a 3-pounder, is an average fish.*

When fishing topwater patterns during the day, go with size 6 or 8 poppers. Davis likes to use a black popper on overcast days and a medium yellow, red, or white popper on clear, sunny days. If going subsurface with a Dahlberg diver, try a size 6 or 8, black or tan pattern. In a pinch, Davis goes with a black and yellow Dahlberg. If fishing leeches, which can produce nice catches of sizable largemouths, try a black or brown rabbit hair leech on a size 6 or 8 hook. Extend the tail so you offer a 3- or 4-inch creature. The bass will certainly notice it.

"When I fish poppers, I like to go with a couple short, quick strips, then a 4- or 5-second pause," Davis says. "The fish normally take when the popper stops and sits for just a moment. With the Dahlberg diver and leeches, I use longer strips and a short pause. Bass usually take the instant it starts moving again."

Whether fishing poppers, divers, or leeches, you'll want to bring a fairly hefty rod to the reservoir. Six-weight rods will work, but they are a little light. A better choice would be 7-, 8-, and even 9-weight rods—sizable sticks that allow an angler to cast large flies effortlessly, and they allow solid hook sets. Off a weight-forward or bass taper fly line, attach a 9- or 10-foot section of 10-pound test leader, which allows an angler to set the hook without fear of breaking a fish off. It also allows for confident retrieval of flies that hang in the brush and weeds.

While there really isn't a bad time to fish bass at Potholes Reservoir, there is a prime time that can't be beat for large fish. According to Davis, that time is during early fall.

"If I could only fish the reservoir for two weeks a year, I'd pick September 15 through October 1," he says. "At that time of the year, the water is cooling, and the fish are in really good shape. They probably average 2 or 3 pounds, and they feed hard because they can sense winter coming along. That's definitely the best time of the year to catch them on the surface."

Some of the best bass fishing at Potholes is located along the islands and sand dunes that dot the western half of the lake. To reach those areas, flyfishers need a boat, preferably one of those souped-up bass boats that you see on TV. If you don't have one, take a cartopper and a 15-horse outboard motor. You can kick a float tube to that section of the lake, but a heavy wind makes the return trip nearly impossible. Plus it's just a little dangers—water skiers and Ski-Doo enthusiasts hammer the reservoir during summer. Fortunately, they clear out after Labor Day. Boats and tubes can be launched at Mar Don Resort, Potholes State Park, and Medicare Beach.

One option for anglers limited to a float tube is to fish the Job Corps dikes. To reach them, exit Interstate 90 (when heading east) at the Conoco exit. At the stop sign, turn right (west) onto Frontage Road and follow for three-quarters of a mile. Look for some large power poles and a sign that says hunting and fishing access. Turn left onto a gravel road and follow it to a "T." At the "T," turn right and follow it to the dikes. Fish the south side of the dike—the north side is a bird sanctuary and is closed to angling.

"That area is excellent from July through September, and it gets no boat pressure," Davis says. "There are some deep pools that hold fish all year. You can use a sinktip line in the pools, but you'll want to have a floating line along, too. There are some shallow areas that can be covered with poppers."

While bass are the big draw at Potholes Reservoir, flyfishers may also hook large rainbow trout—up to 7 or 8 pounds—and walleye. Bluegill and crappie are also abundant and can be harvested for dinner, but return the bass to the water.

"There are lots of walleye, crappie, bluegill, and trout, so I don't mind when people keep those, but the bass are different," Davis says. "They get hammered on, and it doesn't take long to knock down a population. The only time I let people keep bass is when they catch one that is 6 pounds or more. Those fish aren't prime spawners, so they aren't missed."

To reach Potholes Reservoir, follow I-90 east from Seattle or west from Spokane to Moses Lake. Follow Hwy 17 south to its junction with Hwy 262. Turn west on 262 and follow to the reservoir.

# Lake Facts: Potholes Reservoir

## Seasons
- Open year-round.
- Statewide rules apply.

## Special Regulations
- No more than 25 crappie or bluegill in combination.

## Species
- Largemouth bass
- Crappie
- Bluegill
- Walleye
- Trout

## Lake Characteristics
- Bass fishing is the big draw here. Largemouth to 6 pounds or more are possible.
- Most anglers concentrate efforts from mid-June, as the water warms, through October.

## Access
- Easy boat launch access via Mar Don Resort, Potholes State Park, and Medicare Beach.
- To cover most of the water, a boat or float tube is need. A float tube is limiting and also dangerous when recreational boaters are on the water.
- Some walleye and trout can be taken from shore at the dam.

# Quail Lake

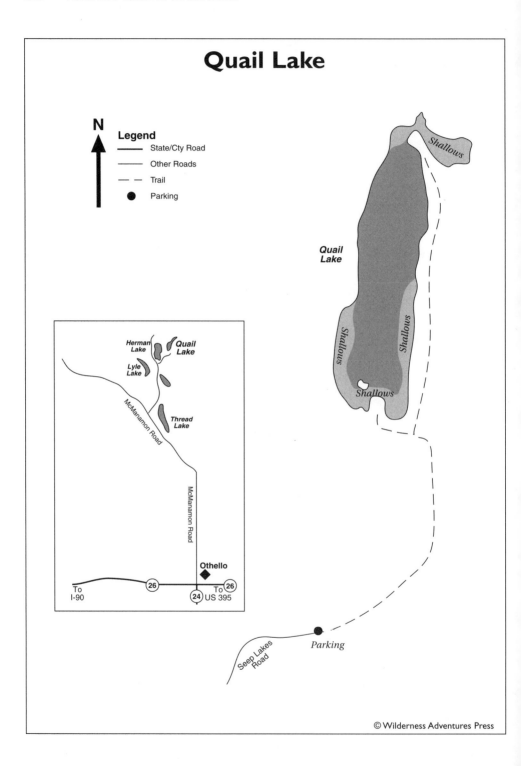

**Legend**
State/Cty Road
Other Roads
Trail
Parking

Quail Lake

Shallows
Shallows
Shallows
Shallows

Herman Lake
Quail Lake
Lyle Lake
McManamon Road
Thread Lake
McManamon Road
Othello
26
To I-90
24
26
To US 395

Parking
Seep Lakes Road

© Wilderness Adventures Press

# THE SEEP LAKES: QUAIL LAKE

We had only been in our float tubes for 15 minutes, and already I had misgivings about Quail Lake.

We hadn't touched a fish or even seen a trout in the water, let alone a simple rise ring on the surface, which would have been a clear indication that the lake hadn't been rotenoned (poisoned)! At the moment, the health of the lake was in serious doubt.

The lack of fish wasn't a huge surprise to me. The previous evening, while waiting for T.R. McCrystal to complete his winter drive north from Bend, Oregon, to Washington's Seep Lakes, I had wandered in the dark around the edge of the lake. The wind was absolutely dead, and the surface of Quail stood motionless—not a mark of breeze, which was good, if not entirely common. However, what caught my attention was a lack of rise rings, which I could have spotted a quarter-mile away. Not good. In fact, it made me wonder if Quail and these other Seep Lakes, including Herman, Teal, and Sage, had been fished out. Had Quail been poached to death by the locals? I shook my head, started for my truck and hoped the situation looked better in the morning.

That's when I realized it was awfully dark out in the desert, and the moon just wasn't coming up. My truck is black, and all of a sudden everything looked the same; black here, black there, black, black everywhere. I picked the best looking direction and started walking.

Somehow I managed to find my truck, and shortly after, T.R. arrived. Twelve hours later we were immersed in water, bobbing around in float tubes, searching for the elusive Quail Lake rainbow. That's when T.R. issued this statement: "Oh yea, there is a leak in these waders. And it's right in the crotch."

That wasn't good. Overnight the temperature had dropped 15 degrees, and now (the morning of February 21) the wind had Quail whipped into a sea of whitecaps. Waves broke over the back of our tubes, showering our jackets and wool caps with spray. Of course, this all would have been bearable had we found some trout. Unfortunately, we made two passes around the lake, using a variety of flies and probing different depths, without drawing a strike. Calling it quits, we sat at the edge of the lake through one large cigar each, giving the fish another chance to show themselves. But they never materialized. So much for Quail Lake and its big trout.

Quail Lake rests out in central Washington's sagebrush and basalt lava-flow desert north of Othello. It's part of the Columbia National Wildlife Refuge, which includes the Seep Lakes chain, formed when O'Sullivan Dam was built to create Potholes Reservoir. After completion, the water seeped up through the basalt, creating lots of new lakes. Since that time, all sorts of fish, including trout, have been planted into their waters.

Like many of the lakes—there are more than 70 of them—Quail is a shallow, fertile environment that grows trout quickly. Other lakes in the area also produce fast-growing trout along with a smattering of warmwater fishes, such as bass, crappie, bluegill, the nasty sunfish, and the dreaded walleye. Few, if any, of the lakes support self-sustaining trout populations, but that doesn't really matter—Washington Department of Fish and Wildlife stocks most of the lakes annually, and the bass and panfish get by on their own.

Most of the lakes are put-and-take venues that rarely provide fish over 12 inches. However, some of those trout survive their first season in the water—meaning they don't end up in the frying pan or in the garbage—and turn into 14- to 18-inch holdovers. Those fish that survive more than two or three seasons weigh 5 pounds or more and are a kick to catch. But that is the rare fish.

Quail is different: It's managed as a year-round fishery protected by catch-and-release, flyfishing-only regulations, so it offers better numbers of large trout.

While T.R. and I came up empty during our February excursion to Quail Lake, it can produce nice catches, including some large rainbow and brown trout at certain times of the year, mostly prominent after the water warms in March and April and insect hatches begin in earnest. Quail and the other Seep Lakes follow nearly identical hatch schedules. Information that you garner from Quail can be applied to any of the Seep Lakes.

Prime hatches begin in mid-March with the first heavy emergences of midges. Early in the season, meaning February, March and April, concentrate efforts near the shoreline. That's where photosynthesis takes place and aquatic plant life flourishes. Where there is aquatic plant life you'll find lots of aquatic insects. And where you find insects, you'll find fish.

Most anglers use midge patterns under a strike indicator, and that is a good choice at Quail. Attach a midge larvae or pupa, size 14, 16, or 18, under the indicator and retrieve it with a terribly slow line coil around your hand. Nine- to 12-foot leaders tapered to 4X or 5X should do the trick.

If you are going to test the deep water areas, spool a sinking line and tie on a leech or woolly bugger. Scuds, damsel nymphs, and Chironomid pupa can also be fished through the deep sections. Because Seep Lakes trout are lethargic in February, March, and April, you'll want to use a relatively slow strip retrieve no matter what pattern you offer.

When fishing the Seep Lakes, look for solid Callibaetis mayfly emergences and maybe even some Baetis and pale morning duns in late April, May, and June. Callibaetis emergences and spinnerfalls are equally important, so bring emerger, dun, and spinner patterns.

A stocked fly box should include Stalcup CDC biot Callibaetis comparaduns, gray sparkle duns, Callibaetis cripples, and downwing Callibaetis spinners. A selection of hare's ear and pheasant tail nymphs can be used when there is no visible hatch or spinnerfall on the water. All Callibaetis patterns should be fished off 5X tippet. If the trout seem picky, go to 6X.

Damselflies also catch the eye of Seep Lakes trout beginning in late May and extending into July. Damsel nymphs like the marabou damsel are the best offering when damsels are about, but a braided butt damsel, cast along the shoreline reeds, also draws hearty takes. Damsel nymphs can be fished off of 4X or 5X tippet. Damsel

*The Seep Lakes kick out some dandy holdover rainbows.*
*Here, the author hoists a 5-pounder.*

dries should be worked off of 4X tippet, which allows retrieval of your fly when it snags in the grass. If the fish are picky, go to 5X and count on losing some patterns to the weeds, not to mention a fly or two to large trout.

Scuds, dragonflies, leeches, and minnows are also prime trout prey in these desert lakes. Make sure that you bring a selection of flies to cover those food items. Size 6 and 8 brown, black, and olive leeches are particularly effective when fished off of sinktip and full-sink lines.

Quality fishing holds up at Quail and other nearby lakes into early July. After that point, extending into early September, the lakes warm up under a hot eastern Washington sun, and the fishing goes to hell. Fortunately, it perks up in September and remains productive through October.

At Quail, January and February, from my experience, can be rather difficult times, but I have friends who have caught some dandy trout from the lake then.

My favorite time to visit Quail and its surrounding waters is in late May and early June, when Callibaetis and damselflies are active and trout are trying their best to pack on weight after enduring the winter on tiny insects.

*T.R. McCrystal waiting out the blow at central Washington's Quail Lake.*

Many of the Seep Lakes are open year-round, but they get hammered by the bait and tackle crew. Others open March 1, and they, too, get hammered. If you don't mind hanging out with the other persuasion (i.e., those who prefer to eat rather than release trout), give some of the other lakes a try, such as Sage, Warden, and Widgeon.

Most of the easily accessible lakes have boat ramps and primitive campsites. Others, like Quail, require a short hike to reach. Those are the waters that fish best throughout the season.

Although most of the Seep Lakes can be fished from shore, a small boat or float tube offers anglers more access. In some areas, a lake can be almost impossible to reach, due to a pile of reeds and tules crouched up against shore. You can't get an aluminum or wood boat onto Quail Lake, but pontoon boats and float tubes work well there.

As mentioned, there are crude campgrounds at most of the lakes. Camping can also be found at Mar Don Resort. It offers a cafe, bar, groceries, and tent and RV sites. Potholes State Park is another option. It offers tent sites and about 60 RV sites.

To reach Quail Lake and the Seep Lakes chain, follow McManaman Road north out of Othello. Follow for nearly 5 miles to a public fishing access on the right side of the road. Follow that road about a mile to a sign for Quail and Herman Lakes. There is a parking lot at the south end of Herman. The trail to Quail begins there. Walk through the gate and head left, past the shoreline of Herman, to Quail. Note: the sign on the highway can be missed if you do not pay attention. Also, watch out for snakes and loads of ticks—they love my Labradors—during the warm months.

Note: you may want to contact Washington Department of Fish and Wildlife before visiting the Seep Lakes. All of the lakes endure a monotonous routine of feast and famine. Illegal introductions of sunfish and other warmwater species can destroy trout fishing for some time. After my trip to Quail Lake with T.R., I called a biologist and found out that sunfish had infiltrated the water and that the trout population, if not totally nonexistent, was very limited—maybe only a couple big toads in the entire lake. A simple phone call, as I found out the hard way, can save you from a fruitless trip. The Ephrata Fish and Wildlife office number is 509-754-4624.

# Lake Facts: The Seeps Lakes

## Seasons
- Many are open year-round.
- Other lakes open in late April.

## Special Regulations
- A few lakes are managed under special regulations, but standard statewide rules apply at most.
- Quail Lake offers flyfishing only. Strictly catch and release.
- Selective gear rules apply.

## Species
- Rainbow and brown trout
- Largemouth bass
- Crappie
- Bluegill
- Sunfish

## Lake Characteristics
- The Seep Lakes are small fertile waters that grow trout quickly.
- Holdover fish measure at least 16 inches long, and any fish that reaches its third year of life should weigh 4 pounds or more.
- Excellent insect hatches keep anglers busy. Look for Callibaetis, Baetis, pale morning dun, damselfly, and midge action.

## Access
- Most of the Seep Lakes offer boat launches; however, some require a short hike to reach.
- A float tube or small boat really helps anglers cover the water.

# SEEPS LAKES MAJOR HATCHES

| Insect | J | F | M | A | M | J | J | A | S | O | N | D | Flies |
|---|---|---|---|---|---|---|---|---|---|---|---|---|---|
| Chironomid | ■ | ■ | ■ | | | | | | | | | | Brassie #14–20; Chan's Chironomid #14–18; Gulper Special #14–18; Palomino Midge #16–18; Biot Midge #16–18; Suspender Midge #16–18 |
| Damselfly | | | | | ■ | ■ | ■ | | | | | | Nyergess Nymph #4–10; Six-pack #6–10; Marabou Damsel #6–10; Burk's Olive Damsel #6–10; Braided Butt Damsel #6–10 |
| Callibaetis | | | | | | ■ | ■ | ■ | ■ | | | | CB Spinner #14–18; CDC Biot Callibaetis #14–18; AK's CB Spinner #14–18; Hare's Ear #12–18; CB Cripple #14–16 |
| Scuds | ■ | ■ | ■ | ■ | ■ | ■ | ■ | ■ | ■ | ■ | ■ | ■ | Bighorn Scud #14–16 |
| Leeches | ■ | ■ | ■ | ■ | ■ | ■ | ■ | ■ | ■ | ■ | ■ | ■ | Canadian Mohair Leech #6–8; Kaufmann's Mini Leech #6–8; Marabou Leech #4–8 |
| Caddis | | | | | ■ | ■ | | | ■ | ■ | | | Traveling Sedge #4–8; LaFontaine Emergent Sparkle Pupa #14–16; X-Caddis #12–16; Diving Caddis #12–16; Prince Nymph #12–16 |

# Lake Lenice, Nunnally Lake, and Merry Lake

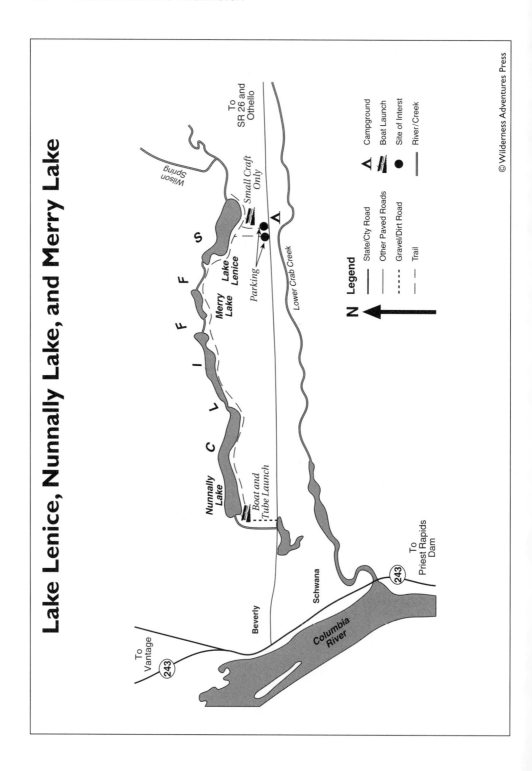

Legend

N

State/Cty Road
Other Paved Roads
Gravel/Dirt Road
Trail

△ Campground
Boat Launch
● Site of Interst
River/Creek

To Vantage
243
Beverly
Schwana
Columbia River
243
To Priest Rapids Dam

Nunnally Lake
Boat and Tube Launch
C L I F F S
Merry Lake
Lake Lenice
Parking
Small Craft Only
Lower Crab Creek
To SR 26 and Othello
Wilson Spring

© Wilderness Adventures Press

# LAKE LENICE

At first it was just a little itch, a nagging sensation on my left thigh. Ten minutes later, I was developing a problem, my fingernails scratching double-time, clawing at my leg, attempting to alleviate extreme discomfort.

I looked at Torrey Cenis, bobbing placidly in his float tube, casting diligently to a pod of rainbow trout, bare legs dangling down in the drink, and asked, "Hey, man, do you itch?"

He looked at me, reached between his legs and answered, "Yeah, kinda. And it's getting worse."

A few minutes later we were scratching wildly, kicking as hard as we could for the far shore, Torrey screaming, "Wait up, man, something's in the water, and it's eating the hell out of me."

I yelled to my dad, Fred, who was fishing from shore, "Get to the truck, quick. We're getting out of here. Hurry."

If dad hadn't had the truck keys in his vest, he would have been left in the dust, stuck at Lake Lenice to fish on his own.

There are worse places to be abandoned. Lake Lenice is a rainbow trout factory that supports many large fish in the 16- to 20-inch range. It rests out in the central Washington scabland, southeast of Vantage and east of Wanapum Dam, and it could easily entertain a dedicated flyfisher for a week or more if he chose to stay or was unceremoniously abandoned.

Lenice and its neighbors, Nunnally and Merry Lakes, were formed when irrigation water wound down Crab Creek Canyon and hatched an armada of tiny, shimmering blue jewels that stand out in stark contrast to the dry desert that surrounds them.

Shortly after filling, each lake sprouted plentiful weed growth, and a plethora of insects immediately called them home. Naturally, fishermen convinced Washington Department of Fish and Wildlife to dump hard-fighting Kamloops rainbows from British Columbia into the fertile lakes. It was every angler's hope that the fish might grow to immense proportions, as they do in B.C., and provide a trophy trout opportunity in Washington's desert.

At first they did just that. The fish grew rapidly to 5 pounds, with only a few anglers getting in on the act. But the Kamloops provided a short shelf life—two years—and never equaled the enormous size of their relatives across the border. Unfortunately, it was determined that the Columbia Basin was too warm for Kamloops trout. Anglers mourned.

Luckily for those fishermen and an armada of fly casters today, Fish and Wildlife released a hardy California strain of rainbow into Lenice, Nunnally, and Merry in the 1970s, and a prime flyfishing ground hatched. Those fish continue to entertain anglers today.

The trout are annually released in May as 2-inch fry and can grow to 14 inches by the following April on a gourmet menu of caddisflies, damselflies, midges, Callibaetis mayflies, minnows, and leeches. By their second year, rainbows range between 16 to

20 inches with a few larger specimens thrown in. As a very tempting bonus, Merry, Nunnally, and Lenice also host some hefty brown trout that prowl the depths, keeping anglers honest about knots and tippet strength.

While there is no bad time to visit Lenice or its neighboring lakes, which all open March 1 and close November 30, the best fishing at Lenice is tied to insect hatches. Of those hatches, there is no better offering than the damselfly emergence, which extends from late May through late July. Merry and Nunnally Lakes follow identical emergence schedules.

Imagine, if you will, a cheap Tokyo horror flick with a wave of Japanese soldiers marching in unison, taking on Godzilla. Lenice's damsels resemble those soldiers in sheer numbers. And whatever the reason—mythic monster threatening them or just the urge to head ashore and reproduce—they move from dense weedbeds to shore by the hundreds of thousands. That migration is an amazing event. Whether you are a serious entomologist or just a weekend observer, you'll find the damsel movement on par with Africa's wildebeest migration and Alaska's caribou crossing.

What most fascinates flyfishers about the damsel movement is a rainbow trout's propensity to smash every one of those insects that it encounters. It's as though the fish hold a personal vendetta against the insects. Or, more likely, they just like the taste of damsels, much like my regard for microbrews and cheese.

Whatever the reason, anglers are eager to take advantage of the gluttony, and it's during that time that 30- and even 40-fish days are possible.

According to Bob Archer, who works at Gary's Fly Shop in Yakima and frequently fishes Lenice, the damselfly emergence is the one insect offering that he would try to catch if he could only fish Lenice one week during the year. That won't be a surprise to those lucky anglers who've also enjoyed Lenice's damsel hatch—once you hit it, you'll want to return every year.

"The damsels are definitely the best hatch," Archer says. "If you are squeamish about bugs, you don't even want to get close to the water. They'll crawl all over your waders and float tube. At that time, you can spot lots of fish cruising across the shallow flats areas. Then you've got to get out in front of them with a fly - it's a classic sight-fishing scenario, and I love it.

"I'd say 90 percent of the guys out here fish underneath the surface during damsels, but you can get them on top," Archer adds. "A braided butt damsel will work, and it's pretty exciting to see a large trout come up to the surface to smack one of those things."

During the damselfly emergence, there really is not a bad place to fish. Damsels are spread throughout the water, and naturally the fish are dispersed, too. However, if you were to judge the prime fishing area by the concentration of float tubes, you'd think the fish were restricted to a small portion of the lake—most anglers congregate in the east half. Often 30 or more dot the surface of Lenice, most hovering over some cool springs that are hidden in deep water.

With so many flyfishers congregated in one area, invariably, tangled lines occur. But arguments are rare—the fishing fraternity at Lenice is pleasant and cooperative,

*Lake Lenice is one of Washington's premier trout lakes. Here, Brooke Wight puts the hurt on a large rainbow.*

with many anglers venturing up from Oregon or over from western Washington. It's an atmosphere where most people are landing their share of fish, and for those who are not, advice and a few free flies are not hard to come by. Just don't push your luck —don't troll a fly through a group of float-tubers and don't cast over people's lines. If somebody hooks a fish, get your fly out of the water and allow him to land the fish. Watch the show, offer some encouragement. Snap a photo if they request. Just use common courtesy.

A typical summer day at Lenice begins with a Chironomid hatch at or before daylight. When you stop on a ledge above the lake, you'll see rising fish everywhere. At that time, size 18 and 20 adult and emergent midge imitations work well.

You'll want to stick with midge patterns until the sun reaches above the surrounding hills to cast its glare and, most importantly, its warmth over the water. When it does, damsels become active, and fish switch from small midges to the damsel smorgasbord.

Try working nymphs to start with. Nyergess nymphs, marabou damsel nymphs, and six-pack nymphs are effective offerings. Try these patterns at a variety of depths until you find the thermocline where trout are concentrated. Using a countdown method is your most effective method to locate the "sweet spot."

During damsels, David Ashmore, a dedicated flyfisher who worked at the Avid Angler fly shop with me in the late 1980s and introduced me to Lenice, prefers to fish a high density line that takes a fly to the bottom quickly and keeps it there on the retrieve. Most anglers prefer to paddle back and forth in a small section of the lake, essentially trolling a fly, but Ashmore covers the entire lake using the countdown method to keep a fly just above the weeds. With most of the line off the reel, Ashmore retrieves in short, quick, even strips with an occasional 2- or 3-second pause. Once, I witnessed Ashmore land 10 beautiful rainbows on ten successive casts when a nearby angler (yours truly) caught one fish. Since that day, I've used Ashmore's tactics, and I, too, have landed lots of fish. My best day brought 32 rainbows to net. A large tally should not be expected when fishing Lenice, but it can occasionally occur.

Another weapon of Ashmore's is the Nyergess nymph. As mentioned, many nymph patterns work well at Lenice, but nothing works like the Nyergess.

Gil Nyergess of Bothell, Washington, developed the Nyergess nymph, and he specifically designed it to imitate scuds. But that doesn't seem to bother the damsel-chomping fish in Lenice. The Nyergess is tied with brown-palmered hackle over a dark olive, chenille body. The top and side hackles are cut off. Only the underside hackle remains. The Nyergess is both an effective pattern and very easy to tie.

The Nyergess works best in deep water, but it also draws strikes in shallow areas where fish are visibly cruising along the bottom.

In the shallows, most of the trout will sit tight-bellied against the bottom, refusing to take any fly, even if it brushes up against their nose. An angler must determine which fish are feeding and then place a fly at the proper depth and slightly ahead of a trout.

Any fish that is swimming—not just lying on the bottom—is probably feeding. To make sure, look for the white interior of the mouth. If you see it, the fish is sucking something down. Most often it will be a damsel nymph. If a trout suddenly rises in spectacular fashion it is probably taking a blue damsel off the surface.

If dry-fly action is your game, you can visit the shoreline areas and cast braided butt damsels into the shallows.

Blue damsels on the wing will concentrate near the green marsh grass and cattails that adorn much of the lake's edge. That's where you'll find the fish, too. In fact, an angler may lose his breath the first time he sets eyes on 40 or 50 big rainbows sitting over cool spring vents in the shallows— all within a short cast. The vents are located in a few spots around the lake, including the eastern end where I like to cast dries.

Lenice's damsel hatch peaks in late June and tapers off in late July. If you can't visit Lenice during that time, don't fret—the lake offers many productive hatches throughout the year.

From March 1, when the lake opens, through late April, Chironomids are the main food for trout. Their importance peaks again in October and remains until

*Here, the author releases one of Lenice's large rainbows.*

closing day, November 31. Miniscule midge patterns, such as size 16, 18, and 20 brassies, palomino midges, blood midges, serendipities, and Swannundaze midges, all draw strikes. These patterns are fished off long, 10- to 20-foot leaders with tippets down to 6X. Split shot or Twist-Ons can be added to the leader to achieve various depths. Fishing the midge hatches can be productive, but it is awfully monotonous.

Typically, when fishing midges, an angler casts his floating fly line, then slowly retrieves the fly by coiling line around his hand. Or he casts a line and lets a midge pupa sit under the surface below a strike indicator. That type of fishing reminds me too much of my youth and bores me to death. Fortunately, during the early season, there are options that do not require so much patience.

Lenice, Nunnally, and Merry all harbor good numbers of minnows and leeches. Anglers can cast streamer patterns, such as woolly buggers, zonkers, muddler minnows, mohair leeches, marabou leeches, and rabbit-strip leeches, to the banks and strip-retrieve them back to their float tubes. Strikes can be jarring and some of the largest fish—rainbows to 4 pounds, browns to 6 pounds—are landed in that fashion.

To enhance your chance for big browns, night fishing is a must. But even at night do not expect to fish alone. Often a dozen or more anglers will fish the dark hours, all gathered in a midnight ritual that may or may not produce a huge brown but will certainly provide an exciting diversion from the norm.

*Brooke Wight fights a big Lake Lenice rainbow
as a summer thunderhead passes by.*

Joe Foster, a regional biologist for Washington Department of Fish and Wildlife in Ephrata, says, "The biggest browns may go over 24 inches, but they are hard to catch. They'll feed mostly on insects, but I'm sure they hit the rainbow fry in the spring as well. I personally can't catch the things, and it would be like winning the Lotto if I did, but I know some guys who get them."

Especially in the spring, big ugly patterns like woolly buggers and zonkers are the best bet for browns. They are most effective at night and just after rainbow fry appetizers are released in May. The same countdown-strip method that Ashmore uses on rainbows during daylight will work for browns at night. But your best bet may be to throw minnow imitations into the shallows and strip them over dropoffs—truly heart-wrenching action in the moonglow.

In June, Lenice sees its first hatches of Callibaetis mayflies, an insect that draws the lake's rainbows to the surface. According to Archer, Callibaetis are present from June through mid-September, and they offer some of the best dry-fly fishing opportunities.

"The Callibaetis range from size 14 to 18, and they really bring fish up top," he says. "There are a lot of dry-fly patterns that will match Callibaetis, but I like Callibaetis cripple and sparkle duns. A parachute Adams will also work, as will Callibaetis nymphs. If you are going to fish dry flies and emergers, go with a leader that is no less than 10 feet long that tapers down to 6X or 7X. The lake has some heavy moss, so holding a fish on light tippet can be difficult, but that's the tradeoff."

Callibaetis can be found on the surface any time during the day, but they are most active between 11AM and 5PM. As the Callibaetis hatch quiets down, keep an eye out for the caddis emergence, which can provide some fast action in the late afternoon and evening hours.

"The hatches are sporadic through summer, but you can usually count on them in the evenings through July and August," Archer says. "You'll see most of the action close to the banks. I like to fish a size 16 or 18 LaFontaine sparkle emerger or a caddis pupa, and they seem especially good around dusk on evenings that have a full moon.

"The fish work in really shallow water, like 6 inches deep, and at times they really go crazy," Archer says. "Sometimes you'll think they are going to jump right in the tube with you."

Out in the desert, a trout is not the only thing that might crawl into your lap.

In fact, despite the prime fishing, visiting the desert and dealing with its attributes is not always so rosy. Out in the desert, wind, dust, and heat are the order of the day. And the dust may be the worst of the three.

The heat may make you thirsty, the wind may blow you off the water, but the dust will parch your mouth and throat, burn your lungs, and sting the hell out of your eyes. When you pass a truck on that dusty, dirt road leading into Lenice, you will die of dust poisoning if you don't roll up the window. It always pays to keep a few or more cold beverages on ice in the cooler behind the seat—an insurance policy in case your reactions are slow or your accomplice is snoozing in the passenger seat when a hay truck barrels by. But an angler's greatest worry in the desert comes in the form of venomous creatures.

Torrey Cenis, my father Fred, and I pulled into the parking area near Lenice one July evening, planning to hit the lake early in the morning. As I sat in the back of the pickup tying some god-awful-looking six-packs, Dad and Torrey worked on setting up a tent.

That task was even more difficult in the light of a half-moon and after two pitchers of brew in Ellensburg, followed by three cans for Torrey and me while gaining energy for our projects. Dad was dismayed—shocked—to see his son and his son's good friend shotgunning beers and war-whooping out into the night. But out there in the sage and dust, Torrey and Dad worked diligently on the tent until one of those venomous creatures interrupted the act.

"My God," cried Cenis. "You didn't tell me there's scorpions out here. Look at that sucker."

So I did.

Standing poised at the entrance of the tent, a two-inch scorpion with a nasty stinger held us at bay. Dad, having tasted less beer than Cenis and I and wanting to show the young bucks how it's done, deftly scooted the scorpion out of the way with a brush of his foot. Cenis and I zipped the front flap of our fortress and headed back to the truck for a shot of something strong—more to fight off the barrage of taunts flung our way by my father than to deal with the inevitable—spending a night with a pile of blood-thirsty scorpions. Torrey asked if a scorpion pattern might work in the morning! The back of the truck, where Dad planned to sleep, was worth a pocketful of gold.

Even when on the lake, an angler should not feel entirely safe. One angler told me she watched a big rattler slither across Lenice's surface, (thankfully) gliding just past her float tube. On other occasions rattlesnakes and bullsnakes are sighted on the quarter-mile, walk-in-only path to the lake. However, if you can reach the lake unscathed, you'll quickly dismiss unpleasant thoughts. Lenice, especially, is a treat to fish.

One late May afternoon, I visited Lenice and watched the surroundings fade into evening. Out in front, 200 rising trout rings rippled the surface. Rainbows practically frothed the water in a twilight feeding frenzy under a growing moon. Blue damsels and caddis hovered enticingly—precariously—over the water as large trout darted up out of long swaying shards of weed growth to inhale them greedily.

Overhead, bats flashed through the dusky sky as the sun set behind a coarse, volcanic ridge above the Columbia River. I continued casting to dreamy rainbows. The nocturnal desert creatures arose to start their search for food. Coyotes serenaded my angling addiction.

After dark I stripped a brown woolly bugger over a dropoff and then held on tight as a fish picked off the fly, headed into a deep channel, and took off for the Columbia River—no doubt a brown. When the leader snapped, I reeled in a few yards of backing and the sinktip line. I popped open a beer to settle my nerves and listened to the night sounds.

Two casts later another fish picked off the bugger, charged into submerged weeds (a frequent ploy), and broke me off. I was fully pissed off, and another brew was in order.

Later I cast to a swirl in the shallows. A surge of water came up behind the fly, turned into shimmering white against the moonlight, and revealed itself as a 17-inch brown, cartwheeling in the shallows. High intensity fishing for those willing to brave the elements. However, night fishing isn't always a sure thing. I've spent several frustrating nights plying the water diligently, only to come up empty-handed. I don't know why a skunking occasionally happens, but for whatever reason, the occasional goose egg should not be too disconcerting.

What could ruin your visit is the dreaded itch that pushed Torrey and me off the water as though we had outboards attached to our float tubes.

Swimmer's itch, an infestation of tiny parasites that burrow under the skin, is common on many waters in Washington and should be considered each time you decide to fish a lake without waders. Typically, swimmer's itch is most prevalent during late summer when lake temperatures are highest. As Torrey and I found out, the itch is maddening—if a pistol had been in the glove box of the truck, my father might have found two empty shell casings and two corpses when he arrived to drive Torrey and me to the nearest store—we needed itch cream in the worst way.

As bad as I itched, I could only laugh at Torrey's plight. My itch ended where the elastic band on my briefs cut off those blasted parasite's access to my crotch. Torrey, underwearless on the water, was feeling a harsher bite.

*Brooke Wight releasing a large rainbow. Lenice's rainbows average 14 inches, but there are plenty of fish, such as this one, that stretch 17 inches or more.*

As long as you can avoid venomous creatures and that unbelievable itch, Lenice is a great place to fish, whether you nail 20 rainbows in a day or just manage to catch a few. The lake offers challenges for beginners and experts, whether casting from a tube, small boat, or shore, and the fish put up a good fight even during the heat of summer. And maybe most appealing, Lenice is dependable.

In the realm of northwest angling, Lenice ranks right up there with other destination fly waters. The beautiful rainbows and chunky browns may not be as large as those in waters like Klamath Lake in Oregon or Clark Canyon Reservoir in Montana, but for consistent numbers, Lenice reigns supreme.

Note: In 1999 or 2000, Lenice is scheduled to be chemically treated to remove an unwanted population of sunfish. Generally, after being treated, a fertile lake like Lenice will recover within two seasons. Check with your local fly shop or call Washington Department of Fish and Wildlife before visiting.

# Lake Facts:
# Lake Lenice, Nunnally Lake, Merry Lake

## Seasons
- March 1 to October 31.

## Special Regulations
- One fish a day, no minimum size limit.
- Selective gear rules apply.
- Outlet of Nunnally Lake closed.

## Species
- Rainbow and brown trout to 20-plus inches. Most fish average 14 to 17 inches.

## Lake Characteristics
- Fertile water and extensive vegetation growth facilitates massive aquatic insect populations.
- These lakes offer terrific nymph, streamer, and dry-fly options.
- They fish best in late spring and early summer and again during fall.

## Access
- These lakes provide easy hike-in access off Beverly/Crab Creek Road.
- There is some shore access offered to wade fishers, but each lake is best fished from a float tube or small pram.
- If you opt for a pram, you will need to roll it in on wheels to Lenice.

# LENICE, NUNNALLY, AND MERRY LAKES MAJOR HATCHES

| Insect | J | F | M | A | M | J | J | A | S | O | N | D | Flies |
|---|---|---|---|---|---|---|---|---|---|---|---|---|---|
| Damselfly | | | | | | ■ | ■ | | | | | | Nyergess Nymph #4–10; Bark's Olive Damsel #6–10; Six-pack #6–10; Braided Butt Damsel #4–6; Olive Marabou Damsel #6–8; Sheep Creek Special #6–10 |
| Chironomid | | | ■ | ■ | ■ | ■ | ■ | ■ | ■ | ■ | | | Chan's Chironomid #14–18; Palomino Midge #14–18; Brassie #16–18; Griffith's Gnat #16–18; Midge Emerger #14–20; Serendipity #16–20 |
| Streamers | | | ■ | ■ | ■ | ■ | ■ | ■ | ■ | ■ | | | Woolly Bugger #4–8; Woolhead Sculpin #16–18; Egg-sucking Leeches #4–8 |
| Callibaetis | | | | | ■ | ■ | ■ | ■ | | | | | CB Cripple #14–18; Sparkle Dun #16–18; Parachute Adams #14–18; Hare's Ear Nymph #12–16; Spinner #14–18 |
| Scuds | | | ■ | ■ | ■ | ■ | ■ | ■ | ■ | | | | Bighorn Scud #14 & 16 |
| Leeches | | | ■ | ■ | ■ | ■ | ■ | ■ | ■ | ■ | | | Canadian Mohair Leech #6–8; Kaufmann's Mini Leech #6–8; Marabou Leech #4–8 |
| Caddis | | | | | ■ | ■ | | | | ■ | | | Traveling Sedge #14–18; LaFontaine Emergent Sparkle Pupa #14–16; X-Caddis #12–16; Diving Caddis #12–16; Prince Nymph #12–16 |

*Note: The legal season for Lake Lenice and Nunnally and Merry Lakes is  March 1–October 31.*

# COLUMBIA BASIN HUB CITIES*
# Moses Lake
### Elevation–1,046 • Population–13,320 (26,000 within 5-mile radius)

## ACCOMMODATIONS
**Best Western Hallmark Inn,** 3000 West Marina Drive / 509-765-9211 / Cable TV, pool, kitchen, sauna
**Holiday Inn,** 1745 East Kittleson / 509-766-2000 / Cable TV, pool, kitchen, sauna
**Motel 6,** 2822 West Wapato / 509-766-0250 / Cable TV pool, sauna

## CAMPGROUNDS AND RV PARKS
**MarDon Resort,** 8198 Highway 262 East / 509-346-2651 / RV sites, tent sites, laundry, store, shower
**Potholes State Park,** 7037 State Road 262 / 509-346-9491 / RV sites, tent sites, laundry, shower
**Big Sun Resort,** 2300 West Marina / 509-765-8294 / 50 RV sites, hot showers, tent sites, boat launch, laundry
**Willows Trailer Village,** 1347 Road M Southeast / 509-765-7531 / RV sites, laundry, showers, full hook-ups

## RESTAURANTS
**Bob's Cafe at the Inn,** 1807 East Kittleson Road / 509-765-3211 / Breakfast, beer and wine, cocktails, orders to go, open 24 hours
**Golden Corral Steak House,** 930 Stratford Road / 509-765-0565 / Breakfast, lunch, dinner, orders to go
**El Abuelo Restaurant,** 1075 West Broadway Avenue / 509-765-0606
**Hallmark Inn,** 3000 West Marina Drive / 509-765-9211
**Michaels on the Lake,** 910 West Broadway Avenue / 509-765-1611
**Porter House Restaurant and Lounge,** 217 North Elder Street / 509-766-0308

## FLY SHOPS AND SPORTING GOODS
**McCoy Tackle Co.,** 3190 Bell Road Northeast / 509-766-6388
**K-mart,** 1020 North Stratford Road / 509-766-0120
**Wal-mart,** 1005 North Stratford Road / 509-765-8979

## AUTO REPAIR
**D&W Auto Repair,** 805 South Broadway Avenue / 509-488-9580 / Engine overhaul, brakes, tune-ups, transmission and clutch repair
**Mike Bauer Auto Service,** 3700 Broadway / 509-766-1868
**McFarland's Repair,** 3102 Bell Road Northeast / 509-765-6198

* See also Richland and Kennewick in the Eastern Washington Rivers section.

## AUTO RENTAL

**Budget Rent-A-Car,** 7610 Andrews Street Northeast (Grant County Airport) /
509-762-6116

**Practical Rent-A-Car,** 6389 Patton Boulevard Northeast / 509-762-2488

## AIR SERVICE

**Grant County Airport** / 509-762-5363

## MEDICAL

**Samaritan Hospital,** 801 Wheeler Road / 509-765-5606

## FOR MORE INFORMATION

Moses Lake Area Chamber of Commerce
324 South Pioneer Way
Moses Lake, WA 98837
509-765-7888

# Ephrata
### Elevation–1,275 • Population–6,000

## ACCOMMODATIONS
**Columbia Motel,** 1257 Basin Street Southwest / 509-754-5226
**Hi U Motel,** 732 Basin Street Northwest / 509-754-3602
**Lariat Motel,** 1639 Basin Street Southwest / 509-754-2437
**Sharlyn Motel,** 848 Basin Street Southwest / 509-754-3575
**Travelodge,** 31 Basin Street Southwest / 509-754-4651

## CAMPGROUNDS AND RV PARKS
**Oasis Resort & Golf,** 2541 Basin Street Southwest / 509-754-5102
**Stars & Stripes RV Park,** 5707 Hwy 28 West / 509-787-1062

## RESTAURANTS
**Bamboo Shoot,** 263 Basin Street Northwest / 509-754-5539
**The Country Deli,** 245 Basin Street Northwest / 509-754-3143
**Inca Mexican Restaurant,** 514 Basin Street Northwest / 509-754-0813
**Lee's Landmark Number Two,** 130 1st Avenue Northwest / 509-754-2808
**Time Out,** 1095 Basin Street Southwest / 509-754-1111

## VETERINARIANS
**Animal Tracks Veterinary Clinic,** 1529 Basin Street Southwest / 509-754-3282
**Ephrata Veterinary Clinic,** 2129 Basin Street Southwest / 509-754-3128

## FLY SHOPS AND SPORTING GOODS
**K-mart,** 1020 North Stratford Road (Moses Lake) / 509-766-0120

## AUTO REPAIR
**D & B Automotive,** 1884 Basin Street Southwest / 509-754-5120
**Ephrata Auto & RV Repair,** 1224 Basin Street Southwest / 509-754-4201
**Rocky's Auto Clinic,** 858 Basin Street Southwest / 509-754-4902

## MEDICAL
**Columbia Basin Hospital,** 200 Southeast Boulevard / 509-754-4631

## FOR MORE INFORMATION
Ephrata Chamber of Commerce
90 Alder Street Northwest
Ephrata, WA 98823
509-754-4656

# Northern Washington Lakes

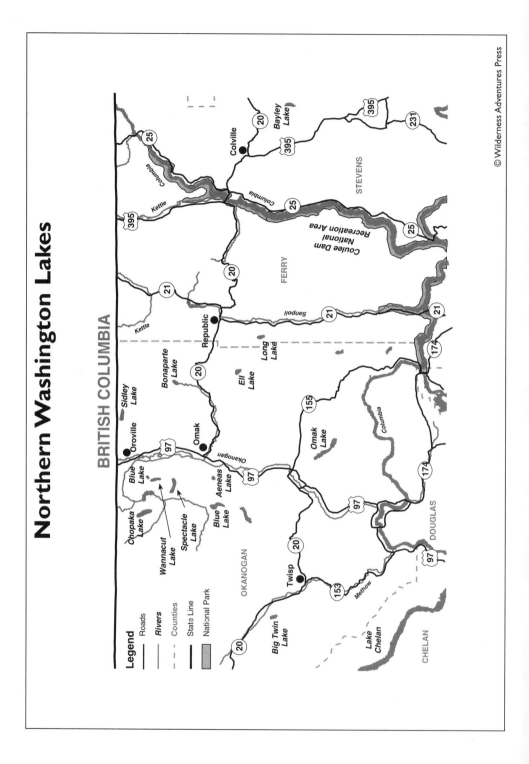

# The Northern Washington Lakes

If you're looking for some solitude and you don't mind fishing stillwaters and small creeks, northern Washington is where you want to be.

Unlike much of the state, this section remains relatively isolated from the major population centers, and life here is a little more laid-back.

A long drive from just about anywhere, northern Washington's lakes, including several flyfishing-only waters, offer excellent chances to hook rainbow trout ranging from 16 to 20 inches, with possibilities existing to take trout much larger than that.

Northern Washington's most highly regarded trout lake is Chopaka. Flyfishing-only regulations and a 1-fish harvest limit keep this water producing obscene numbers of 14- to 20-inch rainbows, despite the pressure it receives. Visit Chopaka during late spring or early summer, and you'll be amazed at how many float tubes and prams dot the water. There's not much relief through the dog days of summer or during the wonderful fall season, either. That's OK. Flyfishers make good company, and if there are just too many people on the lake for your liking, there are nearby opportunities that may be devoid of anglers.

Aeneas Lake is also managed under flyfishing-only regs, and it offers lots of rainbows in the 2- to 3-pound range. It, too, receives plenty of pressure, but the angling quality remains high. Spend a good day on Aeneas, and you are likely to bring a dozen or more large trout to net.

Lesser known waters, yet nearly as productive, are Ell Lake, Bayley Lake, and Long Lake, among others. They also pump out large trout and are managed with restrictive regulations.

While there is a distinct lure to a flyfishing-only water, don't overlook options on area lakes that are managed under general regulations. At times, fishing can be excellent at Wannacut, Spectacle, Blue, Bonaparte, Jameson, and and a host of other stillwaters.

Yes, you will have to dodge the marshmallow-tossing, baitchucking masses at some of those lakes, but you can locate isolated bays where the competition is minimal and the fishing excellent. Plus, you might turn a few spinfishers onto the merits of flyfishing.

If you are looking for really large trout, say to 18 pounds, you may find that opportunity in northern Washington, too. Omak Lake rests on the Colville Indian Reservation, and it harbors Lahontan cutthroat trout. Fished less than the Columbia Basin's Lake Lenore, which also offers Lahontans, Omak provides 4- to 7-pound fish with some regularity, and crowds are not a problem.

Northeast Washington also provides excellent stream fishing opportunities, with many creeks and rivers offering rainbow, cutthroat and brown trout, plus mountain whitefish (see central and eastern Washington rivers and creeks section).

While flyfishers who are located near the population centers of Washington may pass on the northern section of the state, indicating that it is just too far out there for a weekend trip, those in the know regard that long drive as a minimal inconvenience when considering the quality fishing available. When you find the time, hit northern Washington with your 4- or 5-weight fly rod, a float tube and a box of nymphs, streamers, and dry flies. Have a week or two to blow, or you'll end up telling yourself, "I just didn't have enough time!"

# CHOPAKA LAKE

Northeast Washington is a stillwater flyfisher's paradise. The area is sprinkled with quality trout waters that range in size from intimate little lakes to large, windswept reservoirs.

In these waters, flyfishers may land big rainbows, wily browns, and some gigantic Lahontan cutthroat, all species that grow big on a steady diet of aquatic insects and minnows. Firmly entrenched at the top of northeast Washington's flyfishing heap is Chopaka Lake, a 160-acre gem of a rainbow trout fishery that has beckoned Washington's top flyfishers to its banks for more than 30 years.

Chopaka rests just south of the British Columbia/Washington border north of Omak and Tonasket. As indicated, it's inhabited by lots of feisty rainbow trout that run to good size—3-pounders are commonly caught, and larger fish are possible. A few bass have been illegally introduced into Chopaka, so they may also be encountered. If you catch one, give it the coup de grâce and fry it for dinner.

It's doubtful that you could find a more beautiful setting than the one Chopaka occupies: It's perched on a bench above the Sinlahekin Valley with the picturesque Cascade Mountains and rolling pine tree-covered hills dominating the western and northern views. Sagebrush flats and more pine tree-laced hills race off to the south and east. Mule and white-tailed deer are often sighted near the edge of the lake. Cattle graze placidly on the surrounding hills. Occasionally they are startled by the presence of a black bear. Often, especially during summer, a loon's wild cry echoes over the lake. Ravens, ospreys, and various waterfowl also call Chopaka home.

If I were a parent, I would make it a point to take my children to Chopaka every summer and introduce them to flyfishing. If they didn't want to flyfish, I'd head out on the water by myself and turn the kids loose; the area just begs to be explored, and there is little trouble to be found in the surrounding hills, other than the sting of a yellowjacket or a scraped up knee.

Although there are many eastern Washington lakes that provide flyfishing nearly equal to Chopaka, they are not embedded in the Washington flyfishing mindset. Chopaka is different: whether you are an old sage or just starting out with a fly rod, you'll hear about Chopaka from guys at the local fly shop, and at some point, you'll get out the map, tell the spouse you're leaving for a few days, get in the truck and drive there, if for nothing else, to validate all those tall tales you've heard. The long drive should be worth your effort. Chopaka's trout are aggressive, and they aren't so shy that they won't feed up top, which is a trait that separates Chopaka from other lakes. Its Callibaetis mayfly emergence and spinnerfall, and the dry-fly action they produce, is legendary.

However, don't expect to have the lake to yourself when you arrive at Chopaka. Despite its distance from any major population center, including a heavily-rutted mountain road that anglers must negotiate to reach the lake, it gets pounded throughout the season, which opens the last Saturday in April and closes October 31.

# Chopaka Lake

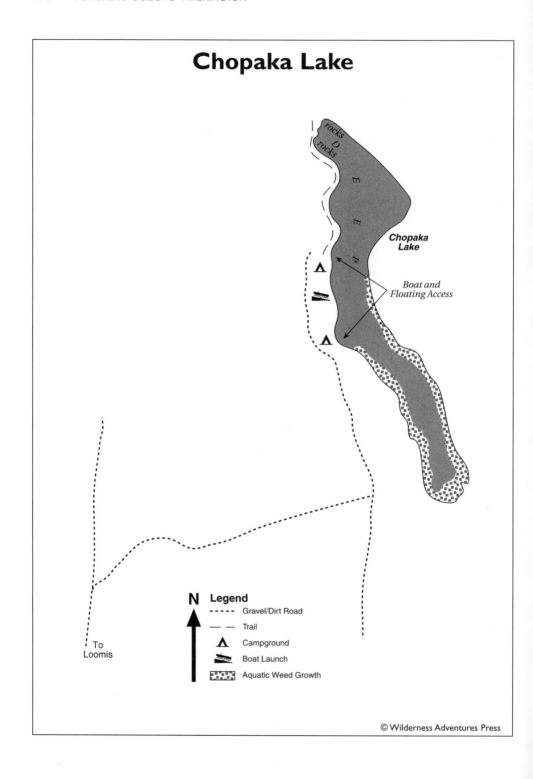

Chopaka Lake

Boat and
Floating Access

N

**Legend**
- - - - Gravel/Dirt Road
— — Trail
Λ Campground
Boat Launch
Aquatic Weed Growth

To
Loomis

© Wilderness Adventures Press

Fortunately, the lake maintains its quality flyfishing throughout the season due to a 1-fish limit and flyfishing-only regulations. Motors are prohibited on the lake, so most people use float tubes or small prams guided by oars. That keeps the serenity in place.

When I first visited the lake, I remember feeling like I was way out there. I passed no cars when ascending the long, rutted dirt road to the lake, which scattered the contents on my dashboard, not to mention all of the gear in the back of my truck. I thought, foolishly, that maybe I'd have the lake to myself. When I dropped off a hill above Chopaka, praying that my brakes wouldn't go out, I could see how naive I had been: It was June 18, and float tubes and boats covered the south end of the lake. A tent city had cropped up on the lake's west shore. In all, there may have been 50 or more people camped.

That was fine—the fish were feeding on the surface, and there were plenty of places to work the shore without interruption from other anglers. In fact, no matter how crowded the lake may be, you can usually find some solitude at Chopaka's north end where deep water keeps most flyfishers away. That does not mean you can't catch fish there on sinktip and full-sink lines. Occasionally, you might even find fish up top scarfing big mayflies or caddis.

According to Rick Baker, who lives in Tonasket and is a member of the Okanogan Flyfishing Club, Chopaka is worth floating a fly on, whether you encounter crowded conditions or not.

"Chopaka is located in a gorgeous spot, and it's quite unique," he says. "It's on the east slope of the Cascades, and you go from alpine timber to some of the most arid country in Washington, so the weather is always nice. Storms break up as they come over the Cascades, so you can have a sunny day in Loomis (located about 12 miles from Chopaka) when it's rainy everywhere else in the state.

"However, I've never seen so many people on a lake so far away from anything," Baker adds. "I don't fish the lake very often any more, but it can fish really good, so when I do make a trip to Chopaka, it's usually worth it."

Aquatic insect hatches dictate quality fishing at Chopaka, and they begin in April with emergences of midges, also called Chironomids.

Standard Chironomid patterns work well here. A handful of size 16 and 18 pupa and larvae, tied in various colors, such as black, red, and tan, should put fish in your net. Popular patterns include brassies, serendipities, pheasant tails, Kaufmann's Chironomid pupa, disco midges, and palomino midges.

Although Chopaka's midge hatches are most pronounced in late April, May, and June, there are still some midges around during summer. In late April, May, and June, expect midge emergences throughout the day. During July and August, expect midges to come off early in the day, sometimes getting going before 7AM. They reappear in the evening, and fishing can be quite productive as the sun drops behind the mountains.

When fishing midge patterns at Chopaka, most flyfishers place the flies under a strike indicator. When using this type of setup, place your fly, or flies, about 3 feet under the indicator. If you don't get strikes, increase the amount of tippet below the indicator until you find the depth where trout are working. Typically, they'll feed near the surface.

If a full-scale rise occurs, try midge emergers in size 16 and 18. Dry flies of similar size, such as a Griffith's gnat or gulper special, may also draw strikes when cast ahead of a rising trout.

When fishing midges during the early season at Chopaka, 5X leaders work fine. As late May and June arrive, trout can be super selective, and you may need to go with a slimmer tippet in the 6X range to draw strikes.

If you don't want to get up early in the morning to meet the midge hatches, opting instead for a few extra hours in the sleeping bag, don't worry—you can be lazy and still find good fishing at Chopaka.

Chopaka's most noted hatch is an emergence of Callibaetis mayflies that gets going in May and lasts through summer. Peak hatches arrive in May and June. July and August offer some Callibaetis action. September revitalizes the insects, and quality emergences reappear with the bugs rating slightly smaller (size 18) than they were in the early season (size 14 and 16).

Anglers who encounter Callibaetis need to understand that the emergence and spinnerfall are important events. Each phase requires fly imitations that specifically represent the proper stage of the insect. Emergences—when nymphs swim from the bottom vegetation to the surface where they shed their nymphal shucks, then take to the air—are particularly productive.

You can identify an emergence, which can come off at any time of the day but usually arrives in midmorning and again in the evening, by the presence of Callibaetis duns on the water. You'll see their tent-like wings sticking up off the surface. Attached to some of their fannies will be a nymphal shuck, which they shed like a rattlesnake slithering out of its skin. It's at that time, when those flies are twitching on the surface, their fannies stuck in the water, their wings too wet to take to the air, that they are most vulnerable to trout.

To match that phase of the hatch, try a size 16 or 18 Callibaetis cripple or a Stalcup CDC biot comparadun. These patterns will take fish at Chopaka during Callibaetis emergences. Slate gray sparkle duns are a nice follow-up pattern once a few fat rainbows take off with your cripples and comparaduns.

One pattern that old-timers and those who appreciate tradition may want to include in their arsenal is the Chopaka May, a time-tested pattern developed by Boyd Aigner of Bothell, Washington. It, too, imitates the Callibaetis dun and can be fished effectively throughout an emergence. To make it super-effective, most flyfishers clip the hackle below the hook so that the fly rides low in the water, just like a natural. Here are tying instructions for the Chopaka May:

- **Hook:** Mustad 94840
- **Tail:** Moose body hair
- **Body:** Gray poly or blue heron wing fibers
- **Wing:** Single upright deer hair
- **Hackle:** Dun, clipped across bottom if desired

*Located in northern Washington's beautiful mountain scenery, Chopaka offers large rainbow trout and dependable insect emergences.*

Callibaetis spinnerfalls—when Callibaetis return to the lake to deposit eggs, then die (downwing fashion on the water) can arrive at any time of the day at Chopaka. However, they generally come off in the afternoon. Spinnerfalls can provide some wonderful hours on the water, but your cripples and sparkle duns may not do the trick due to the presence of a trailing shuck on these patterns.

During spinnerfalls, opt for a specific spinner pattern, such as an AK Best quill body Callibaetis spinner or a CDC biot Callibaetis spinner. Again, 5X or 6X leaders and tippets will be required, especially if the surface of the lake lacks wind and is flat. That situation gives trout ample time to inspect an offering before they sink their teeth into it.

While trout may rise throughout the lake during Callibaetis emergences and spinnerfalls, some of the best fishing arrives at the south end of the lake in the shallows. Excellent options also occur across the lake from the campground. To reach the south end, anglers must put in at the campground. It's not a bad trip when you head for the south end in a float tube, but it's a heck of a kick back, especially if the wind picks up. For that reason, I usually forgo the south end unless I have a boat—rowing against the wind is easier than trying to kick a float tube along.

To reach the north end, you can kick a float tube or row a boat. Another option is to hike with your float tube to the north end and work your way back along the west or east shores.

During periods when Callibaetis are not present on the surface, flyfishers can drag mayfly nymphs over submerged weedbeds or cast toward shore with the same patterns and slowly retrieve them.

Some popular subsurface patterns include hare's ear nymphs, pheasant tail nymphs, Callibaetis quill nymphs, Carey specials, and Sheep Creek specials.

During slow hours, leeches, woolly buggers, damsel nymphs, and scuds also draw strikes. All of the above can be fished in the deeper water off sinktip and full-sink lines, or they can be worked off a floating line near the surface. If using a sinking line, use a short, 3- or 4-foot leader. If fishing nymphs off a floating line, extend your leader to 12 feet.

Chopaka also receives a good damselfly hatch, which begins by mid-May and lasts through mid-June. A few damsels will be present throughout summer.

Standard damsel patterns, such as a marabou damsel, work well at Chopaka. Popular Northwest patterns, such as a Sheep Creek special or Nyergess nymph, also draw strikes during the damsel hatch.

For Baker, wet fly and streamer fishing is the way to go at Chopaka. In fact, instead of casting dry flies, he prefers to offer some unorthodox patterns down near the bottom of the lake. By doing so, he catches some large trout.

"Early in the year, I use a shrimp pattern (scud) or a leech," he says. "A Gordon grizzly is also a good wet fly. It doesn't have the characteristics of anything I've seen, but it knocks them dead. During the damsel hatch, I like to use a green Carey (special).

"When nothing else is working, one of my secrets is to go with a full-sink line and a Joe's hopper—any time of the year. I don't know why it works, but an older man told me that trick, and it gets them. I start out by using a green, yellow, or black woolly bugger. If I get a hit on the yellow bugger, I switch to the hopper. The fish really key on color here, and once you find out what they are looking for, you can get them pretty good. If they want green, I go with a shrimp or lime Carey. If they want black, I go with a marabou leech."

In May some caddisflies start showing up along the shores of Chopaka, and their presence lasts through the season. Early in the year, they are smallish, dark flies, rating about size 16. Later in the year, they run to good size, some of them stretching to size 8 or 10. At that time, large caddis patterns, stripped across the surface, can draw hearty strikes from some of Chopaka's largest rainbows, all fat and sassy from a strong summer feeding binge.

To imitate a big caddis correctly, here's what you do: Cast as much line off your reel as possible, tuck the butt of the rod under your arm, drop the rod tip to the water, then strip the line with both hands as fast as you can.

During fall, anglers should encounter some Baetis mayflies, also called blue-winged olives, on Chopaka's surface. They can be matched with size 18 and 20 olive sparkle duns, cripples, and even the simple, yet very effective, parachute Adams. The Baetis hatches are most pronounced on chilly, misty fall afternoons.

If you choose to visit Chopaka or any other northeast Washington trout lake, be prepared when you arrive—there are no fly shops in the area, so you need to stock up on fly patterns, tying material, leaders, tippets, and anything else you might need, before you arrive. Insect repellent, sunblock, food, and drink can be purchased at most of the small towns sprinkled throughout that wonderful country.

Note: The dirt road from Loomis to Chopaka Lake is notorious for banging up vehicles and scattering gear. It's very steep and rutted. You may want to take a moment to secure gear before heading up that grade. Also, make sure you have a good spare tire with you. Before leaving Chopaka Lake and heading back down the steep grade, test your brakes and check your master cylinder for brake fluid. Sure death rests ahead of you if your brakes go out when traveling down that long hill.

No matter what anyone tells you about Chopaka Lake ("It's too crowded," "The fish are too picky"), every flyfisher deserves a trip to this location. The fish run to good size and are prone to eat dry flies off the surface, and the Sinlahekin Valley is a special, beautiful place to see. In my mind, those are tough options to beat.

To reach Chopaka, follow Highway 97 to Tonasket. About midway through Tonasket, turn left at the Loomis/Nighthawk Recreation sign. Follow that road to the stop sign and turn right. Follow Loomis-Oroville Road through Loomis. About a mile out of town turn left at the sign for Chopaka Lake. Another mile down the road, follow the dirt road on the right—that is where your uphill grind begins. Follow the road about 5 miles to a "Y" intersection and turn right. The road takes you downhill about 2 miles directly to the campground on the west shore of Chopaka. There is no fee to camp, but you'll want to arrive early and secure a spot if visiting on a holiday weekend. Even standard weekends in May and June may have a full campground.

# Lake Facts: Chopaka Lake

### Seasons
- Last Saturday in April through October 31.

### Special Regulations
- Flyfishing only.
- One fish limit, no size restriction.
- Use of motors prohibited.

### Species
- Rainbow trout that average 12 to 15 inches, with plenty of fish stretching to 18 inches or more.

### Lake Characteristics
- A midelevation mountain lake, Chopaka offers lots of strong-fighting rainbows and excellent insect hatches to match.
- Look for midges, damselflies, Baetis, and the big draw at Chopaka, the Callibaetis emergence in May and June.
- If there is one single characteristic that applies to Chopaka, it's this: crowded. Expect company when you fish here.

### Access
- A long, steep dirt road leads out of the Sinlahekin Valley and up to the lake. Before commencing on your venture up the road, batten down all loose items. If you don't, your truck will resemble chaos. During evil-weather years, the road may not be passable when the lake opens, but by mid-May a vehicle can usually make it through.
- Once you reach the lake, boats and float tubes can be launched along the west shore. There is limited shore fishing here, but you'll want to have a boat, canoe, or float tube at your disposal.
- Camping sites are scattered along the west shore.

## CHOPAKA LAKE MAJOR HATCHES

| Insect | J | F | M | A | M | J | J | A | S | O | N | D | Flies |
|---|---|---|---|---|---|---|---|---|---|---|---|---|---|
| Callibaetis | | | | | █ | █ | | | █ | | | | CB Cripple #14–18; Stalcup CDC Biot CB #14–18; Sparkle Dun #14–18; Hare's Ear #12–18; Pheasant Tail Nymph #14–18; Parachute Adams #14–18 |
| Chironomid | | | | █ | █ | █ | █ | █ | █ | █ | | | Gulper Special #14–20; Griffith's Gnat #14–20; Biot Midge Emerger #14–20; Palomino Midge #14–20; Brassie #14–20; Suspender Midge #16–20; Blood Midge #16–20 |
| Damselfly | | | | | | █ | █ | | | | | | Nyergess Nymph #4–10; Six-pack #4–10; Burk's Olive Damsel #4–10; Marabou Damsel #4–10; Braided Butt Damsel #4–8 |
| Scuds | | | | █ | █ | █ | █ | █ | █ | █ | | | Bighorn Scud #14–16; Epoxy Scud #12–16 |
| Leeches | | | | █ | █ | █ | █ | █ | █ | █ | | | Canadian Mohair Leech #4–8; Marabou Leech #4–8; Mini Leech #6–10 |
| Streamers | | | | █ | █ | █ | █ | █ | █ | █ | | | Egg-sucking Leech #4–10; Woolly Bugger #4–6; Woolhead Sculpin #4–6 |
| Grasshoppers | | | | | | | █ | █ | | | | | Joe's Hopper #4–8 (drowned or dry) |
| Caddis | | | | | █ | █ | █ | | █ | | | | Elk Hair Caddis #16–18; LaFontaine Sparkle Emerger #16–18; x-Caddis #16–18; Free-living Caddis Larva #14–18; Stranahan's Caddis Variant #16–18 |

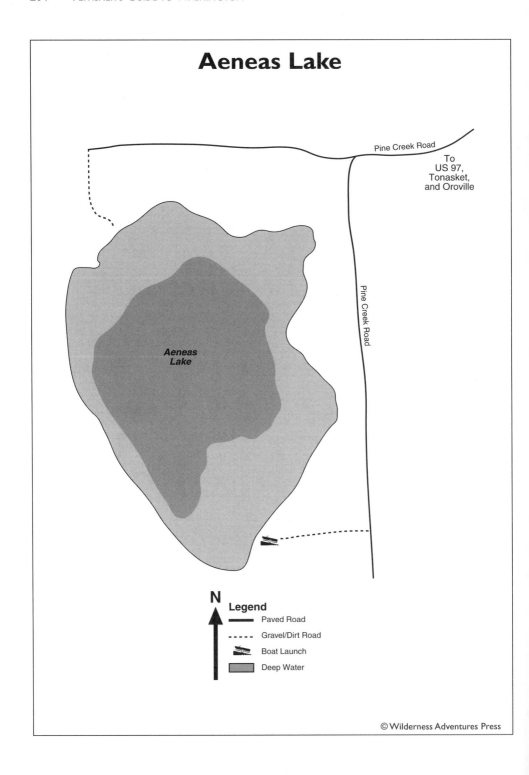

# AENEAS LAKE

Another must pilgrimage for Washington flyfishers, Aeneas is managed under flyfishing-only regulations.

However, don't think you won't see a few trout die here. Statewide harvest limits apply, which means anglers can take 5 trout from the lake each day if they choose.

If you are looking for a 5-trout limit to take home and fry, you should look elsewhere. At Aeneas, flyfishers release almost every fish they catch, keeping only a fish that might be irrevocably gill-hooked and faced with an uncertain recovery. If you cruise around the lake bonking fish, you'll get some pretty evil looks and probably a few comments, too. Who knows; when you get back to your rig, the tires might be flat.

The reason for a cold shoulder: Catch and release plays an integral role in the Aeneas fishery, and it is the prime reason why the lake produces so many gorgeous 16- to 20-inch rainbow trout. Place a few fish on a stringer here and you will clearly demonstrate that you don't understand fisheries management and the value of catching a fish more than once.

Anyway, Aeneas is worth fishing even if you have to battle crowds during the prime summer weekends.

Aeneas is located just southwest of Tonasket, which makes it much more accessible during the early season than Chopaka. For that reason, many flyfishers work Aeneas right after the last Saturday in April opener, rather than battling up the hill to Chopaka. And fishing can be good at Aeneas early on.

Midges hatch from opening day through the season, and they are followed by decent hatches of Callibaetis mayflies and damselflies in May and June. Damselflies can provide especially good action, and during their emergence, some of Aeneas' top anglers tally 20-fish days. Caddis can also be found on the water or buzzing around the bankside bushes during late May through August. Grasshoppers also draw strikes when fished near the edge of the lake in August, September and even on the warm days of October.

The lake also hosts an abundance of scuds and olive scud patterns, with size 12, 14, 16, and 18 taking their fair share of fish. In fact, if you arrive at Aeneas and are baffled by a hatch, just tie on a scud—fish feed on them every day of the year.

Flyfishing at Aeneas is best during the early season and extending into July. When the water heats up under incessant summer sun and aquatic weed growth proliferates, the lake's rainbows shut down. A few fish can be taken in the cool morning and evening hours, but it's pretty slow. The action starts up again in September when the water temperature cools and weeds recede. At that time, Callibaetis patterns work well, along with the venerable woolly bugger and marabou leech. Of course, scuds draw strikes, too.

While most of the flyfishing pressure is directed at Aeneas' shallow water areas, especially around the north end, you can ply the depths of this 60-acre lake and take fish. Of course, you'll need a full-sink line, a short leader, and some big leech patterns. Try to work patterns near the bottom with 10 quick strips, a pause, then another 10 strips.

Aeneas is noted for its rainbow trout, but it now hosts a population of browns, as well. Browns were introduced to the lake to keep rough fish populations in check. It's believed that they will grow to good size, with some reaching 4 or 5 pounds. Could you imagine what they'd look like if there were a 1-fish limit in place?

Rainbow trout in Aeneas are no slouches—they average 15 to 18 inches with lots of fish available in the 20-inch range. Reports indicate that they grow an inch a month in Aeneas' fertile waters.

Because Aeneas is not a large lake, a float tube works fine for covering it. A small boat or pram is an excellent option, too. No motors are allowed.

Again, when heading to Aeneas Lake, pick up all the flies, leaders, and tying material that you need. Food and drink can be found in Tonasket. There are a few primitive campsites located at Aeneas that are held on a first-come, first-serve basis. Motel lodging can be found in Tonasket.

To reach Aeneas, follow the Loomis/Nighthawk recreation road out of Tonasket. At the "T," turn left and follow the Loomis-Oroville Road for a half-mile. Turn right on Pine Creek Road and follow it for a few miles to the Aeneas Lake access.

# Lake Facts: Aeneas Lake

### Seasons
- Last Saturday in April through October 31.

### Special Regulations
- Flyfishing only.
- No motors allowed.

### Species
- Rainbow trout

### Lake Characteristics
- Heavily hit by the flyfishing crowd, Aeneas manages to produce good catches of 14- to 17-inch rainbows with a few bigger fish thrown in on the side.
- Excellent midge, Callibaetis, and damselfly hatches offer excellent early-season opportunities.
- The lake slows during July and August but fishes well during fall.

### Access
- There is some shore fishing available, but Aeneas is best fished from a float tube or boat.
- A boat launch exists at the southeast end of the lake.

# Ell Lake

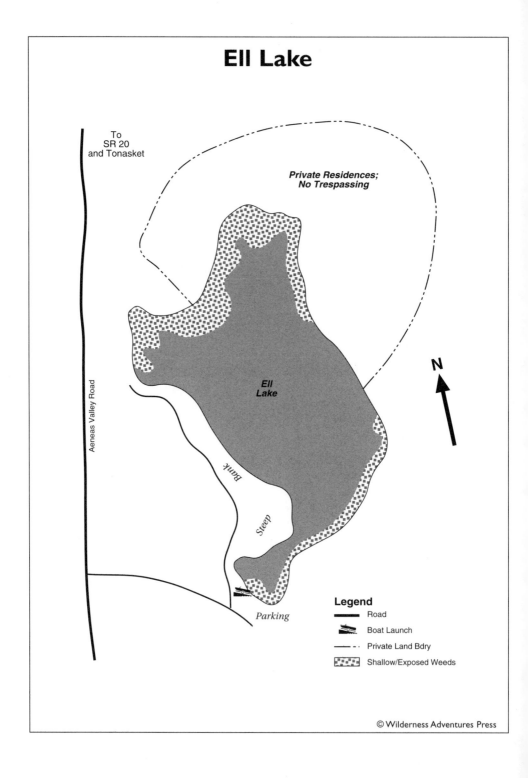

To
SR 20
and Tonasket

*Private Residences;
No Trespassing*

Aeneas Valley Road

*Ell
Lake*

*Bank*

*Steep*

*Parking*

N

## Legend

| | |
|---|---|
| ▬▬▬ | Road |
| ⛵ | Boat Launch |
| — · — · — | Private Land Bdry |
| ▨▨▨ | Shallow/Exposed Weeds |

© Wilderness Adventures Press

# ELL LAKE

Less loved than Aeneas or Chopaka, Ell Lake provides some excellent options for large rainbow trout without massive crowds that can confuse matters on the other well-known waters.

Ell rests in the gorgeous Aeneas Valley, just off the Aeneas Valley Road southeast of Tonasket. It's not a large lake, rating just 24 acres, and it's not deep. In fact, its deepest spot is just 19 feet down from the surface, and most areas are 1 feet deep or less. The shallow depth facilitates massive aquatic weed growth, providing plenty of cheap housing for aquatic insects. Due to massive populations of scuds, damselflies, midges, and Callibaetis mayflies, Ell's rainbow trout grow fast and fight strong. Catching an 18-incher from Ell is not uncommon. The average fish probably goes about 12 to 14 inches. Twenty-inch-plus trout are possible.

When I first visited the lake on a pleasant June afternoon, a few Callibaetis spinners lay spent-wing on the water, and lots of blue damselflies hovered around the bankside vegetation. Throughout the lake, rainbow trout noses pushed through the surface, sucking in Callibaetis. Occasionally, a fish would leap clear into the air, detonating on a damsel.

I tied on a Callibaetis spinner, cast it to the weedbed right next to the boat launch site and hooked up with a 16-inch rainbow on my first cast. I released the fish, kicked my tube another 50 yards up the south shore and hooked another fish of equal size. Ell Lake, I quickly determined, was worthy of more serious inspection. So I did the natural thing: I fished hard the rest of the afternoon and evening, camped at nearby Long Lake, and returned in the morning to another excellent day of Callibaetis and damsel action.

Because of its small size, Ell would be quickly fished out if the baitchucking, fish-bonking masses were allowed to lob their offerings into its water. Fortunately, the lake is managed under special regulations: there is a 1-fish limit and single, barbless hooked artificial flies and lures are required. No bait. No treble hooks. No motors. No problems.

Ell is really an easy lake to fish, although its trout occasionally contract a case of lockjaw. However, due to Ell's size and depth, the fish can't hide, and if you place an offering in front of their noses enough times, they'll finally take.

Ell opens the last Saturday in April, and the season extends through October 31. It fishes well early and late in the season. In July and August, weed growth can make fishing difficult.

Expect midges on the surface from opening day through the season. Their emergences should be most pronounced in May and June, but midges are a key ingredient in a trout's diet all season.

Ell's trout can be taken on top when midges are present with a size 16, 18, or 20 parachute Adams, Griffith's gnat, or gulper special. However, fishing midge pupa under a strike indicator or below a dry fly, just off the weedbeds, is most effective.

Callibaetis begin showing up on Ell in early May, and their emergence peaks by the third week of the month. They are present on Ell's surface through the summer, but the prime times to catch the emergence and spinnerfall is definitely during May and June. Standard Callibaetis patterns work here, and those listed for Lake Chopaka, a size 16 or 18 Callibaetis cripple, olive sparkle duns, spent-wing spinners, a Stalcup CDC biot comparadun, or a Chopaka May work fine.

Damsels make a strong appearance at Ell beginning in early to mid-May. Their numbers are healthy through June, extending into July on occasion.

Damsel fishing at Ell can be an absolute blast. When I've fished Ell, always during the early season, I've enjoyed terrific action on damsel dries, cast right in among the exposed weeds and lily pads. Occasionally, an Ell Lake rainbow gets so excited about the prospect of a damsel dinner, it throws its entire body clear of the surface and lands on a fly. Of course, when I see a fish come out of the water like that, I give a reflex yank on the fly and rip it right out of the trout's mouth. I suppose there are worse pitfalls in life.

Braided butt damsels work very well when mimicking adult damselflies. You may want to fish them off of a 4X tippet rather than the standard 5X or 6X. The 4X is stronger and offers the opportunity to retrieve a fly that hangs up in the weeds from a distance. Separating a fly from the weeds with 5X or 6X tippet invites departure.

Subsurface, Ell's rainbows are very fond of Nyergess nymphs and marabou damsels. One pattern that I find super effective on Ell and other area lakes is Andy Burk's olive damsel pattern. Here are the tying instructions for that nymph:

- **Hook:** TMC 9300, size 10 or 12
- **Thread:** Olive 6/0
- **Eyes:** 50-pound monofilament burned black
- **Tail:** Tuft of olive marabou tied to end of abdomen
- **Abdomen:** Olive Ultra Chenille
- **Wingcase:** Turkey tail
- **Thorax:** Brown or olive dubbing

You can work damsel patterns off a sinktip line, but you probably want to avoid a full-sink—the lake's bottom is covered with weeds, and taking them off your hook on every cast not only diminishes your chance to catch fish, but it is a pain in the ass. Even if you only have a floating line to fish damsel nymphs with, you'll be fine. Just extend the tippet, depending on the depth of water you want to fish. Generally, a 10- or 12-foot leader with a weighted fly works fine.

Caddisflies are also present at Ell beginning in June. Their presence lasts through the summer, and they are most effective when fished in the late afternoon and evening hours. Flyfishers should expect to encounter various caddis species. A selection of elk hair caddis and emergent sparkle pupa in various colors, size 16 and 18, should do the trick in most cases. However, the giant sedge is also present at Ell, and fish may key on these big insects that skate across the surface, creating a ripple that can be seen several dozen yards away. A giant caddis pattern, say size 6, 8, or 10, should bring fish to the top when giant sedge are present.

Scuds are fairly dense at Ell, and when everything else turns off, you can often turn a fish on by offering a size 14 or 16 scud. Downtime between hatches can also

*Ell Lake offers large rainbow trout, excellent aquatic insect emergences, and a measure of solitude—what more can you ask for?*

be spent working leech patterns near the weedbeds. Olive, black, brown, and red leeches draw strikes. Size 6 and 8 leeches seem to be most effective.

Access to Ell is easy, whether launching a float tube, a raft, or a small boat, since a boat launch exists at the south end of the lake. There is also plenty of parking and an outhouse that comes in handy. There are several houses near the lake, and their inhabitants probably don't appreciate watching flyfishers drop their waders all the time. I don't like sani-cans any better than the next guy in line holding his nose, but we should use this one out of courtesy.

To reach Ell, follow Highway 20 east out of Tonasket and turn right (south) on the Aeneas Valley Road. Ell is located about 6 miles south of Highway 20, and a sign clearly marks its presence.

There is no food or fly material available anywhere near Ell, so stock up before you head out to fish. Some primitive campsites can be found at Ell. A campground exists just north of Ell at Long Lake that offers some nice tent and trailer sites.

# Lake Facts: Ell Lake

### Seasons
- Last Saturday in April through October 31.

### Special Regulations
- One fish limit, no size restriction.
- Selective gear rules apply.
- No motors allowed.

### Species
- Rainbow trout to 18 inches.

### Lake Characteristics
- A real sleeper, Ell offers good-sized fish and plenty of aquatic insects to match. Damselflies, dragonflies, midges, Callibaetis, Baetis, and even a few pale morning duns emerge here. Leeches and scuds are also present.
- The lake is very shallow, and weed growth is a problem during summer months.
- May and June are productive times, but the lake slumps in July and August. Fortunately, it turns on in mid-September and remains productive through October.

### Access
- Easily reached from Aeneas Valley Road, Ell offers some shore fishing, but private land surrounds some of the lake.
- To fully explore the water, a small boat or float tube is the way to go.
- A boat launch exists at the south end of the lake.

# SPECTACLE LAKE

Spectacle Lake is another favorite for the guys who prefer to fish bait or troll pop-gear and a worm. Three resorts that are located on the banks of the lake facilitate those anglers.

But Spectacle does offer some good options on rainbow trout—good-sized fish —for the fly caster. Foremost, Spectacle opens on March 1, which allows anglers on the water earlier than most Okanogan area lakes.

When the season opens, expect lots of company but also solid midge emergences. Midge larvae and pupa, fished under strike indicators in the shallow water areas, will take fish. Streamers, such as woolly buggers and zonkers, also draw strikes early in the season. Olive, brown, and black leeches, tied on size 4, long shank hooks, are good searching patterns, too.

In May and June, Callibaetis mayflies and damselflies bring trout into the shallow, weedy areas to eat. Standard nymphs, such as marabou damsels, hare's ears, and pheasant tails draw strikes under the surface. Up top, a Callibaetis cripple, sparkle dun, or parachute Adams should bring rises.

By July, Spectacle's rainbows take a siesta, and the fishing season closes July 31. Fish to 18 inches are commonly caught in Spectacle. A few holdovers in the 5-pound range show up each season, too.

To reach Spectacle, take the Loomis-Oroville Road west out of Tonasket. The lake is located on the left side of the road, and you can't miss it—resort advertisements dominate the roadside scenery. Campsites can be found at all of the resorts.

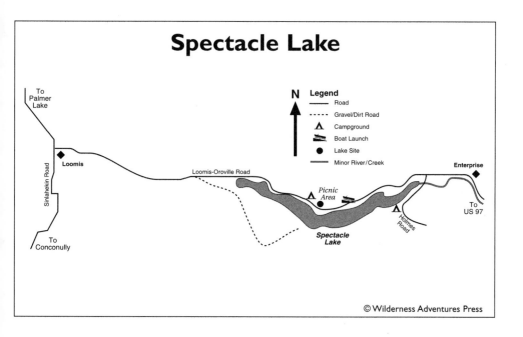

# Wannacut Lake

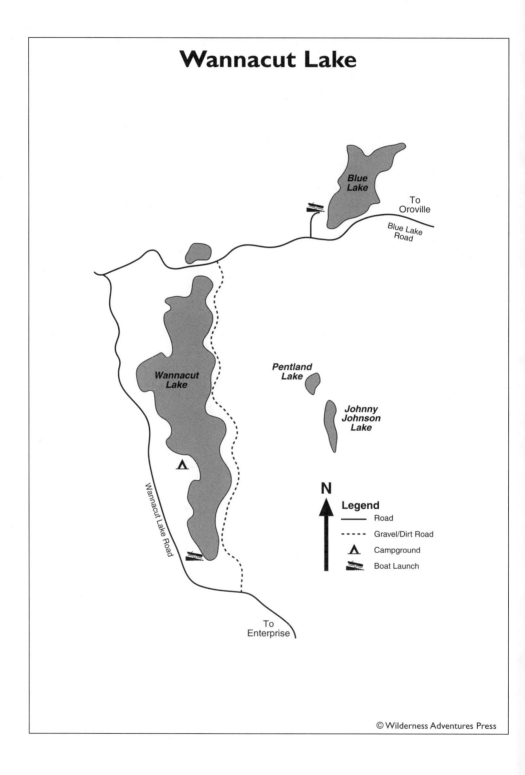

Blue
Lake

To
Oroville

Blue Lake
Road

Wannacut
Lake

Pentland
Lake

Johnny
Johnson
Lake

Wannacut Lake Road

N

Legend
Road
Gravel/Dirt Road
Campground
Boat Launch

To
Enterprise

© Wilderness Adventures Press

*Wannacut offers decent opportunities for rainbow trout that may stretch from 15 inches to 5 pounds.*

# Wannacut Lake

Located just west of Blue Lake and north of Spectacle Lake, Wannacut Lake is another water that is heavily hit by the bait and tackle crowd. However, it does see its share of flyfishers, and for good reason. Wannacut rests in a beautiful setting, its rainbow trout run large and its aquatic insect population is diverse.

Most flyfishers hit the north and south ends of the lake, where shallow water facilitates dense aquatic weed growth. That's where the insects live. However, I've had good luck catching some very pretty rainbows, up to 20 inches, on the west shore in little bays and coves. Streamers and nymphs, I've found, fished off of sink-tip lines, work best in those areas.

Wannacut opens the last Saturday in April, and midges should be present from opening day through the season, which closes October 31.

Most flyfishers work larvae, pupa, and emergers under strike indicators and enjoy good success. I prefer to fish mayfly nymph imitations, such as a flashback pheasant tail or hare's ear, off of sinktip and full-sink lines. I vary my retrieve until I discover at what speed and depth the fish will take it.

Floating lines also come in handy at Wannacut, because it does offer pretty good Callibaetis and damselfly hatches. Callibaetis cripples, sparkle duns, and comparaduns bring trout to the top. Braided butt blue damsels will also bring fish up when plopped over, or even into, the weeds.

The lake does get a little weedy during July and August, but fishing continues to be productive in the morning and evening hours. All-day action returns in September and continues through October.

To reach Wannacut, follow the Loomis-Oroville road out of Tonasket. Just before you reach Spectacle Lake, turn north on Wannacut Lake Road and follow for about 5 miles. The lake and Sun Cove Resort, which offers RV and tent camping sites, are on the right side of the road.

# BLUE LAKE
## (SOUTHWEST OF OROVILLE)

Of all the Blue Lakes I've fished, the one located just southwest of Oroville in Okanogan County is probably my favorite. Maybe that's because it's always treated me right, beginning with its offering of a 4-pound Lahontan cutthroat trout during the first hour that I ever cast a fly at the place. Or maybe it's because I always fish Blue, which is often deserted, after a day or two at Chopaka, which, it seems, is always crowded. It's a nice change of pace.

The fact that you can catch fish at Blue Lake is no small miracle. Like Lake Lenore, Omak Lake, and Grimes Lake, Blue was considered too alkaline for trout to survive…until Lahontan cutthroat were planted. Lahontans took quickly to the lake, and today their numbers are strong. On a good day at Blue Lake, a competent angler may land 10 to 15 fish. On a poor day, several trout may come to net.

Solid numbers of large trout are directly related to special regulations that apply to this lake: single barbless lures and flies and a 1-fish limit. No motors are allowed.

Blue Lake covers about 112 acres, so it's not huge, but it is large enough to take some time to cover. Small prams or cartoppers are adequate craft at Blue, as are float tubes. It takes more time to cover the water from a float tube, but it's still an effective way to get at the fish. Bank fishing is a possibility, but it restricts an angler from reaching all of the prime water.

Blue Lake is a fertile environment that offers plenty of aquatic insects. Midges, damsels, scuds, dragonflies, caddis, Callibaetis, and Baetis all make appearances here. And the fish know it.

Lahontans, in general, are fish eaters. However, don't think that they won't eat squadrons of damsels, midges and Callibaetis when the opportunity arrives.

Midges are present from opening day, the last Saturday in April, through the season, which closes October 31. Standard midge patterns, such as emergers and pupa, draw strikes when fished under a strike indicator. Adult midges, fished on the surface, don't draw many strikes at Blue.

If you go with the strike indicator and midge pupa method, concentrate efforts near shore. Blue is a deep lake, and its bottom drops off steeply in most areas. Exceptions exist at the south end of the lake and the northwest bay. In the middle, the lake is over 100 feet deep!

Damsels come off at Blue in May and June, and fish feed heavily on the nymphal form. Standard damsel nymphs, such as the marabou damsel, work well here—Lahontans aren't that picky.

Again, the shallow water areas offer the best success with damsels. While passing from one shallow area to another, stay close to shore and work your offerings near the bottom off of sinktip or full-sink lines.

Callibaetis nymphs are commonly eaten by Blue Lake's Lahontans, but the adults don't get the fish too excited. Occasionally you'll see a fish roll on the surface and inhale size 14 or 16 mayfly duns or spinners, but that is a rare occasion.

# Blue Lake (Southwest of Oroville)

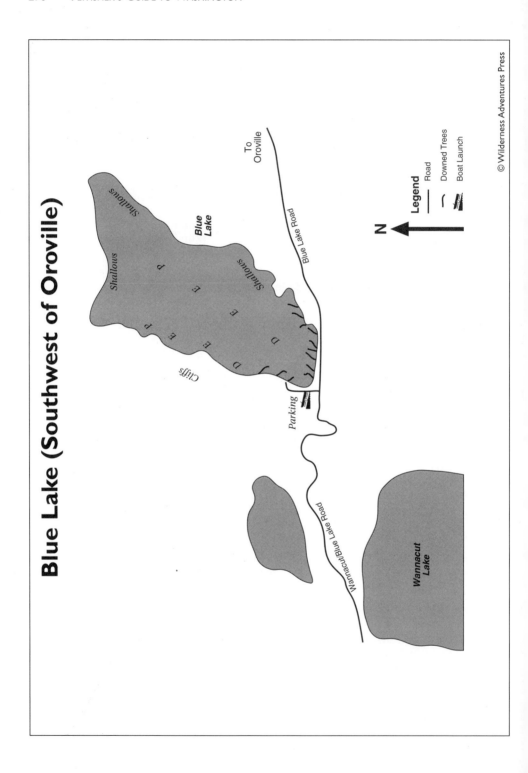

*Blue Lake is easily accessible and offers large Lahontan cutthroat trout.*

Better to stay underneath with mayfly nymphs, such as a size 14 hare's ear or pheasant tail.

While insect imitations work well at Blue, streamers and leeches draw the most attention from Lahontans.

Marabou leeches, egg-sucking leeches, woolly buggers, zonkers, and sculpins—really anything fishy or buggy looking—should draw strikes.

One of the best places to fish these patterns is right next to the dirt road (Blue Lake Road) that follows the south end of the lake. Sunken trees, with some limbs exposed, offer excellent habitat for small fish, not to mention aquatic insects. Big Lahontans prowl the area searching for a meal.

When fishing near the trees, I cast alongside the branches and quickly strip a streamer back to my tube. If I don't want to risk losing a pattern on a limb, I cast parallel to the ends of the trees in slightly deeper water. Lahontans run big in Blue Lake, up to 8 or 10 pounds, and I've taken some nice 4- and 5-pounders on streamer patterns worked near the trees.

Because of the Lahontan's size, you may want to beef up when selecting a rod for Blue Lake. You can handle fish on a 9-foot, 4-weight, but it makes more sense to use a 5- or 6-weight. A heavier rod allows an angler to cast heavy flies farther and more precisely, plus the extra backbone facilitates quick fights and releasing trout.

Blue Lake is not difficult to find. It's located just northeast of Wannacut Lake. If arriving from a trip to Chopaka or Spectacle Lakes, turn north off the highway and follow the signs to Wannacut Lake. Follow the road around Wannacut and up a hill. At the bottom of that hill, right around a sharp bend in the road lies Blue.

# Lake Facts: Blue Lake
## (Southwest of Oroville)

### Seasons
- Last Saturday in April through October 31.

### Special Regulations
- One-fish limit, no size restriction.
- Selective gear rules apply.
- Electric motors allowed.

### Species
- Lahontan cutthroat trout to good size; 4-pound fish are not uncommon, and larger fish exist.

### Lake Characteristics
- Decent insect emergences, including damselfly, midges, and Callibaetis keep the lake's cutthroat active.
- Most of the lake is deep, except around its edges, so a sinktip or full-sink line benefits an angler.

### Access
- Some shore options, but a boat or float tube is the way to go.
- A boat access exists at the south end of the lake, just off the Blue Lake-Wannacut Lake Road.

# SIDLEY LAKE

Sidley is one of a handful of Washington lakes that remains open year-round. Due to that distinction, Sidley is a good place to look for some sizable rainbow trout during the early season in March and April, before most lakes open.

Covering just about 120 acres, Sidley, which rests on the Canadian border east of Oroville, is a great place to launch a 12-foot boat or small pram to flyfish for rainbows. Motors are allowed on the lake.

In March and April, you'll want to wear some heavy clothing, possibly a stocking hat and gloves, and toss midge pupa and emerger patterns.

The standard patterns, such as a suspender midge, Chan's Chironomid, or palomino midge, should draw strikes. These patterns should be fished under a strike indicator or dropped under a small, size 16 or 18 dry fly, such as a Griffith's gnat or parachute Adams.

During April and May at Sidley, anglers will encounter Callibaetis mayflies and damselflies. Nymphs, such as a size 14 hare's ear, will cover the Callibaetis. On the surface, try Callibaetis emergers, such as the cripple or sparkle dun. If you see lots of damselflies hovering around the surface, tie on a damsel nymph and work it through the shallows off a sinktip line.

Whether you show up at Sidley during the early season or at any other time, you are likely to encounter other anglers. And don't be surprised if they aren't fishing with fly rods—the lake is managed under a 2-fish, any size limit. Unfortunately, that limit is usually comprised of a couple fish stretching between 16 and 20 inches. Sidley's trout are healthy and strong, and they average 12 to 16 inches. Several fish longer than 20 inches show up each season.

To reach Sidley from Oroville, turn off Hwy 97 onto Tonasket Creek Road. Follow about 8 miles east and turn north on the County Road to Molson. Follow signs to Molson Lakes. Sidley Lake is just beyond Molson Lakes.

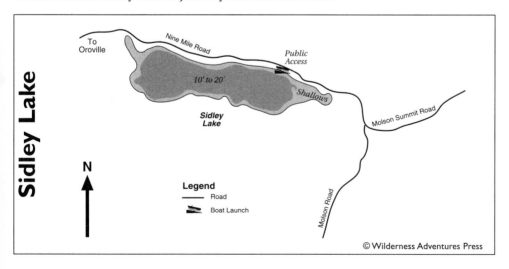

# Bonaparte Lake

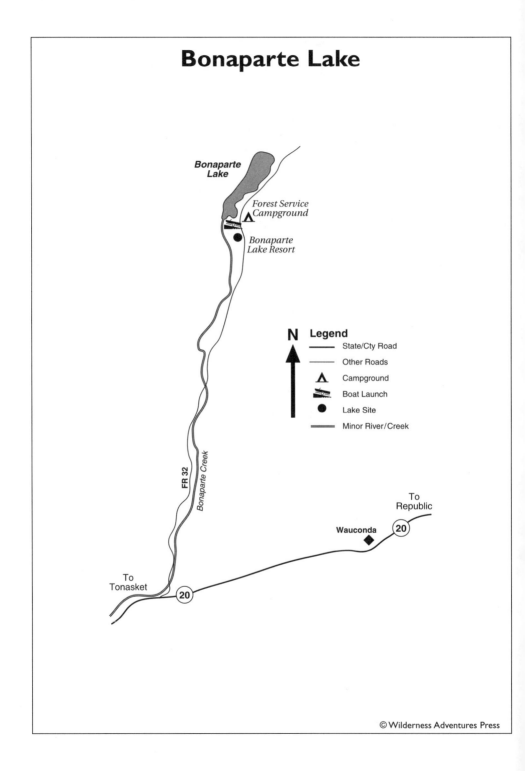

**Bonaparte Lake**

Forest Service Campground

Bonaparte Lake Resort

**N**

**Legend**
State/Cty Road
Other Roads
Campground
Boat Launch
Lake Site
Minor River/Creek

FR 32

Bonaparte Creek

To Republic

Wauconda

20

To Tonasket

20

© Wilderness Adventures Press

# BONAPARTE LAKE

One of Washington's best-known trout lakes, Bonaparte sees its share of anglers. For that reason, you can't expect solitude when fishing here. A resort rests on the lake, and the water gets pounded throughout the year-round season.

But Bonaparte is a good option for those who don't mind company and the common sight of a trout getting whacked on the head. Bonaparte is managed under statewide rules, including a 5-trout limit. Only one fish may stretch more than 20 inches.

Bonaparte covers 160 acres, and it hosts lake trout (mackinaw), brook trout, and rainbow trout. The lake trout reach 30 pounds, and rainbows often reach 5 pounds, some a little more.

Because of its depth, Bonaparte isn't your classic flyfishing lake. If you want to catch trout here, you have to get out the heavy artillery, meaning full-sink lines and large, weighted streamers.

Bonaparte is usually covered with ice during winter, but it recedes sometime in April, and by May the lake is ice-free. Flyfishing for lake trout can be productive right after ice-out when the big brutes are often found in shallower depths, around rock outcrops near shore.

Flyfishing for rainbows is also productive after ice-out. Anglers who work large streamers just off shore can usually pick up a fish or two a day, solid ones at that, in the early season.

As May and June give way to the sweltering heat of summer, most of Bonaparte's trout head into the depths, and flyfishing options diminish. Fall brings the fish back into the shallower areas where full-sink lines can again put anglers in contact with fish.

A selection of flies for Bonaparte reads like a flyfishing purist's list from hell: size 2 and 4 woolly buggers, white zonkers, sculpins, and kokanee salmon imitations draw strikes.

To reach Bonaparte from Tonasket, follow Hwy 20 east 18 miles to the turnoff for Bonaparte Lake. Follow that road about 7 miles to the lake. Bonaparte Lake Resort has tent and RV sites, cabins, and groceries. Bonaparte Lake Campground, which is managed by the Forest Service, also offers campsites.

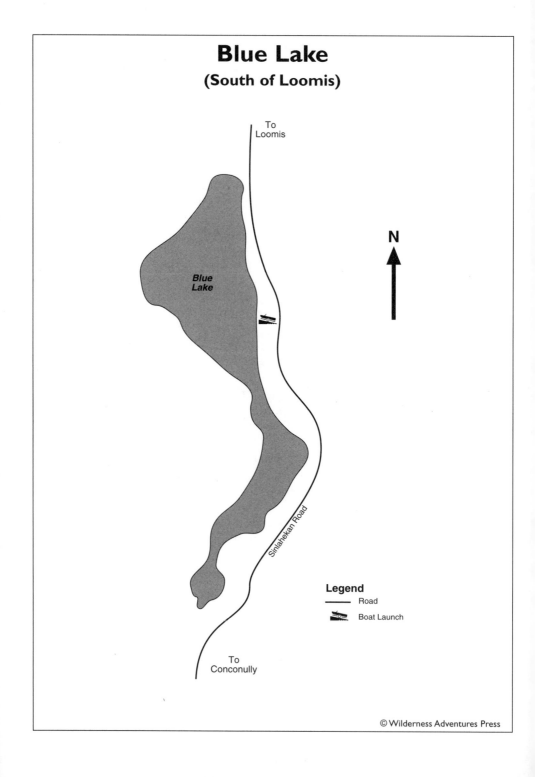

# Blue Lake
## (South of Loomis)

To
Loomis

N

Blue
Lake

Sinlahekan Road

**Legend**
—— Road
Boat Launch

To
Conconully

# BLUE LAKE
## (South of Loomis)

While this Blue Lake doesn't offer huge Lahontan cutthroat as the lake of the same name farther north, it does offer some chunky rainbows and is managed under a strict 1-fish limit, single barbless flies, and artificial lures only. Electric motors are allowed on the lake.

Blue Lake sits in the gorgeous Sinlahekin Valley, and wildlife is in the area. White-tailed deer, mule deer, and bighorn sheep can be spotted on the slopes above the lake.

In the water, Blue offers rainbow trout that commonly reach 16 inches, with lots of fish running larger than that.

Aquatic insect hatches determine the quality of fishing here. Fortunately, there are some good hatches to match.

The lake opens the last Saturday in April and stays open through October. Midges dominate the show during the first couple of weeks of the season. Callibaetis mayflies make their appearance in mid-May, and their presence remains through summer. Damselflies are also important insects at Blue, and the lake's trout have no trouble hammering standard olive marabou damsels, size 6 and 8. Scuds also end up in the belly of trout, so take a few scud patterns in case the damsels and Callibaetis taper off.

During fall, streamer patterns work wonders at Blue, especially for the lake's largest rainbows, which stretch to 24 inches.

Egg-sucking leeches, woolly buggers, brown sculpins and shiner patterns work well. Fish those off sinktip and full-sink lines.

To reach Blue Lake, turn south at Loomis and follow the Sinlahekin Road about 6 miles to Blue. Public access sites exist at the north and south ends of the lake. Some primitive campsites can be found at the access points.

The lake covers about 160 acres, so bring a boat or float tube if you can. Watercraft, and the increased mobility they offer, can only improve your luck.

# Lake Facts: Blue Lake
## (South of Loomis)

### Seasons
- Last Saturday in April through October 31.

### Special Regulations
- One-fish limit, no size restriction.
- Selective gear rules apply.
- Electric motors allowed.

### Species
- Rainbow trout

### Lake Characteristics
- This lake offers some very nice trout in the 14- to 18-inch range.
- Like other northern Washington lakes, it's very fertile and offers excellent midge, damselfly, Callibaetis, and Baetis hatches.
- Leeches, scuds, and minnows are also abundant.

### Access
- Best fished from a float tube or boat, Blue also offers some shore fishing.
- Boat launches can be found at the south end and the northeast side of the lake.

# BIG TWIN LAKE

Although the trolling crowd hits Big Twin hard, the lake is managed under artificial fly and lure restrictions, and it allows a 1-fish limit. The restrictions keep the quality of trout high. That's why it's not uncommon to catch several rainbows to 18 or 20 inches, with a big Lahontan cutthroat thrown in on the side, when fishing Big Twin.

Big Twin, which opens the last Saturday in April and closes October 31, is located just a couple miles south of Winthrop in the Methow Valley.

Due to the presence of Lahontan cutthroat, this lake can be fished in a crude fashion, with large woolly buggers, weighted sculpin imitations, and zonkers drawing strikes. You don't have to match the hatch to catch fish here, although an angler who can switch from the big, ugly patterns that Lahontans like to an insect imitation is going to hit the rainbows pretty hard, too.

Midges, Callibaetis, caddis, and damselflies are all encountered at Big Twin. Standard nymph and dry-fly patterns should draw strikes. Look for midges, Callibaetis, and damsels in May and June. Caddis may be present, too. Hatches taper off a little during July and August, then rebound with solid Callibaetis and midge emergences in September. If no hatch is present, go with scud imitations or the aforementioned streamer patterns—cutthroat can't keep their teeth off them.

To reach Big Twin, which is a gorgeous 80-acre lake surrounded by forested hills and higher mountains, follow Hwy 20 through Winthrop. At the end of town, follow Twin Lakes Road about 3 miles to the Big Twin Lake Campground. Follow the road a half-mile to the public access site.

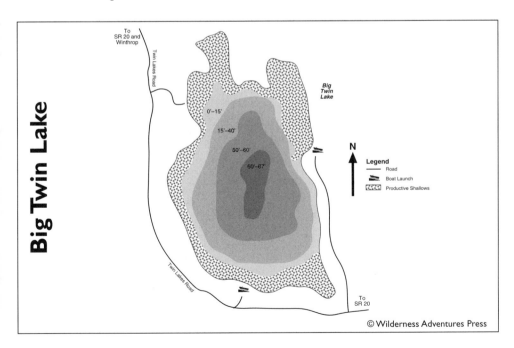

# Omak Lake

To
Omak

To
SR 155
and Omak

COLVILLE
INDIAN
RESERVATION

C L I F F S

S T E E P   B A N K S

Omak
Lake

**N**

**Legend**
—— Road
----- Gravel/Dirt Road
Boat Launch

© Wilderness Adventures Press

# OMAK LAKE

When Lahontan cutthroat trout and Washington state are mentioned in the same sentence, most anglers immediately think Lake Lenore.

Lenore was Washington's first killer Lahontan cutthroat fishery, and it's still kicking out some monster trout, but it isn't the only Evergreen state water that holds those appealing attributes. In fact, in recent years Omak Lake has exhibited equal prowess. Fortunately, the masses haven't reached its banks, unlike Lake Lenore's shores, which hold hundreds of wade anglers, with many more bobbing around the surface in float tubes and boats during the prime spring months.

Due to its proximity to western Washington and its massive urban concentrations, Lenore gets pounded. Omak Lake, on the other hand, rests in northcentral Washington, a long drive from Seattle and other major cities, such as Spokane and Missoula, Montana. If you live in western Washington and want to fish Omak Lake, you better have a four-day weekend to blow—it's a 6-hour drive to the banks of Omak Lake from Seattle. No doubt, the drive is worth it, but because of the hours involved behind the steering wheel, trophy trout hunters fish for Omak's Lahontans in relative solitude compared to the combat angling option at Lenore.

The best time to fish Omak, for quality fishing and lack of competition, is during the catch-and-release season, which runs from April 1 to June 30. During that time, spinfishers are few. If you do see anglers on the water, they most likely belong to your clan and will be clutching a 5- to 7-weight fly rod in their casting hand.

Omak Lake lies on the Colville Indian Reservation about 100 miles north and just slightly east of Wenatchee. It's a fairly narrow, 6.5-mile long body of water that rates about 3,300 surface acres and measures about 300 feet at its deepest point. Lahontans are distributed throughout the lake, but they are most pronounced and most accessible to flyfishers in the shallow areas, which are mostly in the lake's northern and southern sections. The north shores drop off quickly and are relatively deep. However, some good wade access occurs in the north bays. Mission access at East Bay is a good spot, as is Nicholson Beach at West Bay. At the northern tip of the lake, a ramp allows boat access.

To reach the north end, follow Hwy 155 about a mile east, then follow Omak Creek Road for about 5 miles. As the pavement turns to dirt, a road takes off down the hill to the lake and beaches.

Some fish are at the east and west banks, but they, too, are steep and difficult to reach. The south end of the lake is accessible via a road that parallels it. Anglers can park off the highway and hike down to the lake, hopefully timing their arrival with the presence of a pod of midge-scarfing Lahontans.

"Omak Lake is great because you hardly ever see another fisherman," says Rick Baker of Tonasket, who frequently ventures to Omak Lake. "When the dragonfly larvae are active, you can't beat it. If you hit it on the right day, you can't keep the cutthroat off your line—and I'm talking about hooking and releasing 40 fish in a day between 3 and 7 pounds.

"I like to fish a sandbar on the west side of the lake," Baker adds. "You can walk the sandbar 500 yards out into the lake, and either side of the sandbar is good. I cast to one side or the other depending on the wind. Usually there are good hatches of dragonflies and damselflies on the hot days after Memorial Day weekend. But after the Fourth of July, fishing trails off. It picks back up in the fall."

Flyfishers who choose to challenge Omak Lake should be prepared to battle some large fish. First introduced to Omak in 1968 from the Hagerman Fish Hatchery in south-central Idaho and subsequent plants from Heenan Lake, Nevada, cutthroat grew large on a steady diet of redside shiners, sculpins, peamouths, and bridgelip suckers. A healthy aquatic insect supply also adds weight to the fish.

In 1993, an 18-pound, 4-ounce cutthroat was landed and stands as the Washington state record. Imagine that cutt connected to your 4-weight! Beginning in 1970, the Colville Tribal Fish Hatchery has annually added about 60,000 to 100,000 juvenile cutthroat, keeping the fishery healthy.

Due to the potential size of Omak's cutthroat, anglers should pass on the 4-weight rods and throw nothing smaller than a 5-weight. It actually pays to carry several rods and several lines with you. If you find glassy conditions and fish feeding on midges, a 5-weight with a floating line should work fine. If there is no surface activity, you may want to switch to a sinktip or full-sink line and probe the depths with a streamer. If windy conditions are encountered (at some point during the day, the wind will come up), run back to your rig and whip out the 6- or 7-weight fly rod and attach a sinktip or full-sink line to it.

If you fish the northern sections of the lake, a full-sink is a good choice due to the quick dropoff from the shorelines. If fishing the bays or shallow south lake sections, try a moderate sinktip line.

Omak's cutthroat are not very leader-shy, and they seem quite happy to pound just about any offering if it looks fishy or buggy. Streamer patterns in size 2, 4, 6, and 10, lead-eyed woolly buggers (red, black, brown, olive, and crystal flash patterns are good choices), matuka sculpins, muddler minnows, Mickey Finns, zonkers (white, black and green gets them), and rabbit-strip leeches, all draw strikes. Those patterns can be fished off of short (3 or 4 feet) leaders. Six to 10-pound Maxima works well.

If fishing insect imitations, a lighter, longer leader, say a 9- or 10-foot leader, tapered to 3X, 4X or 5X, may be required. Omak's insect emergences begin with midges in April, and they remain on the water through the season. On hot days, look for a midge emergence early in the morning. When the weather is cooler, they may come off in the afternoon. Their size varies, but midges in the size 16 to 20 range should be expected. Keep pupa and emerger patterns in your fly arsenal. Midges are most effectively fished under a strike indicator using a terribly slow, twist retrieve— not the type of fishing that I can endure for very long.

Omak Lake also witnesses a prime damselfly emergence in May and June, and quite a few large fish key on those half-inch to inch-long olive/brown insects. Standard damsel patterns, such as an olive marabou damsel, draw strikes. My favorite damsel patterns include marabous, Nyergess nymphs, and six-packs that

*Many northern Washington lakes offer large Lahontan cutthroat trout.*
*This one, taken by the author, ate a leech pattern.*

can be fished off a floating or sinktip line and are most effective when worked through the shallow areas where trout drill them just before they reach shore.

A few mayflies may be encountered on the water sporadically. Pale morning duns and Callibaetis catch the Lahontan's attention, too, but neither emergence is considered heavy. If you see a few duns on the water and fish rising, a parachute Adams, Callibaetis cripple, or a gray sparkle dun may tempt trout.

Whether fishing streamers or aquatic insect imitations, Omak flyfishers don't have to launch a boat or float tube on the water to enjoy success. However, a boat or float tube does allow an angler lots of access to water that the wade fisher just can't reach. If the wind isn't blowing too hard, I always dump a tube in the water and prowl the shorelines.

Whether casting from a tube or wade fishing, polarized glasses can really help you locate fish. No matter what stillwater you visit, carry a pair of glasses and use them. Search the bottom for cruising fish—often you'll spot pods of big cutthroat working the shallows, or you might sight a single or two diligently cruising the flats. If you can spot a fish and place a streamer in front of its snout, your future looks bright.

To fish Omak Lake, you don't need a Washington Department of Fish and Wildlife license. However, you do need a permit from the Colville Fish and Wildlife Department. You can write the tribe at PO Box 150, Nespelem, WA 99155, or call at 509-634-8845. They can send you a fishing regulations booklet and answer any questions you have about the reservation and Omak Lake. Camping is not allowed, but there are comfortable motels nearby in Omak that make for a comfortable overnight stay. At the time of publication, it cost $15 for a 3-day fishing reservation permit, $20 for 7 days, and $30 for the season license.

While that may sound like a steep price to fish one lake, realize that the average Omak Lake Lahontan stretches 16 to 18 inches. Twenty-inch-plus fish are commonly caught. Five-to 7-pound Lahontans don't even turn too many heads. A 10-pound or better cutthroat is considered a real good one.

Few stillwaters offer trout equaling such impressive dimensions. That's why a trip to Omak Lake should be on the hit list of every dedicated Washington flyfisher. Your travel time and reservation permit cost is well worth it. Who knows, you may even land the next state record cutthroat. If so, take a length and girth measurement, snap a photo, and send that fish back where it belongs—in the lake.

Omak Lake is open to angling all year, and it usually remains ice-free during winter. Lahontans can be taken during winter, but their appetite perks up in April as the first heavy midge emergences take place. Fishing remains strong into early July when fish dive a little deeper to avoid warm surface temperatures. In the fall, they again move into the shallows, and fishing can be terrific.

To reach Omak Lake, take U.S. 97 to Omak. Turn east on State Route 155, then turn right (south) and follow Omak Lake Road over Antoine Pass to the lake.

# Lake Facts: Omak Lake

**Seasons**
- Year-round.

**Special Regulations**
- Catch and release from April 1 through June 30.

**Species**
- Lahontan cutthroat trout

**Lake Characteristics**
- Narrow and deep, Omak provides excellent fishing around its shallow water shoals and bays.
- Lahontans love fish, so streamer patterns, such as woolly buggers or zonkers, work best here.
- Some Callibaetis, midges, and damselflies may be present, and fish can turn their attention to them when they emerge.
- Early season and late season options are best.
- Fishing slows down in July and August when Lahontans dive deep.

**Access**
- Decent wade access for flyfishers who don't own a boat or float tube.
- The south end of the lake and the bays at the north end provide good options.
- A boat ramp exists at the north end.

# Long Lake

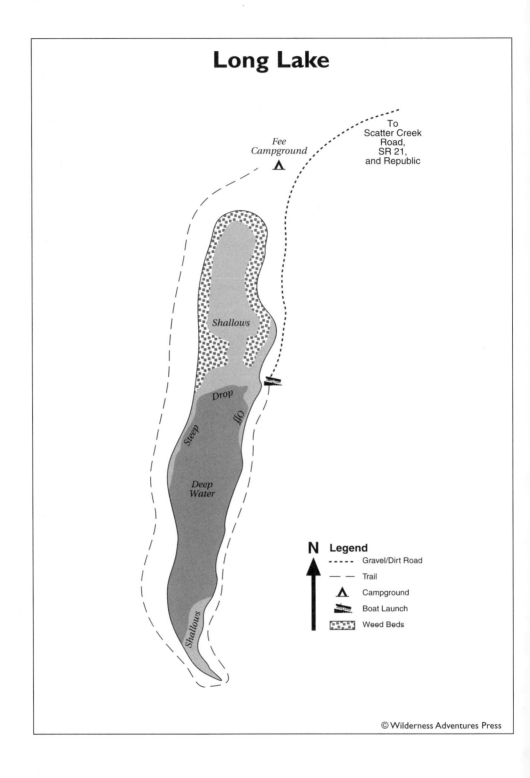

To
Scatter Creek
Road,
SR 21,
and Republic

*Fee Campground*

*Shallows*

*Drop Off*

*Steep*

*Deep Water*

*Shallows*

**N**

**Legend**
- - - - - Gravel/Dirt Road
— — — Trail
**Λ** Campground
Boat Launch
Weed Beds

© Wilderness Adventures Press

# LONG LAKE

There are several lakes in the Okanogan area that answer to the first name Long, but the best one sits in a beautiful mountain valley between steep slopes on either side, just south of Republic, Washington. If you are looking for fast action on naive cutthroat trout, this is the place to go.

Once you visit Long Lake, I'm sure you will place it in your mind as one of the most scenic spots you've ever been. On the west side, arid slopes, riddled with cliffs, rise from the lake. On the east side, the slopes are heavily timbered. The lake itself offers beautiful blue, clear water that gets deep very quickly when you work out from shore. In fact, it's the type of dropoff that gives me the willies. When my legs are dangling down in the drink below a float tube, I wonder just what might prowl in the depths. Nobody ever told me I have a lack of imagination.

Some flyfishers who hit Long have an equal imagination, if their boasts of 20-inch plus cutthroat on every other cast is any indication. Long may have a few fish over 20 inches cruising in its depths, but it is not a lake where you can go out and expect to catch a fish meeting those appealing dimensions. Instead, expect to catch lots of 8- to 13-inch cutthroat, most of them on dry flies. Occasionally you might net a 16-incher.

"Long is a great dry-fly lake," says Rick Baker, who fishes the lake often. "That makes it an excellent option for first-time flyfishers. You can really gain confidence here because cutthroat eat just about anything that floats. Elk hair caddis, a parachute Adams, mosquitoes, midges…everything works."

Baker tells no lie. Long's cutthroat seem to feed off the surface all day long, in any kind of weather, and I've never found them very particular when offered a dry fly.

Prime fishing can be found at the north end of the lake, just in front of the public access site. A shallow, 5- to 10-foot deep flat that bumps up against tules greets anglers there. A couple of dozen yards out, the bottom falls away, and the depth drops to 25 feet. The dropoff holds fish, and if for some reason cutthroat aren't scarfing flies off the top, you can put on a sinktip or full-sink line and work caddis pupa, scuds, woolly buggers, damsel nymphs and standard mayfly nymphs, such as a hare's ear or pheasant tail, with good success.

Near the access site there is a narrow channel, perhaps 5 feet deep, that carves through the tules and allows entrance into the very north end of the lake, a shallower area also circled by tules, that also hosts good numbers of fish.

The east and west shorelines drop off quickly and provide little in the way of productive shallows. However, a trail circles the lake and offers the enterprising angler an option to pack a float tube to the seldom-fished south end where some excellent shallows exist.

Mornings and evenings provide the best action at Long, but even the afternoon hours are productive. General fly patterns such as the elk-hair caddis and Adams work great. Specific patterns such as a sparkle dun, midge emerger, Callibaetis cripple, and Callibaetis comparadun, tied in various sizes, are so much the better.

*Giant caddis bring hearty rises from rainbow and cutthroat trout
on many northern Washington lakes.*

While Long fishes well throughout the season, May, June and September are the prime times to take trout here. The largest fish are usually landed in September.

To reach Long Lake, take Highway 21 south from Republic toward Keller Ferry. Turn left onto Scatter Creek Road and follow to the sign, which is clearly marked, for Long Lake. There is a fee campground at the very north end of Long. Crude campsites are sprinkled around in the surrounding mountains. Motels are available in Republic.

If you camp in the area, follow proper bear precautions. There are many black bears in the area that would just love to make a meal out of your cooler.

# Lake Facts: Long Lake

### Seasons
• Last Saturday in April through September 30.

### Special Regulations
• Flyfishing only.
• No motors.

### Species
• Cutthroat trout to 13 or 14 inches.

### Lake Characteristics
• A deep mountain lake, Long is packed with cutthroat. They can be taken off the surface on small dry flies or underneath with the assistance of a sinktip or full-sink line.
• Most cutts run 6 to 10 inches, but a few fish may stretch to 14 inches or more.
• A wonderful, pristine mountain lake that offers views galore.

### Access
• You need a small boat, canoe, or float tube for Long Lake.
• A boat launch and parking area exist at the northeast end of the lake.
• A fee campground can be found at the north end of Long Lake.

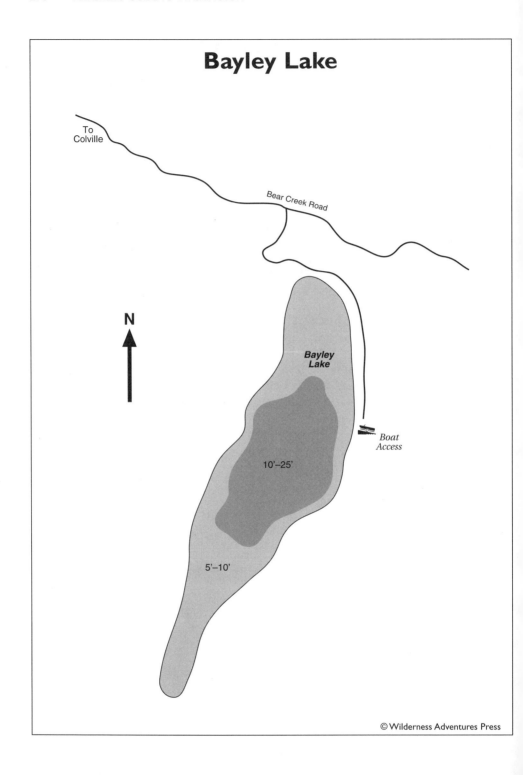

# Bayley Lake

To Colville

Bear Creek Road

N

Bayley Lake

10'–25'

5'–10'

Boat Access

© Wilderness Adventures Press

# BAYLEY LAKE

Due to its abundant aquatic weed growth, which spawns massive insect hatches, Bayley Lake's rainbow trout grow fast. The lake also hosts some brook trout, which, as brookies go, grow to good size.

The average size of Bayley's fish ranges between 12 and 14 inches, but some hog rainbows in the 20-inch range are a distinct possibility when fishing this lake. And fortunately, the fish are afforded some protection by laws governing the water—fly-fishing only, 1-fish (14 inches or better) limit from the last Saturday in April through July 4. After July 4, extending through the October 31 closing date, it's catch and release only. Motors are not allowed on the lake.

Bayley, which rests on the Little Pend Oreille National Wildlife Refuge southeast of Colville, is an excellent location to burn a couple of days in late spring and early summer and again in September and October—its prime fishing seasons.

Bayley covers about 70 acres and is 25 to 30 feet deep in some places. In most areas, the lake runs 10 to 15 feet deep, and that's where you will find rainbows during the early season and again in September and October. When the water warms during summer, rainbows and brook trout head for deep water where sinktip and full-sink lines are needed to reach the fish.

However, in May and June, when the water temperature is still cool, emergences of damselflies and Callibaetis mayflies, not to mention midges and some Baetis activity, get the fish going.

For the angler, these hatches are easy to match and identify. If Callibaetis are coming off, you'll see them struggling to free themselves from their nymphal shucks. Tie on a parachute Adams, gray sparkle dun, Callibaetis cripple, or gray compara-dun, and you're in there.

To match damsels, you'll want to fish nymphs off sinktip lines in the shallow areas. A brown or olive marabou damsel nymph, size 6, 8, or 10, ought to do the trick.

Scuds and leeches are also important food items for Bayley's trout, and patterns imitating them should draw strikes every day of the year.

In late August and September, trout eagerly take grasshoppers that stray onto the water. Placing a grasshopper up against the bank or over one of the lake's numerous dropoffs can bring instant, hearty surface rises. Callibaetis again bring trout to the surface in September and October.

Due to its protective regulations and a relatively demanding drive to get there, Bayley's trout are some of the nicest fish you'll find in northeast Washington. To reach Bayley follow Highway 20 east out of Colville for about 9 miles to a sign for the Little Pend Oreille Wildlife Refuge. Turn south at the sign and follow Narcisse Creek Road 2 miles to Bear Creek Road. Turn left onto Bear Creek Road and follow for 5 miles until you come to a dirt road that veers right and places you at the north end of the lake.

Some shore fishing is available, but the best way to test Bayley is from a float tube, which offers unlimited access to this 17-acre lake.

# NORTHERN WASHINGTON HUB CITIES

# Omak

### Elevation–835 • Population–2,050

Best known for its Omak Stampede and Suicide horse race, Omak is a great place to access northeast Washington's underrated trout fishing.

## ACCOMMODATIONS

**Motel Nicholas,** 527 East Grape / 509-826-4611 / Queen size beds, phone, cable TV

**Stampede Motel,** 215 West 4th / 509-826-1161 / Cable TV, kitchens, one to three bed units

## CAMPGROUNDS AND RV PARKS

**Omak Eastside Park,** from jct US 97 & Hwy 155, ¼ mile northwest on 155 / 509-826-0804 / 72 RV full hook-up sites, tent sites, restrooms, pool

**Log Cabin Trailer Court,** 509 Okoma Drive / 509-826-2422 / Restrooms, laundromat

## RESTAURANTS

**The Breadline Cafe,** 102 Ash Street / 509-826-5836 / Sunday and Monday: breakfast and lunch; Tuesday through Saturday: breakfast, lunch, dinner / Homemade bread, burgers, steaks, full bar, soda fountain, espresso

**North Country Pub,** 15 South Main / 360-826-4271 / Steak, pizza, salad bar, sandwiches, cocktails

**Tequila's,** 635 Okoma Drive / 509-826-5417 / Open 7 days / 12 combination lunches, 27 combination dinners, fajitas, chicken/beef dishes, T-bone steaks

## FLY SHOPS AND SPORTING GOODS

**Cascade Outfitters,** 16 South Main Street / 509-826-4148

**Wal-mart,** 900 Engh Road / 509-826-6002

## AUTO REPAIR

**Damskov,** 707 Okoma Drive / 509-826-2000

## AIR SERVICE

**Omak City Airport,** 202 Omak Airport Road / 509-826-6270 / Lighted airstrip, charter flights, hangar parking, mechanical service, 80-100 octane fuel

Closest Commercial Service: Spokane

## MEDICAL

**Mid-Valley Hospital,** 810 Valley Way / 509-826-1760

## For More Information

Omak Chamber of Commerce
401 Omak Avenue
Omak, WA 98841
509-826-1880

# Oroville
### Elevation–1,000 • Population–1,500

## ACCOMMODATIONS
**Camaray Motel,** 1320 Main Street / 509-476-3684
**Red Apple Inn,** Hwy 97 & 18th / 509-476-3694

## CAMPGROUNDS AND RV PARKS
**Eisen RV Park Reservations,** 1903 Main Street / 509-476-2663
**Sun Cove Resort & Guest Ranch,** 93 East Wannacut Lane / 509-476-2223

## RESTAURANTS
**DJ's Restaurant,** 923 Ironwood Street / 509-476-2056
**Fao's Restaurant & Lounge,** 1412 Main Street / 509-476-4142
**Peerless,** 1401 Main Street / 509-476-4344
**Sun Cove Resort & Guest Ranch,** 93 East Wannacut Lane / 509-476-2223

## VETERINARIANS
**Alpine Veterinary Clinic,** 33276 Hwy 97 C / 509-476-3730
**Ark Animal Clinic,** 33061 US 97 / 509-476-4343

## FLY SHOPS AND SPORTING GOODS
**Darrel's Sporting Goods,** 1417 Main Street / 509-486-0827

## AUTO REPAIR
**Max's Service Center,** 2002 Main Street / 509-476-2581
**Paul's Service,** Hwy 97 / 509-476-2241
**Thompson Towing,** Rt. 2, Box 1248 / 509-476-3948

## AIRPORT
**Oroville Municipal Airport,** 23 Airport Road / 509-476-9976

## MEDICAL
**Pioneer Medical Center,** 608 Central Avenue / 509-476-3631

## FOR MORE INFORMATION
Oroville Chamber of Commerce
1730 Main Street
Oroville, WA 98844
509-476-2739

# Republic

## ACCOMMODATIONS

**Black Beach Resort,** 848 Black Beach Road / 509-775-3989
**Cottonwoods Motel,** 852 South Clark Avenue / 509-775-3371
**Fisherman's Cove Resort,** 1157 Fisherman's Cove Road / 509-775-3641
**Klondike Motel,** 150 North Clark Street / 509-775-3555

## CAMPGROUNDS AND RV PARKS

**Pine Point Resort,** 1060 Pine Point Road / 509-775-3643
**Tiffany's Resort,** 1026 Tiffany Road / 509-775-3152
**Fisherman's Cove Resort,** 1157 Fisherman's Cove Road / 509-775-3641
**Pine Point Resort,** 1060 Pine Point Road / 509-775-3643
**Tiffany's Resort,** 1026 Tiffany Road / 509-775-3152

## RESTAURANTS

**Hitchin' Post Restaurant & Lounge,** 652 South Clark Avenue / 509-775-2221
**Hometown Pizza,** 680 South Keller / 509-775-2557
**The Other Place,** 645 South Clark Avenue / 509-775-2907
**Republic's Fine Dining Restaurant & Lounge,** 908 South Clark Avenue /
    509-775-2305
**Wild Rose Cafe,** 644 South Clark Avenue / 509-775-2096

## VETERINARIANS

**All Creatures Veterinary,** 1447 South Clark Avenue / 509-775-3544

## FLY SHOPS AND SPORTING GOODS

**Republic Sportshop,** 298 Hwy 20 East / 509-775-3040

## AUTO REPAIR

**Cromwell's Auto Repair,** 322 Hwy 21 North / 509-775-2993
**Doug's Automotive,** 420 Hwy 20 East / 509-775-2201
**Smith & Sons Automotive Repair,** 665 South Newton Street / 509-775-3941

## MEDICAL

**Ferry County Memorial Hospital,** 470 Klondike Road / 509-775-3153

# Colville
### Elevation–2,000 • Population–4,650

## ACCOMMODATIONS
**Beaver Lodge Resort & Campground,** 2430 Highway 20 East / 509-684-5657
**Benny's Colville Inn,** 915 South Main Street / 509-684-2517
**Care Free Guest Ranch Bed & Breakfast,** 786 Arden Butte Road / 509-684-4739
**Comfort Inn,** 166 Northeast Canning Drive / 509-684-2010
**Maple at Sixth Bed & Breakfast,** 407 East 6th Avenue / 509-684-5251

## CAMPGROUNDS
**Beaver Lodge Resort & Campground,** 2430 Highway 20 East / 509-684-5657
**Homeland RV Park & Campground,** 4706 Northport Waneta Road / 509-732-4367

## RESTAURANTS
**Crossroads Bar & Grill,** 616 Highway 395 South / 509-684-8544
**The Depot,** 651 North Railroad Street / 509-685-1181
**King Cole's Steak House,** 100 South Main Street / 509-684-2345
**Red Bull Steak House,** 542 South Main Street / 509-684-6651
**Ruffed Grouse Restaurant,** 955 South Main Street / 509-685-1308
**The Whistle Stop,** 695 North Hwy / 509-684-3424
**Woody's of Colville,** 986 South Main Street / 509-684-4458

## VETERINARIANS
**Colville Animal Hospital,** 572 South Main Street / 509-684-2102
**Terry Richards, Veterinarian,** 572 South Main Street / 509-684-2102

## FLY SHOPS AND SPORTING GODS
**Clark's All Sports,** 557 South Main Street / 509-684-5069
**Wal-Mart,** 810 North Hwy 395 / 509-684-3209

## AUTO REPAIR
**Colville Auto Repair,** 505 South Main Street / 509-684-3581
**Earl's Auto Hospital,** 200 South Railroad Street / 509-684-2500
**Dave Weaver Garage,** 281 West 3rd / 509-684-6524

## MEDICAL
**Mount Carmel Hospital,** 982 East Columbia Avenue / 509-684-2561 / 24-hour
service)

## FOR MORE INFORMATION
Colville Chamber Of Commerce
121 East Astor Avenue
Colville, WA 99114
509-684-5973

# Eastern Washington Rivers

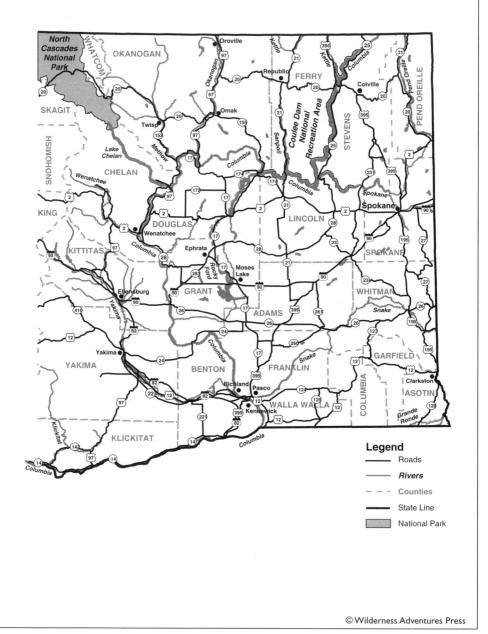

**Legend**

— Roads
— *Rivers*
– – – Counties
— State Line
▨ National Park

© Wilderness Adventures Press

# Eastern Washington Rivers

Although not highlighted in national flyfishing publications, eastern Washington offers excellent stream fishing options, similar to those available on some of the acclaimed Rocky Mountain waters.

Test Rocky Ford on an overcast January day, and you may wonder why Montana's rivers, such as Rock Creek, the Gallatin, and Madison, seem such a winter draw. Rocky Ford offers large rainbows during winter—trout to 5 pounds or more—that greedily feed off the surface. Cast hoppers along the wade-only water during summer, and you may be thrilled to see a 5-pounder detonate on your offering. On a slow day, a couple fish to 20 inches can be expected.

During the summer and fall seasons, there may not be a finer river to spend your time on than the Yakima. It's a sparkling, medium-sized stream that rushes off the flanks of the Cascade Mountains and offers lots of aquatic insect hatches and plenty of solid rainbow trout. Possibly the best way to fish the Yakima is by drift boat or raft, and on a good float, an angler may catch and release a couple dozen trout that range from 8 to 24 inches—all on dry flies.

In northern Washington, two undiscovered streams, the Sanpoil and Kettle Rivers, offer excellent rainbow and brown trout options. And these fisheries stand to improve in years to come due to restrictive regulations that are now in place. In their upper reaches, the Sanpoil and Kettle offer scrappy rainbows in the 6- to 16-inch range. In their lower sections, the rivers offer some meaty brown trout that seem fairly eager to swallow large woolly buggers and weighted sculpins. Four to 5-pound browns show up every season, especially in the nets of those who specifically target them.

Even the residents of eastern Washington's major population center, Spokane, find excellent fishing options right out their back doors. Those who pass on northern Idaho's and western Montana's tasty treats find large rainbow trout and some sizable brown trout in the Spokane River, which flows right through the city. The best water exists from Spokane upstream to the Idaho border, where the river is managed as a wild trout fishery. If you test that section during a major caddis emergence, you won't soon forget the fishing.

While eastern Washington offers excellent trout options, it also provides anadromous fish. In fact, steelhead ascend many eastside rivers with the Grande Ronde, Klickitat, Wenatchee (when it's open), and Methow offering the best options. Eastern Washington's steelhead are determined, hard-fighting fish that test an angler's equipment and skill to the max. A first steelhead on the fly rod can lead to a lifelong devotion. When you head out for one of these streams, realize that you may set yourself up for a lifelong passion, your winter hours spent daydreaming about 10-pound sea-run rainbows, and fine-tuning excuses for your spouse. Your late summer and fall days, hopefully, will be spent in the water, swinging nymphs or even surface flies to steelhead.

For those who prefer moving water to stagnant stillwaters, eastern Washington offers plenty of action. Grab your 4-weight and some dry flies or fetch an 8-weight and a box of steelhead patterns and head out on the river-you shouldn't be disappointed.

# KLICKITAT RIVER

On the map, the Klickitat River winds off Goat Rocks Wilderness and Conrad Glacier before slicing south through the Yakima Indian Reservation under the watchful gaze of Mount Adams, an active volcano.

From there, the river carves through a beautiful canyon before exiting into the Columbia River at Lyle.

While a map accurately depicts the river's physical wanderings, it can't depict the hold the river has on the minds and hearts of those who ply this river regularly as Dan Little does.

Little lives on the banks of the Klickitat during summer and fall, runs a flyfishing guide service (R.B.F. Excursions) on its water, and is absolutely in love with this prime king salmon and steelhead stream. In fact, Little says he couldn't think of a better place to be.

"I've fished a lot of rivers, from the Olympic Peninsula to Canada to Alaska, and when I'm an old man, my best memories will come from this river," Little says. "This is where my heart is, and that's why I make the river my home. It's just a beautiful, scenic place with lots of wildlife and some awesome king salmon and steelhead in it."

Little is so fond of the Klickitat that he rates it a better fishery than Oregon's revered Deschutes River, which flows into the south side of the Columbia, just east of the Dalles. The Deschutes is recognized by flyfishers from all over the Northwest, while the Klickitat is more of a local stream, its treats usually reserved for those who live close to the river.

That's OK with Little and those who fish the river frequently. Although it's not a real secret, the Klickitat certainly doesn't draw the crowds that steelhead and salmon anglers find on many Northwest streams.

Steelhead are present in the Klickitat from opening day, June 1, through the season, which closes November 30.

Because the Klickitat is a glacial-fed river, early-season options (June, July, and early August) can be hampered by stream flow and water clarity, especially when the temperature scoots into the 90-degree range. At that time, visibility may rate just a few inches. That makes it tough to find steelhead or king salmon with a fly. An angler practically has to touch a steelie's nose with a fly to get a take.

However, there remain some options even when the river kicks out of shape. Anglers just need to know what they're looking for.

"When the temperature hits the 90- to 100-degree mark, the river goes out during the day," Little says. "But there is about a 2- to 4-hour window each day when the fishing can be pretty good. It occurs from cool temperatures the evening before. Your location on the river determines when the window occurs-it might be 10AM or perhaps not until afternoon. If you are in a riffle where fish are holding when the water clears, you'll get them."

# Klickitat River

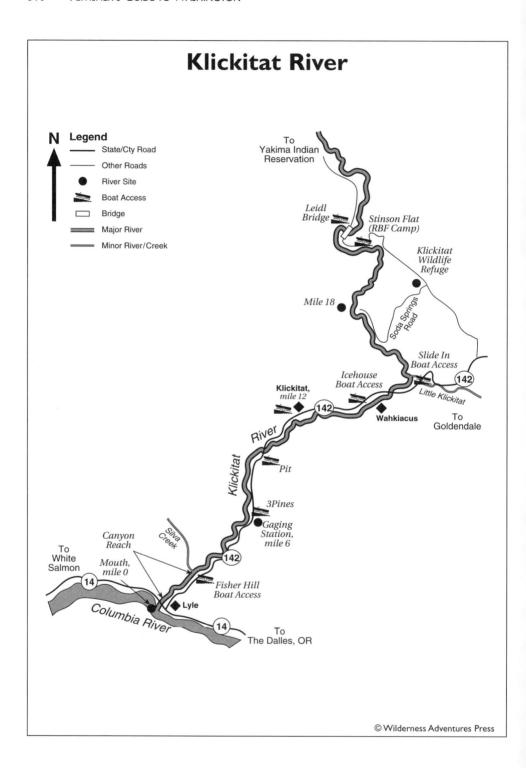

**Legend**

| | |
|---|---|
| State/Cty Road |
| Other Roads |
| River Site |
| Boat Access |
| Bridge |
| Major River |
| Minor River/Creek |

N

To Yakima Indian Reservation

Leidl Bridge

Stinson Flat (RBF Camp)

Klickitat Wildlife Refuge

Mile 18

Soda Springs Road

Slide In Boat Access

Icehouse Boat Access

142

Little Klickitat

Klickitat, mile 12

142

Wahkiacus

To Goldendale

Pit

3Pines

Klickitat River

Gaging Station, mile 6

Silva Creek

Canyon Reach

To White Salmon

Mouth, mile 0

14

142

Fisher Hill Boat Access

Columbia River

Lyle

14

To The Dalles, OR

© Wilderness Adventures Press

During June and early July, the Klickitat's steelhead are mostly comprised of hatchery stock. But by mid-July, a run of native metalheads push their snouts into the river and provide excellent fishing until even more natives run into the river in September.

"Natives that enter in July are really hot fish," Little says. "They fight like hell, and you can really tell the difference between them and the hatchery fish. The natives run 12 to 14 pounds on average-really strong, big fish-and you have to release every one you catch.

"These native Klickitat fish are really adapted to take flies, so you can use nymph tactics with a dead drift, as you would on a trout," Little adds. "From July through mid-September, I use nymph techniques and only one fly-a drowned, weighted Joe's or Dave's hopper. The fish's latent memory makes them really key on those bugs. They don't spawn until spring so they must eat to survive while they are in the river. When they take a hopper there's no doubt about it-they take it wholeheartedly. I fish hopper patterns off a floating line with a 9-foot leader tapered to 12-pound test. I'll attach the fly under a corky, which is used as a strike indicator."

During summer, in the heat of the day, the Klickitat's steelhead move into fast riffles. In the morning and evening, anglers may find them in the tailouts of pools, but most often they will hold in the fast water where the river is better oxygenated and a steady supply of food washes by.

While it's true there are good numbers of steelhead in the river throughout the season, with the exception of the first week or two of June when numbers are a little paltry, steelhead fishing becomes a little dicey in August due to the presence of king salmon in big numbers.

In fact, according to Little, there are so many kings around, it becomes difficult to get a fly to a steelhead before a king eats it, sending an angler off to the races, chasing some monstrous brute down the river, putting a near-breaking-point bend in his 6-, 7-, or 8-weight fly rod.

One nice thing about the Klickitat, whether fishing for steelhead or salmon from a boat or just wading, is access. There are plenty of places to dump a boat in or hike to the river.

Prime floats on the upper sections include Summit Creek to Leidl or Stinson; Leidl or Stinson to Slide In. Excellent lower river floats include Slide In to Icehouse, Klickitat, or Pit; Icehouse to Pit or Three Pines; Klickitat to Pit or Three Pines. Caution: the entire river funnels into a rock canyon at Fisher Hill Boat Access. The river narrows to no wider than drift boat and is impassable.

"The float from Stinson to Slide In is my float, that's my home," Little says. "The water has lots of riffles and the gradient is heavy, so it's fast. Through that area, it's experts only as far as boats go."

As far as wade-fishing options go, there's really no limit. The river is very wade-able, and State Route 142 parallels the Klickitat for most of its length. Side roads, bridge crossings, and public access points allow anglers a chance at the river.

*A Klickitat River king salmon. (Photo by Dan Little)*

However, there is little access to the canyon due to the highway cutting east away from the river and not rejoining it for about 6 miles.

Access, for those who don't mind walking a mile and a half, is available from Soda Springs Road. If you take that route, you'll meet the water in the middle of the canyon reach. Another good option is to hike or mountain bike along a closed logging road that parallels about 6 miles of the Klickitat's west bank. The road is paved, but it may be washed out in certain sections. Just be careful when you maneuver around those areas. Access to the road is from Wahkiacus Bridge. The road follows the west bank and moves north.

When fishing the river, take a few moments to raise your eyes from the water and search the surrounding hills for wildlife. Few houses exist near the river, but deer, beaver, muskrats, grouse, and yes, rattlesnakes are seen on a regular basis.

Although Little rates the Klickitat's entire season "good" for steelhead, if he was forced to choose just two weeks of the year to fish the river (a proposition, I must

*Dan Little, a Klickitat River guide, hoists a large, native summer-run steelhead.*

add, he didn't like), he'd take any two weeks in July or the last week of October and the first week of November.

If visiting in July, anglers confront the prospect of watching the river go out, but that is the tradeoff for getting shots at fresh, hot native fish. In late October and early November, it's a good bet that the river will be in prime shape, the weather cool in the morning and evening, absolutely perfect during the day. The water will be low and clear, and the fish will be active, trying their damnedest to put on some weight before winter really sets in and drops their metabolism to near inactivity.

"Late October into November is when I've really experienced some great fishing," Little says. "At that time, I've had my clients with two fish on at a time. We've even taken up to 10 or 12 fish in a day. It's awesome."

At that time, Little drops the nymph tactics of summer and opts for the traditional wet fly steelhead swing, covering much of the slower water, especially the tailouts of pools. Steelhead are seen holding in the riffles less frequently. In fact, as fall weather cools the water, steelhead seek slower water where their lower metabolism can sustain them.

"If I'm going with a wet fly swing, I'll fish a general practitioner or a doctor doom off sinktip lines," Little says. "The doctor doom, a sand shrimp-like imitation, is a fly that I developed, then turned over to Calib Whitmore of Cabin River Flies, who ties them for me. I use it a lot from July, when the kings enter the river, throughout the season. If I'm not using a hopper, I use the doctor doom."

Another fly that Little wouldn't be without on the water is the time-tested muddler minnow. The muddler takes trout in the Rocky Mountains, draws strikes from salmon in Alaska, and it would probably raise a tarpon in the Florida Keys if anyone ever gave it a try. It can be fished wet or dry. Little soaks it near the bottom of the Klickitat and says that day in/day out, it's probably the most effective fly on the river.

"It's a nasty fly and I love it," Little says. "If I had to use only one fly all year, I'd probably take the muddler, because it works in all types of water all year long. If I were allowed three flies, it would be the muddler minnow for the early season, a hopper during summer, and the doctor doom in fall. I'd tie the muddler on a 1/0 hook."

While the Klickitat's run of steelhead is not likely ever to be compared with big-name Western rivers, such as the Deschutes, Stillaguamish, or Skagit, it offers some extra-strong native fish and some less distinct geological attributes that influence fishing on the river.

"I feel that our fish are even more susceptible to a fly rod than the Deschutes run," Little says. "We may not have the numbers of fish that the Deschutes gets, but our fish are bigger and aren't in the sunlight all day. We're on the north side of the Columbia, with steep hills surrounding the river, and the sun just doesn't hit the water as much as it does on the Deschutes. I catch 90 percent of my fish in the heat of the day. On the Deschutes, I find that the fish become difficult during midday. Often, they go down and won't take a fly. That's not the case on the Klickitat."

Washington's dedicated flyfishers would be foolish not to make a trip to the Klickitat to test its wonderful run of summer steelhead. Throw in the river's run of huge king salmon, and you're really missing the boat if you don't cast a line here.

The Klickitat's king salmon begin pushing their snouts into the river by mid-July. By the first week of August, there are plenty of fish in the lower river's deeper holes, which offer cooler water than the upstream shallows. In fact, during the early king season, fish stack up in four or five major holes, and fishing pressure on them can be fairly intense. To avoid that, flyfishers need to test second-rate holes where a few kings-not the mother lode-may be found. Hey, that's OK. How many kings do you want to fight? Hooked on an 8- or 9-weight rod, one king will make your arms sore and tear up your tackle.

Kings continue their return in late August and September, when they can be found throughout the river, even in some shallow, riffled water. That's when Little really likes to headhunt.

"I target kings in the deep holes early in the season, but I catch most of my fish in September and October when the water cools and fish move into shallow water,"

*A gorgeous Klickitat steelhead. (Photo by Dan Little)*

Little says. "(One) year I caught 10 fish over 50 pounds with the largest going 63 pounds. Forty to 50 percent of our kings will be 5-year old fish." One season, Little ran a 38-pound average on kings!

Kings are comprised mostly of wild stock, maybe 1,000 to 1,400 fish each year. Unfortunately, Washington Department of Fish and Wildlife makes no distinction between the true fish and its hatchery imposters, so any fish can be harvested after August 1. Little, other knowledgeable anglers, and I encourage release of all kings, not to mention the river's steelhead.

For tackle, anglers can handle smaller kings on 6- and 7-weight rods, but an 8-, 9-, or even 10-weight rod is better suited for such a strong, powerful fish. An 8-weight is an excellent choice, because a steelhead might also take a fly-you still get a good fight from a steelhead on this rod, and you can also send a little muscle into a king salmon with it.

A solid reel with plenty of backing (approximately 250 yards) is also a requirement for kings. Wind a Type 2 or Type 3 sinktip line that will allow deep drifts through the holes. A 3- or 4-foot section of 20-pound monofilament that serves as your leader should be attached to the end of the line.

Once a king is hooked, Little encourages anglers to fight it hard, keeping heavy pressure on the rod throughout the fight.

"You can't just let him sit in the hole and rest," Little says. "You have to move him. I like to get downstream of a fish and really put the pressure on. You can't fight these fish to total exhaustion. They need to be hooked, fought, and released in a reasonable time-frame...or else they'll die."

Standard king salmon flies work well on the Klickitat, but Little's tried-and-true pattern is the doctor doom. Mickey Finns, general practitioners, and marabou flies, especially those tied with red feathers, take their fair share of king salmon, too.

The Klickitat also receives a run of coho salmon, but its significance is minimal for a flyfisher. Coho arrive in October and November, but they are most commonly taken by trollers running a flatfish or a sand shrimp at the river's mouth. To the person casting a fly specifically for coho, I pose this question: What's wrong with all the steelhead finning upstream in the river?

Although not often covered in the big-name sporting magazines, the Klickitat River is a true northwest gem and deserves your attention, whether you want to throw a line for native steelhead or giant king salmon. If you spend as much time on this stream as Dan Little does, you, too, might find this river running straight through your heart—it can be that good.

To reach the Klickitat, follow State Route 14 to Lyle. Turn north at Lyle onto State Route 142, which parallels the river for about 20 miles. Little can be reached at 509-965-6308.

# Stream Facts: Klickitat

### Seasons and Special Regulations
- Steelhead: Open June 1 through November 30.
- Whitefish: December 1 through March 31.
- Salmon: Open August 1 through January 1 (Exceptions apply; please consult current fishing regulations).

### Species
- Steelhead and king salmon are the big draw.
- A few coho push into the lower river, but they are not very attractive to the flyfisher.

### Stream Characteristics
- A broad river near its confluence with the Columbia, the Klickitat quickly molds into a fine steelhead and salmon stream.
- Deep pools are complemented by swift riffles.
- The river also offers a deep canyon that produces fish.

### Access
- Boat anglers are allowed the best access, but there are plenty of places all along the river where a wade angler can hit the water.

# Yakima River

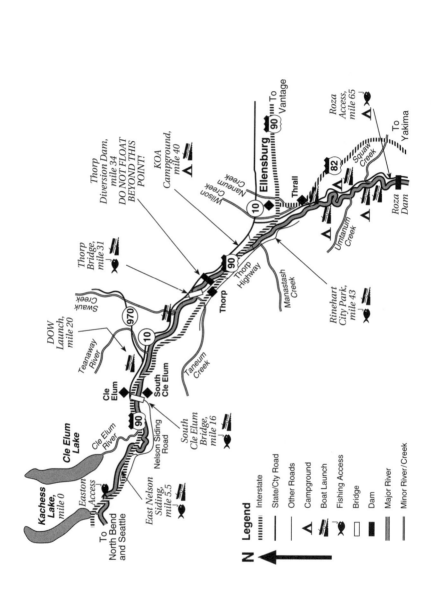

**Legend**

- Interstate
- State/Cty Road
- Other Roads
- Campground
- Boat Launch
- Fishing Access
- Bridge
- Dam
- Major River
- Minor River/Creek

N

# Yakima River

I have seen Torrey Cenis do a lot of crazy things, but none more dangerous than floating down the Yakima River on an iceberg.

It was February, 20 degrees, and we were nymphing for the Yakima's outstanding population of wild rainbow trout. Torrey liked the looks of a deep, softwater run along the downstream bank, but thick brush prevented him from testing it. When a large chunk of ice floated by, Torrey climbed on and drifted downstream, popping casts toward the bank. That he didn't drown or die of hypothermia, via a spill in the river, is somewhat of a miracle.

The Yakima River begins in the Cascade Mountains just west of Cle Elum at Keechelus (pronounced *cathless*) Lake. Through its course, which runs southeast to Ellensburg before slicing through a beautiful canyon and finally arriving in Yakima, the river offers the dry-fly, nymph, or streamer fisher miles of excellent, varied water and plenty of aquatic and terrestrial insects to match.

In Washington, the Yakima is as close to a Rocky Mountain trout stream as you're going to get. Hover over a map of the Rockies and drop this trout stream where you like—it wouldn't be out of place or overlooked whether you let it go in Wyoming, Montana, Idaho, Utah, or Colorado. The Yakima is a pleasure to fish, and it offers just as many sexy holes and eager trout as many of the famous streams in the Rockies.

However, the Yakima hasn't always captured the attention flyfishers. In fact, the river has just recently turned into an excellent trout fishery. The metamorphosis from a lark to a legitimate blue ribbon stream began in 1983 with a decision to end hatchery supplements and begin a naturally reproducing, wild trout program. Regulation changes culminated in 1990 when the 50-mile section between Easton and Roza Dam was designated catch and release. In 1991, this stretch was opened year-round. In tandem with those regulations, that stretch is governed by no bait, single, barbless hook restrictions.

Today, it is not uncommon to raise 15 to 20 trout over 12 inches in a day on the Yakima's special regulation water. But anglers must understand the river's nuances, including the impact that water levels have on angler success and the presence or absence of aquatic insects, which, unlike westside salmon and steelhead streams, controls the habits of trout on the Yakima.

The Yakima's best hatches begin with an emergence of golden stoneflies in March, and their presence can send trout into a feeding frenzy. If a flyfisher is lucky enough to hit this hatch when everything, meaning water conditions and temperature, are perfect, they'll likely never forget the experience.

Put yourself there: The Yakima is running low and clear, with maybe just a hint of color from a recent rain. The banks are mostly barren of snow, and the vegetation is just beginning to dress itself in spring and summer foliage. The sun occasionally peaks out from behind dark, moisture-laden cumulus clouds to reveal mule deer and bighorn sheep munching grass on the surrounding slopes. You launch your raft, put your buddy behind the oars (it's fair, he got the last cup of coffee), and reach into

*The Yakima River offers some of Washington's best*
*match-the-hatch rainbow trout fishing.*

your fly vest. You produce a box of stoneflies-fully loaded from a winter spent tying (you did tie didn't you?)—and select a size 8 or 10 golden stimulator. You dress it with Gink or Aquel fly floatent and tie it to the tip of a 9-foot leader, tapered to 4X or 5X tippet. Your first cast lands dangerously close to the bank (right where it needs to be) and gingerly bobs with the current, which takes it under an overhanging willow tree. Of course, a monster rainbow (hey, this story is taking place in my mind, and I can choose the ending) pushes its nasty snout through the surface film and introduces itself to your stimulator, via a healthy chomp. You set the hook, let out a serious war-whoop that vibrates off canyon walls, then fight the fish skillfully, not applying too much pressure, but definitely making the big fish work against the bend of your fly rod. In three minutes you've witnessed six jumps, two reel-screeching runs, and a serious attempt by a trout to part your leader and your company by scraping its jaw on a submerged boulder. But you weather the barrage, and soon you have a 21-inch rainbow resting in the net, ready for release.

That's the Yakima in March under the best circumstances and it's my opinion that you should try to place yourself there as soon as possible.

The golden stone emergence (not the giant stone, *H. pacifica*, rather a smaller version in the size 10 range) can begin in early March, or it may not be present until the later part of the month depending on weather. Prime conditions would be a series of warm days that raise the water temperature to 45 degrees or more. When that happens golden stonefly nymphs crawl from the large submerged midriver boulders to shallow bankside areas. Trout, in unison, move to those areas to meet them.

A size 10 or 12 golden stonefly nymph will draw strikes when bounced along the bottom rocks. Usually, a chunk or two of split shot, attached to the leader, will help the nymph reach bottom. Lead can also be tied directly to the hook if you tie your nymphs. If you buy flies and nymphs from a shop, ask for weighted golden stone nymphs. A good shop will supply you with weighted nymphs whether they have any on hand or not. You may have to wait overnight for them, but it might be worth the time.

Stonefly nymphs generally work well during the morning hours. In the afternoon, as air temperature heats up, bugs that have crawled out of the water onto bankside vegetation will break through their carapaces, dry their wings, and take flight. They are clumsy flyers and often smack into the water. When they do that, a fish is usually waiting. Don't expect to see blizzards of golden stones as you might on Montana's Rock Creek. But that doesn't mean the fish won't know what they're looking at throughout the Easton to Roza Dam stretch.

According to Jack Mitchell, who guides extensively on the Yakima when he's not chasing trout in Argentina, the Yakima's golden stone emergence does not demand numerous fly patterns or stealth. When the fish are on, they're on, and it doesn't take much to draw them to the surface.

"I don't throw a lot of patterns," Mitchell says. "I like to use a yellow or orange stimulator with rubberlegs, or I try a dirty olive/yellow double-wing or an orange double-wing. If the fish are picky and are not taking the general attractors, I use a realistic stimulator that has a fly foam wing under a sparse deer overwing. And I like to move it. Sometimes the fish want a dead-drift, but usually we fish the stoneflies with controlled twitches and the fish really like it."

If you choose to fish under the surface with a golden stone nymph, you may want to attach a 10-inch section of 4X leader to the bend of the hook and tie on an *Ameledus* mayfly nymph to the end of that, whether you see fish rising for that substantial bug or not. According to Mitchell, the *Ameledus* catches a trout's attention during late winter and early spring.

"I don't think many people realize just how many Ameledus the trout eat, because you don't see fish taking them on the surface," he says. "They emerge right along with the March brown drakes, so you can cover both insects with a a size 12 olive hare's ear or a traditional soft hackle. I just let wet flies swing through the riffles on a quartering downstream cast and they nail it."

During March, April, and May, you may also see the Baetis mayfly, also called a blue-winged olive, especially on warm afternoons. Although diminutive in size (Baetis range from size 16 to 18), they draw trout to the surface and can offer some of the best dry-fly action of the year.

To match Baetis, try a size 16 or 18 parachute Adams or a transitional dun (an excellent flatwater offering tied by Rene Harrop of St. Anthony, Idaho, that works extremely well when trout snub their snouts at a parachute Adams and demand an emerger pattern). Sparkle duns in similar sizes also draw strikes, as do hare's ear, brassie, lightning bug, pheasant tail, and flashback pheasant tail nymphs. Because all Baetis patterns are relatively small, fish them in the surface film or deep off 10-foot leaders with 5X or 6X tippets.

During late April, anglers begin to see the Yakima's first caddis hatches, just as the water temperature rises to the 50- to 53-degree range.

"Once the water temperature warms to 50 degrees, you'll start seeing caddis," Mitchell says. "Usually in early May, the water reaches 53 degrees, and you see a blizzard hatch that lasts a week to three weeks. "At that time, look for the emergence during midday, between 11AM and 5PM."

As summer progresses, flyfishers will see the caddis emergence arrive later in the day. By August, caddis activity will mostly occur during the last hour of light and extend into the evening.

Early season caddis are mostly comprised of Grannom caddis. As the season progresses, the species change. To name all of the caddis species present in the Yakima could blow the mind of most flyfishers, so I won't do that. What flyfishers do need to know about caddis is this: The size of the insect, not color or the ability to rip off its Latin title on command, is most crucial. To match size, hit the river with caddis patterns in a variety of sizes, ranging from 12 to 20, and study the water. (As a general rule, caddis get smaller as the season progresses). When you spot a few caddis, take note of their size and tie on a similarly proportioned imitation and rock 'em.

If you were to watch Mitchell approach a caddis hatch, you would see him repeatedly pull a peacock-bodied elk hair caddis from his fly box.

"The peacock caddis is the ticket," he says. "If you put the fly in there nice, a fish is going to eat it. We also fish a parachute caddis with a polywing because it's easy to see. A low-riding caddis pupae (a LaFontaine sparkle emerger works well) is also a fly that we use a lot. I'd carry a few in size 12 to 20 that range in color from olive, to gray to tan."

Mitchell isn't the only angler to discover the merit of an elk hair caddis. My father and I make frequent ventures to the Yakima, and invariably, an elk hair caddis is the first fly my father pulls from his box. And with good reason: He's caught a number of sweet rainbows from the Thorpe area, not to mention some memorable leapers in the canyon section, on that easily-tied pattern.

In September and October, as water temperature cools and the level drops, caddis hatches again occur closer to midday, often between 10AM and 2PM, and some of the emerging bugs may be the giant October caddis, although good numbers of small gray caddis continue emerging midday.

During late September, October and early November, anglers should find the big caddis collecting in the backwaters, eddies, and the inside corners of current lines, especially upstream from Thorpe.

"I think overall, the best caddis hatches occur in the Canyon section," Mitchell says. "But the October caddis seams to come off best upriver. "When they emerge, I like to throw a big, orange, rubberleg stimulator trailed by a parachute Adams to match any Baetis that might also be hatching."

*A fall float through the canyon stretch of the Yakima River.*

While caddis provide opportunity almost all season, flyfishers only have a short time to take advantage of the early season mayfly hatches, which include a substantial emergence of pale morning duns and green and brown drakes.

Pale morning duns should be present from late May through mid-July with a peak in June. Emergences generally begin around 1PM and continue through 4PM. Standard mayfly patterns, such as parachute PMDs, extended body PMDs, sparkle duns, comparaduns, hare's ear, pheasant-tail, and flashback nymphs, work wonders. Note: In regard to all mayflies on the Yakima, spinnerfalls tend to be far less significant than emergences.

While the true PMD hatch dies in mid-July, anglers can still chase some cahill-looking creatures and pale evening duns most summer evenings after 6 or 7PM. If you do see them, fish the riffles with standard PMD patterns or an X-caddis. An X-caddis should match all caddis species and it doubles as a downwing or drowned mayfly imitation.

While you can find that wonderful PMD and caddis activity in the Yakima Canyon during June, you may want to pull yourself away from that section and fish upstream between Thorpe and Easton if you hear any mention of salmonflies or green and brown drakes. Due to feeder streams that can taint the water below Thorpe, salmonflies and drakes come off best upstream of Thorpe and are worth trying to intercept.

"You can find a lot of people in the canyon during June fishing PMDs and caddis," Mitchell says. "If you want to escape the crowd, I'd move upstream and throw size 6 dry salmonflies or a big drake.

"You don't really see too many salmonflies, maybe 20 to 100 a day, but the fish imprint on them and eat them.

"Usually you begin seeing them in late May, and they can last until mid- to late July. The peak is the last two weeks of June. I usually fish dry flies during the hatch, but a big, black Kaufmann stonefly with rubberlegs is good, too."

When fishing salmonflies, keep an eye out for green drakes (*E. doddsi*) and brown drakes. Drakes, according to Mitchell, bring to net many of the largest fish in the river. However, before you schedule a trip around this hatch, realize that it's difficult to hit.

"If you hit the right day, you may see 40 to 60 fish over 14 inches," Mitchell boasts. "When you catch the hatch, you catch it. But there are only a few days that it really comes off and only in certain sections, so it's frustrating. I'd say your best bet lies in the Cle Elum to Thorpe section."

Of all the killer Yakima River hatches, Mitchell rates the drake emergence as his favorite. That does not mean it offers the most consistent fishing. During June the Yakima may rise or fall depending on irrigation demand, which can knock hatch schedules out of whack while literally destroying a visiting angler's options. However, as mentioned, hitting the hatch is an angler's nirvana.

"If I could choose only one hatch of the year to fish, I'd choose drakes," Mitchell admits. "People don't realize what that hatch is like, what it does to the fish. They absolutely hammer them. And at the same time, there are salmonflies. I catch a lot of big fish during that time, and it's a blast."

If an angler does find drakes present, tie on a size 10 or 12 extended body green drake and hold on.

Regarding the size of Yakima River trout, don't hit the water with inflated expectations—the Yakima is not a trophy trout stream on par with Montana's Beaverhead and Missouri or Idaho's Henry's Fork or Silver Creek. However, with that said, realize that there are some dandy rainbows about and on any given cast, an angler might hook a hog ranging from 16 to 22 inches. If you are looking for big numbers of fish in that size range, launch your boat somewhere else because you are setting yourself up for disappointment. Instead, drift along the river, through the dimples of rising trout, and cast dry flies to the bank. The Yakima has a hell of a lot to offer if you just settle down and enjoy it.

According to Jim Cummins, a district fish biologist for Washington Department of Fish and Wildlife in Yakima, some anglers are disappointed in the size of Yakima trout, but he insists that the system is at or near carrying capacity and it just does not facilitate the growth of huge trout.

"Some people are disappointed that there are not larger trout, but the population is at its capacity, and the food supply just doesn't let them grow much larger than what we are seeing," he says. "There are some fish over 15 inches, but there just aren't many of them. When we went to strictly catch and release, there were expectations of many larger trout, but that has not happened."

One reason the Yakima may not support vast numbers of large fish is the relatively unnatural flows affecting the river, especially during summer, fall, and winter seasons.

"The Yakima is a very fertile system, but we have concerns that fluctuation in water levels resulting from irrigation demand may have an effect on the fishery," Cummins says. "Such fluctuations can strand aquatic insects. I don't think it's a huge issue, but it is a concern."

According to Washington Department of Fish and Wildlife, trout populations are highest in the upper canyon, which is one of five sections that are annually sampled in the catch and release waters between Easton and Roza.

For instance, there are about 784 rainbows a mile in the upper canyon, with 208 ranging over 10 inches. The largest trout sampled in that section measured 18 inches. Here is the the breakdown for other Yakima sections:

- Lower Canyon: 479 trout per mile, 118 over 10 inches with the largest rating 24 inches
- Ellensburg: 691 trout per mile, 236 over 10 inches with the largest measuring 22 inches
- Thorp: 470 per mile, 136 over 10 inches, the largest measuring 24 inches
- Cle Elum: 627 per mile, 233 over 10 inches and the largest stretching 23 inches.

Although they are few and far between, you can catch large fish on the Yakima. If you must catch a hog-dog to be happy, visit during late winter and spring when the Yakima's mature rainbows and some large cutthroat make their annual upriver movement to reach prime spawning grounds.

"There is definitely a net upstream movement in the spring with a lot of fish relocating from the canyon section to the area around Ellensburg," says Kenneth Ham, a biologist for WF&W. "Spawning season runs from February through April with a peak in March, and we see the fish travel extensively from above and below the Ellensburg area. Some of the fish are big, 15 to 17-inch, cutthroat."

In unison with the drake and salmonfly emergence, the Yakima begins to offer a surface smorgasbord of terrestrial insects, such as ants and beetles, that draw trout to the top through September. Sunken ants and beetles should work throughout the season, and grasshoppers grab a trout's attention in July, August, and September, especially along the brushy or grassy banks where those unfortunate creatures lose their grip and fall into the water.

Anglers should also see plenty of yellow sallies (small, size 16 and 18 stoneflies) during the summer months. Sallies often draw trout to the surface in riffled sections. If they are present, try a yellow humpy, stimulator or even an elk hair caddis-the fish eat them greedily. However, as is the case with any hatch you hit

*Susette Hartman, Brooke Wight, and Lynanne Bergman pose
with a typical Yakima River rainbow.*

between June and October, water conditions can seriously hamper angling options—remember, unfortunately, on the Yakima, farmers and ranchers hoard the water.

During high water, fishing becomes difficult, especially if a flyfisher is looking for large fish, which are prone to sticking their noses under the banks until the water subsides.

Due to the Yakima's unpredictable flows, wading is often difficult. In fact, wading anglers are placing themselves at serious risk if they enter the water during peak flows, which may exceed 3,500 cfs. Due to that danger, floating the river in a raft, drift boat, or pontoon boat offers the best opportunity to fish in relative safety. It also boosts success. If you decide to enter the river in a float tube, you are guilty of committing slow suicide. Prime wading occurs between 400 and 2,000 cfs.

During the high flows of August and September, flyfishers will likely spot some giant golden stoneflies (*H. pacifica*) on the river's surface. According to Mitchell, the golden stone is worth matching.

"It's a big son of a bitch," he says. "And it's mostly an evening game. You can fish it during the day, but it's most active at night. The male is wingless, but the female has wings. Obviously, the male really cruises around on the water, and trout drill them.

"When the golden stones are out—for that matter throughout August and September—all I fish is a size 6 tan or orange rubberleg. I like to cast quartering downstream, lift the tip, and let the fly skate. These Yakima trout really seem to like a fly that moves, and it's the easiest way to catch fish. There's not a lot of technique needed."

No matter what hatch anglers choose to chase on the Yakima, light trout rods will do the trick. My personal favorite is a Scott 9-foot, 4-weight. It is a two-piece, fast action rod that allows delicate presentations with small mayfly and caddis patterns, yet it holds enough strength to turn over a big stonefly offering. It also offers enough power to toss large, weighted streamers, such as woolly buggers, as long as I don't try to throw them to from one bank to the other. The Scott 4-weight also offers the stability to throw a weight-forward line through a fair amount of wind, which can be encountered any day on the Yakima (during summer, wind can blow you right off the river).

If you don't have a 4-weight in your arsenal, don't fret. A 5- or 6-weight rod works great, too. In fact, I've enjoyed excellent success with a 9-foot, 5-weight Orvis Trident and a 9-foot, 6-weight Sage RPL.

The Yakima's mayfly hatches wind down in October and November with scattered emergences of Baetis and mahogany duns (*Paraleptophlebia*), a size 16 dark bug that rainbows really rip into. The fall Baetis is much smaller than the spring Baetis with its effective imitations being tied onto size 20 and 22 hooks. Long, light tippets and serious stealth during the low, clear fall flows is required.

In late November, mayflies die and the Yakima winds into its winter rhythm, which offers freezing temperatures, snow, and ice, and fortunately for the hard-core flyfisher, some decent midge hatches.

While winter midge fishing is not going to provide the thrills of spring, summer and fall fishing, it can be productive.

Anglers should arm themselves with plenty of minuscule midge patterns, strike indicators, long leaders, light tippets and, yeah, patience.

Look for the Yakima's rainbows to work midges in the slackwater areas, such as back eddies, inside riffle corners, and eddies. Size 20 and 22 paramidges with goose biot bodies, parachute Adams', Griffith's gnats, and suspender midges will draw strikes up top. Blood midges, serendipities, palomino midges, and brassies should draw strikes under the surface, especially if a strike indicator is attached to the leader above the fly. The strike indicator will announce the subtle bite of a trout during winter. Adjust the distance between strike indicator and fly depending on the depth and speed of the water.

While midge patterns draw strikes during winter, streamers should not be forgotten. Actually, no matter what season you choose to fish the Yakima, big, subsurface patterns, such as size 2 and 4 woolly buggers, olive sculpins, zonkers, and crayfish, will draw strikes. Mitchell's favorite pattern, a sculpin, incorporates a spun deer hair head with an olive rabbit strip body and 20 turns of lead on the hook. Fished off a 15-foot sinktip line, this combination is deadly in the deep, slackwater sections and dropoff areas where large fish often set up camp.

Because trout are lethargic during winter, slow the retrieve of a streamer or offer long, downstream looping casts that drag the fly sideways across the river.

If you do choose to fish the winter season, don't try floating down the river on an iceberg and make sure you fill your Thermos with hot chocolate, tea, or straight coffee instead of a mix of coffee and whiskey, such as Torrey and I did when we fished the river on that cold, February day mentioned earlier.

While the Yakima River, its abundance, and varied insect hatches can challenge even the most avid anglers, it truly is a river for everyone.

Unlike Washington's salmon and steelhead rivers, the Yakima offers a relaxing and laid-back day on the water, floating among the dimple rings of trout. There is nothing more thrilling than watching a trout race to the surface and pummel a dry fly. If you are looking for a sure bet, check water conditions first and then visit the Yakima River, Washington's true rainbow trout gem. You won't be disappointed.

# Stream Facts: Yakima River

## Seasons and Special Regulations
- Entire River: Closed to fishing for steelhead.
- From mouth to Roza Dam: June 1 to March 31 for trout; 2-trout limit with a 12-inch minimum.
- From Roza Dam to Easton Dam: Open year-round for trout. Catch and release only with selective gear rules in effect.
- From Easton Dam to Keechelus Dam: Open year-round. Selective gear rules in effect.

## Species
- Rainbow, cutthroat, and brown trout. Most fish average 8 to 14 inches, but some stretch past 20 inches.

## Stream Characteristics
- Washington's premier trout stream, the Yakima can be choked with anglers and recreational floaters through the prime summer months. However, early spring and fall, when sunbathers are off the water, can offer excellent opportunities.
- The Yakima offers lots of aquatic insect hatches to match: Golden stones, yellow sallies, Baetis, pale morning dun, green drake and Callibaetis mayflies, plus midges, crustaceans, and minnows are all prey of Yakima's trout.

## Access
- Very wadeable, especially through the Yakima Canyon before or after runoff. However, maybe the best way to sample the river is via boat or raft.
- There are numerous public access sites located throughout the length of the river.
- Vehicle shuttles can be arranged by local fly shops.

## YAKIMA RIVER MAJOR HATCHES

| Insect | J | F | M | A | M | J | J | A | S | O | N | D | Flies |
|---|---|---|---|---|---|---|---|---|---|---|---|---|---|
| Golden Stone | | | | ■ | ■ | | | | | | | | Rubberleg Yellow Stimulator #4–12; Golden Stonefly Nymph #6–12; Kaufmann's Stonefly Nymph #6–12; Fluttering Stone #6–12 |
| Baetis | | | ■ | ■ | ■ | | | | ■ | ■ | | | Sparkle Dun #16–20; Cripple #16–20; CDC Biot Baetis #16–20; Baetis Spinner #16–20; Hare's Ear & Pheasant Tail Nymphs #16–20; Parachute Adams #16–20; Lightning Bug #16–20 |
| Ameledus | | | ■ | ■ | | | | | | | | | Olive Hare's Ear #12 |
| Caddis | | | | ■ | ■ | ■ | ■ | ■ | ■ | ■ | | | Stranahan's Caddis Variant #16–18; Peacock Body Elk Hair #12–20; LaFontaine Sparkle Emerger #12–20; X-Caddis #12–20; Free Living Caddis #12–16; Elk Hair Caddis #14–18; Giant October Caddis #4–6 |
| March Brown Drakes | | | | ■ | ■ | | | | | | | | Parachute Adams #12–16; March Brown Dun #14–16; Cripple #14–16; Sparkle Dun #14–16; Hare's Ear #14–16; Pheasant Tail #14–16 |
| Pale Morning Duns | | | | | | ■ | ■ | | | | | | Parachute PMD #16–18; Parachute Adams #16–18; Hare's Ear Nymph #16–18; Pheasant Tail Nymph #16–18; PMD Cripple #16–18; Sparkle Dun #16–18; PMD Thorax #16–18 |

## YAKIMA RIVER MAJOR HATCHES (cont.)

| Insect | J | F | M | A | M | J | J | A | S | O | N | D | Flies |
|---|---|---|---|---|---|---|---|---|---|---|---|---|---|
| Yellow Sally | | | | | | X | X | | | | | | Yellow Humpy #14–16; Irresistible #14–16; Stimulator #14–16 |
| Salmonfly | | | | | X | X | | | | | | | Turck's Tarantula #24; Bird's Stone #2–4; Kauffman's Stone #2–4; Improved Sofa Pillow #2–4; Bitch Creek Nymph #2–4; Stimulator #2–4 |
| Green & Brown Drakes | | | | | | X | X | | | | | | Extended Body Drake #10–12; Cripple #10–12; Parachute Adams #10–12; Sparkle Dun #10–12; Hare's Ear & Pheasant Tail Nymphs #10–12 |
| Terrestrials | | | | | | | | X | X | | | | Joe's Hopper #2–8; Madame X #2–8; Parachute Ant #14–16; Foam Beetle #14–16 |
| Midges/Chironomid | X | X | X | X | X | X | X | X | X | X | X | X | Brassie #16–24; Suspender Midge #16–24; Palomino Midge #16–24; Blood Midge #16–24; Griffith's Gnat #16–24; Biot Midge Emerger #16–24 |
| Streamer | X | X | X | X | X | X | X | X | X | X | X | X | Egg-sucking Leech #2–6; Woolly Bugger #2–6; Woolhead Sculpin #2–6; Muddler Minnow #2–8; Zonker #2–6 |

# WENATCHEE RIVER

When you live in western Washington, where residents endure eight rain-soaked months each year, you contract a reptile's appeal for sunshine.

During winter, spring, and early summer, west side residents dream of that bright orange orb that used to rise in the sky. They yearn for soft, warm winds and arid country with forests that they can hike through without engaging in hand-to-hand combat with devils club and spiked blackberry vines. They begin to despise the fat, thick green forest where cold rain trickles off big branches and deposits water down the nape of your neck.

There are many areas of eastern Washington that offer respite from the damp, west side coastal air, but to me, no area offers such a relaxing, healing atmosphere as the pine forest and apple orchard country surrounding the Wenatchee River. It's there, between the pine tree-sprinkled hillsides under the watchful gaze of the North Cascade Mountains that many west-siders go to chase steelhead and to soak in sunshine during late summer and fall. We realize that another long, soggy winter is just around the corner, so we peel off our T-shirts, slip a fly vest over bare skin, lather on sunscreen, and hit the river like young children let loose in a candy factory, leaping from rock to rock, casting to likely looking runs with a downstream swing, teasing steelhead from the crystal clear water. Fishing the Wenatchee is a laid-back affair.

The Wenatchee River begins in the high Cascades in a circular bowl formed by the Wenatchee and Entiat Mountains. In that bowl sits Lake Wenatchee, a deep, elongated, natural impoundment that stores the river's flow through the seasons.

At the lake outlet, the Wenatchee is born and it rushes downhill, slicing between open pine tree slopes, curling around riverbank cottonwoods, and dodging exposed boulders before entering Tumwater Canyon, about 15 miles downstream from the lake. At the entrance of Tumwater Canyon, the Wenatchee's face turns angry with increased flow and turbidity from Hatchery Creek, Fall Creek and Cabin Creek. At the outlet of the canyon, about 6 miles downstream from its origin, the lower Wenatchee begins. It's there, on the lower river, as it slips past the towns of Leavenworth, Peshastin, Dryden, and Cashmere, all the while providing sustenance to the apple orchards that line the river's banks, that most flyfishers congregate during fall.

Through its course, the Wenatchee offers some of the best fall flyfishing for summer-run steelhead in the state. Unfortunately, due to numerous dams on the Columbia River and some relatively shallow thinking this century, the Wenatchee's distinct native fish are mostly extinct or, at least, so genetically terrorized by the current hatchery runs that nobody would be able to identify the real thing if it came up and bit them in the ass, let alone if it inhaled their fly. In 1997 the Wenatchee River steelhead was listed as a threatened species. Due to dams and genetic drift, the Wenatchee can be closed to fishing from one season to the next, depending on the size of its steelhead run. It always pays to call ahead before you visit the river.

Despite its problems, the Wenatchee's awesome scenery, the mild fall weather, and the size and character of the river make it a fine place to throw a fly. During the

# Wenatchee River
## Lake Wenatchee to Leavenworth

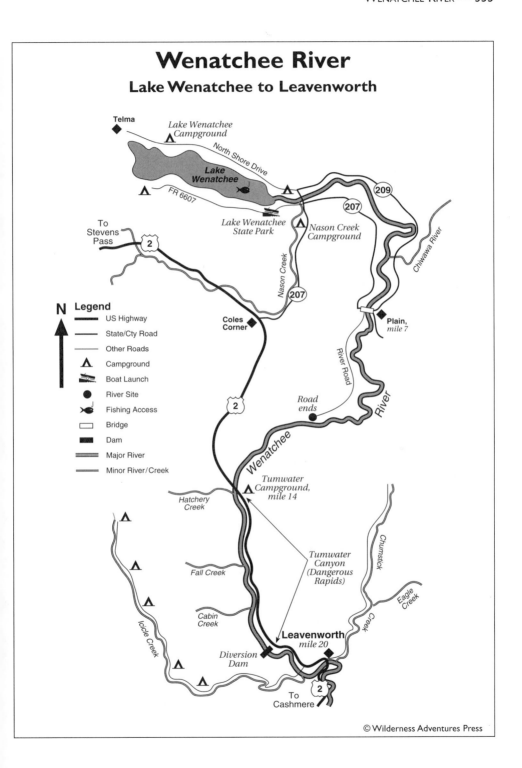

**Legend**

| | |
|---|---|
| | US Highway |
| | State/Cty Road |
| | Other Roads |
| ⋀ | Campground |
| | Boat Launch |
| ● | River Site |
| | Fishing Access |
| ▢ | Bridge |
| | Dam |
| | Major River |
| | Minor River/Creek |

Telma

Lake Wenatchee Campground

North Shore Drive

Lake Wenatchee

FR 6607

209

207

To Stevens Pass

2

Lake Wenatchee State Park

Nason Creek Campground

Nason Creek

Chiwawa River

207

Coles Corner

Plain, mile 7

River Road

Road ends

River

2

Wenatchee

Tumwater Campground, mile 14

Hatchery Creek

Tumwater Canyon (Dangerous Rapids)

Chumstick

Fall Creek

Eagle Creek

Cabin Creek

Icicle Creek

Leavenworth mile 20

Creek

Diversion Dam

2

To Cashmere

© Wilderness Adventures Press

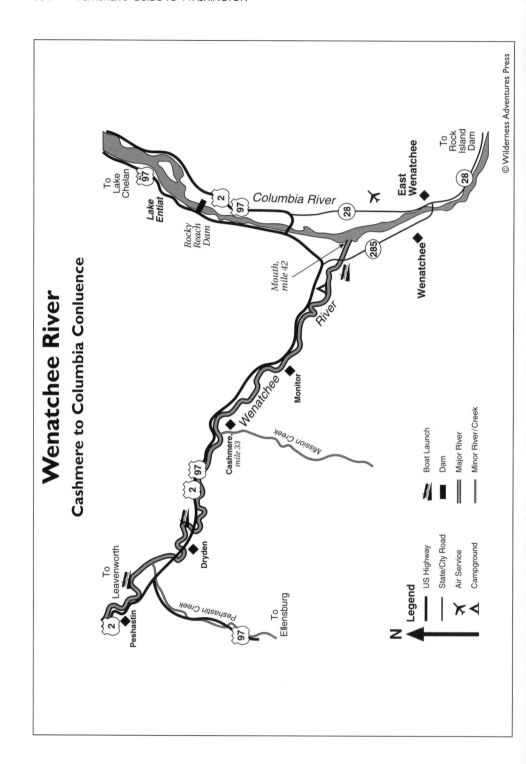

# Wenatchee River
## Cashmere to Columbia Confluence

To Lake Chelan

To Rock Island Dam

East Wenatchee

Columbia River

Lake Entiat

Rocky Reach Dam

Wenatchee

Mouth, mile 42

Wenatchee River

Monitor

Mission Creek

Cashmere, mile 33

Dryden

To Leavenworth

Peshastin Creek

Peshastin

To Ellensburg

© Wilderness Adventures Press

**Legend**

N

US Highway
State/Cty Road
Air Service
Campground

Boat Launch
Dam
Major River
Minor River/Creek

best years the river may see close to 10,000 fish return. During a poor year, less than 1,000 show up. An average year produces about 5,000 fish and that's plenty of steelhead to keep flyfishers busy.

While there is rarely a poor day to visit the Wenatchee—the area receives less than 10 inches of precipitation each year—if you are looking for steelhead, you must pay attention to river flows. It can be drawn down drastically because the apple orchards rely on the Wenatchee River for irrigation water. From August through October, anywhere from 16 to 28 percent of the river is drained for irrigation purposes. When that happens, the river drops and the water temperature soars. Steelhead don't like that combination. In fact, any fish that is unfortunate enough to be caught in the system likely will seek sanctuary in cold tributary streams or dive to the bottom of deep pools. They may be active during the cool morning and evening hours, but they will not be agressive when the sun is on the water. Fish that may be ascending the Columbia, their noses pointed toward the Wenatchee, mill in front of the river's mouth, waiting patiently for conditions to improve. They can taste the warm water and they don't like it one bit.

However, sometime in late September or early October, irrigators decrease their water demand and the river rises and cools. When that happens, those fish that have waited patiently in the Columbia suddenly shoot upstream into the Wenatchee. Most flyfishers agree that prime conditions occur when the river flows at or near 950 cubic feet a second. Prime water temperatures range between 42 and 49 degrees.

Steelhead spread out through the entire Wenatchee system, including its major tributaries, such as Peshastin Creek, Icicle Creek, Nason Creek, Beaver Creek, Mission Creek, Little Wenatchee River, Chiwawa River, and Chumstick Creek; however, the greatest concentrations and some of the best flyfishing opportunities arrive below the mouth of Tumwater Canyon.

Tumwater Canyon itself offers beautiful deep water, but it can be difficult to reach from shore and is no place to be casting a fly from a raft or drift boat. Some of its rapids are rated class VI, best reserved for whitewater enthusiasts.

Much of the canyon, which is extremely beautiful, can be reached from US 2. Anglers who negotiate the steep banks are treated with some demanding pocketwater fishing. Steelhead often hold in the slackwater pockets and behind large, exposed boulders. Standard nymph techniques, just like you use for trout, work here.

If you are lucky enough to hook a steelhead in the canyon, you've got your hands full—they'll peel 50 yards of line off your reel like nothing, then hit fast water and strip some more. Negotiating a rocky bank, one hand holding a fly rod high, the other groping for a handhold, all the while cars race past honking their encouragement, makes for a memorable day astream. When fishing the canyon, anglers must pray that a fish remains in the hole where it was hooked—if it heads downstream, a flyfisher is pretty much toast.

The upper river above the canyon sees some movement of steelhead, including a decent run into Nason Creek, but it's not a good place to float a raft or boat during fall due to low flows and exposed rocks. Therefore, many anglers pass it up on their way to the lower river. That can be a mistake, because the upper section holds some awfully nice water that has, on more than one occasion, provided a wild fight off the end of my rod, be it a steelhead or Dolly Varden char (Dollies are occasionally caught in the system, but fishing specifically for Dolly Varden is prohibited, so any Dolly hooked and landed must be immediately released).

The upper river is highly approachable, meaning it is easily waded in many spots and it hosts some perfect riffles, runs and pools. For the summer-run steelhead angler, this is a good place to throw a 6 or 7-weight rod. Farther downstream, 7- and 8-weight rods loaded with sinktip lines are the preferred weapon. If you do choose to fish the upper river, make sure you wear felt-soled wading boots with studs on the bottom. In fact, felt-soled boots and studs are a good idea no matter where you fish the river since its bottom is rocky and slick. No need to take an unplanned skid along the bottom rocks. If your legs are not as strong as they used to be, a wading staff is not a bad idea. Three millimeter high back neoprene waders are also a required item. During late September, October, and early November, days along the Wenatchee start chilly, maybe with a little frost on the grass and some ice along shore. In the afternoon, temperatures can heat up to the mid-70s or low 80s. The temperature drops quick when the sun moves off the water, and neoprene waders manage to stave off the chill.

Some of the best water on the upper river may be reached by following the Wenatchee River Road, which parallels the water and may be found by following the cement bridge across the river at Plain. Head east or west, whichever you prefer. Both directions offer ample access and some killer water.

While the upper river and Tumwater Canyon are noted steelhead haunts, most anglers bypass those areas and head for the lower river, which extends about 30 miles east of Leavenworth, a quaint Bavarian-style resort town, downstream to the Wenatchee's end at the Columbia River. There, in the lower river, where the riffles are just a little broader and the tailouts a little longer, is where most anglers prefer to ply the water. Armed with 7 and 8-weight rods, sinktip lines and an assortment of colorful flies, anglers would be hard-pressed to find better steelhead flywater: the Wenatchee runs dark blue, accentuated by broad, choppy white riffles and some mysteriously dark, deep pools. The surrounding hills, lit up in crimson and gold, complement the lush green orchards. Occasionally, snow dusts the surrounding mountains, leaving a white layer across the tops of the pine trees until a bright, penetrating sun melts it off in the afternoon. If you look overhead you'll find Canada geese and mallard ducks winging their way by on southern migrations. Occasionally, a shot may ring out in the forest—hunters collecting their winter meat supply. On days like that, you might wonder how much real estate is going for in the area.

Steelhead begin showing in the Wenatchee in late August and early September, but most flyfishers hold back until late September or early October when most of the run pushes into the river. Even during good years, when as many as 10,000 fish push into the system, catching a Wenatchee steelhead is not a piece of cake. Similar to steelhead fishing everywhere, on the Wenatchee, anglers must identify productive water and pass up on the second-rate stuff.

Look for runs and glides that offer a relatively moderate speed and rate between 4 and 7 feet deep. On the lower river, tailouts of pools offer prime water as does pocketwater in the canyon. During sunny weather, no matter where you choose to fish, prime time occurs in the mornings and early afternoons and again in the evening. Midday hours, when the sun shines bright, pushes steelhead into deep water or makes them extremely difficult to approach.

Whether the sun is high or not, take your time when approaching a run and don't wade quickly into the water. Instead, move slowly up to a run and cast into the shallows. Whether you approach from downstream or above is a matter of personal preference.

"I don't think the Wenatchee's steelhead like choppy riffles, so they lie in relatively calm water where they can see things pretty well," says Joe Theiss of East Wenatchee, who grew up along the river and has fished for steelhead all his life. "I usually enter the water at the rear of a pool and work up on fish. Many times you find them right where the pool fans out and gets shallow before turning into another riffle. If you just wade into that shallow water aimlessly and crunch around, you'll spook the fish.

"You also want to pay close attention to the slicks," Theiss adds. "By the time steelhead get to the Wenatchee, they are pretty tired from coming up the Columbia and they like to rest. Anyplace where they can duck out of the fast current and find a place to rest is worth exploring."

While the Wenatchee is not an immense river, it does require a steelhead flyfisher to cast a line 50 feet or more. Some of that distance can be alleviated by wading deep, but we all know what that welcomes.

To achieve long casts and to successfully mend a large portion of line, most Wenatchee flyfishers use a 7- or 8-weight, single-handed rod. Sinktip lines are required to reach down, 4 to 6 feet, to bottom with a fly.

A few Wenatchee flyfishers chase steelhead with floating lines and dry flies or subsurface patterns that skim just under the water. When fishing in that manner, takes can be thrilling.

In fact, Theiss says some of his best action has taken place on top of the water with a grasshopper pattern. Contrary to what many steelhead anglers believe, big anadromous rainbows do eat when they enter freshwater.

"They do eat when they are in the Wenatchee," Theiss says. "I've caught a lot of steelhead on grasshoppers, and I've even caught them on stoneflies, too."

If wading deep or distance casting is not your deal, you may want to float the river. By cruising the river in a boat or raft, flyfishers can reach water that they normally could not—water that is out of the range of even the best distance casters.

Drift boats work fine on some sections of the Wenatchee, namely the lower river, but an inflatable raft is the ideal vehicle for this river. Due to its shallow depth and rocky bottom in many places, a drift boat often bangs its way down the stream. A raft generally draws less water and often floats right over rocks that a drift boat would drill. When a raft does bang into a rock, it isn't a noisy affair, and no dent is left in the side of the boat.

Some prime floats on the lower Wenatchee include the stretch from Cashmere to the Sleepy Hollow Bridge, which is pretty much restricted to rafts. Another good drift would take you from Monitor to the mouth of the Columbia.

Whether you float the river or wade fish, you must offer a steelhead what it is looking for. Thankfully, on the Wenatchee, fly selection is far less important than placing an offering in front of a steelhead's snout.

"I don't even know the names of many of the flies that I've used over the years," Theiss says. "I don't really think it's important. I like a size 6 or 8 fly with an orange body and little white on it. That's about all I use. When the fish are in, it always works. Sometimes you have to run it past them many times, but eventually they'll take."

Popular classic flies for the Wenatchee include the purple peril, silver hilton, general practitioner, fall favorite, purple, black, and orange marabous and the steelumbia, a time-tested Wenatchee river offering that was created by Stan Stalling in 1945.

When fishing any of those flies, most anglers tie the fly to the leader with a riffling hitch, which presents the fly broadside to a fish and initiates more strikes than a fly tied on with a basic improved cinch knot. The riffling hitch is especially productive when flies are fished quartering downstream. As the fly swings across the river, it does so in the broadside position, which makes the fly most visible to the fish and easy to inhale. At the end of a drift, some Wenatchee River anglers like to quickly strip off a few feet of line before retrieving their fly. Sometimes steelhead will take at that time.

The Wenatchee also receives a run of spring Chinook but again, their numbers fluctuate dramatically each year and the season is often closed. If the fish do return in good numbers, flyfishers find them most often in May and June. Because chinook, also called king salmon, range between 15 and 30 pounds, flyfishers require heavy rods—nothing less than an 8-weight for sure. Leaders should be constructed of 15- or 20-pound Maxima line. Look for those fish to congregate in deep pools and runs. Use sinktip lines to drop an offering, like a Mickey Finn, to the bottom. If you do hook a fish, hold on—there's nothing in freshwater as powerful as a lively chinook.

While the Wenatchee's steelhead and chinook salmon runs have taken a hit from the Columbia River's numerous dams, anglers still find a few fish ascending the river each year. Maybe the future holds better offerings. Maybe it doesn't. Only time will tell. No matter how many fish are in the system, the Wenatchee is a beautiful treat to fish, and it's one heck of a sunny retreat from western Washington. If you are fortunate enough to catch a Wenatchee River steelhead or spring chinook, thank the Gods, consider how far your friend has traveled to meet you, and gently release it back to the river. No need to end the journey prematurely.

# Stream Facts: Wenatchee River

### Seasons and special regulations
- From Mouth to Lake Wenatchee: All game fish open June 1 to August 31. Winter whitefish open December 1 through March 31.
- River closed to steelhead, depending on yearly returns. Check current regulations and restrictions.

### Species
- Rainbow trout (mostly stocked)
- Steelhead trout
- Chinook salmon
- Dolly Varden
- Whitefish

### Stream Characteristics
- The Wenatchee offers wonderful water throughout.
- Just below Wenatchee Lake, it's shallow and fast.
- Through Tumwater Canyon, it's deep and roily.
- The river broadens at Leavenworth and is best accessed by boat or raft extending to its confluence with the Columbia River.

### Access
- You don't want to run a drift boat through its upper reaches, but boats and rafts are excellent options below Tumwater Canyon. Wade anglers can hit the river throughout its length, but it is best waded in its upper reaches.

# Methow River

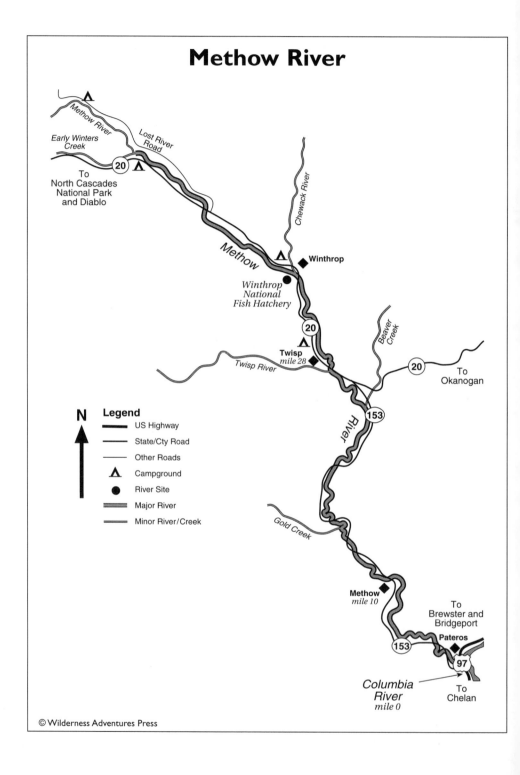

Legend
- US Highway
- State/Cty Road
- Other Roads
- Campground
- River Site
- Major River
- Minor River/Creek

N

Early Winters Creek

Methow River

Lost River Road

To North Cascades National Park and Diablo

Chewack River

Methow

Winthrop

Winthrop National Fish Hatchery

Twisp River

Twisp
mile 28

Beaver Creek

To Okanogan

River

Gold Creek

Methow
mile 10

To Brewster and Bridgeport

Pateros

Columbia River
mile 0

To Chelan

© Wilderness Adventures Press

# METHOW RIVER

Not unlike the Wenatchee, the Methow River offers some excellent steelhead options when it is open. Its fish are also listed as threatened, and the future of steelhead and fishing opportunities are uncertain.

If the river does bounce back to productive levels, don't pass by the Methow in late August, September, October or November. During the best years, runs rate between 10,000 and 15,000 fish. Anything near 7,000 or 8,000 fish is considered a bumper crop. During a poor year, the river still hosts a couple thousand fish. What is truly amazing is that as many as 400,000 steelhead smolts have been planted in the Methow, and of those fish, as you can see, only a few return. The dams, you know.

When fishing steelhead on the Methow, fly pattern is not as important as presentation. To fish the Methow effectively, you'll need a sinktip line, a short 3- or 4-foot leader, and standard fall flies, such as the fall favorite, comet, steelumbia, purple peril, silver hilton, and any of the colorful marabou patterns.

The Methow originates north of the Lake Chelan Sawtooth Wilderness Area and North Cascades National Park, flowing southeast past the towns of Winthrop, Twisp, and Methow before plunging into the Columbia River at Pateros. While steelhead can be found throughout the system, most flycasters concentrate on the middle and lower sections. The mouth of the river is best left to boat and gear fishermen.

Like the Wenatchee's fish, Methow steelhead like to rest on their way upstream. Look for fish resting behind boulders, on inside corners of riffles, and especially at the tailouts of pools. The standard steelhead swing most often draws strikes, but dead-drifting a fly through a middepth run also produces takes.

To reach the Methow from western Washington, follow US 2 over Stevens Pass. At Wenatchee turn north and follow US 97 along the Columbia River to Pateros. From Spokane, follow US 2 east to Orondo and turn north on US 97. Follow 97 to Chelan Falls, where a bridge crosses the Columbia. Continue following 97 north to Pateros.

# Rocky Ford Creek

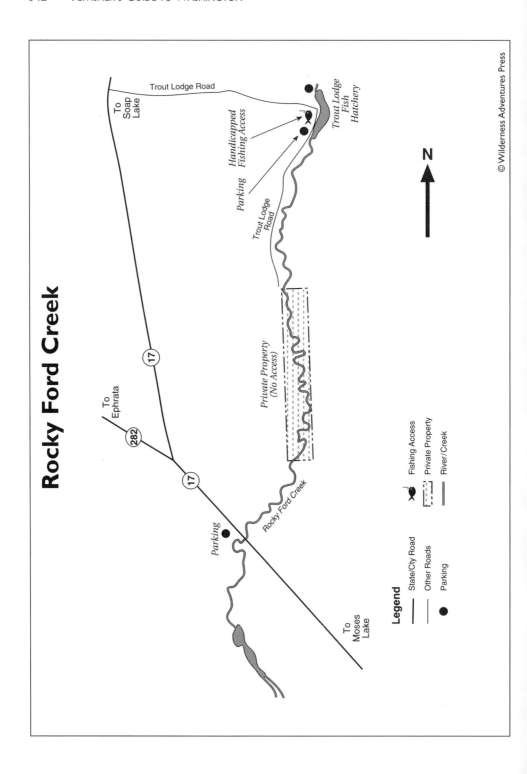

Trout Lodge Road

To Soap Lake

Handicapped Fishing Access

Parking

Trout Lodge Road

Trout Lodge Fish Hatchery

N

© Wilderness Adventures Press

To Ephrata

17

282

17

Private Property (No Access)

Parking

Rocky Ford Creek

To Moses Lake

**Legend**

| | State/Cty Road |
| | Other Roads |
| ● | Parking |
| | Fishing Access |
| | Private Property |
| | River/Creek |

# ROCKY FORD CREEK

It's one of those gray January days in Seattle when you think the cloud ceiling might drop another ten feet and suffocate the city. Greenhouse effect, my ass.

It's been that way for a week—one downpour after another, the Space Needle consumed in gloom. Due to the clouds, the rain, and the wind, western Washington's steelhead streams are blown out, and the thought of bouncing around Pass Lake in a float tube (about the only option), just isn't turning my crank.

But the clouds are pushing on my head, and I know I've got to escape the city, run from the weather, and most pressing, I've got to catch a fish soon or I'm going to die from withdrawal. I've already got a bad case of the shakes, and I'm sure my casting has gone to hell. It's been days since I've been on the water. What I need is a few long, hard-core sessions reconnoitering with Señor Trout.

I pick up the phone, dial information, and in moments I'm speaking with a good friend, T.R. McCrystal.

"I'm going crazy, I've got to catch a fish," I tell him. "How long would it take to drive from Bend (Oregon) to central Washington?"

"About 5 long hours, and I've got a class in the morning."

"Rainbows to 25 inches, midges hatching, cheap cigars, and beer. It's Washington's best spring creek. One of the best places in the West to catch a 5-pound rainbow trout. You in?"

"How we going to find each other? Should we meet at a bar?"

"No," I tell him adamantly. "Let's just meet at Rocky Ford. Tie leeches, olive scuds, and brassies. And bring your stove so we can make coffee. It's supposed to snow."

Rocky Ford, located in central Washington's Columbia Basin near Ephrata, is a delicate, often demanding flyfishing-only spring creek that cuts through a narrow coulee amid scabrock, howling coyotes, and a fortress of tall cattails. To Washington anglers, that setting offers some of the state's best fishing. There is ample public access, including excellent disabled person options, and every cast promises a chance to hook a legitimate hog—a rainbow trout or rainbow/cutthroat hybrid exceeding 5 pounds. Lesser numbers of Atlantic salmon also exist. Diverse aquatic and terrestrial insect hatches, which bring the large rainbows to the surface for lunch, are icing on a flyfisher's cake.

However, even with those offerings, Rocky Ford's trout are not pushovers, and catching a 4- or 5-pound fish isn't going to happen every day, especially for beginners. Rocky Ford's rainbows see thousands of artificial flies cast over their snouts each season, and at times, they can be perfectly maddening to hook. On other occasions, they seem adequately willing to cooperate.

For accomplished flyfishers, each day might offer a dozen or more fish to the net. Beginners and moderately experienced anglers should be content with a half-dozen fish a day, maybe even fewer.

As a bonus, the creek is open year-round, and due to its springfed nature, its temperature is constant and relatively warm—it never freezes. That does not mean

*T.R. McCrystal landing
a large rainbow at
Rocky Ford Creek.*

that ice won't form in your guides when casting a wet line on a cold winter day. In fact, to fish Rocky Ford effectively during the cold months, you have to be persistent —numb, aching feet and hands must simply be dealt with, which means you just have to accept the pain.

By doing so, anglers can fish the creek during its least crowded season, when anglers are few, the trout many, and insect hatches, if not diverse, are productive and predictable.

That's the situation T.R. and I found when he raced up from Bend and I escaped the big city. After shaking hands on the bank of the creek, T.R. and I surveyed our situation. Wind lapped at the nape of our necks, drizzle raced down our shirts, mud and ice had turned the ground into a boot-sucking quagmire, and, delightfully, there were so many fish rising, we would have trouble picking one target. Remember, when flyfishing, as in duck hunting, flock shooting is not advised.

*The author with a typical
Rocky Ford rainbow.*

Carefully approaching the creek, we sighted lots of fish in the crystal clear, spring creek current. We approached from below, tied on 10-foot leaders that tapered to 6X, knotted size 18 black midge imitations to the end of them, and dead-drifted them over rises. That's all it took. We hooked and landed maybe a dozen fish each in an hour, all between 7 and 12 inches, before deciding that a large fish or two was definitely a priority. So we packed our gear and hiked downstream, looking for likely spots where we could reach the water without wading—unlike every other western water I'm aware of, wading is not allowed or tolerated, whether the game warden is around or not, at Rocky Ford.

T.R. stepped out to an elevated launching pad and cast a brown leech, another excellent spring creek offering, into the water. Shortly, I heard T.R. holler. I grabbed the camera and ran down the bank—he wouldn't shout if he hooked a small fish. When I arrived, T.R. was gently cradling a big, fat rainbow that stretched 21 inches (we taped it) and weighed 3 or 4 pounds. We'll never know for sure—T.R. twisted the fly out of the trout's mouth and gently released it to fight again. He could have kept the rainbow—prior to 1998, regulations allowed anglers to take one fish a day over 18 inches—but that would have been robbing the next guy in line from such a spirited fight and the opportunity to see such a large fish close up. Now, Rocky Ford is being managed with catch-and-release-only regulations, along with a barbless hook requirement.

For the rest of the day, T.R. and I caught and released a few more hogs, some on leeches, some on subsurface midge imitations like brassies before heading for the truck. Later that evening, while T.R. belted out one last war-whoop, we tossed our Therma-Rests and sleeping bags onto the handicapped fishing dock and turned in for the frosty night.

Winter, especially on weekdays, is my favorite time to test Rocky Ford Creek, because angler numbers are down and fishing remains productive. However, there is really not a bad time to fish the creek—it produces varied insect hatches throughout the year, especially during the spring season.

If you choose to fish during winter, bring a light rod in the 4- to 6-weight range and load its reel with a weight-forward floating line. Attach a 10-foot leader that tapers to 5X or 6X.

Depending on a number of variables, including weather and the idiosyncracies of trout, you may be able to catch fish on the surface during winter, but most often you must tie on a subsurface offering. If you see fish rolling on the surface, tie on a midge imitation, such as a Griffith's gnat, suspender midge, or parachute Adams, in sizes ranging from 16 to 20, and dead-drift it over rising fish. If you see few fish rising, try underneath the surface with small midge imitations, such as brassies, palomino midges, serendipities, and blood midges. Another excellent winter pattern —for that matter any time of the year—is a size 18 olive scud.

Whether fishing midges or a scud, most anglers place a strike indicator above the fly to detect subtle strikes. Because Rocky Ford is shallow and its current relatively slow, you need not place your indicator more than 4 feet above the fly. Allow the indicator and fly to dead-drift and set the hook quickly when the indicator flinches.

If fishing small flies under an indicator is not your gig, tie on a size 8 olive, brown, or black marabou leech or woolly bugger. Cast as far out as you can (made difficult by backcast-snaring cattails and brush) and allow the leech or bugger to sink to the bottom.

Vary your retrieve: Try short, quick strips or slowly twist the fly line around your hand. One method may work in the morning, another in the afternoon. A trout's preference changes often, so play around with your retrieve until you find what they're after.

As winter loses its grip on central Washington, usually in late February and early March, anglers deluge Rocky Ford. If you are a sociable creature, you probably won't be bothered by their presence. However, if you subscribe to the solitary angling club, stay clear.

*T.R. McCrystal surveys Rocky Ford Creek with Moose and Shadow.*

"As soon as the weather warms up, we see an awful lot of people over here," says Joe Foster, a regional biologist for Washington Department of Fish and Wildlife in Ephrata. "Other places in the West, like Idaho, Montana, and British Columbia, are still snowbound in March, and people are eager to get back outside after being indoors all winter. This is one place where they can come and fish, and it gets pounded. But the fishing is good. We see Baetis and Callibaetis and even some caddisflies in March and April."

Of those hatches, look for the Baetis emergence to be most significant, but don't overlook the others.

"You'll see some Baetis on the good days during winter, but they really pick up around the first part of March and last through the summer," says Darc Noble, who works at Blue Dun Fly Shop in Wenatchee. "You start seeing Callibaetis by the end of March. They pick up in April, and they are present through summer, too. You also see sporadic Trico hatches, which can be heavy at times, in July, August, and early September. Sometimes the Trico hatches are heavy, and the fish sure do feed on them."

You don't have to throw small mayfly patterns to catch Rocky Ford's rainbows during summer. The smart angler will always keep a few hoppers, ants, and beetles in his fly boxes, along with a generous supply of damselfly nymphs and adults.

"You start seeing a few damsels in April, but they really get going in late May and June," says Noble, who keeps a detailed journal of his days on the creek. "Fishing the damsels can be a blast. I like to walk along the shore and sight-fish to cruisers using adult damsel patterns."

During a dry, warm year, grasshoppers start feeding trout by late June and their presence remains a focal point for fish through September. Hoppers cling to the shoreline vegetation during the evening and morning hours, becoming active as the sun rises each day. Their activity peaks in the afternoon. At that time, hoppers try to fly across the creek. Some of them make it, others don't. You get the picture.

While there is nothing quite like watching a huge rainbow rise to the surface and pummel a hopper, Noble wouldn't include the hopper in his fly box if he was limited to fishing just three flies on the creek.

"If I was limited to three flies, one of those would definitely be a size 14, dirty olive scud," he says. "I catch more fish on that pattern than any other, and it works all year. I'd also pick a hare's ear, size 14, and an adult damselfly, size 6 or 8. There are other patterns that I would like to have, but you could catch fish through the seasons on those."

While Rocky Ford provides many great days for Washington's anglers, unfortunately, it is a system that will likely go through boom and bust cycles every 7 to 10 years.

Rocky Ford's trout history dates back to the early 1940s when a hatchery was erected on its banks. A decent fishery was spawned, but it faded with the crumbling hatchery. Today, Rocky Ford is enduring its third wave of hatcheries, with one at its springfed headwaters and another located a few miles downstream.

In 1987 Washington Department of Fish and Wildlife erected a dam on lower Rocky Ford Creek near its confluence with Moses Lake. The intent of the dam was to keep rough fish, especially carp, from entering Rocky Ford to compete with trout. After the dam was completed, WFW chemically treated the creek, which wiped out almost all of the carp and other undesirable species, such as suckers, sunfish, and shiners. In 1988 the creek was planted with trout, and the fishery flourished. Another plant of trout in the early 1990s supplemented the fish that had been harvested by anglers or had perished by natural causes. At that time, with lots of fish available in the 5-pound range, Rocky Ford's reputation grew throughout the West.

Unfortunately, since that time, the creek has diminished in productivity and popularity. The reason: harvest by legal anglers and greedy poachers, plus the resurgence of carp.

"Right now (1998), the status of the creek is mediocre," says Foster. "We've got carp back in the system on the lower end and there are also lots of suckers near the first hatchery. The lower reaches of the creek just don't produce anymore. I don't think that we will ever be able to remove every single carp from the system, so I anticipate this cycle to occur every 7 to 10 years."

That shouldn't overly concern dedicated anglers. It just means that Rocky Ford may have a year or two downtime in its ability to pump out huge rainbows. For instance, rainbow trout are planted in Rocky Ford when they measure between 3 and 5 inches. By the end of their first year, they measure around 12 to 14 inches. By their second year, they stretch 17 to 20 inches, and by their third year, they are full-blown hogs that measure about 24 inches long. In Rocky Ford, a trout's life expectancy is 4 or 5 years, so they hold the potential to reach 27 or 28 inches and weigh, perhaps, 7 or 8 pounds.

While rainbows offer all the excitement an angler needs, it's hard not to dream about brown trout and their potential in the creek. Brown trout are notorious fish eaters and they would likely lessen the carp population, maybe to the extent of postponing or eliminating altogether the need to chemically treat the system every decade. Plus, brown trout just hold a special appeal for trout anglers: They are the ultimate test of fly selection, presentation, and angling skill. And they get big. For now, we brown trout supporters must wait patently and accept all that the rainbows have to offer. However, in the future, we may see browns in the system.

"I want to plant brown trout in Rocky Ford," Foster says. "I think they would do well and offer even more opportunity for anglers. But we work tightly with the hatcheries, and they don't want to increase the odds of their hatcheries becoming infected with a disease. Brown trout are notorious for having a bacterial kidney disease. If I could find some browns that were certified disease free, I'd put them in, but that just hasn't happened yet."

One thing that most anglers will dislike at Rocky Ford is the amount of litter on its banks. I have never fished a flyfishing-only water that has been more tainted with items ranging from leader packages to empty beer cans. When T.R. and I fished the creek one winter, T.R. filled a plastic bag with litter on his way back from the water. The only way the problem can be remedied is for all of us to pick up after those few anglers who don't give a damn about littering.

In the realm of western trout angling, Rocky Ford ranks right up there with the most famous waters when it comes to producing overly plump fish. It may not have the brown trout that Idaho's Silver Creek offers, and it might not have the spectacular scenery that surrounds you while fishing Montana's Paradise Valley spring creeks or Wyoming's Flat Creek, but Rocky Ford is Washington's finest donation to western trophy trout fishing. That's enough to keep me going back.

# Stream Facts: Rocky Ford Creek

### Seasons
• Open year-round.

### Special Regulations
• Catch and release, flyfishing only.
• No wading (fishing from bank only).

### Species
• Rainbow trout stretching between 8 inches and 8 pounds
• Atlantic salmon

### Stream Characteristics
• A true spring creek, Rocky Ford offers wary trout that feed on small insects.
• Midges, damselflies, scudes, dragonflies, Baetis, and Callibaetis mayflies all draw the attention of large rainbows.
• Grasshoppers, ants, and leeches all draw strikes, too.
• Rocky Ford offers one of the best shots at a large rainbow trout in Washington that may test the skill of the most experienced angler. However, on a good day, 20 or more fish may come to net.

### Access
• Easy access via Department of Fish and Wildlife access point at the north end of the stream. There is also a handicapped access dock located there.
• Flyfishers may also drive a half-mile past the first access to a dirt parking lot. From there, a short hike takes anglers to the stream.
• Anglers are not allowed to wade into the creek, but waders should be worn anyway, because trails along the banks are muddy and wet.

# ROCKY FORD CREEK MAJOR HATCHES

| Insect | J | F | M | A | M | J | J | A | S | O | N | D | Flies |
|---|---|---|---|---|---|---|---|---|---|---|---|---|---|
| Chironomid | ■ | ■ | ■ | ■ | ■ | ■ | ■ | ■ | ■ | ■ | ■ | ■ | Brassie #16–24; Suspender Midge #16–24; Palomino Midge #16–24; Blood Midge #16–24; Griffith's Gnat #16–24; Biot Midge Emerger #16–24 |
| Pale Morning Dun | | | | | | ■ | ■ | | | | | | Parachute Adams #16–18; Pheasant Tail #16–18; Sparkle Dun #16–18; Hare's Ear #16–18; Cripple #16–18 |
| Grasshoppers | | | | | | | ■ | ■ | ■ | | | | Joe's Hopper #4–8; Parachute Hopper #4–8; Chernobyl Hopper #4–8 |
| Leeches | ■ | ■ | ■ | ■ | ■ | ■ | ■ | ■ | ■ | ■ | ■ | ■ | Canadian Brown Mohair Leech #6–8; Brown or Olive Marabou Leech #4–10; Rabbit Strip Leech #4–8 |
| Streamers | ■ | ■ | ■ | ■ | ■ | ■ | ■ | ■ | ■ | ■ | ■ | ■ | Brown or Black Woolly Bugger #4–8; Woolhead Sculpin #4–8; Epoxy Minnow #4–8; Egg-sucking Leech #4–10 |
| Baetis | ■ | ■ | ■ | ■ | | | | | ■ | ■ | ■ | | Olive Sparkle Dun #16–22; Olive Cripple #16–20; Olive Hare's Ear #16–20; Pheasant Tail #16–20 |
| Scud | ■ | ■ | ■ | ■ | ■ | ■ | ■ | ■ | ■ | ■ | ■ | ■ | Olive Scue #18–20; Bighorn Scud #16–20 |
| Callibaetis | | | | | | ■ | ■ | ■ | ■ | | | | CB Spinner #14–18; CDC Biot Callibaetis #14–18; AK's CB Spinner #14–18; Hare's Ear #12–18; CB Cripple #14–16 |
| Caddis | | | | | ■ | ■ | ■ | ■ | ■ | | | | LaFontaine Emergent Sparkle Pupa #14–18; X-Caddis #14–18; Diving Caddis #14–18; Slow Wter Caddis #14–18; Hemingway Caddis #16–20; Caddis Variant #16–18 |
| Trico | | | | | | | | ■ | ■ | ■ | | | CDC Trico #18–24; Parachute Adams #18–24; Female Trico #18–24 |
| Damselfly | | | | | ■ | ■ | ■ | ■ | | | | | Nyergess Nymph #6–12; Six-pack #6–10; Burk's Olive Damsel #8–12; Braided Butt Damsel #4–10; Sheep Creek Special #6–10 |

# Sanpoil River

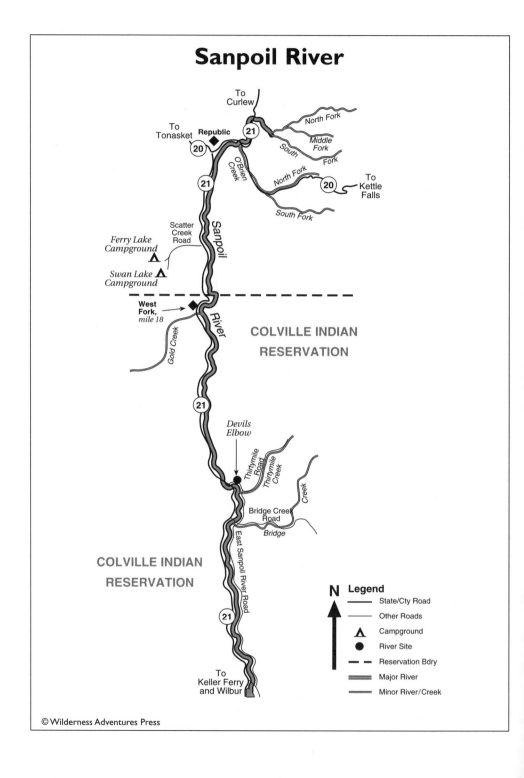

To
Curlew

To
Tonasket

**Republic**

21

20

North Fork

Middle
Fork

South
Fork

O'Brien Creek

North Fork

20

To
Kettle
Falls

South Fork

Scatter
Creek
Road

Ferry Lake
Campground

Swan Lake
Campground

Sanpoil

River

**West
Fork,**
mile 18

Gold Creek

COLVILLE INDIAN
RESERVATION

21

Devils
Elbow

Thirtymile
Road

Thirtymile
Creek

Creek

Bridge Creek
Road

Bridge

East Sanpoil River Road

COLVILLE INDIAN
RESERVATION

21

To
Keller Ferry
and Wilbur

**N**

**Legend**
State/Cty Road
Other Roads
Λ  Campground
●  River Site
- - -  Reservation Bdry
Major River
Minor River/Creek

© Wilderness Adventures Press

# SANPOIL RIVER

A beautiful little freestone stream that flows south from Republic, the Sanpoil River suffers from general harvest regulations and frequent contamination from Republic's sewer treatment plant, which is located just off the bank of the river.

However, the Sanpoil still provides some decent opportunity for flycasters, most notably after runoff in late June or early July.

The Sanpoil offers rainbow, brown, and brook trout in fair numbers and access, via Hwys 20 and 21, is excellent. However, the Sanpoil is cluttered with downfalls and logjams, so it probably isn't a river you want to float, unless you take the time to walk a 5- or 10-mile section to check for obstruction. And you really don't have to do that —the river rates about 25 or 30 yards wide in most places, and it can be easily waded and covered with a long cast after spring runoff subsides.

At that time, look for significant pale morning dun, yellow sally, and golden stonefly emergences. Caddis are also present in good numbers, especially in the evenings when they fire out of the bankside brush and hover over the river.

Dry-fly patterns, such as an Adams, sparkle dun, or cripple, match the mayflies. To match caddis, try an elk hair caddis, X-caddis, caddis variant, or LaFontaine sparkle emerger. Golden stones can be matched by a royal stimulator or a Henry's Fork golden stone. To imitate the smaller stoneflies, which are particularly dense around riffles, try a yellow humpy, small stimulator, Madame X, lime trude, or a Turck's tarantula.

The upper river, including a major tributary (O'Brien Creek) fishes well for brook trout and small rainbows. There is decent access to the stream at bridge crossings and where it parallels the highway, but much of it runs through private pasture and permission must be secured to fish some prime water. Downstream from Republic, the river parallels Hwy 21, which offers frequent access. Again, some stretches run through private land, and permission is needed to fish this water. Through this stretch, brown trout start showing up in the catch and can run to good size, many extending between 16 and 20 inches, with a few true hogs thrown in on the side.

Just north of West Fork, the Sanpoil carves into the Colville Indian Reservation, and a tribal permit is required to fish this section, which extends about 33 miles downstream to its Lake Roosevelt.

The reservation section is probably the best water on the river and well worth the purchase of a tribal permit. Large brown trout fin in the deep holes and under the cutbanks and logjams. Big rainbow trout move out of Lake Roosevelt and into the lower Sanpoil during the spring spawn. Some of those fish take up residence and remain in the river all year.

According to Curt Vail, a biologist for Washington Department of Fish and Wildlife, the lower Sanpoil is the place to fish.

"I think the lower river is better than the upper section because you do get some large fish—rainbows between 16 and 20 inches, running upstream," he says. "The

*The Sanpoil River is an undiscovered rainbow and brown trout fishery.*

upper river has a nice population of brookies and rainbows, but it can get fished pretty hard. The lower river, through the reservation, produces much larger fish and hardly anyone hits it."

If you hit the lower Sanpoil, work large streamers through the deep pools and near undercut banks and logjams. In the evening, big browns can sometimes be taken on top with emergent and adult caddis patterns. Look for subtle rises, often with just the snout of a trout visible.

# Stream Facts: Sanpoil River

### Seasons and Special Regulations
- Catch and release only from Nineteen Mile Bridge to Colville Indian Reservation boundary.

### Species
- Rainbow, brown, and brook trout. Rainbows and brook trout range from 6 to 16 inches, while brown trout can stretch 20 inches or more.

### Stream Characteristics
- Brushy along its banks, the Sanpoil offers excellent caddis habitat, and fish feed heavily on them during summer months.
- Rainbows and brook trout also hammer caddis, along with pale morning duns and Baetis.
- The upper river harbors mostly small trout, with an occasional 16-incher.
- The lower river, below the reservation boundary, has larger fish, some arriving from Lake Roosevelt.

### Access
- Excellent access is available via Hwy 21.
- Permission is needed to gain access over private land in some sections.
- A reservation permit is required to fish sections that pass through Indian land.

## SANPOIL RIVER MAJOR HATCHES

| Insect | J | F | M | A | M | J | J | A | S | O | N | D | Flies |
|--------|---|---|---|---|---|---|---|---|---|---|---|---|-------|
| Caddis | | | | | | | | | ■ | ■ | | | Elk Hair Caddis #16–18; LaFontaine Sparkle Emerger #16–18; X-Caddis #16–18; Free-living Caddis Larva #14–18; Stranahan's Caddis Variant #16–18 |
| Pale Morning Dun | | | | | | | | ■ | ■ | | | | Parachute PMD #16–18; Parachute Adams #16–18; Hare's Ear Nymph #16–18; Pheasant Tail Nymph #16–18; PMD Cripple #16–18; Sparkle Dun #16–18; PMD Thorax #16–18 |
| Golden Stone/Yellow Sally | | | | | | ■ | ■ | | | | | | Royal Stimulator #8–14; Elk Hair Caddis #14–18; Yellow Humpy #14–16; Black Stonefly Nymph #6–14 |
| Streamers | | | | ■ | | | | | | | ■ | | Woolly Bugger #4–8; Zonker #4–8; Woolhead Sculpin #2–4; Epoxy Minnow #4–6; Rabbit Strip Leech #4–6; Egg-sucking Leech #2–6 |
| Baetis | | | | ■ | | | | | ■ | | | | Sparkle Dun #16–20; Cripple #16–20; CDC Biot Baetis #16–20; Baetis Spinner #16–20; Hare's Ear & Pheasant Tail Nymphs #16–20; Parachute Adams #16–20; Lightning Bug #16–20 |
| Terrestrials | | | | | | | | ■ | ■ | | | | Joe's Hopper #2–8; Chernobyl Hopper #4–8; Parachute Black Ant #14–20; Foam Beetle #14–16 |
| For Whitefish | ■ | ■ | ■ | ■ | ■ | ■ | ■ | ■ | ■ | ■ | ■ | ■ | Beadhead Prince Nymph #12–18; Flashback Pheasant Tail #14–18; Beadhead Stonefly Nymph #8–14 |

# KETTLE RIVER

When flyfishers talk about stream options for quality trout in Washington, the Yakima River, which has been extensively written about in the flyfishing magazines, is always mentioned.

When considering other first-rate Evergreen state trout streams, people usually draw a blank. That's unfortunate because Washington does offer options, and one of its best is the Kettle River.

The Kettle flows south out of British Columbia into northeast Washington before making a north turn at Curlew. Ten miles downstream, it reenters Canada then breaks back into Washington at Laurier. From there it flows south about 22 miles before entering Lake Roosevelt.

Flyfishers should feel fortunate that the river dips into Washington, and we should commend Curt Vail, a Kettle River biologist for Washington Department of Fish and Wildlife. It's his interest in the river and his knowledge of its potential that swayed regulation changes in the early 1990s. That's when the Kettle went from a year-round fishery, with standard trout harvest regulations, to a 2 trout over 12 inches, single, barbless hooks and no bait requirement. It's strictly catch and release on trout from November 1 through May 31. These regulations, as well as the practice of taking rainbow from the Kettle's tributaries, raising them in a nearby lake, and then releasing them into the Kettle when they are 3 or 4 inches, have dramatically improved the fishery.

"Right now, the Kettle is a pretty good flyfishing river with lots of rainbows and some large browns," Vail says. "We tried 20 years ago to get restrictive regulations here, and people shot it down. This river was in dire need of (new regulations), so I'm excited that we have them now. It used to be that we couldn't keep a fish alive long enough to allow it to spawn. They were getting harvested before they ever got a chance. Now we are seeing a lot of mature fish spawning on their own. At some point, we may be able to stop our stocking program and go strictly to wild trout management."

Prime fishing begins on the Kettle as runoff subsides in late June. At that time, look for solid caddisfly emergences along with golden stoneflies, yellow sallies, and a few pale morning duns. During solid insect emergences, which last through summer and fall, the Kettle's trout, especially rainbows, aren't too picky about fly imitations. However, there is a lack of cover (including woody debris) in the river, and it's a relatively shallow stream. Trout congregate near the riffles, sometimes at the head, sometimes at the tail and sometimes on the sides or in the riffle itself for cover. In the shallow water, a poor cast can spook them, so long, light leaders are recommended.

"When the water starts dropping in July, there are guys who catch and release up to 20 fish in an hour," Vail says. "At that time, with the water still up, the fish hold close to the banks. As summer progresses you'll find them in the riffles and slick glides. When they are in the riffles, they can be cautiously approached. When they get in the glides, they're real spooky and a bad cast can put them down.

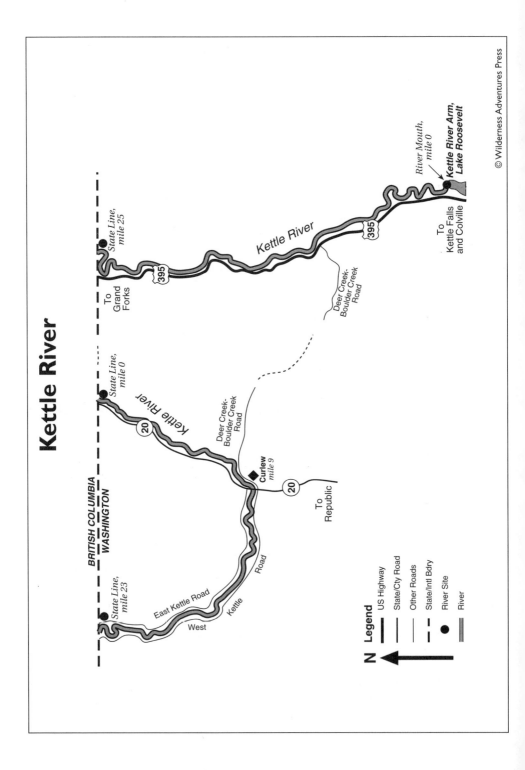

Kettle River

*The Kettle River is full of whitefish, which provide an excellent winter diversion. Here, John Huber poses with a whitefish while Shadow inspects.*

"Through summer, we use, almost exclusively, small dry flies, size 16 or smaller. During fall we still have caddis and mayflies, but we also get some small black ants on the water. Sometimes we see so many ants they almost overpower the fisherman. You almost have to muscle a fly past all those ants and into a trout's mouth."

While most of the river shapes up by July, several factors can push the Kettle back out of shape. First, Curlew Creek, which enters the Kettle at Curlew about 12 miles from the Canadian border, pumps a lot of sediment into the river. The 10-mile section of water from Curlew extending north to the Canadian border remain out of shape longer than the section upstream from Curlew.

However, the section of river extending from the Canadian border at Ferry downstream to Curlew, can blow out if thunderstorms dump rain and hail in British Columbia, as they often do. It's not uncommon to fish perfect conditions one day, only to find the river a foot or more higher and cloudy the following morning. When that happens, don't fret—you can still catch fish if you work the inside corners of riffles and slack pockets against the banks with small nymphs, such as a beadhead hare's ear or pheasant tail. Also, the river clears quickly, so conditions may improve by the afternoon if another deluge doesn't besiege the river.

Most of the rainbows that you'll catch on the Kettle measure 12 inches or less, but there is a burgeoning population of fish that stretch 12 inches with a few rating 16 inches or longer. Brown trout, which established themselves in the river after a single plant of just 3,000 fish in the late 1970s, run up to 20 inches or more.

Rainbows are scattered throughout the river, but browns are more common on the lower end, where the river broadens and the deep water habitat that browns prefer becomes more abundant.

Fall is an especially good time to chase brown trout on the Kettle. The river is low and clear, the browns are active due to their inherent urge to spawn, and they concentrate near the mouths of tributary streams, such as Boundary Creek, Toroda Creek, and Curlew Creek. Working large streamers, such as weighted woolly buggers, sculpins and zonkers, through the deeper holes, medium depth runs, and the pools at the mouths of tributary streams is a good tactic for browns. On the very lower end of the river, below Barstow Bridge, where restrictive regulations end, brown trout can be taken on those same streamers along with walleyes, which move into the river from Lake Roosevelt.

"Just because we don't have the restrictive regulations on the lower river doesn't mean it's no good," Vail says. "The quality of trout fishing does go down below Barstow Bridge, but there are some smallmouth bass and walleye and brown trout to catch. We even see some pretty nice rainbows to 16 inches or more move out of Lake Roosevelt and into the lower Kettle."

Flyfishers encounter good fishing throughout the special regulation water, but the highest density of rainbows can be found in the upper 10 miles of stream above Curlew. Fortunately, the section from Ferry to Curlew can be floated in a raft or pontoon boat.

"Floating the river is definitely the best way to go," Vail says. "There's plenty of wade access off the east and west Kettle roads, but with a raft you can hit all of the good water. And the Kettle is not a difficult river to float. It offers a medium gradient with moderate velocity. There are not many obstructions so it's very relaxing.

"You could dump a small boat, raft, or pontoon boat in on the gravel bank within a hundred yards of Midway, British Columbia, and float down to Curlew, where you can take out at the city park. There's also a take-out point just above Curlew on the west Curlew road."

There are also excellent floats downstream from Curlew, extending all the way to Barstow. Crude access for put-in and take-out exist in several places. It is advisable to scout the river before dumping a boat or raft in it. Some of the accesses may disappear during high water from one year to the next. One option is to ask local landowners if it's OK to take out on their property. It's a hit and miss proposition, but if you get permission and treat those people properly (meaning you give them a gift, such as a bottle of wine), they are likely to allow your presence again.

Winter is also a good time to fish the Kettle. Anglers can catch and release trout and bring home a pile of mountain whitefish for the smokehouse if they want. Whitefish congregate in the deep and middepth pools. They are fond of subsurface nymphs, such as hare's ears, pheasant tails, and, especially, beadhead Prince nymphs.

While the Kettle may never attract the attention that Washington's top trout venue, the Yakima River, gets, it is a wonderful stream that is on the rise. With special regulations in place, the Kettle should only get better.

# Stream Facts: Kettle River

### Seasons and Special Regulations
- Open year-round.
- Catch and release only from Barstow Bridge upstream to Canadian border, November 1 through May 31.
- Two-trout limit, with 12-inch minimum, June 1 through October 31.

### Species
- Rainbow and brown trout. Most fish average 10 to 13 inches, but some hog browns to 20 inches plus show up on occasion, mostly from the lower river.

### Stream Characteristics
- An excellent stream to float in a raft or pontoon boat, the Kettle offers decent insect hatches to match, and its trout key on them.
- Caddis, pale morning duns, Baetis, and a few drake mayflies bring fish to the surface.
- Large streamers and nymphs are better suited for brown trout, which hold in the deeper holes under logjams and below undercut banks.

### Access
- Wade access to the river is good via the west and east Kettle roads.
- Raft put-in and take-out sites are also available and are evenly dispersed along the river every 5 to 10 miles.

## KETTLE RIVER MAJOR HATCHES

| Insect | J | F | M | A | M | J | J | A | S | O | N | D | Flies |
|---|---|---|---|---|---|---|---|---|---|---|---|---|---|
| Caddis | | | | | | | | | ■ | | | | Elk Hair Caddis #16–18; LaFontaine Sparkle Emerger #16–18; X-Caddis #16–18; Free-living Caddis Larva #14–18; Stranahan's Caddis Variant #16–18 |
| Pale Morning Dun | | | | | | | | ■ | | | | | Parachute PMD #16–18; Parachute Adams #16–18; Hare's Ear Nymph #16–18; Pheasant Tail Nymph #16–18; PMD Cripple #16–18; Sparkle Dun #16–18; PMD Thorax #16–18 |
| Golden Stone/Yellow Sally | | | | | | | ■ | | | | | | Royal Stimulator #8–14; Elk Hair Caddis #14–18; Yellow Humpy #14–16; Black Stonefly Nymph #6–14 |
| Streamers | | | | ■ | ■ | ■ | ■ | ■ | ■ | ■ | ■ | | Woolly Bugger #4–8; Zonker #4–8; Woolhead Sculpin #2–4; Epoxy Minnow #4–6; Rabbit Strip Leech #4–6; Egg-sucking Leech #2–6 |
| Baetis | | | | | ■ | | | ■ | | | ■ | | Sparkle Dun #16–20; Cripple #16–20; CDC Biot Baetis #16–20; Baetis Spinner #16–20; Hare's Ear & Pheasant Tail Nymphs #16–20; Parachute Adams #16–20; Lightning Bug #16–20 |
| Terrestrials | | | | | | | | ■ | ■ | | | | Joe's Hopper #2–8; Chernobyl Hopper #4–8; Parachute Black Ant #14–20; Foam Beetle #14–16 |
| For Whitefish | ■ | | | | | | | | | | | ■ | Beadhead Prince Nymph #12–18; Flashback Pheasant Tail #14–18; Beadhead Stonefly Nymph #8–14 |

# Spokane River

A 2-hour drive from Spokane places far-eastern Washington anglers in the midst of northern Idaho's justly famous mountain cutthroat trout streams, such as Kelly Creek and the North Fork Clearwater and St. Joe Rivers, where big, bushy dry flies easily entice large cutthroat to the surface.

A 3-hour drive from Spokane drops eastern Washington flyfishers onto Montana's Clark Fork River, where a plethora of aquatic insect emergences draw large rainbow trout to the top during summer and fall. For that reason, Spokane's local stream, the Spokane River, is often overlooked by anglers who are too busy heading out of state to notice excellent options right under their noses.

Oh, don't get me wrong—no biologist or well-traveled flyfisher is going to favorably compare the Spokane River to such Rocky Mountain gems. But for anglers who invest the time to understand their home river, some rich rewards, in the form of large rainbow and brown trout, are possible.

Quality flyfishing, including excellent access to the river, extends from the Idaho/Washington border near Post Falls, Idaho, downstream through Spokane. In that section, a one fish limit (none under 12 inches) and selective gear restrictions apply. There are also excellent flyfishing options extending from Spokane downstream to the mouth of the Little Spokane River. From that point downstream the Spokane broadens out, warms up, and is essentially a warmwater lake fishery (called Lake Spokane) that offers bass and walleye, mostly for the bait and tackle crew.

As mentioned, access to the big Spokane is abundant throughout the river's course, and it provides some good insect hatches to match. And, unlike those Idaho and Montana streams, you probably won't find hordes of competition when you launch a boat or plant a wading boot in the river. In the era since *A River Runs Through It*, there's a lot to be said for that quality.

When choosing a time to fish the Spokane, anglers need to consider several factors, including water temperature, clarity, and velocity. If the river is too hot, as it can be in July, August, and September, or if the water is muddy and running Mach 3 speed, as it can during spring, an angler is mostly out of luck.

However, if you can hit the river just as the water drops during spring or as it cools during fall, insect emergences, especially caddisflies, can be heavy and the fishing can be outstanding. On a good day, a flyfisher's dreams of those prominent Rocky Mountain streams can be quickly halted.

"The Spokane is probably not as good as those streams in Montana on average, but the guys who know when and how to fish the river do really well," says Bob Peck, Spokane River biologist for Washington Department of Fish and Wildlife. "The average rainbow or brown goes about 14 inches and a real nice one is 17 or 18 inches long. There are some that are quite a bit larger. During our electrofishing surveys, we've seen fish to 22 or 23 inches, but I know there are fish in there to 6 or 7 pounds."

Larry Cowles, an avid Spokane River flyfisher who works at Silverbow Fly Shop in Spokane agrees.

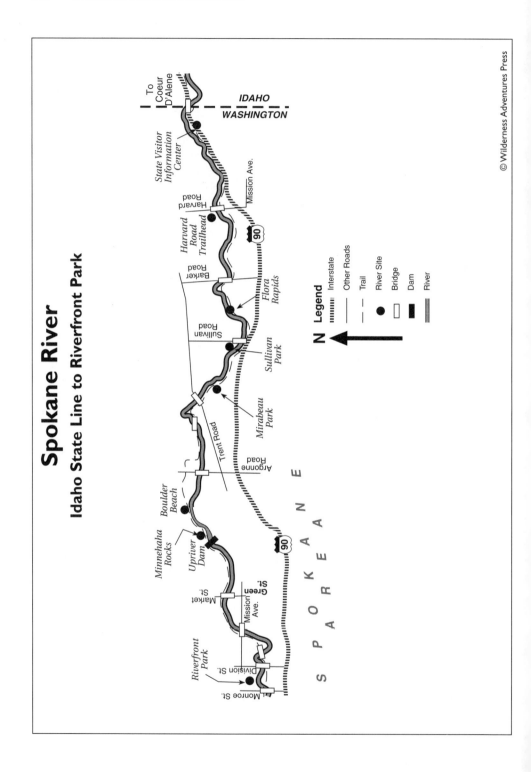

# Spokane River
## Idaho State Line to Riverfront Park

To Coeur D'Alene

IDAHO
WASHINGTON

State Visitor Information Center

Harvard Road

Mission Ave.

Harvard Road Trailhead

90

Barker Road

Flora Rapids

Sullivan Road

Sullivan Park

Mirabeau Park

Trent Road

Argonne Road

Boulder Beach

Minnehaha Rocks

Upriver Dam

90

Market St.

Green St.

Mission Ave.

Riverfront Park

Division St.

Monroe St.

S P O K A N E

N

**Legend**

||||| Interstate

— — — Other Roads

|||||||| Trail

● River Site

☐ Bridge

■ Dam

River

© Wilderness Adventures Press

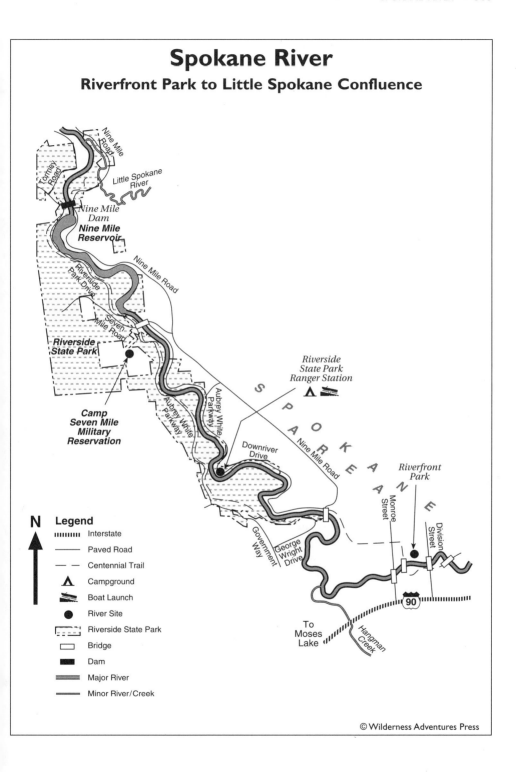

# Spokane River
## Riverfront Park to Little Spokane Confluence

Little Spokane River

Tormey Road

Nine Mile Road

Nine Mile Dam
**Nine Mile Reservoir**

Riverside Park Drive

Nine Mile Road

Seven Mile Road

**Riverside State Park**

**Camp Seven Mile Military Reservation**

Aubrey White Parkway

Aubrey White Parkway

Downriver Drive

Government Way

George Wright Drive

Riverside State Park Ranger Station

S P O K A N E

Nine Mile Road

Riverfront Park

Monroe Street

Division Street

To Moses Lake

Hangman Creek

90

**N**

**Legend**

| | |
|---|---|
| ⊪⊪⊪⊪ | Interstate |
| —— | Paved Road |
| – – – | Centennial Trail |
| ▲ | Campground |
| 🚤 | Boat Launch |
| ● | River Site |
| ⬚ | Riverside State Park |
| ▭ | Bridge |
| ▬ | Dam |
| ▬▬ | Major River |
| —— | Minor River/Creek |

© Wilderness Adventures Press

"I mostly catch fish between 10 inches and 3 or 4 pounds, but I've seen some guys with fish that would weigh between 5 and 8 pounds," Cowles says. "In the upper river between the Idaho border and Spokane, the fish are all naturally spawned—there's no stocking. Those fish are really pretty and really strong. They look like Alaska's rainbow trout."

Those rainbows are believed to be descendants of steelhead and are specifically adapted to the Spokane River and its challenging environment. For that reason, the upper section of river has not been stocked with hatchery trout since the 1980s. One might ask why a 1-fish limit remains on the river—why not entirely catch and release?

According to Eric Johnson, a fisheries biologist for Washington Water Power, the one fish limit is not what limits the upper Spokane's fishery. Instead, water conditions and poaching are the trout's biggest obstacles.

"When we have hot, dry years, the water temperature can rise as high as 80 degrees, and that is lethal to rainbow trout. Even brown trout, which make up about 10 percent of the population, may not survive in those conditions. In the 1980s we had nearly 2,000 trout a mile in the upper river, but we had the hot, dry years in the late 1980s and early 1990s that knocked the population down to about 200 trout a mile. The other problem we have is people who don't release their fish, and those are the guys who disobey the no-bait regulations. You still see a fair number of people fishing bait and hauling away 5 or 6 good size adult fish. I guess they don't understand how important, how diverse, the rainbow trout in this river are. Native fish can't be replaced by hatchery stock. That's why almost all of them should be released. If we lose them, the river won't be very good."

If you see somebody fishing bait on the upper river, give them an earful and don't bow down to their ignorant plea of "Gosh, when did it go to no bait?" Instead, grab your cell phone and call Fish and Wildlife at their Spokane office (509-456-4088) or call the poaching hotline at 1-800-477-6224. If we all report violations and word gets out that you'll get busted if you fish bait on the Spokane River, maybe those knotheads will stay home. Or maybe they'll do the right thing and fish a water that allows bait fishing for trout.

For the flyfisher, there are several important hatches to match on the upper river that begin with caddisflies the day the river opens to fishing on June 1.

Although caddis can bring trout to the surface any hour of the day, their presence is greatest just before dusk and that's when the trout get really fired up about them.

According to Peck, Johnson, and Cowles, the Spokane is first and foremost a caddisfly river, and caddis hatches offer the best opportunity of the year to take the river's rainbows and browns on a dry fly.

"Caddisflies are the big-ticket item on the Spokane and I think the largest caddis hatches occur during the first couple weeks of June," Johnson says. "At that time, the flows are declining and the bugs really get going in the evenings. That's when you'll find the fish really active up top feeding. We see several species of caddis come off, but the main one is the *Hydropsyche*."

*Ian Cenis, a stellar Spokane River flyfisher, hoists a plump, spring-caught brown trout. (Photo courtesy Ian Cenis)*

Although caddis hatches are most prominent during June, Cowles says that caddis are present through summer and late evening—just as the sun drops behind the surrounding hills and air temperature diminishes is when they drop out of the bankside brush and take flight over the river.

"Usually, you can count on caddis if you're on the river a half-hour before dark," Cowles says. "When it comes off, you can find fish in the slackwater just below a run or in the pockets along the banks, especially under overhanging vegetation."

Standard caddis patterns, such as the elk hair caddis, Hemingway caddis, Goddard caddis, and even the royal trude, draw strikes on the Spokane, but the new, innovative patterns are much better. In fact, patterns that imitate emerging caddis pupa, rather than adult caddis, are the ticket just before dark.

The spotted sedge (*Hydropsyche*) that you'll encounter on the river is about a size 12, mottled-wing insect with a brown or dull yellow body, almost a rust color. To match them, flyfishers should take plenty of LaFontaine sparkle emergers that slam trout when traditional caddis imitations, such as an elk hair caddis, are shunned.

When fishing emerger patterns, such as the sparkle pupa or an X-caddis, flyfishers should imitate the pupa, which rest half in, half out of the water.

When the pupa emerges, it is a fully-formed insect that is encased in a transparent sheath. The sparkle pupa is tied with Antron yarn, which mimics the sheath and holds tiny air bubbles like the actual insect. Floatant should be applied to the deer hair wing of the emergent sparkle pupa, and the pattern should be dead-drifted.

If the sparkle pupa or X-caddis fails, try a diving caddis. Fished wet, just under the surface and dead-drifted, it can be a real killer when the sparkle pupa occasionally fails.

Keep an eye out for egg-laying female caddis, too. Generally, they are seen in the air before fish begin rising. During the last hour of light, females return to the river to deposit their eggs. That is when the fish key on them.

If you fish the Spokane during the day, try size 12, 14 or 16 free-living caddis larvae. Bright green is one of the most productive colors. Of course, Prince nymphs, hare's ear nymphs, pheasant tails, and a variety of beadhead offerings also draw takes.

"Beadhead nymphs work really well on the river," Cowles says. "I like the Prince nymph best, but hare's ears and pheasant tails also work well. I like to work those nymphs in the slack water just above the riffles or in the riffles themselves."

The Spokane also receives a healthy dose of mayfly emergences and the most prominent of those beautiful, dainty creatures is the pale morning dun, which comes off in June and July.

To match PMDs, tie on a size 16 PMD cripple, sparkle dun, extended body comparadun, or a parachute Adams. Underneath the surface, try a hare's ear nymph, pheasant tail nymph, or a halfback emerger. PMD populations are most dense near fast water riffles so concentrate efforts in those areas. Work nymphs near the bottom under a strike indicator. Apply split shot to the leader as needed—the deeper the water, the more split shot you'll need.

During fall, as the water cools, Baetis mayflies also appear, and trout can turn significant attention to them. Tiny patterns, such as size18 blue-winged olives, parachute Adams', olive sparkle duns, Baetis cripples, and comparaduns work well.

"We usually start to spill water out of Post Falls (dam) just after Labor Day," Johnson says. "As the flows pick back up, the water cools and the trout get active again. That's when you start to see the mayflies again, and Baetis are the most pronounced. As long as the water temperature remains cool, fishing can be good through the end of the season. You won't see rising fish like you would in June, but there are enough fish eating off the surface to keep things interesting."

Expect the presence of Baetis to be most pronounced during fall afternoons when air temperature is warmest. They remain on the river until the upper Spokane's season closes October 31. The lower river, which follows a similar hatch schedule is open year-round.

*Ian Cenis poses with a prime Spokane River rainbow prior to release. He took the fish near Sullivan Bridge. (Photo courtesy Ian Cenis)*

When fishing the Spokane, no matter what time of the year, anglers in the know will keep a few streamer patterns in their fly boxes. Muddler minnows are particularly effective on the Spokane, but woolly buggers, zonkers, and egg-sucking leeches are also good patterns.

Streamers, heavily weighted and fished through the deep pools and riffles, are just what the doctor ordered if you're looking for large brown trout. Brown trout, especially the large variety over 18 inches, subsist mostly on other small fish. They hammer streamers when given the opportunity. If fishing specifically for large browns, bring a stout 6- or 7-weight rod to the Spokane. The extra power allows an angler to cast large, heavy flies and fight a big fish quickly when hooked.

While most brown trout are located in the upper river above Spokane, there are some strung out in the lower river, too. In that section, hit the feeder creek mouths and deep pools during fall. Any streamer swung in front of them is likely to draw attention and, hopefully, a grab.

As mentioned, the Spokane warms considerably during the summer months. That event sends trout scurrying for cover, attempting to escape lethal water temperatures. Fortunately, the Spokane offers respite, and the fish know where it is—so should you.

"The Spokane aquifer offers the only cool water to the river," Johnson says. "In places it can double the flow of the river so it's significant. It flows in at about 50 degrees, and trout move from all over the river to find that water. During low-water years, that flow is especially important. If you find the springs during summer, you'll find the fish stacked up, and you can have a good time. Most of the springs are located between Sullivan Bridge and the Marabou Park area. That's only about a mile and a half area, so the fish are really concentrated."

No matter what time of year anglers choose to fish the Spokane, they must make an important decision: wade or float the river?

There is plenty of wade access located all along the upper river via the Spokane trail system, but boat take-outs are few. Those that do exist are crude—trailered boats would be difficult to haul out of the river.

For that reason, most anglers who float the river do so in pontoon boats, which can be easily hauled up a bank and deposited in the back of a pickup truck or strapped to the top of a car.

For the wade-fisher, access is excellent, but water conditions can make stepping into the river a risky proposition, especially early in the season when so many caddis are on the water and rising fish make braving the high flow seem so appealing. However, the Spokane is not a river to be taken lightly—it can kill the unwary. If you do choose to wade, realize that the Spokane's bottom is rocky, and unwary waders can trip over a rock and plunge head-first into the water. Make sure you wear a wading belt, cinched tight, and don't be so proud that you won't use a wading staff. Work the banks and don't worry about the deeper water in the middle of the river—most of the fish are located on the banks eating caddis and wading deep only facilitates an unwelcome skid along the bottom rocks.

While the Spokane may never achieve the notoriety of its Idaho and Montana neighbors, it is a good trout stream that offers a unique brand of rainbow. Its brown trout run to good size, and it even offers a stray brook trout or two. Access to the river is excellent and that Twentieth Century flyfishing nemesis—crowds—is usually not an issue here. Take a summer afternoon and evening this year, tie an X-caddis or a woolly bugger to your 5X tippet, and give the Spokane a good chance to prove itself. Given the opportunity, the Spokane should represent itself nicely.

# Stream Facts: Spokane River

### Seasons and Special Regulations
- From Monroe Street Dam to upriver dam: open year-round, statewide rules apply.
- From upriver dam to Idaho state line: Open June 1 through October 31, 1-fish limit with 12-inch minimum in effect. Selective gear rules apply to this section, except motors are allowed.

### Species
- Rainbow and brown trout. Rainbows dominate the population, but big browns can be taken from the deep holes.

### Stream Characteristics
- The upper river offers the best action for flyfishers.
- Caddis are the main forage base for the river's trout, so evening action through the summer season can be excellent.
- Fall Baetis hatches offer good action, too. Standard nymphs, such as beadhead hare's ears, Princes, and pheasant tails, draw strikes when the fish aren't up top.
- Streamers draw takes from large brown trout.

### Access
- Wade-fishers can reach the upper river via the Spokane River Trail.
- During high water, wading can be difficult.
- Pontoon boats and small rafts are the best option during high water, but public put-ins and take-outs are rare, so be ready to pack your floating craft up a steep bank to your rig.

## SPOKANE RIVER MAJOR HATCHES

| Insect | J | F | M | A | M | J | J | A | S | O | N | D | Flies |
|---|---|---|---|---|---|---|---|---|---|---|---|---|---|
| Caddis | | | | | | | ▌ | ▌ | | | | | Stranahan's Caddis Variant #16–18; Elk Hair Caddis #14–18; X-Caddis #14–18; Free-living Caddis #14–18; Egg-laying Female Caddis #14–18; Prince Nymph #14–18 |
| Pale Morning Dun | | | | | | ▌ | | ▌ | | | | | PMD Cripple #16–18; Sparkle Dun #16–18; Thorax PMD #16–18; Parachute Adams #16–18; Hare's Ear #14–18; Pheasant Tail #14–18; Halfback Emerger #16–18 |
| Baetis | | | | | | | | | ▌ | ▌ | | | Baetis Parachute #16–18; Olive Sparkle Dun #16–18; Parachute Adams #16–20; Hare's Ear #16–20; Pheasant Tail #16–20 |
| Streamer | ▌ | | | | | | | | | | | | Woolly Bugger #4–8; Zonker #4–8; Woolhead Sculpin #4–8; Muddler Minnow #4–8 |

# GRANDE RONDE RIVER

In a forgotten corner of Washington state, far from the bustle of big city life, twists one of the West's best steelhead streams, a place where the chance to take a large fish on a surface fly can't be beat.

Beginning in northeast Oregon before slicing across the Washington border near Anatone, the Grande Ronde River and its summer-run steelhead are notorious for their aggressive surface feeding.

In the progression of steelhead flyfishers, tempting a 5 to 10-pound fish from the depths to inhale a surface fly rates as one of angling's most orgasmic (yeah, that's what I said) events. In the realm of North American angling, taking a steelhead on a dry fly rates right up there with catching a permit on the Florida flats or sticking a big Atlantic salmon from a Gaspé Peninsula stream. It's that good.

Maybe that's why a faithful following (and I mean a lot of them) travels long distances to reach the Ronde each fall. The river, tucked away in the relatively desolate southeast corner of Washington state, is really close to nothing: Walla Walla is an hour's drive west; Spokane is three hours north; and Lewiston, Idaho, is an hour drive from the Ronde's prime fillet water. Western Washington's and Oregon's metropolitan areas are a 7-hour drive drive. And it should also be mentioned that when the Ronde's steelhead fishing peaks in September, October, and November, the area's roads and driving conditions in general, especially along the Columbia River Gorge, deteriorate. Even with bad conditions, those who are in the know rarely consider the drive too long or the road conditions too bad to postpone a trip to this river. Hunting for steelhead can drive a typically sane person to do extreme things.

That was my situation one early November day when weather forecasts predicted that the roads would be "ice riddled." Travelers could expect blowing and drifting snow across the eastern half of the state. I weighed my single status, decided my Labradors could live out their lives with my parents if required, and fired up the Ford. Ten hours later, white knuckles curled around the steering wheel, I negotiated down a terrific grade, covered with black ice and snow, above the Grande Ronde River.

Once waist-deep in the river, my driving concerns faded, and I only wondered how much of the cold—the kind that slowly creeps into your bones—I could take. By the fourth drift my hands were tightening up and I could already feel a cool spot inside my waders—surely a hole.

I may have exited the river shortly after that revelation, but my line stopped short on the downstream swing and I felt the terrific rhythmic pulse of a strong fish.

That's when a strange, yet familiar sensation crept through my soul—each time I hook a steelhead, there is a split second of elation, followed by several moments of severe anxiety.

Hooking a steelhead on a fly reminds me of early romance, those times when exploring new territory can be suspenseful but unquestionably rewarding. With steelhead it's no different. The hook-up is thrilling, but your date with Señor

# Grande Ronde River

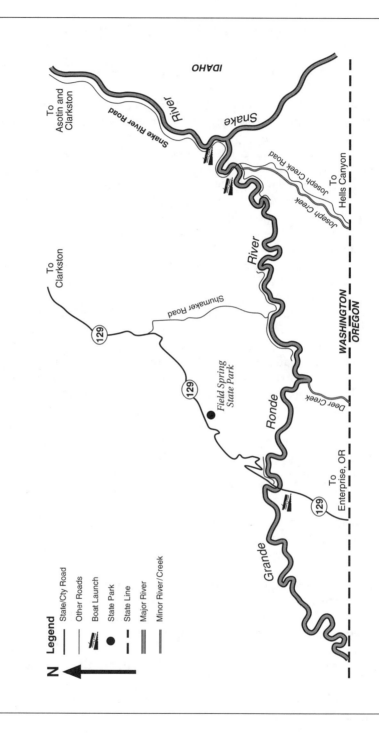

*Southeast Washington's scenic Grande Ronde River. (Photo by John Huber)*

Metalhead is in severe question right from the start: will that big fish throw the hook, part the leader, or leap skyward and bid adieu with a flip of its tail?

Fortunately for me, that Grande Ronde steelhead held to the depths and failed to part my leader on a rock. Several minutes after the hook-up, I was able to slip him into the shallows, briefly admire the 6-pound buck, twist a comet out of his mouth, then watch him fade away into aqua orbit.

As mentioned, the Grande Ronde begins in Oregon at the base of the Elkhorn Mountains. From there, it rushes northeast toward Washington, gaining in size from its tributary streams, such as the Minam, Wenaha, and Wallowa.

In Oregon, the river is heavily forested in many areas, but its nature changes when it drops into the 4,000-foot deep canyons and arid desert country that is synonymous with the lower river and southeast Washington.

In Washington, the Ronde flows unimpeded for 25 miles before emptying its water into the Snake River at Heller Bar. In the stretch that runs from the Oregon border to the Snake, the Ronde slices its way through desert canyons, its twists and turns creating some of the tastiest glides and runs a steelhead flyfisher could ever feast on. In fact, the desert itself, while drastically different from coastal forests where salmon and steelhead are typically pursued, is something to behold.

The desert, which is often called "wasteland" by some, has always fascinated me. I would visit the desert if I was the only creature within a hundred miles just to see its wildflowers and rock formations and to smell the sagebrush. But it is the desert creatures, such as rattlesnakes, scorpions, black widows, coyotes, and mule deer, that offer the most appeal. The option to fish steelhead in a small ribbon of life-sustaining water is just icing on the cake. Sitting next to the river at dusk, a long way from the chaos of humanity, listening to water gurgle and splash, watching the stars rise while being serenaded by coyotes puts an exclamation point on a good day.

To reach the Grande Ronde, steelhead must negotiate a variety of obstacles. The fact that any fish find the river of their birth is amazing. Most Grande Ronde steelhead enter the Columbia River near Astoria, Oregon, in June and July. From there, it's a 250-mile upstream journey past eager anglers and four massive dams before they even reach the mouth of the Snake River. From there, sensing a certain taste in the water, they travel another 130 miles and jump four more dams to reach the Ronde. Talk about the pits! And you thought a little traffic on weekday commutes was bad.

A few fish start trickling into the Ronde by late August, and the bulk of the run follows in September and October. It's at that time, in late September and throughout October, even extending through November during mild years, that the river can be seen in its prime.

Grande Ronde steelhead are not huge by coastal stream standards—most fish measure between 24 and 30 inches long, with an occasional brute pushing 12 pounds.

According to Art Viola, a Grande Ronde biologist for Washington Department of Fish and Wildlife, two-thirds of the run is comprised of one-salt steelhead that weigh between 4 and 5 pounds. One-third of the run is made up of two-salt fish that weigh between 6 and 9 pounds. Small numbers of three-salt fish, which may reach 12 or even 14 pounds, show up each season, too. Those sizes are not large by steelhead standards. However, don't be discouraged by those dimmensions; Grande Ronde steelhead fight valiantly, and each one landed is a treasure. If you consider the difficulties the fish encounter trying to reach the river, you'll realize what a treat you've found each time you land a fish, no matter how long it measures. It's truly amazing that a steelhead can negotiate all of those dams to find its birthplace. Talk about a sex drive.

During good years, biologists count about 4,000 Washington-origin steelhead returning to the river. Another 4,000 swim through Washington to reach their natal grounds in Oregon. Other fish, bound for Idaho's Salmon River, often enter the Ronde by mistake, much to the delight of Washington's fly rodders.

The Grande Ronde's steelhead are a bit of an anomaly. While other inland populations suffer in decline, such as Idaho's Snake and Salmon River fish, the Ronde prospers. Typically, the Ronde does not have poor returns: if the river has a poor season, it's a matter of less than ideal water conditions rather than a bad return of fish.

*Mike Witthar hefts a Grande Ronde steelhead caught on a spey rod.*
*(Photo by John Huber)*

The Ronde is considered fishable when water clarity rates a foot or more. When the water is murky, go with bright flies. Chartreuse marabous, polar shrimp, and freight trains draw strikes. In clear conditions, work black and purple marabou flies. Skunks and fall favorites also work well.

Concerning steelhead flies for the Grande Ronde, the standard rule applies: it's more a matter of presenting a fly in a tantalizing way than picking a particular fly that sends steelhead into some sort of feeding frenzy. Have confidence in your fly, fish it diligently, and you will catch fish.

To fish the Ronde effectively, use a sinktip line off a 6-, 7- or 8-weight rod. Leaders should be short, in the 3- and 4-foot range. Eight- or 10-pound Maxima is a good leader choice. Try to keep your fly near the bottom and let it swing across the current. Takes often occur as the fly finishes its swing and stops directly below an angler. Don't get anxious and lift your fly before you fish the entire drift.

Of course, subsurface flies aren't the only option. In fact, during prime conditions in September, October, and even early November, when the water is often low and clear and before it cools, topwater flies, such as bombers, wakers, and a fly called the after-dinner mint (tied with a purple and green sparkle braided body, a spun deer hair head and a heavy elk or moose hair wing) should draw fish to the top. However, fishing steelhead with a surface fly demands research and patience—and, of course, a floating line.

The anglers who are most effective with a surface fly know exactly where steelhead hold day in and day out. They cover the water with knowledge that fish are resting just a few feet under the fly and may, at any time, rise to the surface for a meal. That knowledge facilitates confidence when blind-casting to steelhead.

Those of the dry-fly persuasion should hit the river early in the morning and watch for steelhead rolling on the surface. If you see a fish or two, set up camp for the day and work your surface fly religiously. When you see a big sea-run rainbow rise from the depths, part the surface with its snout, and take off with your offering like it had just snatched a woman's purse, you'll realize that all your effort was worth it. You might even check in with the local real estate office and ask, "Isn't this place primed for a little fly shop?"

Where steelhead typically hold in the Ronde is where steelhead hold no matter where they are found. Anglers should pay close attention to the tailouts of pools, middepth runs and slicks, and soft water behind obstructions, such as boulders. Basically, look for soft water and you may find a steelhead resting in it. Because the Grande Ronde's bottom is made up of ledges and shelves, anglers must probe those areas thoroughly, even if fast water skates over the top of those lies. Steelhead often duck into a crevice or hold behind a ledge, avoiding the main current.

While steelhead fishing can be excellent throughout the Grande Ronde, there are several places that draw most anglers for a couple of good reasons: concentrations of fish and limited river access.

One such place is the catch-and-release, special regulation water that extends from the mouth of the river upstream 2.5 miles. In that section, anglers find some absolutely classic steelhead water that beckons each day of fall. Due to that draw, the C&R section can be clogged with anglers any day of the season. If you know that fish are sitting in a prime run, get there very early in the morning if you want to make the first pass through.

Another area that draws anglers is the Cottonwood acclimation ponds near Bogan's Oasis, where Cottonwood Creek flows into the river. It's there that many of the hatchery steelhead return each year, often congregating *en masse* at the ponds. Plus, Oregon-bound fish must pass through, and they add to the mix. When the water is clear, there may not be a better spot to fish the river, if you can put up with the crowds.

Because access is so severely limited on the Ronde, some anglers float the river and find glorious runs to fish for themselves—Washington's stream access law allows anglers to fish anywhere as long as they remain below the high water mark. If you plan to float the river, there are several considerations you must first explore.

First, there is a section of river that funnels between two rocks, often called "chicken-out rapids," that can destroy a good trip if not a life. A drift boat with oars extended will not fit through the gap. For that reason, most drifters line their boat through the gorge. Second, floating the Ronde requires time. Most of the floats are two days, meaning you must carry enough equipment to camp overnight.

One excellent float takes an angler from the Oregon border downstream to the Hwy 3 bridge or Cottonwood. Another option is to put in at Bogan's Oasis—a Grande Ronde institution that, by the way, runs shuttles, prepares lunches and offers camping—and float to the mouth of the river, which is a two-day drift through some wonderful sections of water.

The Grande Ronde sees its greatest angling pressure during September, October, and November, but it also draws the eye of steelheaders again in February, March, and early April. At that time, after a lengthy winter, river conditions improve and fish go back on the move.

"In mid-February through the end of the season on April 15, guys do best near Cottonwood," Viola says. "It really gets good if the water conditions hold. Typically, you are alright if you fish from mid-February through mid-March. The longer you wait to fish the river the bigger risk you take with water conditions."

While it is definitely not as convenient to visit as many other steelhead streams in Washington, the Grande Ronde offers an irreplaceable mix of arid desert scenery and determined fish. If you spend enough time on the river, eventually you'll catch steelhead on dry flies.

There are many paths to reach the Grande Ronde from western Washington, but each of them eventually leads to Clarkston, Washington. From there, take State Route 129 south past Anatone. The highway crosses the river about six miles north of the Oregon border. From there, Grande Ronde Road parallels the north side of the river. To reach the lower Ronde, follow the Snake River Road south from Clarkston.

Because of the distances you must travel to get to the river, it always pays to call ahead. Nothing worse, as we all know, than arriving someplace with high expectations just to find the river blown out. So call Bogan's Oasis (509-256-3372) to check on conditions. Bogan's offers guided steelhead trips, makes lunches for anglers, and sells all the necessities. They also have a few cabins for rent and room for several campers to stay in their yard.

# Stream Facts: Grande Ronde River

## Seasons and Special Regulations
- From mouth to county road bridge (about 2.5 miles upstream): Open year round; catch-and-release only on steelhead. Selective gear rules September 1 through May 31.
- From county road bridge to Oregon state line and all tributaries: Open for trout June 1 through August 31. Steelhead fishing opens September 1 and extends through April 15. Barbless hooks required. All tributaries closed to fishing for steelhead.

## Species
- Steelhead.

## Stream Characteristics
- One of Washington's most revered steelhead waters, the Grande Ronde offers a prime summer and fall run with fish averaging 6 to 12 pounds.
- Noted for their appetite for surface flies, steelhead are equally inclined to munch standard subsurface steelhead flies.

## Access
- Access is limited on the Ronde.
- Those who choose to float the river in a boat or raft usually spend two days on the water.
- Good wade fishing can be found on the lower river and near Cottonwood hatchery.
- Much of the river runs through private land. Knocking on a door could pan out, but southeast Washington is farming and ranching country, you know.

# EASTERN WASHINGTON HUB CITIES*
# Yakima
### Elevation–1,068 • Population–60,000

## ACCOMMODATIONS

**Cavanaugh's at Yakima Center,** 607 East Yakima Avenue / 509-248-5900 / 155 units, pool, sauna, restaurant

**Econo-Lodge,** 1022 North 1st Street / 509-453-5615 / 40 units, pool, sauna, spa, cable TV

**Quality Inn,** 12 Valley Mall Boulevard / 509-248-6924 / 85 units, pool spa, sauna, cable TV

## CAMPGROUNDS AND RV PARKS

**Trailer Inns RV Park,** 1610 North First Street / 509-452-9561 / Bus service to downtown, full hook-ups, pool, laundry, spa, sauna

**Yakima Sportsman State Park,** 904 Keys Road / 509-575-2774 / RV hook-ups, tent sites

## RESTAURANTS

**Black Angus,** 501 North First Street / 509-248-4540 / Steaks, salad, seafood, cocktails

**Grant's Pub,** 32 North Front Street / 509-575-1900 / Steaks, burgers, beer, wine

**International House of Pancakes,** 15 East Yakima Avenue / 509-453-7263 / Breakfast, lunch, dinner

**Santiago's Gourmet Mexican Restaurant,** 111 East Yakima Avenue / 509-453-1644

## FLY SHOPS AND SPORTING GOODS

**Chinook Sporting Goods,** 901 South 1st Street / 509-452-8205 / Some flyfishing equipment

**Gary's Fly Shoppe and Yakima River Outfitters,** 1210 West Lincoln / 509-457-3474

**K-mart,** 2304 East Nob Hill Boulevard / 509-248-1990

**Wal-mart,** 1600 West Chestnut Avenue / 509-248-3448

**Big 5 Sporting Goods,** 2801 West Nob Hill Boulevard / 509-453-6040

**Bi-Mart,** 309 South 5th Avenue / 509-454-4030

**Bi-Mart,** 1207 North 40th Avenue / 509-457-1650

## AUTO REPAIR

**Alamo Service and Muffler Center,** 132 South 2nd Street / 509-453-1218

**C and J Car Clinic,** 1602 South 36th Avenue / 509-248-7412

**Firestone Tire & Service Centers,** 202 South 1st Street / 509-457-6191

**Rick's Garage,** 210 West Mead Avenue / 509-452-4104

\* See also Columbia Basin—Moses Lake; and Northern Lakes—Republic and Colville

## AUTO RENTAL

**Budget Car & Truck Rental,** 17 West Washington Avenue / 509-248-6767
**Enterprise Rent–A-Car,** 312 West Nob Hill Boulevard / 509-248-2170
**Hertz Rent-A-Car,** Yakima Municipal Airport / 509-452-9965
**Sears Car & Truck Rental,** 17 West Washington Avenue / 509-453-5212
**U-Save Auto Rental,** 1117 West Lincoln Avenue / 509-452-5555

## AIRPORT

**Yakima Air Terminal,** 2400 West Washington Avenue / 509-575-6149

## MEDICAL

**Memorial Hospital Emergency Department,** 2811 Tieton Drive / 509-575-8100
**Providence Yakima Medical Center,** 110 South 9th Avenue / 509-575-5066

## FOR MORE INFORMATION

Yakima Chamber of Commerce
P.O. Box 1490
Yakima, WA 98907
509-248-2021

Yakima Valley Visitors and Convention Bureau
10 North 8th Street
Yakima, WA 98901
509-575-1300

# Ellensburg
### Elevation–1,500 • Population–12,570

Located next to the Yakima River, Ellensburg offers excellent accomodations for those anglers visiting the Yakima, Cle Elum and Teanaway rivers. A western town with western flavor, accompanied by Central Washington University, Ellensuburg offers a nice mix of old and new.

## ACCOMMODATIONS
**Best Western Ellensburg Inn,** 1713 Canyon Road / 509-925-9801
**Super 8,** 1500 Canyon Road / 800-800-8000 or 509-962-6888
**Thunderbird Motel & Restaurant,** 403 West 8th Avenue / 800-843-3492

## CAMPGROUNDS AND RV PARKS
**R&R Resort,** Exit 109 east of Ellensburg / 509-933-1500 / 80 RV sites, full hook-ups, 50 rooms, laundry
**Ellensburg KOA,** Route 1 / 509-925-9319 / Camp on Yakima River, restrooms, hot showers, store, laundry, full RV hook-ups, tent sites

## RESTAURANTS
**Red Robin,** 101 Umptanum / 509-925-9898 / Seafood, steaks, pasta
**Valley Cafe,** 105 West 3rd Avenue / 509-925-3050 / Breakfast, lunch, dinner
**The Copper Kettle,** 210 West 8th Avenue / 509-925-5644
**Rodeo City Bar BQ,** 204 North Main / 509-962-3770
**Taco Time,** 724 East 8th Avenue / 509-925-4000

## FLY SHOPS AND SPORTING GOODS
**Cooper's Fly Shop,** 310 North Main / 509-962-5259
**Kittitas County Trading Co.,** 103 North Main / 509-925-1109
**Mountain High Sports,** 105 East 4th Avenue / 509-925-4626
**Worley-Bugger Fly Co.,** 811 4th Parallel / 888-950-FISH / worleybuggerflyco.com
**Bi-Mart,** 608 East Mountain View Drive / 509-925-6971

## AUTO REPAIR
**Autoworks,** 205 East 2nd Avenue / 509-962-2868
**D & M Motors & Towing,** 205 North Main Street / 509-925-4151
**Independent Auto Repair,** 208 West Tacoma Avenue / 509-925-5539
**University Auto,** 7th & Pearl / 509-925-1455

## AUTO RENTAL
**Budget Rent-A-Car,** 7th & Pearl / 800-735-2886 or 509-925-1455

## AIR SERVICE
**Midstate Aviation at Bower's Field,** 1101 Bowers Road / 509-962-7850 / 5,500-foot runway, commercial and private aircraft

## MEDICAL
**Kittitas Valley Community Hospital,** 603 South Chestnut / 509-962-9841

## FOR MORE INFORMATION
Ellensburg Chamber of Commerce
436 North Sprague
Ellensburg, WA 98926
509-962-6148

# Wenatchee
## Elevation–600 • Population–65,000

### ACCOMMODATIONS
**Chieftain Motel & Restaurant,** 1005 North Wenatchee Avenue / 509-663-8141
**Holiday Lodge,** 610 North Wenatchee Avenue / 509-663-8167
**Orchard Inn,** 1401 North Miller Street / 509-662-3443
**Red Lion Inn,** 1225 North Wenatchee Avenue / 509-663-0711
**The Uptowner,** 101 North Mission Street / 509-663-8516
**Warm Springs Inn Bed & Breakfast,** 1611 Love Lane / 509-662-8365

### CAMPGROUNDS AND RV PARKS
**Ohme Gardens County Park,** 3327 Ohme Road / 509-662-5785
**Steamboat Rock State Park,** 12 miles south of Grand Coulee / 509-633-1304
**Wenatchee River County Park,** 3 miles west of Wenatchee on Hwy 2 & 97 / 509-662-2525

### RESTAURANTS
**Anchor Bay Steak & Seafood Co.,** 123 Easy / 509-663-1755
**Azteca Artesania Mexicanas,** 19 North Wenatchee Avenue / 509-662-1640
**The Carriage House Pub & Cafe,** 2 Horan Road / 509-663-0018
**Greathouse Springs Cafe,** 1505 North Miller Street / 509-664-5162
**Hart's British Fish & Chips,** 609 North Wenatchee Avenue / 509-662-7004
**McGlinn's Public House,** 111 Orondo Avenue / 509-663-9073
**Prospector Pies Restaurant & Bar,** 731 North Wenatchee Avenue / 509-662-1118
**Shari's,** 1516 North Wenatchee Avenue / 509-662-7811
**Smitty's Pancake & Steak House,** 1621 North Wenatchee Avenue / 509-662-2784
**Visconti's Italian Restaurant,** 1737 North Wenatchee Avenue / 509-662-5013

### VETERINARIANS
**Appleland Pet Clinic,** 600 North Mission Street / 509-663-8508
**Cascade Veterinary Clinic,** 2127 North Wenatchee Avenue / 509-663-0793
**Countryside Veterinary Clinic,** 1604 North Wenatchee Avenue / 509-662-3478

### FLY SHOPS AND SPORTING GOODS
**Blue Dun Fly Shop,** 25 North Wenatchee Avenue / 509-664-2416
**Big 5 Sporting Goods,** 159 Easy Street / 509-663-1332 / Some flyfishing equipment
**Wal-Mart,** 2000 North Wenatchee Avenue / 509-664-2448
**Bi-Mart,** 780 East Grant Road / 508-884-1141

### AUTO REPAIR
**Dick's Towing & Repair,** 110 Thurston Street / 509-663-1623
**Hampton's Auto Repair,** 22 South Buchanan Avenue # 6041 / 509-665-8513
**Mechanic On Wheels,** 1312 9th Street / 509-663-4053
**Vic's Auto Repair,** 1322 South Columbia Street / 509-662-8327

## AUTO RENTAL

**Budget Car & Truck Rental,** Downtown,  / 509-663-0293

**U-Save Auto Rental,** 908 South Wenatchee Avenue / 509-663-0587

## MEDICAL

**Central Washington Hospital,** 526 North Chelan Avenue / 509-665-6087

**Wenatchee Valley Clinic,** 820 North Chelan Avenue / 509-663-8711

## FOR MORE INFORMATION

Wenatchee Chamber of Commerce
2 South Chelan Avenue
Wenatchee, WA 98801
509-662-2116

# Twisp
### Elevation–1,500 • Population–1,000

## ACCOMMODATIONS
Blue Spruce Motel, 1405 Hwy 20 / 509-997-8852
Idle-a-While Motel, 505 North Hwy 20 / 509-997-3222
Sportsman Motel, 1010 Hwy 20 East / 509-997-2911

## CAMPGROUNDS AND RV PARKS
Riverbend RV Park, 19961 State Route 20 / 509-997-3500
Sportsman Motel, 1010 Hwy 20 East / 509-997-2911

## RESTAURANTS
Mick & Miki's Red Cedar Bar, 110 Glover / 509-997-6425
The Roadhouse Diner / 509-997-4015
Rosey's Branding Iron Restaurant & Lounge, 123 Glover / 509-997-3576
Wagon Wheel Cafe / 509-997-4671

## VETERINARIANS
Valley Veterinary Clinic, Hwy 20 / 509-997-8452

## FLY SHOPS AND SPORTING GOODS
Mazama Fly Shop, 48 Lost River Road, Mazama / 509-996-3674
Valley Hardware / 509-997-3355

## AUTO REPAIR
Coyote Ridge Automotive Repair & Sales / 509-997-3454
Gardner Auto Repair, 204 East 2nd Ave / 509-997-2115
Les Schwab Tires, 219 South Hwy 20 / 509-997-2026

## MEDICAL
Methow Valley Family Practice, 51 East 2nd Avenue / 509-997-2011

## FOR MORE INFORMATION
Twisp Chamber of Commerce
201 Hwy 20 South
Twisp, WA 98856
509-997-2926

# Spokane
**Elevation–2,000 • Population–404,920**

## ACCOMMODATIONS
**Apple Tree Inn,** 9508 North Division / 509-838-4411 / Swimming pool, kitchens
**Hampton Inn,** 2010 Assembly / 509-747-8722 / Continental breakfast, free movies, continental breakfast, free airport shuttle
**Downtowner Motel,** three blocks from city center / 509-838-4411 / Cable TV
**Cavanaugh's,** North 700 Division / 509-326-5577 / Restaurant, cable TV
**Best Western,** 120 West Third Avenue / 509-747-2011 / Close to downtown and restaurants, continental breakfast, pool, cable TV

## CAMPGROUNDS AND RV PARKS
**Park Lane RV Park,** 4412 East Sprague / 509-535-1626 / Phone, full hook-ups, TV, laundry, BBQ, sauna, no tents
**KOA Campground,** 3025 North Barker / 509-924-4722 / Pool, full hook-ups, laundry, store, cabins, showers, cable TV
**Alpine Campground,** I-90 Exit 293 / 509-928-2700 / Showers, store, pool, 14 motel units, basketball, tent camping

## RESTAURANTS
**Chapter Eleven,** 7720 East Sprague / 509-928-1787 / Prime rib, salads
**Milford's,** 719 North Monroe Street / 509-326-7251 / Fresh seafood from the Northwest, full bar
**Perkin's,** North 5903 Division, breakfast, lunch, dinner, 24 hours /
**The Calgary Steak House,** East 3040 Sprague / 509-535-7502 / Prime beef, salad, seafood, pasta
**Cucina! Cucina! Italian Cafe,** 707 West Main Avenue / 509-838-3388 / Italian dishes, salad, bar

## FLY SHOPS AND SPORTING GOODS
**Fly Fishing Specialists,** 5727 East Sprague / 509-535-7681 / Full service shop
**Silver Bow Fly Shop,** 1003 East Trent Avenue / 509-483-1772 / Full service shop
**The Outdoor Sportsman,** 1602 North Division Street / 509-328-1556
**Propp's Rod & Fly Shop,** 135 South Sherman Street / 509-838-3474 / Full service shop
**The Sport Cove Fly Shop,** 5727 East Sprague / 509-535-7681
**Water Hole Sports Shop,** 1428 East Francis Avenue / 509-484-1041
Also, in Coeur D'Alene, Idaho:
**Joe Roope's Castaway Fly Fishing Shop,** 350 West Bosanko/ 208-765-3133
**Fins and Feathers Fly Shop,** 1816½ Sherman Avenue / 208-667-9304

## AUTO REPAIR
**Auto Specialty Center,** East 3118 Gordon / 509-487-7211
**Perfection Tire & Automotive,** 604 East 2nd / 509-747-1164

**Firestone Tire & Service Center,** E10717 Sprague / 509-924-7853
**Napa Auto Care Center,** N109 University Road / 509-926-1808
**Wally's Towing & Repair,** 3619 North Cement Road / 509-924-7635

## AUTO RENTAL

**Alamo Rent-A-Car,** 5516 West Sunset Hwy / 509-624-9501
**Avis Rent-A-Car,** Spokane International Airport / 509-747-8081
**Dollar Rent-A-Car,** Spokane International Airport / 509-727-2191
**Enterprise Rent-A-Car,** 101 North Argonne Road / 509-926-4321
**Hertz Rent-A-Car,** Spokane International Airport / 509-747-3101

## AIR SERVICE

**Spokane International Airport** / 509-455-6429 / Alaska, Air Canada, Delta, Horizon, Northwest, Southwest, United

## MEDICAL

**Deaconess Medical Center,** 800 West 5th Avenue / 509-458-5800
**Holy Family Hospital,** 5633 North Lidgerwood Street / 509-482-0111
**Sacred Medical Medical Center,** 101 West 8th Avenue / 509-455-3131
**Valley Hospital and Medical Center,** N1414 Houk / 509-922-9489

## FOR MORE INFORMATION

Spokane Area Chamber of Commerce
1020 West Riverside Avenue
Spokane, WA 99210
509-624-1393

Spokane Valley Chamber of Commerce
East 10303 Sprague
Spokane, WA 99201
509-924-4994

# Richland

### Elevation–340 • Population–35,990 (122,800 in Benton County)

## ACCOMMODATIONS

**Best Western Tower Inn,** 1515 George Washington Way / 509-946-4121 / Cable TV, pool, spa

**Desert Gold Motel,** 611 Columbia Drive Southeast / 509-627-1000 / Cable TV, laundry, swimming pool, continental breakfast

**Dunes Motel,** 1751 Fowler Street / 509-783-8181 / Cable TV

## CAMPGROUNDS AND RV PARKS

**Desert Gold RV Park,** 611 Columbia Drive Southeast / 509-627-1000 / Full hook-ups, laundry, restrooms with showers, weekly rate, hot tub, pool

## RESTAURANTS

**Baron's Beef and Brew,** 1034 Lee Boulevard / 509-946-5500 / Burgers, Philly steak sandwich, halibut, chicken, hot wings, salad, large selection of import beers

**McDougall's,** 1705 Columbia Drive / 509-735-6418 / Salads, sandwiches, burgers, pizza, soups, seafood

**Giacci's Italian,** 94 Lee Boulevard / 509-946-4855 / Pasta, pizza / Lunch 11AM– 8PM; Dinner 5PM– 9PM

## FLY SHOPS AND SPORTING GOODS

**Bill's Fishin' Hole,** 2131 Van Giesen Street / 509-942-2399

**R & R Tackle and Fly Shop,** 109 East Woodin Road (Sunnyside) / 509-837-2332

## AUTO REPAIR

**Motoring Services,** 327 Wellsian Way / 509-943-0441

**P&K Auto Service,** 1415 Gillespie / 509-943-1141

## AUTO RENTAL

**Budget Rent-A-Car,** 500 Wellsian Way / 509-946-5144

## AIR SERVICE

**Bogert International,** 1901 Terminal Drive / 509-943-4800

## MEDICAL

**Kadlec Medical Center,** 888 Swift Boulevard / 509-946-4611

## FOR MORE INFORMATION

Richland Chamber of Commerce
515 Lee Boulevard
Richland, WA 99352
509-946-1651

# Kennewick
### Elevation–340 • Population–48,010

## ACCOMMODATIONS
**Cavanaugh's,** 1101 North Columbia Center Boulevard / 509-783-0611 / Restaurant, lounge, pool, cable TV
**Super 8 Motel,** 626 N. Columbia Center Boulevard / 509-736-6888 / Indoor pool, hot tub, cable TV
**Columbia Motor Inn,** 1133 West Columbia Drive / 509-586-4739 / Cable TV, breakfast

## CAMPGROUNDS AND RV PARKS
**Columbia Mobile Village,** 4901 West Clearwater Avenue / 509-783-3314
**Maxey's Mobile Home Park,** 3708 West Clearwater Avenue / 509-783-6411

## RESTAURANTS
**Abby's Legendary Pizza,** 3014 West Kennewick Avenue / 509-735-0395
**Applebee's Grill and Bar,** 606 North Columbia Center Boulevard / 509-783-0300 / Salads, steaks, wraps, pasta, burgers
**Cedars,** 7 Clover / 509-582-2143 / Steaks, seafood, prime rib, pasta, cocktails
**Elly's Family Restaurant,** 3790 West Van Giesen / 509-967-2633 / Burgers, sandwiches, breakfast, lunch, dinner
**Stinky's Drive-In,** 2521 West Kennewick Avenue / 509-585-9339 / Burgers, salad

## FLY SHOPS AND SPORTING GOODS
**Clearwater Fly Shop,** 417 West 1st Avenue / 509-582-1001 / Fully stocked shop
**Hole in the Wall,** 7509 West Deschutes Avenue / 509-783-1111
**Phil's Sporting Goods, Inc.,** 3806 West Court Street, Pasco / 509-547-9084
**Sporthaus,** 326 North Columbia Center Boulevard / 509-735-7555
**Tri Sports,** 1413 North Young Street / 509-783-9203

## AUTO REPAIR
**Hi-Land Garage,** 215 North Union / 509-783-2512
**A-1 Automotive Repair,** 620 East 3rd Avenue / 509-582-6504
**Auto Works,** 10 West 4th Avenue / 509-586-7794

## AUTO RENTAL
**Enterprise Rent-A-Car,** 4304 West Clearwater Avenue / 509-735-2700

## AIR SERVICE
**Kennewick Airport** / 509-735-2875

## MEDICAL
**Kennewick General Hospital,** 900 South Auburn / 509-586-6111

**FOR MORE INFORMATION**

Kennewick Chamber of Commerce
P.O. Box 6986
3180 West Clearwater
Kennewick, WA 99336
509-736-0510

# Walla Walla

## Elevation–949 • Population–29,000

## ACCOMMODATIONS

**Best Western,** 7 East Oak / 509-525-4700 / Pool, cable TV, hot tub, continental breakfast

**Travelodge,** 421 East Main Street / 509-529-4940 / Free local calls, pool and spa, in room coffee, refrigerators

**Comfort Inn,** 520 North 2nd Avenue / 509-525-2522 / Pool and spa, cable TV, kitchenettes, continental breakfast

## CAMPGROUNDS AND RV PARKS

**RV Resort Four Seasons,** 1440 Dalles Military Road / 509-529-6072 / Full hook-ups, laundry

**RV Resort Four Seasons,** 1255 Country Club Road / 509-529-7026 / Full hook-ups, laundry

## RESTAURANTS

**La Casita,** 428 Ash Street / 509-525-2598 / Mexican dishes, cocktails, beer, wine

**Mr. Ed's,** 2555 Isaacs / 509-525-8440 / Breakfast, lunch, dinner / 5am-8pm / Take out available

**Pastime Cafe,** 215 West Main / 509-525-0873 / Baked lasagne, spaghetti, ravioli with meatball, cocktails / Breakfast, lunch, dinner, 5;30am-12am, closed Sundays

## FLY SHOPS AND SPORTING GOODS

**Drumheller Sports Center,** 7 West Alder / 509-525-8772 / General hunting and fishing equipment, some fly fishing material, rods, lines and reels

**Bi-Mart,** 1649 Plaza Way / 509-529-8840

## AUTO REPAIR

**Cantrell's Automotive,** 910-1 South 9th Avenue #2 / 509-525-9262

**Dean's Automotive,** 919 North 9th Avenue / 509-525-1646

**Lauderdale Auto Repair,** 704 West Pine Street / 509-525-7211

## AUTO RENTAL

**Budget Rent-A-Car,** Walla Walla Regional Airport / 509-525-8811

**Dollar Rent-A-Car,** 214 East Rose Street / 509-527-0812

**Enterprise Rent-A-Car,** 491 North Wilbur Avenue / 509-529-1988

**Hertz Rent-A-Car,** Walla Walla Regional Airport / 509-522-3321

## AIR SERVICE

**Walla Walla Regional Airport,** 310 A Street / 509-529-0843

## MEDICAL

**Walla Walla General Hospital,** 1025 South 2nd Avenue / 509-525-0480

## FOR MORE INFORMATION

Walla Walla Area Chamber of Commerce
29 East Sumach Street
Walla Walla, WA 99362
509-525-0850

# Clarkston

**Elevation–7,000 • Population–736**

## ACCOMMODATIONS

Best Western Rivertree Inn, 1257 Bridge Street / 509-758-9551
Golden Key Motel, 1376 Bridge Street / 509-758-5566
Southshore Landing Restaurant & Lounge, 700 Port Drive / 509-758-9500
Sunset Motel, 1200 Bridge Street / 509-758-2517

## CAMPGROUNDS AND RV PARKS

Hillview RV Park, 1224 Bridge Street / 509-758-6299

## RESTAURANTS

Bread Basket, 839 6th Street / 509-758-8533
Paolino's, 900 6th Street / 509-751-9454
Phoenix Mountain Restaurant, 701 6th Street / 509-758-9618
Southshore Landing Restaurant & Lounge, 700 Port Drive / 509-758-9500

## VETERINARIANS

Clarkston Veterinary Clinic, 1409 Peaslee Avenue / 509-758-9669
Riverview Animal Clinic, 1552 5th Street / 509-758-5022

## FLY SHOPS AND SPORTING GOODS

Schurman's True Value Hardware, 801 6th Street / 509-758-6411
Wal-Mart, 2981 Thain Grade (Lewiston, ID) / 208-746-8364

## AUTO REPAIR

15th Street Auto Service, 505 15th Street / 509-758-7878
Bud's Auto Repair, 2589 19th Street / 509-758-0162
Lewis Auto Repair, Inc., 1328 Fair Street / 509-758-8674
Pro-tech Automotive, 1484 16th Avenue / 509-751-9650

## HOSPITAL

Tri-State Memorial Hospital, 1221 Highland Avenue / 509-758-5511

## FOR MORE INFORMATION

Clarkston Chamber of Commerce
502 Bridge Street
Clarkston, WA 99403
509-758-7712

# Washington Game Fish

## SEA-RUN CUTTHROAT TROUT

In saltwater and in streams that drain coastal Washington, sea-run cutthroat are readily available. They are beautiful, aggressive fish that are noted for their strength, especially when pursued with light fly rods in the 4- to 6-weight range.

Sea-run cutthroat can be found in most coastal streams and may be present any month. However, the best sea-run action takes place during fall when the first big rains of the season raise river flows and send fish pushing upstream.

Sea-runs are fond of aquatic insects and can be taken on dry flies in saltwater and in freshwater. Nymphs also work well for sea-runs, as do streamers.

### Sea-run Cutthroat Identification

**Sea-run Cutthroat Trout, *Onchorhyncus clarki lewisi* (Anadromous)**

In saltwater, sea-run cutthroat are typically bright silver on the sides, with dark olive backs that are heavily spotted. However, sea-runs may also offer an olive/yellow coloration when in saltwater. The key is to look for bright orange slashes under the lower jaw. Typically, sea-runs average 12 inches, but 20-inch specimens, weighing close to 4 or 5 pounds are possible.

In coastal streams, sea-runs often have more color, their stomachs and sides often appearing yellow or olive. They, too, have many spots on their backs. In coastal streams, sea-runs average 8 to 12 inches. Again, larger specimens are available.

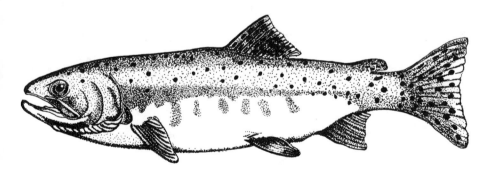

*Sea-run Cutthroat Trout (Oncorhynchus clarki lewisi, anadromous)*

# STEELHEAD TROUT

Steelhead can be found in many of Washington's streams year-round and are the true trophy game fish in the evergreen state. Most steelhead average 5 to 12 pounds, but metalheads to 30 pounds and up have been caught.

Most of Washington's streams offer winter-run steelhead, which ascend the streams as early as November and remain inland as late as April or May. Many other streams offer summer-run steelhead, which are typically smaller in size and push their snouts into freshwater beginning in April, May, or June. They remain in the system as late as December or January. Some of the best summer-run action occurs during fall when water conditions facilitate both wet-fly and dry-fly techniques.

## Steelhead Identification

### Steelhead Trout, *Oncorhynchus mykiss* (Anadromous)

In the saltwater, where few flyfishers attempt to catch steelhead, fish are bright silver with small black dots extending across an olive back. They may retain this appearance in the lower portions of rivers, but as they ascend freshwater, they take on colors more characteristic of their landlocked rainbow trout brothers.

Adults typically range from 20 to 40 inches and sport a red tint on their gillplates. Their gums are white, and they display a wide red stripe that often runs the length of their body, dissipating just before the tail.

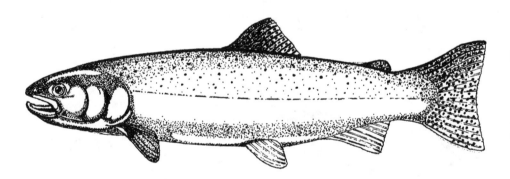

*Steelhead Trout (Oncorhynchus mykiss, anadromous)*

# Chinook Salmon

These large, anadromous fish are true tackle-busters. Found in the coastal streams of western Washington, plus tributaries of the Columbia River, the chinook, also called the king salmon, is a true test for a flyfisher.

Chinook ascend Washington's streams two times a year: during spring and fall. Spring-run chinook can be taken on a fly, but it is their later-arriving cousins that offer the best chance for success.

Ranging in size from 12 to 50 pounds, the typical king runs 15 to 20 pounds. They hold in the deep pools of coastal streams. On occasion, they can be encountered in the middepth runs and riffles.

Kings are not too particular about fly patterns, and flyfishers catch them on the standards, such as large, weighted woolly buggers, Teeny nymphs, and Mickey Finns.

Although king salmon can be found in good numbers on some coastal streams, their populations are dwindling, and Washington's king salmon fisheries may eventually be closed altogether. This fish, it seems, is headed for the Endangered Species List.

## Chinook Identification

### Chinook Salmon, *Oncorhynchus tshawytscha*

The number one giveaway is size. If you catch a salmon over 30 pounds, it's a king. If it's smaller, look for telltale signs, such as a black interior of the mouth; scattered large, black spots across a green back; a forked, fully-spotted tail and an anal fin that is long and shallow with 15 to 19 rays.

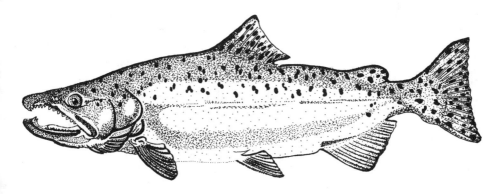

*Chinook Salmon (Oncorhynchus tshawytscha)*

# COHO SALMON

Smaller than their chinook cousins, the coho salmon is often called the best-fighting fish in the sea due to its propensity to leap out of the water and smash the hell out of a flyfisher's tackle.

Typically ranging between 6 and 12 pounds, a large coho may stretch the scale to 20 pounds or more. They are aggressive fish that respond well to chartreuse-colored flies. Some of Washington's best flyfishing for coho takes place in river estuaries where freshwater meets salt. However, opportunities exist in upstream portions of rivers, too.

Coho ascend Washington's coastal streams during late summer and fall. When in the river they turn crimson-hued, with dark heads and exaggerated kypes.

## Coho Identification

### Coho (Silver) Salmon, *Oncorhynchus kisutch*

Coho are bright silver when caught in the saltwater. They turn crimson when ascending freshwater streams. Their mouths are black with white gums. They sport small, scattered spots across their backs (much smaller than found on king salmon), and they have a forked tail with no spots on its lower half. Their anal fin is long and shallow with 12 to 17 rays.

# CHUM SALMON

One of the most aggressive fish in Washington's salt and freshwater, chum salmon can really bend a flyfisher's rod.

The best flyfishing opportunities for chum salmon are found in Puget Sound and Olympic Peninsula streams. Chums, also called the calico salmon due to their tiger-like stripes that are noted on the fish when it enters freshwater, are overly fond of chartreuse streamers and will attack them in shallow water.

Chums are late fall visitors to Washington's streams. Typically, their presence is most noted in November and early December. On most streams, the peak of the run arrives around Thanksgiving, which gives anglers a great holiday fishing option.

Chums average about 10 to 15 pounds with an occasional monster ranging into the 20-pound plus category.

## Chum Salmon Identification

### Chum Salmon, *Oncorhynchus keta*

In saltwater, chum salmon closely resemble coho salmon. However, in freshwater the chum is unmistakable—its has a heavy olive coloration, accented by purple bars that stretch from its back to belly. Also called the dog salmon, chums have large, pronounced teeth on their upper and lower jaws when encountered in freshwater.

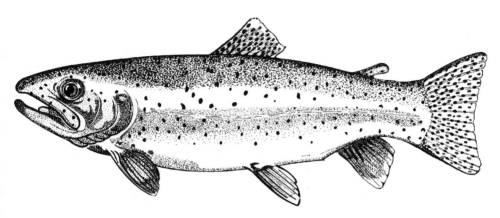

*Rainbow Trout (Oncorhynchus mykiss, nonmigratory)*

## RAINBOW TROUT

Far and away, the most exciting fighter of the trout family, the rainbow, always pulls something from its bag of tricks, from cartwheeling leaps to reel-sizzling runs to repeated dashes away from the net.

It gets its name from the crimson to pinkish-red band along the midline of its flanks. This reddish band may be absent in lake dwellers, which are generally more silver in total appearance. It is marked across its head, back, and upper flanks with many small, irregular black spots that are most heavily concentrated on its squarish tail.

The rainbow trout, *Oncorhyncus mykiss*, was reclassified as part of the Western salmon genus, *Oncorhyncus*, in 1990. Its former classification was with the Atlantic salmon genus, *Salmo*. Its former species name, *gairdneri irideus*, was replaced with *mykiss* because the Japanese description of the rainbow preceded descriptions made in the western United States in the early 1800s.

Generally, the average rainbow is 12 to 16 inches, with the potential in nutrient-rich waters for fish over 24 inches. In trophy lakes, a rare rainbow can reach 20 pounds. Landlocked monsters approaching this size take on the appearance of a potbellied pig.

The rainbow is a spring spawner, like the cutthroat, which leads to hybridization when the species coexist. The rainbow also reaches sexual maturity earlier, at age 2 or 3 years. In hatcheries, they often spawn at 1 year of age. The life span of the rainbow is fairly short. Few live beyond 5 or 6 years of age.

## Rainbow Trout Identification

**Rainbow Trout, *Oncorhyncus mykiss* (Nonmigratory)**

The rainbow's common name comes from a broad swath of crimson to pinkish-red usually seen along the midline of its flanks. The reddish band may be absent in lake dwellers, which are generally more silver in appearance. River rainbow coloration ranges from olive to greenish-blue on back, with white to silvery belly. They are marked with many irregularly-shaped black spots on the head, back, and tail that extend below the midline.

# BROWN TROUT

The brown's scientific name, *Salmo trutta*, declares it as the "true trout." It was introduced into the West in the late 1880s from stocks originating in Scotland and Germany. Many anglers commonly refer to it as a German brown.

Its basic coloration is an overall golden-brown, with the back ranging from dark-brown to greenish-brown, and its sides and belly ranging from light tan to lemon-yellow or white. The back and flanks are marked with many large black or brown spots. The few red spots on the lower flanks are surrounded by light blue-gray halos. There are very few or no spots on its squarish tail.

Longer-lived than North American species, browns have been known to grow to sizes exceeding 30 pounds in the United States and up to 40 pounds in Europe. The U.S. record, 33 pounds, came from the Flaming Gorge Reservoir of the Green River on the southwestern Wyoming-northeastern Utah border.

The older the fish, the bigger and more wary the brown trout. They normally grow about 4 to 6 inches a year the first 3 years. Growth slows to about 2 inches a year after this, but browns have been known to live up to 15 years. Still, depending on environmental variables such as water temperature and available food, size can range widely. Average fish on some streams may range from 10 to 12 inches and up to 2 pounds, which is still a respectable fish. On others, lunkers over 25 inches and 5 to 10 pounds may be common.

The brown's preferred habitat is large rivers and lakes at lower elevations, although it can grow to remarkable size in small streams with adequate cover or deep pools. It is generally thought that the brown is able to adapt to warmer waters than North American species, but the brown's most active periods mirror those of the rainbow. It is active in waters ranging from 45°F to 70°F, with activity peaking at 60 degrees.

Cold water, in fact, spurs the brown's autumn spawning runs. Late October through December is the time trophy hunters most heavily flog the waters.

Browns first spawn at 3 or 4 years of age. A large spawning male can be distinguished from a female by its hooked lower jaw. This morphological adaptation is called a *kype*.

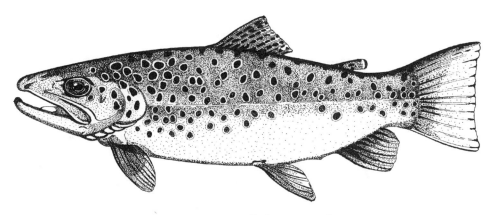

*Brown Trout (Salmo trutta)*

### Brown Trout Identification

**Brown Trout,** *Salmo trutta*

The coloration of a brown trout is generally golden-brown with a dark-brown to greenish-brown back. The sides and belly range from light brown to lemon yellow. There are well-spaced large black or brown spots mixed with a few red spots on the sides with light blue-gray halos. The adipose fin usually has an orange border. There are very few or no spots on the squarish tail.

The brown was introduced to the United States from Europe in the 1800s.

## Brook Trout

Native to East Coast and Canadian waters, the brook trout, *Salvelinus fontinalis*, is actually a char like lake trout, bull trout, Dolly Varden, and Arctic char. Both trout and char belong to the same family, *Salmonidae*. The main difference between the two is that char have light spots on dark backgrounds. Trout have dark spots on light backgrounds. Both prefer cold water environments, but char seek out the coldest water.

Introduced into the West in the 1880s, the brook trout is a resident of pure cold waters of headwater mountain streams and alpine lakes.

Unfortunately, its Eastern reputation as a scrappy fighter is lost to most Western anglers because it tends to overpopulate the waters in which it occurs, thereby stunting its growth. The short growing seasons of alpine lakes also contribute to its diminutive size. But many high country hikers don't mind. They love to catch "plate-size" brookies because they are excellent table fare, often rated as the best among the trout species.

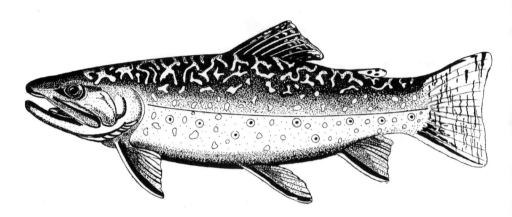

*Brook Trout (Salvelinus fontinalis)*

Average size in most Western waters is 8 to 12 inches, although its potential is much greater. Brook trout sometimes take up residence in lower lakes, reservoirs, and beaver ponds, where they may grow to a substantial size and provide a tussle worthy of their renown as excellent game fish. A 2- or 3 -pounder taken from one of these waters is considered a good-sized fish.

The brook trout's most distinctive markings are white and black edges on the fronts of its lower fins. It is dark green or blue-black on its back, fading to white on the belly. Numerous wavy worm-like lines, or vermiculations, cover its back and dorsal fin. Scattered red spots surrounded by blue halos are seen on its flanks. The belly and lower fins of a spawning male are brilliant red in autumn.

Flyfishers should be aware of two other chars that have a similar appearance to brook trout.

The bull trout, *Salvelinus confluentus*, was previously considered an inland version of the coastal Dolly Varden, *Salvelinus malma*. It has no worm-like markings like the brook trout, and white edges on lower fins are less distinct.

The lake trout, *Salvelinus namaychush*, was introduced into the West in the late 1880s. Also called Mackinaw, it inhabits large, deep lakes, but it is occasionally washed through dams into the rivers below. Its overall coloration is gray. It has no colored spots like the brook trout or the bull trout. The lake trout's tail is deeply forked. The tail of both brook trout and bull trout is square.

Brook trout reach sexual maturity in 2 or 3 years. Its life span ranges from 6 to 10 years, although a fish over 5 is rare. It is a fall spawner and breeds in both streams and lakes. It hybridizes with other trout species. Introduction of the brook trout into the West, habitat loss, and pollution are the main contributors to the demise of the native bull trout throughout much of its former range.

Rarely found in waters with prolonged temperatures above 65°F, it is most active in waters ranging from 45 to 65 degrees. Activity peaks at 58 degrees.

## Brook Trout Identification

**Brook Trout, *Salvelinus fontinalis***

The most distinctive markings on a brook trout are the white and black edges on the front of the lower fins, the wavy or worm-like markings on the back, and scattered red spots surrounded by a blue halo on the flanks. Brook trout are dark green or blue-black on the back and white on the belly. The belly and lower fins turn brilliant red on spawning males in the fall. The tail is square.

Brook trout were introduced to the western United States in the 1880s.

# Bull Trout/Dolly Varden

Once pursued like a coyote with a bounty on its head—even poisoned in attempts to eradicate it—the bull trout has gained newfound respect as a gauge in determining the health of the Pacific Northwest's wild forests and mountain streams. But the bull trout hangs on the brink of extinction.

It is found in only 42 percent of its native streams in Idaho, Montana, Oregon, and Washington. In 1994, the U.S. Fish and Wildlife Service found that bull trout warranted protection under the Endangered Species Act but declined to list it. The decision was repeated in 1995.

There were two reasons given: there are too many other species in danger of extinction; and state political and wildlife officials prefer to attempt saving the species without federal intervention. Programs to protect bull trout and encourage their comeback are under way in all four states.

In their petition for endangered species listing, environmentalists said bull trout populations and habitat were seriously degraded by logging, forest road building, cattle grazing, mining, dam construction, irrigation, pesticides and home construction in floodplains. Other threats to the fish have included overfishing (particularly during spawning runs), poaching, and introduction of nonnative char species that outcompete and hybridize with bull trout.

The bull trout's key importance to the Northwest is their dependence on pristine waters that are clean and silt-free, cold and oxygen-rich. This makes bull trout a prime indicator species for monitoring the health of forest ecosystems and watersheds. Sharing the same wilderness waters are native salmon, steelhead, and cutthroat trout.

Native to inland waters of northwestern North America, the bull trout (*Salvelinus confluentus*) is a char, not a trout. It is long-lived and grows to trophy proportions. An average adult from a large river or lake weighs 3 to 8 pounds. Fish as large as 20 pounds are common. The U.S. record, 32 pounds, came from Northern Idaho's Lake Pend Oreille in 1949.

Formerly lumped with the Dolly Varden (*Salvelinus malma*), the bull trout was reclassified as a separate species in the early 1970s. The Dolly Varden is more common to the coastal waters of Canada and Alaska. Arctic char (found in the Northwest Territories and Alaska), brook trout, and lake trout (native to eastern North American waters), are in the same genus.

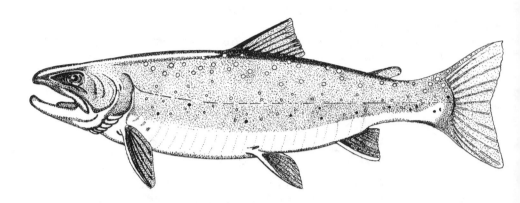

*Bull Trout (Salvelinus confluentus)*

Fall spawners, bull trout are known for migrating 50 to 150 miles to their spawning beds. Sexual maturity occurs at 4 to 5 years of age, and individual fish spawn every 2 or 3 years. Siltation covering redds or water temperatures rising above 41 degrees can be lethal to the eggs.

Washington and Oregon both have significant populations of bull trout. Some along the coast are anadromous and go to sea like salmon and steelhead.

Chars are distinguished from trout by their light spots on a dark background. Trout have dark spots on a light background. The spots on a bull trout's olive-green to bronze back and flanks are pale-yellow, orange, or red. There are no spots on the dorsal fin and no black line on the ventral fin.

## Bull Trout Identification

### Bull Trout, *Salvelinus confluentus*

Bull trout are olive green to brown above and on the sides with shading to white on the belly. They lack the worm-like markings seen on brook trout, and the white border on their fins is less distinct. There are no spots on the dorsal fin. There are yellow spots on the upper body and red or orange spots on the flanks, but no blue halos around spots like a brook trout. The tail is square.

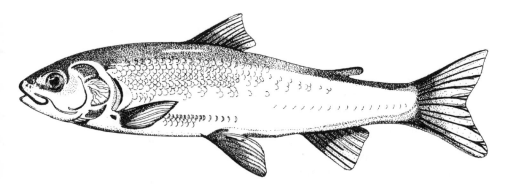

*Mountain Whitefish (Prosopium williamsoni)*

## MOUNTAIN WHITEFISH

One of the most abundant game fish in the West, the whitefish gets little respect from flyfishers.

There is almost a social stigma against taking whitefish wherever they are found. Fishing for whitefish is most popular in winter when they are more active than trout. There are winter whitefish seasons on many drainages, which often become de facto catch-and-release seasons for trout.

Some anglers scorn the whitefish because they presume it competes with trout; however, the two species evolved to occupy separate niches in a shared habitat. There is no biological evidence that high whitefish numbers harm trout populations.

While it is in the same family as trout, salmon, and char (*Salmonidae*), the whitefish's silvery body is slender and almost round in cross-section. It has a small head and tiny mouth, with a slightly overhanging snout. Its scales are large and coarse. Like its cousins, it has an adipose fin.

The average mountain whitefish averages 10 to 12 inches, but on nutrient-rich streams, 18- to 20-inch fish are relatively common.

Whitefish hang out in deep pools and shallow, slow-water runs. They feed actively in riffles on mayfly nymphs and caddis larvae. Surface feeding on adult insects occurs most often toward evening.

Among the best wet flies for whitefish are small green-colored nymphs, caddis larvae, and emergers. Beadhead patterns are very effective. Perhaps because of their small mouths, many whitefish fail to take a dry fly when they strike. These misses can be frustrating, but they are also a sign that actively rising fish aren't trout.

Whitefish spawn in late fall and remain active through the winter. Midge patterns can be productive at this time.

## Whitefish Identification

### Mountain Whitefish, *Prosopium williamsoni*

Light, grayish blue on back, silvery on sides, dull white belly, and scales are large. It has a small mouth without teeth and a body that is almost round in cross-section. Mountain whitefish are native to the western United States.

# BASS

Unlike trout, bass have no adipose fin. The dorsal fin is long and has two distinct parts—stiff spines in front and softer rays in back—and its scales are large and obvious. The key difference between the two black bass species is the size of the mouth. The jaw of the largemouth extends behind the eye, while the jaw of a smallmouth ends in front of the eye.

Largemouth bass (*Micropterus salmodies*) and smallmouth bass (*M. dolomieui*), are members of the sunfish family, *Centrachidae*. It includes the sunfishes, crappies, and other basses. Native to North America, only one member of the family, the Sacramento perch, was originally found west of the Rocky Mountains. Many species have been introduced successfully all over the world.

Largemouths live in warmwater lakes and ponds, as well as quiet backwaters and sloughs of streams. They prefer clear water with good cover, such as weedbeds, reeds, lily pads, or flooded snags, but also do well in somewhat barren irrigation reservoirs with radically fluctuating water levels.

Smallmouth bass inhabit cool, clear lakes and streams with rocky and gravelly bottoms and shoals. Smallmouth size averages 1 to 3 pounds. A 5-pounder is considered a trophy and an 8-pounder a monster.

Both species are photosensitive and retreat to shadowy lies or deeper waters on bright days. They are more active at dawn and dusk and in water temperatures above 50 degrees. Optimum water temperatures are 60 to 70 degrees.

The males of both species jealously guard egg nests and newly hatched young in spring. This determined defense of their progeny against predators makes them very vulnerable to anglers at this time.

## Bass Identification

### Largemouth Bass, *Micropterus salmoides*

Dark green on back and flanks, belly white. Dark, irregular horizontal band along flanks. Upper jaw extends behind eye. Deep notch in dorsal fin.

### Smallmouth Bass, *Micropterus dolomieui*

Dark olive to brown on back, flanks bronze, belly white. Dark ventricle bands on flanks. Eyes reddish. Upper jaw ends in front of eye. Shallow notch in dorsal fin.

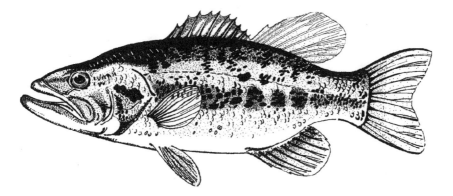

*Largemouth Bass (Micropterus salmoides)*

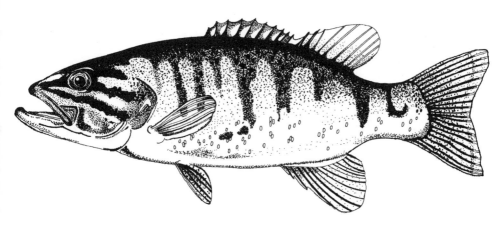

*Smallmouth Bass (Micropterus dolomieui)*

# Planning a Trip

### The Merit of a Guide

Because Washington offers so many varied climates and such drastic changes in weather patterns, my most important recommendation to visiting anglers is to allow as much time as possible for a flyfishing trip. Then add a few days to your visit.

Especially in western Washington, weather influences everything. For instance, when winter storm systems push into the state, river conditions change drastically. Heavy rains either help or hinder anglers, depending on the situation. In the worst case, certain rivers may be blown out completely while others may only offer marginal opportunities. For these reasons, extra time and a flexible itinerary greatly increases a visiting angler's chance for success.

When visiting in late fall, winter, spring, or summer, set your sights on a particular river or lake, but have two or three options if conditions take a turn for the worse. By doing so, you won't walk away feeling cheated.

One of the best ways to fish Washington's waters is with the services of a guide. Most guides know a particular water or two intimately. No matter what the conditions, a guide may have other options. By fishing with a guide, a visiting angler greatly increases his chance to catch fish. Also, by spending a day or two on a particular lake or stream with a guide, an angler may feel sufficiently confident to return alone and fish successfully.

### Rods

Although it's easy to buy a low-grade flyfishing outfit for under $100, purchasing quality equipment should greatly increase your passion for the sport.

Cheap noodle sticks, the kind you find at department stores, are death when the wind comes up, which can happen in Washington any day of the year.

When selecting your equipment, first consider the species of fish you want to chase. If you are focusing on stream or stillwater trout, go with a 9-foot, 4-, 5- or 6-weight rod. If looking for anadromous steelhead, a 7-, 8-, or 9-weight rod is ideal. Single-handed rods work fine, but you may consider a two-handed rod, which allows an angler to cover more water with less effort during a day astream.

Personally, I fish Sage, Thomas and Thomas, Scott, Loomis, and Orvis rods. For stream trout and stillwater trout I use a 9-foot, 4-weight Scott or Thomas and Thomas (Horizon series). If I visit a lake that offers large trout and windy conditions, I go with a 9-foot, 5-weight Orvis Trident, which offers plenty of backbone when I need to punch a cast into the wind. I use a 9-foot, 6-weight Sage for small summer-run steelhead and stillwaters where large trout are encountered. I've landed a 49-pound king salmon and a 42-inch buck steelhead with this rod, but it is best reserved for smaller fish. For winter steelhead and fall salmon, my 9-foot, 8-weight Loomis GL 3 is the ticket.

## Reels

With my 4- and 5-weight rods, I use Able and Marryat reels. With my 6-weight Sage I go with an STH that offers interchangeable spools. On my 8-weight Loomis, I use an Orvis Odyssey+III reel that is smooth and really allows an angler to crank down the drag on a fast-running fish.

## Flies

You can find flies priced under a dollar in many places, but they are apt to fall apart while fishing. I buy most of my flies from quality flyshops; the rest I tie. If you can tie your own flies, more power to you. If not, visit a local flyshop and ask for their best patterns.

## Foul-weather Gear

A good pair of neoprene waders are a must for winter fishing in Washington. Three-millimeter waders will suffice, but 4mm and 5mm, particularly in bootfoot style, offer the most comfort.

During winter, I use a 3mm Orvis, highback guide wader with a stocking foot. When the weather really turns sour and snow blankets the terrain, I go with boot-foot, 5mm Orvis Battenkill waders. Both are rugged waders that keep an angler warm during cold weather, which is an enormous advantage—there's nothing worse than being forced off the stream because you're too cold.

During summer, I wear a pair of Orvis breathable waders that don't overheat me, even under intense sun.

Rain arrives in Washington during all seasons, so I carry a raincoat with me during every trip astream. A Gore-Tex® coat, such as an Orvis or Patagonia, sheds water like a sealskin. It also keeps the wind from cutting into your bones.

## Lines

There are various lines available today, and the general rule is the more you carry the better off you'll be. However, in most situations, you can get away with a floating line.

A floating line is essential when fishing dry flies. For small streams, it is also an ideal nymph line. However, when fishing lakes and large rivers, sinktip and full-sink lines, which help take a fly to the bottom, are very handy. Again, make sure your first fly line is a floater, but add sinking tips to your arsenal as quickly as you can.

## Sunglasses

Beyond the essentials, polarized sunglasses are the most important piece of equipment to a flyfisher. There are several companies that manufacture cheap polarized sunglasses, and you will become acquainted with that fact if you skimp on a cheap pair.

I wear Action Optics sunglasses, made in Ketchum, Idaho, and they always perform well. With polarized glasses, I can spot fish through water that a person without sunglasses couldn't see into due to glare. Spotting fish is extremely important when fishing summer-run steelhead and stillwater trout.

Polarized glasses also help oarsmen negotiate Washington's labyrinthine rivers. By wearing polarized glasses, an oarsman can spot potential underwater obstructions as well as excellent holding water for fish that a person without sunglasses or with a cheap pair of sunglasses would never see.

## Winter Fishing Checklist

_____ Neoprene chest waders

_____ Fleece pants and pullover shirts

_____ Forceps

_____ Stocking hat

_____ Wool socks and liners

_____ Fleece gloves

_____ A Thermos of warm liquid

_____ High energy food, such as Power-Bars and Cliff Bars

_____ Polarized sunglasses

_____ Gore-Tex® raincoat

_____ Flashlight

_____ Camera

## Warm Weather Fishing Checklist

_____ Lightweight waders or quick-drying shorts (Ex Officio offers excellent clothing)

_____ Forceps

_____ Dry-fly floatant

_____ Polarized sunglasses

_____ Long-billed fishing cap

_____ Gore-Tex® raincoat

_____ Sunscreen

_____ Gallon of water

_____ Insect repellent

_____ Flashlight

_____ Camera

_____ Cold beverage on ice in cooler

# Washington Fly Shops

The fly shops and sporting goods stores listed below all carry fly fishing equipment. Many of the sporting goods stores have a limited selection, call ahead for specific items.

**Aberdeen Area**
The Backcast Fly Shop
720 Simpson Avenue
Hoquiam, WA 98550-3610
360-532-6867

**Arlinton**
Hook, Line & Sinker,
3507A 168th Street Ne
360-651-2204

**Auburn Area**
Auburn Sports & Marine
810 Auburn Way North
Auburn, WA 98002-4118
253-833-1440

Diamond Sports Shop
30848 3rd Avenue
Black Diamond, WA 98010-9767
360-886-2027

Shoff's Tackle
214 West Meeker Street
Kent, WA 98032-5821
253-852-4760

**Bellevue**
Kaufmann's Streamborn, Inc
15015 Main Street
425-643-2246

Orvis
911 Bellevue Way
425-452-9138

Altrec
50 116th Avenue SE /
800-369-3949

**Bellingham Area**
The Guides Fly Shop
3960 Suite C, Meridian
Bellingham, WA 98226
360-527-0317  / Fax 360-527-0853

H & H Outdoor Sports
814 Dupont
Bellingham, WA 98225-3103
360-733-2050

R & R Tackle & Fly Shop
109 East Woodin Road
Sunnyside, WA 98944
509-837-2332

Yeagers Sporting Goods
3101 Northwest Ave
360 384-1212

**Bothell**
Swede's Fly Shop
16826 119th Pl NE
425 487-3747

Wetfly.net
1529 201st Place SE Suite B

**Bremerton Area**
Northwest Angler Fly Shop
18830 Front Street
Poulsbo, WA 98370
360-697-7100

Hawk's Poulsbo Sports Center Fly Shop
19424-C 7th Avenue NE
Poulsbo, WA 98370
360-779-5290

Kitsap Sports
10516 Silverdale Way NW
Silverdale, WA 98383
360-698-4808

**Castle Rock Area**
Fish Country Sports Shop
2210 U.S. Highway 12
Ethel, WA 98542-9719

**Chattaroy**
Spring Creek Outfitter's
P.O. Box 478
509-276-9893

**Chehalis**
Sunbird Shopping Center
1757 N. National Avenue
360-748-3337

**Colville**
Clarks All Sports
572 South Main Street
509-684-5069

**Ellensburg**
Worley-Bugger Fly Co.
306 S. Main, Suite 3
888-950-3474
888-950-FISH
worleybuggerflyco.com

**Everett Area**
Fly Smith, The Fly Fishing Outfitters
1515 5th Avenue
Marysville, WA 98270-4700
360-658-9003

John's Sporting Goods
1913 Broadway
425-259-3056

**Federal Way**
The Mad Flyfisher
2020 S 320th St
Bldg A, Suite N
253-945-7414

**Forks**
Olympic Sporting Goods
190 S. Forks Avenue
360-374-6330

**Issaquah**
Creekside Angling Co.
1660 Northwest Gilman Blvd #C5
425-392-3800

Buffalo Bills Sporting Goods
1005 5th Avenue N
425-392-0228

CascadeAngling.com
21316 SE 35th Way
425-557-5830

**Kalama**
Prichard's Western Anglers
2106 Kalama River Road
Kalama, WA 98625
360-673-4690

**Kennewick**
Clearwater Fly Shop
417 W 1st Ave
509-582-1001

**Kent**
Shoff's Tackle
214 West Meeker St
253-852-4760

R.E.I. Inc.
6750 South 228th St.
253-395-3780

**Lacey**
The Fly Fisher
5622 Pacific Avenue SE
360-491-0181

**Lake Forest Park**
Avid Angler
17171 Bothell Way NE, Suite A 130
206-362-4030

**Lake Stevens**
Greg's Custom Fishing Rods
P.O. Box 732, 12405-20th NE
425-335-1391

**Longview**
Bob's Sporting Goods
1111 Hudson
360-425-3870

**Lynden**
The Guide Fly Shop
3960 Guide, Suite C
360-527-0317

Coast to Coast
1736 Front Street
360-354-2291

**Lynnwood**
Ted's Sport Center
15526 Highway 99 West
425-743-950

**Marysville**
Fly Smith
1515 5th Street #B
360-658-9003

**Mazama**
Mazama Store, Inc.
50 Lost River Road
509-996-2855

Mazama Fly Shop
48 Lost River Rd
509-996-3674

**Moses Lake**
Tri-State Outfitters
1224 S. Pioneer Way
509-765-9338

**Oak Harbor**
Cornet Bay Shoppe
275 Cornet Bay Rd
360-675-3635

**Olympia Area**
The Fly Fisher
5622 Pacific Avenue SE
Lacey, WA 98503-1271
360-491-0181

Streamside Anglers Fly Shop
4800 Capitol Blvd. SE
Tumwater, WA 98501-4464
360-709-3337

Puget Sound Sports
527 Devoe Street SE
360-943-4867

Tumwater Sports Center
6200 Capitol Blvd. SE
Tumwater, WA 98501-5288
360-352-5161

**Omak**
Cascade Outfitters
16 South Main Street
Omak, WA 98841
509-826-4148

**Pasco**
Critter's World
5274 Outlet Drive
509 543-9663

Phil's Sporting Goods, Inc.
3806 West Court Street
509-547-9084

**Port Angeles Area**
Greywolf Angler
275953 Highway 101
Gardiner, WA 98382-8722
360-797-7177

Port Townsend Angler
695 Schwartz Road
Nordland, WA 98368
800-435-4410

Quality Fly Fishing Shop
2720 East Highway 101
Port Angeles, WA 98363-9470
360-452-5942

**Poulsbo**
Northwest Angler Fly Shop
18804 Front Street
360-697-7100

**Redmond**
Northwest Fishing Holes Mag
14505 Ne 91st Street
425-883-1919

Sportee's
16725 Cleveland Street
425-882-1333

**Seattle Area**
The Angler's Workshop
1350 Atlantic
Woodland, WA 98674-9485
360-225-6359

Avid Angler Fly Shoppe
11714 15th Northeast
Seattle, WA 98125-5026
206-362-4030

Kaufmann's Streamborn, Inc
1918 4th Avenue
Seattle, WA 98101-1157
206-448-0601

Kaufmann's Streamborn, Inc.
15015 Main Street
Bellevue, WA 98007-5229
425-643-2246

Creekside Angling Company
1660 Northwest Gilman Blvd. # C-5
Issaquah, WA 98027-5340
425-392-3800

The Morning Hatch Fly Shoppe
3640 South Cedar, Suite L
Tacoma, WA 98409-5700
253-472-1070

Orvis Seattle
911 Bellevue Way Northeast
Bellevue, WA 98004-4207
425-452-9138

Patrick's Fly Shop
2237 Eastlake Avenue East
Seattle, WA 98102-3418
206-325-8988

Salmon Bay Tackle Guides & Outfitters
5701 15th Avenue Northwest
Seattle, WA 98107-3004
206-789-9335

Swede's Fly Shop
17419 139th Avenue NE
Woodinville, WA 98072
425-487-3747

Warshal's Sporting Goods
1000 1st Avenue
Seattle, WA 98104
206-624-7301

Outdoor Emporium
420 Pontius North
Seattle, WA 98109-5422
206-624-6550

Ted's Sport Center
15526 Highway 99
Lynnwood, WA 98037-2341
425-743-9505

Outdoor Emporium
420 Pontius Avenue N
206-624-6550

Patrick's Fly Shop
2237 Eastlake Avenue E
206-325-8988

Tightloops.com
4814 18th Avenue SW

Seattle Sports Co.
1415 NW 52nd St.
206-782-0773

On the Fly
10002 Aurora Ave N 2246
206-528-0428

Linc's Fishing Tackle
501 Rainier Ave S
206-324-7600

**Seaview**
Chuck's Fly Shop
1206 36th & L Place
360-642-2589

**Silverdale**
Kitsap Sports
10516 Silverdale Way NW, Suite 110
360-434-4736

**Spokane Area**
Silver Bow Fly Shop
1003 East Trent Avenue
Spokane, WA 99202-2180
509-483-1772

Propp's Rod & Fly Shop
135 South Sherman Street
Spokane, WA 99202
509-838-3474

The Sport Cove Fly Shop
5727 East Sprague
Spokane, WA 99212-0828
509-535-7681

The Outdoor Sportsman
1602 North Division Street
Spokane, WA 99207-2421
509-328-1556

Water Hole Sports Shop
1428 East Francis Avenue
Spokane, WA 99207-3736
509-484-1041

White Elephant
12614 E. Sprague
509-924-3006

Joe Roope's Castaway Fly Fishing Shop
3620 North Fruitland
Coeur D' Alene, ID
509-765-3133

Fins & Feathers Fly Shop
1816 ½ Sherman Avenue
Coeur D' Alene, ID 83816
208-667-9304

**Sunnyside**
R.R. Tackle Fly Shop
109 East Wootin Road
509-837-2332

**Tacoma**
Morning Hatch Fly Shoppe
3640 S. Cedar St., Suite L
253-472-1070

**Tri-Cities**
Clearwater Fly Shop
417 W. 1st Avenue
Kennewick, WA 99336-3926
509-582-1001

Phil's Sporting Goods, Inc.
3806 West Court Street
Pasco, WA 99301-2777
509-547-9084

**Tukwila**
Koen West
18249 Olympic Ave. S
206-575-7544

**Tumwater**
Tumwater Sports Center
6200 Capitol Blvd SE
360-352-5161

**Twisp Area**
Mazama Fly Shop
48 Lost River Road
Mazama, WA 98833
509-996-3674

**Vancouver**
The Greased Line Fly Shoppe
5802 Northeast 88th Street
Vancouver, WA 98665-0941
360-573-9383

**Wenatchee**
Blue Dun Fly Shop
25 Wenatchee Avenue
Wenatchee, WA 98801-2282
509-664-2416

Hooked on Toys
1444 N. Wenatchee
509-663-0740

**Woodland**
Angler's Work Sho
P.O. Box 1044
360-225-6359

Larry's Sport Center
1511 N. Goerig
206-255-9530

**Yakima**
Gary's Fly Shoppe
    & Yakima River Outfitters
1210 West Lincoln
Yakima, WA 98902-2536
509-457-3474

Chinook Sporting Goods
901 S. 1st Street
Yakima, WA 98901-3401
509-452-8205

Gary's Fly Shoppe
1210 W Lincoln
509-972-3880

Chinook Sporting Goods
901 South 1st St
509-452-8205

# Index

# NOTES

# NOTES

# FLY FISHING GUIDE SERIES

If you would like to order additional copies of this book or our other Wilderness Adventures Press guidebooks, please fill out the order form below or call **1-800-925-3339** or *fax 800-390-7558.* Visit our website for a listing of over 2000 sporting books—the largest online: **www.wildadv.com** *Mail To:*

*Wilderness Adventures Press, Inc., 45 Buckskin Road • Belgrade, MT 59714*

☐ **Please send me your quarterly catalog on hunting and fishing books.**

*Ship to:*
Name _____

Address _____

City _____ State _____ Zip _____

Home Phone _____ Work Phone _____

*Payment:* ☐ Check  ☐ Visa  ☐ Mastercard  ☐ Discover  ☐ American Express

Card Number _____ Expiration Date _____

Signature _____

| Qty | Title of Book | Price | Total |
|-----|---------------|-------|-------|
| | Saltwater Angler's Guide to Southern California | $26.95 | |
| | Saltwater Angler's Guide to the Southeast | $26.95 | |
| | Flyfisher's Guide to the Florida Keys | $26.95 | |
| | Flyfisher's Guide to Colorado | $26.95 | |
| | Flyfisher's Guide to Idaho | $26.95 | |
| | Flyfisher's Guide to Michigan | $26.95 | |
| | Flyfisher's Guide to Montana | $26.95 | |
| | Flyfisher's Guide to Northern California | $26.95 | |
| | Flyfisher's Guide to Northern New England | $28.95 | |
| | Flyfisher's Guide to Oregon | $26.95 | |
| | Flyfisher's Guide to Pennsylvania | $28.95 | |
| | Flyfisher's Guide to Washington | $28.95 | |
| | Flyfisher's Guide to Minnesota | $26.95 | |
| | Flyfisher's Guide to Utah | $26.95 | |
| | Flyfisher's Guide to Texas | $26.95 | |
| | Flyfisher's Guide to New York | $26.95 | |
| | Flyfisher's Guide to Virginia | $28.95 | |
| | *Total Order + shipping & handling* | | |

*Shipping and handling: $4.99 for first book,*
*$3.00 per additional book, up to $13.99 maximum*